Shakespeare, Italy, and Transnational Exchange

This interdisciplinary, transhistorical collection brings together international scholars from English literature, Italian studies, performance history, and comparative literature to offer new perspectives on the vibrant engagements between Shakespeare and Italian theatre, literary culture, and politics from the sixteenth to the twenty-first century. Chapters address the intricate, two-way exchange between Shakespeare and Italy: how the artistic and intellectual culture of Renaissance Italy shaped Shakespeare's drama in his own time, and how the afterlife of Shakespeare's work and reputation in Italy since the eighteenth century has permeated Italian drama, poetry, opera, novels, and film. Responding to exciting, recent scholarship on Shakespeare and Italy, as well as transnational theatre, this volume moves beyond conventional source study and familiar questions about influence, location, and adaptation to propose instead a new, evolving paradigm of cultural interchange. Essays in this volume, ranging in methodology from archival research to repertory study, are unified by an interest in how Shakespeare's works represent and enact exchanges across the linguistic, cultural, and political boundaries separating England and Italy. Arranged chronologically, chapters address historically-contingent cultural negotiations: from networks, intertextual dialogues, and exchanges of ideas and people in the early modern period to questions of authenticity and formations of Italian cultural and national identity in the eighteenth and nineteenth century. They also explore problems of originality and ownership in twentieth- and twenty-first-century translations of Shakespeare's works, and new settings and new media in highly personalized revisions that often make a paradoxical return to earlier origins. This book captures, defines, and explains these lively, shifting currents of cultural interchange.

Enza De Francisci is Lecturer in Translation Studies at the University of Glasgow.

Chris Stamatakis is Lecturer in English at University College London.

Routledge Studies in Shakespeare

For a full list of titles in this series, please visit www.routledge.com.

12 **Disability, Health, and Happiness in the Shakespearean Body**
Edited by Sujata Iyengar

13 **Skepticism and Belonging in Shakespeare's Comedy**
Derek Gottlieb

14 **Shakespeare, *Romeo and Juliet*, and Civic Life**
The Boundaries of Civic Space
Edited by Silvia Bigliazzi and Lisanna Calvi

15 **Shakespeare in Hate**
Emotions, Passions, Selfhood
Peter Kishore Saval

16 **Shakespeare and Hospitality**
Ethics, Politics, and Exchange
Edited by David B. Goldstein and Julia Reinhard Lupton

17 **Shakespeare, Cinema, Counter-Culture**
Appropriation and Inversion
Ailsa Grant Ferguson

18 **Shakespeare's Folly**
Philosophy, Humanism, Critical Theory
Sam Hall

19 **Shakespeare's Asian Journeys**
Critical Encounters, Cultural Geographies, and
the Politics of Travel
*Edited by Bi-qi Beatrice Lei, Poonam Trivedi, and
Judy Celine Ick*

20 **Shakespeare, Italy, and Transnational Exchange**
Early Modern to Present
Edited by Enza De Francisci and Chris Stamatakis

Shakespeare, Italy, and Transnational Exchange
Early Modern to Present

Edited by Enza De Francisci
and Chris Stamatakis

LONDON AND NEW YORK

First published 2017 by Routledge

2 Park Square, Milton Park, Abingdon, Oxfordshire OX14 4RN
52 Vanderbilt Avenue, New York, NY 10017

Routledge is an imprint of the Taylor & Francis Group, an informa business

First issued in paperback 2019

Copyright © 2017 Taylor & Francis

The right of the editors to be identified as the authors of the editorial material, and of the authors for their individual chapters, has been asserted in accordance with sections 77 and 78 of the Copyright, Designs and Patents Act 1988.

All rights reserved. No part of this book may be reprinted or reproduced or utilised in any form or by any electronic, mechanical, or other means, now known or hereafter invented, including photocopying and recording, or in any information storage or retrieval system, without permission in writing from the publishers.

Notice:

Product or corporate names may be trademarks or registered trademarks, and are used only for identification and explanation without intent to infringe.

Library of Congress Cataloging-in-Publication Data
CIP data has been applied for.

ISBN: 978-1-138-66891-1 (hbk)
ISBN: 978-0-367-87718-7 (pbk)

Typeset in Sabon
by codeMantra

Contents

Acknowledgements	ix
Foreword	xi
SUSAN BASSNETT	

Introduction	1
CHRIS STAMATAKIS	

PART I
Early Modern Period: Dialogues and Networks   25

1   Shakespeare, Florio, and *Love's Labour's Lost*   27
GIULIA HARDING AND CHRIS STAMATAKIS

2   A Tale of Two Tamings: Reading the Early Modern
Shrew Debate from a Feminist Transnationalist
Perspective   40
CELIA R. CAPUTI

3   Shakespeare and the *Commedia dell'Arte*   53
ROBERT HENKE

4   The Unfinished in Michelangelo and *Othello*   65
ROCCO CORONATO

5   Shakespeare and Italian Republicanism   80
JOHN DRAKAKIS

6   "A kind of conquest": The Erotics and Aesthetics of
Italy in *Cymbeline*   96
SUBHA MUKHERJI

vi *Contents*

PART II
Eighteenth and Nineteenth Centuries: Translation and Collaboration 111

7 The Eighteenth-Century Reception of Shakespeare: Translations and Adaptations for Italian Audiences 113
SANDRA PIETRINI

8 Shakespeare's Reception in Nineteenth-Century Italy: Giulio Carcano's Translation of *Macbeth* 125
GIOVANNA BUONANNO

9 Verdi's Shakespeare: Musical Translations and Authenticity 137
RENÉ WEIS

10 Eleonora Duse as Juliet and Cleopatra 151
ANNA SICA

11 Representations of Italy in the First Hebrew Translations of Shakespeare 166
LILY KAHN

12 Through the Fickle Glass: Rewriting and Rethinking Shakespeare's *Sonnets* in Italy 179
MATTEO BRERA

PART III
Twentieth Century to the Present: Originality and Ownership 193

13 Giovanni Grasso: The *Other* Othello in London 195
ENZA DE FRANCISCI

14 Shakespeare, Vittorini, and the Anti-Fascist Struggle 208
ENRICA MARIA FERRARA

15 Hamlet's Ghost: The Rewriting of Shakespeare in C. E. Gadda 221
GIUSEPPE STELLARDI

Contents vii

16 "The rest which is *not* silence": Shakespeare and
Eugenio Montale   233
CAMILLA CAPORICCI

17 Giorgio Strehler's *Il gioco dei potenti*: A Shakespearean
Master Finds His Voice   246
MACE PERLMAN

18 Shakespeare behind Italian Bars: The Rebibbia Project,
The Tempest, and *Caesar Must Die*   265
MARIANGELA TEMPERA

19 Shakespeare, Tradition, and the Avant-garde in Chiara
Guidi's *Macbeth su Macbeth su Macbeth*   277
SONIA MASSAI AND CHIARA GUIDI

Afterword: Shakespeare, an Infinite Stage   293
PAOLO PUPPA

List of Contributors   297
Index   303

Acknowledgements

Fittingly, this book about exchange is the result of several collaborations and exchanges—spoken and written, formal and informal. It was first inspired by a cross-disciplinary conference, "The International Voice in Shakespeare" (Rose Playhouse, London, September 2013), sponsored by the Mazzini Garibaldi Charitable Foundation and drawing on the invaluable and kind assistance of Pepe Pryke and Florian Mussgnug. From this genesis, the material in this volume evolved considerably, following a series of conversations across continents and disciplines, and the editors would like to thank all those who have contributed to this project. Our thanks, and those of our contributors, are extended to Luke Seaber and Scarlett Baron for, *inter alia*, generous assistance with translations of some rebarbative passages in Italian and French; to innumerable colleagues and friends from UCL—Beci Carver, Helen Hackett, Paul Davis, and Alexander Samson, most notably—who have freely shared their ideas about cultural exchange, and to Colin Burrow, Ruth Scurr, Philip Horne, Richard North, Catherine Keen, Julia Jordan, Claire Pascolini-Campbell, Rob Turner, Roberta Klimt, and George Potts, who have been instrumental in fostering interdisciplinary dialogues; to our several peer-reviewers, not least Anna Laura Lepschy, Giulio Lepschy, Guido Bonsaver, Shirley Vinall, Ian Short, and Adele Bardazzi; and to other anonymous reviewers, unnamed but essential intermediaries in these processes of intellectual exchange. We would like to express our particular gratitude to Liz Levine and Erin Little at Routledge, without whose patience and support this book would not have been possible. The book is dedicated as a memorial tribute to Jane Dunnett, Mariangela Tempera, and Terry d'Alfonso, whose enthusiasm for all things Shakespearean and Anglo-Italian has been a source of constant inspiration to us.

EDF, CS

Note on Translation

Unless otherwise indicated, in each chapter all translations are the author's own.

Foreword

Susan Bassnett

In the Piazza Santa Maria Novella in Florence, there is a plaque on the wall of the Hotel Minerva in honour of Henry Wadsworth Longfellow, describing him as "POETA AMERICANO | NELLE LINGUE NEOLATINE MAESTRO | TRADUTTORE DELLA DIVINA COMMEDIA" [AMERICAN POET, CONSUMMATE MASTER OF THE ROMANCE LANGUAGES, TRANSLATOR OF THE DIVINE COMEDY]. This unusual tribute to a foreign poet highlights Longfellow's work as a translator from many languages, and especially his translation of Dante that appeared in 1867. Not that Longfellow was alone among his contemporaries in translating the *Divina Commedia*, but he was one of the best-known. Indeed, the nineteenth century saw an explosion of English translations of Dante's poem: Henry Boyd's version in 1802 was closely followed by Henry Francis Cary's blank verse translation in 1814. There is a plaque to Cary too, in Westminster Abbey, dubbing him "The Translator of Dante". Dozens of translations followed, published in Britain and the United States, and continue to this day.

Translation theorists such as Itamar Even-Zohar, Lawrence Venuti, and André Lefevere, to name three of the most celebrated, have pointed to the variegated history of translations. There are periods in a culture of intense translation activity, and fallow periods; there are minor writers who acquire canonical status in another literary system when translated, and great writers in the source literary system who, when translated, disappear without trace. There are time lapses, as the fortunes of translated writers rise or fall long after they have first been translated. There are writers who are simply not translated at all, despite their status in the source literary system (Bassnett 2014). The causes of these textual divergences are many and various, and one of the tasks of both Translation Studies and World Literature Studies has been to map them, both synchronically and diachronically. The relationship between Shakespeare and Italy is a rich field for exploration of some of the complex patterns of textual transfer and assimilation that occur through translation.

In the history of translations from Italian into English, we find a great flowering of translational activity in the Middle Ages and Renaissance: the sonnet, the novella, and *ottava rima* entered English literature, and Elizabethan and Jacobean drama drew on manifold Italianate sources.

xii *Susan Bassnett*

Shakespeare located some plots in Italian cities (including Venice, Verona, and Padua), and the broader Italianicity of his work is indisputable: he shaped and refashioned Italian plots, characters, and venues for home consumption, drawing upon the multitude of translated sources available in English, sometimes arriving via French. Through the seventeenth century, there was a slowing down of translations from Italian into English, and gradually the pendulum began swinging in the opposite direction. By the time Cary's translation of Dante appeared, writers such as Edward Gray, James Macpherson, Lord Byron, and Walter Scott had a trans-European readership (including in Italy) and were having a major impact on a new generation of writers. The fascination in England with things Italian of the high English Renaissance had its equivalent in the "Anglomania" of late eighteenth-century Italian literary and cultural circles.

The non-translation into English of Dante's great work was due, partly, to the religious divisions that tore Europe apart during the Reformation and Counter-Reformation. But by the nineteenth century, the mood had shifted, and English translators of Dante found enthusiastic readers. Nevertheless, it was not until the twentieth century, notably with T. S. Eliot and Seamus Heaney, that echoes of Dante could be found in the creations of English-language poets, showing that, finally, the *Divina Commedia* had entered fully into the English literary system. Similarly, though for very different reasons, it took until the nineteenth century for Shakespeare to become a key figure for the Italian public; arguably, the Italian Shakespeare has had greatest success on operatic stages, most notably through Giuseppe Verdi's works. As the reputation of Shakespeare grew in England and across Europe—albeit belatedly, since substantial interest in Shakespeare started to accelerate only in the mid-eighteenth century—so too did his works become absorbed by writers in many languages, including Italian, conferring upon him the status of a global writer canonical in various literary cultures. In Germany, for example, the translations of August Wilhelm von Schlegel and Ludwig Tieck set the benchmark for a German Shakespeare and for future German translations. So great was the popularity of that German Shakespeare that the Danish critic Georg Brandes declared that it was as if Shakespeare, born in England in 1564, had been re-born in Germany in 1767, at the side of Goethe and Schiller (Brandes 1872–90: 2.56–57). Tolstoy, in an essay on Shakespeare published in 1906, declared that Shakespeare's fame originated in Germany, only later migrating to the English (Tolstoy 1970: 236).

Shakespeare in Italy, however, did not easily find a great translator. It could be argued that, despite many excellent translations of individual plays, there has never been a canonical Italian Shakespeare translation— no bad thing in itself, endowing new translators with the freedom to create versions of Shakespeare according to their own criteria. Nevertheless,

Foreword xiii

there is a kind of Shakespearean thread that runs through the work of many Italian writers, some engaging with Shakespeare directly in the original, others encountering him through translation. What characterizes the Italian Shakespeare and makes him distinctive from the Shakespeares who have taken root so powerfully in German, Russian, Czech and, more recently, Japanese and Chinese, is the way in which his work reached an Italian public. In the eighteenth century, Shakespeare's plays tended to be filtered into various European languages via French intermediaries. Italian audiences first encountered some of Shakespeare's plays through translations of versions by Pierre-Antoine de la Place and Jean-François Ducis, whose renderings were formulated expressly to conform to the demands of French classical theatre. Ducis' *Hamlet* (1769), for example, changed the plot and characters, removed central scenes such as the play-within-the-play, and rewrote Shakespeare's original to such an extent that, in a letter to the English actor David Garrick (orchestrator, of course, of the Stratford Jubilee that had, in that same year, 1769, helped inaugurate the cult of Shakespeare), he apologized for the changes, endeavouring to explain why he felt forced to make them. Acknowledging that the Ghost played a major part, as did "the rustic actors and the swordplay", he dismissed these devices as "absolutely inadmissible on our stage"; as a result, he was "forced, in a way, to create a new play" (Heylen 1993: 29). Despite Ducis having no English, the French *Hamlet* was a great success, later translated into other European languages, including Italian in 1772.

The first translation into Italian of a complete play directly from English was *Julius Caesar* in 1756, by Domenico Valentini, Professor of Ecclesiastical History at the University of Siena, who also knew no English, relying on friends who were native speakers for assistance. Valentini, the first in a series of scholar-translators, initiated a philological, text-centric strand of reception, a tradition stretching into the latter years of the twentieth century: notable scholars such as Agostino Lombardo, Alessandro Serpieri, and Nemi D'Agostino have produced bilingual editions of some plays, as have several distinguished Shakespearean editors and critics, including Giorgio Melchiori and Gabriele Baldini. This strand runs in parallel to a second, performance-based mode of reception. Ducis' *Hamlet* was performed in Francesco Gritti's Italian translation in 1774 and ran for nine nights in Venice. Less successful was Antonio Morrocchesi's performance in *Amleto, Principe di Danimarca* in 1791, for one night only. Performances of Ducis' 1772 version of *Romeo and Juliet*, in which he bizarrely incorporated the Conte Ugolino story from Dante's *Inferno*, were better received. This version was translated into Italian in 1774 by Antonio Bonucci, who also wrote a four-act tragedy about Cleopatra.

It was in the nineteenth century that Shakespeare's Italian reception gathered momentum, as a genuine *Italian* Shakespeare began to develop.

xiv *Susan Bassnett*

Given the powerful musical tradition of Italian theatres, operatic versions of (*inter alia*) *Romeo and Juliet* and *Othello* began to appear, as well as ballets based on his best-known plays, including *Macbeth* and *Coriolanus*. It was not until 1856, when Ernesto Rossi, the great *mattatore* actor (a leading light in the emergent tradition of the *grande attore*), performed in *Othello*, using a translation by Giulio Carcano, that Shakespeare began to have a serious impact on Italian theatre audiences. Carcano produced the first verse translation of Shakespeare's complete works (Carlo Rusconi's prose translation had appeared in 1838) using English editions. He also collaborated with actors (including Tommaso Salvini and Adelaide Ristori), thereby ensuring Shakespeare's place in the repertoire of Italy's principal performers who enjoyed a world-wide reputation. In her book on Shakespeare in nineteenth-century Milanese theatre, Hilary Gatti provides a list of performances from 1788 to 1899. The list's repetitiveness is intriguing: the plays most frequently performed until the 1850s are *Hamlet*, *Othello*, *Macbeth*, *Romeo and Juliet*; in 1858 came Salvini's *King Lear*; and, despite occasional performances of *Coriolanus* and *The Merchant of Venice*, there was no enlargement of that repertoire until the later nineteenth century, with productions of *Antony and Cleopatra*, *The Taming of the Shrew*, and *Much Ado about Nothing*. There was, then, by the end of the century a very clear Italian Shakespeare canon, consisting of the great tragedies favoured by the greatest histrionic actors of the Italian stage, and plays with a Roman or Italian setting.

All texts are transformed through translation into something different. The constraints of language necessitate some changes, and new horizons of expectation necessitate others. The dominance of French classical theatre conventions in Italy meant that much of Shakespeare was deemed coarse, vulgar, and so far in violation of norms of good taste that translators were compelled to make radical revisions. Of course, radical alterations were made to accommodate the norms of good taste of English audiences, as the rewritings of Nahum Tate demonstrate, but the conventions of French theatre were observed much more rigidly than on London stages. Moreover, the translation of play-texts presents additional problems, since theatre conventions are not consistent across time or culture. Acting styles and audience expectations vary considerably, as theatre semioticians and translation experts routinely note. For Italian actors, who often insisted on considerable reworking of Shakespeare's originals, what Shakespeare offered was above all else great tragic roles comparable to those afforded by Ancient Greek theatre: Felice Romani, who produced libretti for operas based loosely on both *Romeo and Juliet* and *Hamlet* in the early nineteenth century, saw in Hamlet a northern Orestes and in Gertrude a northern Clytemnestra (Gatti 1964: 17). Ristori made the role of Lady Macbeth one of her most powerful, transforming her into the play's protagonist, Macbeth reduced to her obedient

Foreword xv

supporter. Her version, based on Carcano's text, made the sleepwalking scene the highlight of the play, which ended shortly after that, at the start of Act 5. So successful was this scene that she often performed it as a coda to some completely different play. In 1882, she attempted the role in English for London audiences, but without much critical success. Italian actors on tour often performed a role in their own language, while a supporting cast of local actors performed in their language, a practice that Henry James, for one, found abominable.

Salvini, whose portrayal of Othello was widely acknowledged as remarkable, brought a physicality to the role, and to that of King Lear, another prominent part of his repertoire. Researching his roles in depth, Salvini, in preparing for Othello, read the source from which Shakespeare had derived his own ideas for the play, namely Cinthio's *Gli Hecatommithi*. Salvini wrote about his interpretation, pointing out his dilemma as an actor between accentuating Othello's nobility of soul and great intelligence, and showing how he came to be deceived by Iago. Salvini's passion in the role enthralled international audiences, and the violence with which he despatched poor Desdemona caused ladies to faint.

Verdi's *Otello*, with a libretto by another Italian Shakespeare translator, Arrigo Boito, opened in Milan in 1887. Verdi's *Macbeth* had premièred in 1847, and he was to write *Falstaff* shortly after *Otello*. During his life, he considered other operas based on Shakespeare's works, including *King Lear*, but that project never came to fruition. Writing to Antonio Somma in June 1853, Verdi hints at why, despite his obvious enthusiasm for Shakespeare, he transformed so few of his plays into operas: "vi sono troppi cambiamenti di scena" [there are too many scene changes], he wrote, adding that these irritated him enormously— "mi dava una pena immensa" [it caused me great distress]—and gave the impression of watching a magic lantern show (Gatti 1968: 21). By contrast, the French, Verdi continues, create plays that need only one scene for each act. One of the marked differences between Verdi's *Otello* and Shakespeare's *Othello* is the way the play has been cut to conform to a lesser number of scene changes, increasing the speed of the action, accentuating the diabolical nature of Iago (exactly what Salvini was opposed to!), and giving Iago possibly the most memorable male-voice aria of the opera.

The première of *Otello* had an unexpected result: Arrigo Boito met Eleonora Duse, whose acting style was deliberately antithetical to that of the previous generation's great histrionic actors. In the heat of their new relationship, Boito produced a version of *Antony and Cleopatra* for her which opened in 1888 in Milan: despite its lavish costumes, Duse's growing reputation, and a cultural obsession with Cleopatra and all things Egyptian, the play was savaged by critics. Duse took it to Naples, where once again it was badly received, though the worst review

xvi *Susan Bassnett*

must surely be William Archer's account of the production in London in 1893—a "badly constructed domestic comedy in outlandish costumes". Duse showed nothing in the least sensuous, voluptuous, or languorous: "her very embraces are chilly and she kisses like a canary bird" (Stokes, Booth, and Bassnett 1988: 148).

In the twentieth century, Italian directors enlarged the repertoire, notably in Giorgio Strehler's case, by including many of the history plays, comedies (*Twelfth Night*), and romances (*The Tempest*), while Leo de Berardinis produced powerful experimental versions of some plays. Due to postcolonial interests, *The Tempest* has become more widely known in Italy; Eduardo De Filippo directed a Neapolitan-dialect version of the play in 1984. What distinguishes the Italian Shakespeare from other Shakespeares is the continued engagement with his plays as pieces of theatre. There have been a great many translations, of varying quality, which reflect the norms of the age in which they were produced and the tastes of the readers and audiences for whom they were intended. But it is the theatricality of Italian interpretations of Shakespeare that strikes the strongest chord—whether the ballets and musical versions, or the role-playing of the greatest *mattatore* actors whose legacy lasted well into the twentieth century, as evinced by the Italian cinema, or the sheer boldness of the more recent experimental versions by Italian directors. Things Italian fascinated Shakespeare and his contemporaries (fascinated and repelled, to judge most obviously from public reactions to Machiavelli in the period, even if these masked private sympathies), and Shakespeare, in turn, has come to exert a fascination for Italian culture. These enriching processes are the subject of this book.

Bibliography

Bassnett, Susan. 2014. *Translation*. London.

Brandes, Georg. 1872–1890. *Hovedstrømninger i det 19de Aarhundredes Litteratur*, 6 vols. Copenhagen.

Gatti, Hilary. 1968. *Shakespeare nei teatri milanesi dell'Ottocento*. Bari.

Heylen, Romy. 1993. *Translation, Poetics, and the Stage: Six French Hamlets*. London.

Stokes, John, Michael Booth, and Susan Bassnett. 1988. *Bernhardt, Terry, Duse. The Actress in Her Time*. Cambridge.

Tolstoy, Leo. 1970 [1906]. "Shakespeare and the Drama". *Shakespeare in Europe*, ed. by Oswald LeWinter. Harmondsworth. 214–74.

Introduction

Chris Stamatakis

> They have seemed to be together, thought absent; shook hands, as over a
> vast; and embraced as it were from the ends of opposed winds.
> —*The Winter's Tale*, 1.1.28–31

Intertraffique

Published in London in 1598, John Florio's monumental Italian-English
Dictionarie made available, as its title professed, *A Worlde of Wordes*,
opening up a new linguistic topography for Italophilic English readers.
Shakespeare may well have dipped into this lexicographic aid when min-
ing his Italian sources—elsewhere, he drew upon Florio's parallel-text
language-learning manuals, especially Florio's *Firste Fruites* (1578). This
local, lexical illustration of a border-crossing is mirrored by another dictionary published in London, the two-volume *Dictionary of the English
and Italian Languages* (1760) compiled by the Italian literary critic and
translator Giuseppe Baretti (gratifyingly anglicized to "Joseph Baretti"),
who had spent ten years in England, befriending Samuel Johnson in the
process. Baretti's bilingual dictionary was used by Alessandro Verri,
who completed his translations of *Othello* and *Hamlet* into Italian in
1777, the same year that Baretti published his *Discours sur Shakespeare
et sur monsieur de Voltaire*, which sought, in part through occasional
nods to Johnson's 1765 *Preface to Shakespeare*, to recuperate Shakespeare's works and defend his literary standing from Voltaire's critique.

These two dictionaries offer useful staging-posts in the history of transnational exchange between Shakespeare and Italian literary culture, not
least since they were both composed by linguists whose national identities and cultural affiliations were fluid, spanning the Anglo-Italian di-
vide. Florio, the English-born son of an Italian Protestant refugee, spent
much of his formative childhood in an Italian canton of Switzerland:
the lines subscribed to his portrait in his expanded dictionary of 1611,
Queen Anna's New World of Words—"*Italus ore, Anglus pectore*"
[Italian in his native tongue, English at heart]—attest his in-between,
go-between status. Baretti spent a second period in England, from 1766
till his death in 1789, declaring himself to be "an Englishman forever".

2 Chris Stamatakis

Their dictionaries are emblematic of what lies at the heart of this volume of essays, a diachronic study of exchange between languages and literary cultures. Like these works of lexicography, the chapters gathered here attest the centrality of translation in cultural exchange; the foundational importance of what Bakhtin called, variously, the interaction, "interorientation", or "interanimation" of languages that catalyses the appearance of neologisms and loanwords (Bakhtin 1968: 470); and the role played by intermediaries (lexicographers, commentators, scholars, critics) in the interlingual transactions between nations and cultures. This volume ventures a two-way *translatio studii*—not simply a translation between languages, but also a transfer of knowledge and cultural prestige—and the *longue durée* of transnational exchange between Shakespeare and Italy could even be likened to a process of "double translation", as theorized in Roger Ascham's posthumously-published *Scholemaster*. For Ascham, one-way translation restricts the cultural benefit to "but simple and single commoditie", compared to the "whole proffet" and "commodities of double translation" (Ascham 1570: sigs. L1^v–L3^r). Historically, of course, given the shifting hegemony of Italian and English literature over the early modern period, the direction of cultural transfer in the first instance is from Italy to Shakespeare, who derives material and inspiration from Italian sources; from the eighteenth century onwards, Shakespeare becomes a source in turn to Italian writers, translators, and actors. Yet these obvious chronological shifts notwithstanding, this book contends that at each point of any cultural transfer, there is evidence of a two-way exchange belied by the restrictive terminology of "source" and "influence": like the lemma and definitions in a bilingual dictionary or the two texts constituting a double translation, source and translation are simultaneously present, available for continual collation by the reader. This volume insistently blurs the distinctions between "original" in the sense of returning to a pre-existing origin (*OED*, "original, adj.", 1.a) and "original" in the sense of inaugurating new origins (*OED*, 6.a). A similar rejection of unidirectional influence underlies the theory of intertextuality, a forerunner to which— if only in its cognate etymology—is articulated by Florio himself, who defines "Intertessere" as an interlacing of works: "*to interweaue* [...] *or enterlace with other works*" (Florio 1598: sig. Q4^v). Interlaced works of literature invite an "analogical" mode of reading, favoured by Elizabethans, actively relating a text to its co-present analogues and parallels (Miola 2006: 4).

The purpose of this book is to examine the relationships between Shakespeare and Italian literary, dramatic, and intellectual culture by asking a series of questions centred on the keywords "transnational" and "exchange": is there a currency of cultural exchange, and how should its transactions be valued? Does the term "exchange" sugar-coat what is merely a one-way transaction, a hostile takeover, an appropriation, or is there evidence of a genuine two-way transfer, in which something is

Introduction 3

traded, lent, borrowed, transformed, returned with interest? Is there an anxiety of exchange, as there might be with influence? Are "transnational" encounters possible in Shakespeare's time before the idea of the nation-state has fully materialized? Do transnational exchanges shade into looser, cultural exchanges? In endeavouring to answer these questions, this volume ventures an evolving, shifting paradigm of exchange, one that changes over time, and one that is reconfigured depending on what gets carried over in the exchange—whether Shakespeare's language itself; particular works within his oeuvre; his models of generic hybridity; the more intangible idea of an irregular, transgressive genius; his cultural cachet, or something closer to what Pierre Bourdieu calls, in revealingly economic terms, "cultural capital". The exchanges may be multilateral rather than strictly bilateral—textual and cultural merchandise is often translated through a number of intermediaries, leading to a kind of *contaminatio* of source texts with other literary touchstones, or to an unexpected blending of genres.

Since the coefficients of cultural transaction change over time, this book has been arranged into three sections that are both chronological and thematic. Underpinning the methodological range of the individual chapters—encompassing literary criticism, political history, repertory study, translation theory, and reception studies—is an organizing principle: namely, "exchange" between Shakespeare and Italy in the sense of both a reciprocal transaction (a mercantile trade, an exchange *between* equivalents) and a displacement (a substitution, an exchange of one thing *for* another). Where the former subordinates difference to similitude, the latter addresses resistance in the transaction—the untranslatability of a word or an idea, the replacement of one term by another. The duality is neatly embodied in the name that Lucentio adopts in his guise as a private tutor in *The Taming of the Shrew*, "Cambio", glossed by Florio as both *"an exchange"* and *"a change"* (Florio 1598: sig. E4^r).

Metaphors for translation often liken the activity to a linguistic exchange, whereby the translator acts as a go-between brokering a trade between two languages, cultures, or eras. These image clusters can be traced at least as far back as the early modern period itself. Metaphors of exchange available to Shakespeare and his contemporaries typically take their inspiration from economics, commerce, transport, traffic—fittingly, perhaps, for a theatrical medium whose dramaturgical freight can be quantified as "two hours' traffic", a term synonymous with mercantile trade (*OED*, "traffic, n.", 1.a) but encompassing more figurative meanings of "intercourse, communication" too (*OED*, 3). Early modern English commentaries, Brenda Hosington remarks, frequently theorize the translating process in terms of "merchandise, treasure, wealth, monetary value and coin": such metaphors for translation as a commercial exchange typically "contain some notion of mutuality and reciprocity, of receiving and giving, ideally in equivalent measure", if, in practice, complete parity is harder to achieve (Hosington 2015: 27, 30).

4   *Chris Stamatakis*

Cultural transfer on this nascently-capitalist economic model is subject to patterns of debt and credit, the asymmetry of arbitrage, discrepancies between a commodity's essential worth and its symbolic, relationally-defined value, and the possibilities of loss and gain. Sir John Cheke, in a letter appended to Thomas Hoby's translation of Castiglione's *Il Cortegiano*, expresses anxiety at the translator's introduction of foreign words: the English tongue, "euer borowing and neuer payeng", would be "fain to keep her house as bankrupt" (Hoby 1561: sig. Zz5^r). Countering Cheke's gloomy vexations about one-way indebtedness and the devaluation that results from linguistic quantitative easing, George Chapman described giving "pasport" to unfamiliar or neologistic loan-words in translating *The Iliad*: "if my countrey language were an vsurer [...] hee would thanke mee for enriching him" (Chapman 1598: sig. B2^r), the native linguistic stock increasing in value from his imports and coinages.

These conceits of cultural exchange as a commercial transaction are given their most succinct articulation by the poet and historian Samuel Daniel, Florio's close friend and (possibly) brother-in-law. Daniel's poem "To my deere friend M. *Iohn Florio*", prefacing Florio's translation of Montaigne's essays, compares translation and cultural transfer to a "trans-passage" (Daniel's coinage) into an English "lodging" that naturalizes Montaigne. Daniel maintains that a "happie Pen" circumvents national or cultural isolation by joining an all-inclusive "communitie" which

> *neither* Ocean, *Desarts, Rockes nor Sands*
> *Can keepe from th'intertraffique of the minde,*
> *But that it vents her treasure in all lands,*
> *And doth a most secure commercement finde.*
>
> (Florio 1603: sig. ¶1^v)

Daniel's "intertraffique" (a second coinage) idealizes the exchanges of words and ideas as a kind of reciprocal, equitable trade—a risk-free transaction that "vents" (vends, sells) its "treasure", leading to a guaranteed trade or "commercement" that precludes loss of value. "Intertraffique" dissolves suggestions of hierarchy and asymmetry inherent in the language of "influence", "imitation", "source language" and "target language", "original" and "copy", "precursor" and "epigone", which imply a vertical syntax of ancestry, descent, servility, and belatedness. Admittedly, these terms *do* underwrite some of Shakespeare's portraits of cultural *imitatio*: in *Richard II* (1595), York indicts Richard's court for its assimilation of "[l]ascivious metres" and "[r]eport of fashions in proud Italy",

> Whose manners still our tardy-apish nation
> Limps after in base imitation
>
> (2.1.19–23)

Introduction   5

articulating fears about English susceptibility to the impress of Italian culture, the emergence of the Italianate Englishman, and an "apelike" will-to-copy, as bewailed by William Rankins' obloquy *The English Ape, The Italian Imitation, the Footesteppes of France* (1588). Rankins' lexicon permeates *King John* too, when the zealously patriotic Philip the Bastard voices calls to ward off the "apish and unmannerly approach" of the French (5.2.135). By contrast, the idea of "intertraffique" connotes a more equitable, continuous exchange or collaborative dialectic, and finds an equivalent in Shakespeare's terminology of "interchange". In the emblematic "heraldry" of Lucrece's face, the "sov'reignty" of beauty and virtue is "so great | That oft they interchange each other's seat" (*Lucrece*, ll. 64–70). And Camillo's lines from *The Winter's Tale*, the epigraph to this Introduction, invoke a similarly even-handed exchange, here in the form of an Erasmian epistolary ideal of mutual conversation between absent friends, substituting heraldry with cartography, as the image of "the ends of the opposed winds" summons up the diametrically-opposed points of a compass or map. Partly set, of course, in Italy (Sicilia) and partly in another, counterpointed realm, Shakespeare's play, from this opening scene onwards, revolves around a series of textual, paper exchanges—what, a few lines earlier, Camillo calls "encounters ... attorneyed with interchange of gifts, letters, loving embassies" (1.1.26–28), and what the shape-shifting ballad-seller Autolycus will gesture towards on his first appearance, declaring "My traffic is sheets" (4.3.23)—a textual (if also, in Autolycus' case, sexual) intertraffic.

"What ish my nation?"

This is the question that Macmorris memorably poses in *Henry V* (3.2.123), among the most international of Shakespeare's plays, staging representations of English, French, Scots, Irish, and Welsh, a series of roles all enacted in the earliest performances of the play by, of course, English actors. It has become a commonplace that, in Shakespeare, the "physical borders of England are clear, but its conceptual borders are not" (Lethbridge 1999: 318), and that the writings and theatre of early modern England are rife with "proliferating images of hybridities and cross-overs" (Loomba 2002: 19). For these reasons and others, the very idea of the "nation" is a contested one in this period, its contours not yet ossified into the modern nation-state. As Alexander Samson observes, the nation has had a "notably short, modern history, despite its foundational gesture being a claim to mythic origin", a political entity that has enjoyed arguably only a "brief predominance from the mid-nineteenth century to the twentieth" (Samson 2015: 243). In early modern currency, the term and concept of "nation" were sufficiently capacious to accommodate the sense of "race" or "people" (Henke 2008: 3), a "nation" designating those of a common nativity (*natio*). As such, a nation, as

6 Chris Stamatakis

a relatively coherent group of people, could exist in a new geographic territory, as with the small community of English students—the *natio Anglica* or "English nation"—at Padua's university of law, a "microcosm" of that "sense of national cohesiveness which has long been said to have emerged from confessional strife in the sixteenth century" (Woolfson 1998: 33). Beyond this foundational sense of "nation" as a people, Claire McEachern argues that the term "hovers near" a more recognisable definition of a "principle of political self-determination belonging to a people linked (if in nothing else) by a common government". In a sense, every nation at every time is "proto-national", still in the process of definition—"there is no nation that is *not* a proto-nation". This inherent, systemic fragility notwithstanding, English nationhood could be called "a sixteenth-century phenomenon". Even before its more stable nineteenth-century reification, the "nation" in the sixteenth century exists as a "performative ideal of social unity founded in the ideological affiliation of crown, church, and land" (McEachern 1996: 1, 19, 5).

Even as nations strove for firmer definition (territorial and semantic), no nation was truly complete in itself. As Helen Hackett has argued, building on Stuart Elden's work (2013), while the early modern period was undoubtedly a "time of nation-formation", gauged in part by the "rise of vernacular literatures, and new assertions of national identities and cultures", these nations "defined themselves not only by difference from one another, but also through dialogue" (Hackett 2015: 4). A cosmopolitan, outward-looking purview, an antitype to patriotic insularity, is suggested by Sir Philip Sidney in a posthumously-printed letter of travel advice to Robert Dudley: "For hard sure it is to know England, without you know it by comparing it with some other Countrey; no more than a man can know the swiftnesse of his horse without seeing him well matched" (Sidney 1633: sig. G1^{rv}). Understanding a nation requires, or at least invites, understanding other nations, through a kind of intercultural, transnational collation. National identity is never quite autonomous, but dialogically forged in relation to other national or regional identities. That assumption seems to underlie George Chapman's prefatory address "To the vnderstander" of his translation of part of *The Iliad*. Conscripting an incipient terminology of nationhood, still emergent but also sufficiently well-defined to admit its antitype, Chapman alleges that

> as Italian & French Poems to our studious linguistes, win much of their discountryed affection, as well because the vnderstanding of forreigne tongues is sweete to their apprehension, as that the matter & inuention is pleasing, so my farre fetcht, and as it were beyond sea manner of writing [...] should be much more gracious to their choice conceiptes, then a discourse that fals naked before them, and hath nothing but what mixeth it selfe with ordinarie table talke.
>
> (Chapman 1598: sig. B2^{r})

Introduction 7

Defending his polylingual translation, and lexical difference more generally—not only the defamiliarizing, "farre fetcht", "beyond sea" otherness of his idiom, but also the alterity of Italian and French poems read in their original, "forreigne tongues"—Chapman leaves us with a delightful ambiguity in his neologism "discountryed". It remains unclear how a poem or the experience of reading it could be said to be "discountryed", and who or what is uprooted from their native origins—whether the reader is momentarily deracinated in the act of reading a text in a different language, or whether the text itself becomes discountryed when read by a foreign audience, in its original tongue or in translation. Either way, interlingual transactions negate or elide national boundaries.

A still more tangible manifestation of early modern cosmopolitanism or transnationalism, of discountrying the country, takes the form of an idealized textual "communitie" (in Daniel's terms)—a pan-European republic of letters. The architecture of this virtual commonwealth had its foundations in an international book trade that served as a network of literary and intellectual transmission, and a Europe-wide print market that "traversed national and linguistic boundaries" as if they were, Thomas Betteridge argues, "simply there to be crossed and erased". This humanist model of a "pan-European textual community, without borders" (Betteridge 2007: 1) endured well into the eighteenth century, as articulated by Paolo Rolli, the Italian translator and librettist resident in England for nearly thirty years in the early eighteenth century. An apologist for Shakespeare's style against Voltaire's censures (Rolli 1742: 11–12), and the hand behind the first translation of any passage from Shakespeare ("To be or not to be...") to be printed in Italian ("Essere o no, la gran questione è questa...", Rolli 1739: 97–99), Rolli contended, on the one hand, that national identity was necessarily hemmed in by one's language and parochial purview: "I always thought that the Country of an Author was to be discovered by his Language, or what he related of his Age, Country or himself". Yet on the other he envisaged a cosmopolitan community of literati who transcended local borders: "There is a Degree of Perfection and Taste, which when Authors and Criticks are arriv'd at, make them all of one Nation, call'd the *Commonwealth of Letters*" (Rolli 1728: 12).

The idea of nationhood is doubly loaded in this volume. The "nation" was a porous category not only for Shakespeare and his contemporaries, but it remained for much of the history of the Italian peninsular a theoretical ideal rather than a political actuality. Paradoxically, Italy's "theatrical and literary prestige" in early modern Europe was "inversely proportional to its relatively weak political position [...] as it was carved up by foreign powers" (Henke 2008: 4), and its political, regional fragmentation continued in a variety of forms well into the nineteenth century. Italy as a coherent nation-state emerges only after the rumblings of political unification, orchestrated in part by Garibaldi, in 1861. Prior

8 *Chris Stamatakis*

to unification, Italy had been dismissed by Metternich as no more than a "geographical expression", an agglomeration of unstable regions and states—the Austrian-controlled north, the Papal States of central Italy, the Kingdom of the Two Sicilies in the South. Political parochialism was mirrored linguistically: despite efforts, by the Cinquecento humanist Pietro Bembo, to establish the Florentine of the *tre corone* (Dante, Boccaccio, Petrarch) as an Italian literary standard, after unification only about 10% of the population was fluent in this language (Castellani 1982), since local dialects still dominated (Lepschy and Lepschy 1988). This political and linguistic disunity had implications for Italian theatre too: the lack of a common tongue lent added importance to gesture over speech on the stage, and helped cultivate an actor's theatre—"il teatro dell'attore" (Alonge 1988)—in which audiences were drawn not by the play *per se* but by the star actors, the *grandi attori* (Adelaide Ristori, Ernesto Rossi, Tommaso Salvini, Eleonora Duse), whose performances became the central ingredient of any production. The success enjoyed by these actors on international tours fostered Italian theatre *outside* the nation's borders, in a transnational environment.

"Cultures come into being at their borders", argues Alexander Samson, and "in the spaces between" (Samson 2015: 244). Mary Louise Pratt's coinage, "contact zones", describes a space in which cultures clash and grapple with each other agonistically (Pratt 1991). The phrase invokes a theoretical vogue that risks approximating all cultural activity to a condition of liminality, prizing a *"debordement"* or "overrun" across boundaries (Derrida 1979: 83). The iconography from the early modern period itself might offer a more nuanced analogy for the types of exchange that happen across cultural thresholds. The lexicographic illustration with which this Introduction began might be supplemented by another example of textual practice that emblematizes a two-way cultural exchange, namely parallel-text publication. John Florio's language manuals, to which Shakespeare apparently had recourse, privileged a parallel-text mode of reading, and the format perhaps reaches its apotheosis in Shakespeare's time in John Wolfe's 1588 trilingual *Book of the Courtier*, a feat of printing that brings together Castiglione's Italian (in italic), Gabriel Chappuys' French (in Roman type), and Thomas Hoby's English translation (in black letter) in a tri-column quarto (Hoby 1588). The morphology of the page, as Anne Coldiron has brilliantly demonstrated, visually enacts the cross-cultural threads that Castiglione's book itself celebrates, assisting the reader in experiencing and practising "the very cosmopolitanism its pages advocate": the "printer's formes internationalized the forms of nationhood". This tri-column, polyglot *mise-en-page*—the English text occupying the outer margins, encasing the French (a kind of mediating presence), which in turn encased the Italian (bestriding the gutter)—effects a kind of typographic, linguistic egalitarianism: Hoby's English translation becomes "an equal among versions", Wolfe's implicitly geo-spatial arrangement of texts on the page making visible what Karlheinz Stierle terms the "co-presence of cultures" (Coldiron 2015: 106, 112; Stierle 1996). Three languages, indeed three cultures, are simultaneously present, available for readers to judge and collate; individual national identities are asserted, encoded visually in the different typefaces, but at the same time the page insists on a transnational dialogue between these languages and cultures. This lateral format proved an enduring one in the history of encounters between Shakespeare and Italy. Angelo Olivieri chose, as the format for his 1890 translation of Shakespeare's *Sonnets*, a parallel-text edition that invited his readers to assess for themselves the types of lexical exchange and cultural transpassage effected on the page.

Scheme of the Book

Manfred Pfister's provocative essay, "Shakespeare and Italy, or, The Law of Diminishing Returns" (Pfister 1997), seemed to cast doubt on what more could be derived from comparative, cross-cultural studies of Shakespeare and Italy. This collection of essays, bringing together international scholars—established and emergent—from English literature, Italian studies, drama, and comparative literature, builds on scholarship from over the last twenty years since Pfister's essay and ventures new approaches to the question of the relationship between Shakespeare and Italian artistic culture. The volume is mindful of recent theoretical elaborations on the idea of transnational mobility, such as Greenblatt's model of cultural transfer—the "hidden as well as conspicuous movements of people, objects, images, texts and ideas" (Greenblatt 2010: 250). And it also acknowledges a substantial body of scholarship on Shakespeare and Italy: from comparative studies of early modern Italian and English theatre (notably Andrews 2004), to the copious output of Michele Marrapodi, who has authored or edited studies on Shakespeare's Italian sources (Marrapodi et al. 1997), intertextual relationships between Shakespeare and Italy (Marrapodi 2004), and the adaptation of Italian culture by early modern English dramatists (Marrapodi 2007).

Of most direct bearing on this volume is the special issue of *Shakespeare Yearbook* (1999), co-edited by Marrapodi and Holger Klein, entitled *Shakespeare and Italy*, which opts for a fourfold division. Thematic sections are devoted to the nineteenth- and twentieth-century Italian reception of Shakespeare ("Reception, Appropriation, Translation"); Shakespeare's Italian sources ("Sources and Cultures"); British national identity in Shakespeare's plays, articulated through contact with Italian sources and contexts ("Representation and Misrepresentation"); and the cultural sources of Shakespeare's plays ("Intertextuality"). This present volume, by contrast, ventures a division that is both thematic and chronological, its three sections addressing different types and phases of

10 Chris Stamatakis

exchange. The goal is to historicize exchange, rather than to suggest a single, monolithic paradigm, and to that end Susan Bassnett's Foreword to this collection establishes some of the shifting theoretical and historical contours of cultural exchange that shape the volume. In her succinct catalogue of the key phases of transnational contact between Shakespeare and Italy, encompassing the "Italianicity of Shakespeare's work" and the emergence in the late eighteenth century of an "Italian Shakespeare", Bassnett outlines the complex procedures of textual transfer and adaptation that inform acts of lingual and cultural translation, both on the stage (a performance-based Shakespeare) and on the page (a textual Shakespeare).

1 Early Modern Period: Dialogues and Networks

The first section examines what might be called Shakespeare's "dialectic with Italy [...] or, rather, Italies, since the English view of Italy is a pliable construct" (Marrapodi 1999: 1), and the ways in which English cultural identity is crafted in response to Italian literature and art. Chapters in this section are devoted to Shakespeare's intertextual encounters with Italian literary, dramatic, and intellectual sources, and his engagement with "Italianism" as variously theorized in early modern England. The transnational exchanges (of people and ideas) discussed in this section are conducted through personal networks and textual dialogues. The conditions for these exchanges—which are both more circuitous and imbricated than mere binary transactions between just two parties—were fostered by the blossoming of the Italian book trade in England from the mid-sixteenth century onwards, as momentum gathered for the translation and publication of Italian books in England, especially romances, poetry, and proverbs (Tomita 1999: 97). The London press of John Wolfe, partly trained in Florence's publishing houses, issued a number of literary and dramatic works in Italian, including Pietro Aretino's comedies, Torquato Tasso's *Aminta*, and Giovanni Batista Guarini's tragicomedy *Il Pastor fido*—a vital source for what Robert Henke has termed Shakespeare's "pastoral reformation of tragedy" in the dramaturgy of his late romances (Henke 1997: 103).

Opportunities for intercultural contact were heightened by the movement of Italian merchants and entrepreneurs; by visiting troupes of Italian players from the *commedia dell'arte*, *commedie regolari*, and *favole pastorali*; or sojourns in Italy made by English actors, including Will Kemp, Shakespeare's colleague in the Lord Chamberlain's Men; by itinerant musicians, like Alfonso Ferrabosco; and mobile humanists and diplomats, including the Pasqualigo family, which served the Venetian Republic in London, including Luigi Pasqualigo, who composed a "pastoral play uncannily resembling *A Midsummer Night's Dream*" (Clubb 2011: 282). A Protestant church for Italians in London

Introduction 11

(the Mercers' Church of St Thomas of Acon) afforded a site in which sixteenth-century Italian travellers and immigrants as well as "Italianate English gentlemen" would converge, provoking Roger Ascham's disgruntlement in *The Scholemaster* (Tomita 1999: 99–100). This first section of the book is less interested than previous studies in the Italian settings of Shakespeare's plays, or in positivistic analysis of Shakespeare's specific Italian sources, or even in Shakespeare's engagement with "theatergrams" (Louise George Clubb's coinage for theatrical *topoi*, plot modules, character systems, and framing devices) that made up a common language of European theatre (Clubb 1989; 2011: 283), than in what might be called ideas of "Italianism". Rather than examining the passive absorption of axiomatic Italian lodestones (such as *sprezzatura*, *petrarchismo*, or *virtù*), these chapters address instead the ways in which Italian forms, ideals, and aesthetic qualities are imitated, recast, and made new in Shakespeare's handling.

In "Shakespeare, Florio, and *Love's Labour's Lost*", Giulia Harding and Chris Stamatakis trace one likely conduit by which Shakespeare may have accessed and interpreted some of his Italian source materials, namely through John Florio—the lexicographer, Italian-language tutor, and translator, celebrated in his own time as an "Inglese Italianato" mediating Italian humanistic culture to Elizabethan England. This chapter places Florio in a theatrical network encompassing Leicester's Men and the playwright Robert Wilson; triangulates Florio with the Italian philosophical maverick Giordano Bruno and Sir Philip Sidney; unpacks the Italian subtext of the distinctly Sidneian, "Florioesque" *Love's Labour's Lost*; and deliberates on the ways in which Florio's parallel-text pedagogy emblematizes the dual presence of Italian and English in Shakespeare's plays, as the playwright negotiates the two languages and their literary cultures. The tantalizing suggestions of a personal connection between Florio and Shakespeare notwithstanding, the chapter argues that Florio's Italianism permeates Shakespeare's dramatic writings of the 1590s at a proverbial, intertextual level, and that Florio is a key agent of cultural transaction at the turn of the seventeenth century.

Reconstructing Italian and native English traditions of misogyny, Celia Caputi's chapter, "A Tale of Two Tamings", argues for a "proto-transnationalism" in John Fletcher's *The Tamer Tamed*, which rebuts what might be construed as the misogynistic bias of Shakespeare's *The Taming of the Shrew*. Shakespeare's Paduan setting protected English cultural identity by sublimating the misogynistic violence, cast as Italian, whereas Fletcher's *The Tamer Tamed* transports Shakespeare's now-widowed Petruchio to England and marries him to Maria, who tames this "woman-tamer" in turn. This chapter demonstrates how English national and linguistic identity is inextricable from questions of gender, not least in Fletcher's collocation of "country" and "nation" with what his heroine Maria terms "this gulf of marriage". Placing both plays

12   Chris Stamatakis

in an Anglo-Italian context of "shrew" debates, and glancing sideways to Pietro Aretino's ribald sonnets (*I modi*, accompanied by Marcantonio Raimondi's scurrilous engravings) and his comedy *Il Marescalco* (a play probably accessed by Fletcher via Ben Jonson's *Epicoene*), Caputi assesses the respective "Italianism" of Shakespeare's and Fletcher's plays and their participation in Anglocentric fantasies about Italian culture and gender politics.

Given Shakespeare's indebtedness to a vista of European theatrical traditions, Robert Henke's chapter "Shakespeare and the *Commedia dell'Arte*" assesses the evidence for Shakespeare's recourse to the typologized characters and theatrical conventions of the *commedia dell'arte*—a form of semi-improvised Italian theatre harnessing modular plot outlines. Retracing the transnational movements of actors (both English and Italian), Henke locates Shakespeare's engagement with the *commedia dell'arte* in the context of contemporary theatrical practice (Thomas Heywood, Ben Jonson, Thomas Middleton, *inter alia*), sometimes indirectly via French channels, and considers the satirical, anti-papal applications of the *commedia* in English plays. Analogues for *commedia* types (*Zanni, Pantalone, innamorato, servo*) litter Shakespeare's early comedies, which often celebrate the *commedia*'s capacity for reinvention by announcing their own incessant theatricality and role-playing. Shakespeare's response to this Italian theatrical tradition modulates over his career: while his mature comedies distance themselves from *commedia dell'arte* types and plots, the *commedia* resurfaces, unexpectedly, in Shakespeare's tragedies (especially *Othello*), and even leaves its impress on his late pastoral tragicomedies. *The Tempest* betrays a fascinating proximity to a *commedia dell'arte* scenario ("Arcadia Incantata"), and shows Shakespeare not only transposing but also transforming this dramaturgical inheritance.

Rocco Coronato's chapter, "The Unfinished in Michelangelo and *Othello*", addresses Shakespeare's response to the Italian poetics of the Neoplatonic "Idea" that informs a masterful work of art. Tracing the transmission of this idea of the "Idea" through Italian art and English literary criticism, Coronato discusses how debates over the artificer's "internal design" (*disegno interno*) are broached in *L'idea de' pittori* (1607) by Federigo Zuccaro, resident at Elizabeth's court in 1575, and in Giovanni Paolo Lomazzo's seminal treatise on painting, translated into English (1598). This shared critical discourse in Italy and England on the role of *disegno, ingegno*, and the unfinished, and the debates on ideal beauty and the artist's *concetto* (Sidney's "fore-conceit") form a transnational intertext with which Shakespeare's *Othello* is engaged. The play is saturated with the lexicon of Neoplatonic "Ideas" and Michelangelo's *non finito* (embodied most obviously in Iago). This chapter provocatively suggests that, in Iago's case, the idea or *concetto* might finally remain buried beneath the surface, irrecoverable and unknowable—a

Introduction 13

chastening conclusion for cultural exchange, if the idea to be imitated remains ultimately obscured, inscrutable, unintelligible, untranslatable.

Othello is the test case—with Shakespeare's other Venetian play, *The Merchant of Venice*—for another Anglo-Italian ideological debate in John Drakakis' chapter, "Shakespeare and Italian Republicanism". Shakespeare demythologizes Venice's reputation as a thriving republic, exposing instead a political system marked by radical self-division and duplicity. Discussing the fluidity of the term "republic" in English political discourse (subtended by Aristotle's *Politics*, newly Englished in 1598), and tracing the emergent mythology of Venice as a commercial centre economically reliant on outsiders like Shylock, Drakakis argues that early modern Venice became a canvas on which the domestic political anxieties of Elizabethan and early Jacobean London were displaced. Both plays exploit the axiomatic Jacobean continuity between domesticity (the household) and the wider polity (the community), within both of which lurks irreparable division. Both plays show the tendency for "accommodation" of strangers to fail: Othello and Shylock remain, culturally and racially, both insiders and outsiders, leaving the tension between accommodation and insuperable alterity unresolved.

The final chapter in this section, "'A kind of conquest': The Erotics and Aesthetics of Italy in *Cymbeline*", defines the Italianism of *Cymbeline* as an aesthetic impulse originating in Italian tragicomedy and permeating Shakespeare's late romances. Subha Mukherji delves into this play's portrait of the subtle Iachimo, a Renaissance Italian interloping in Roman Britain and flitting back and forth between these two geopolitical realms, telescoping historical time, geographical space, and literary, aesthetic identities. "Italy" is not just a place, but a set of generic affiliations: Italian national types are bound up with Italian literary forms (such as tragicomedy) and stylistic modalities (including narrative dilation, deferral, self-consciousness, self-pleasuring artifice, and Ovidian erotic energy). These aesthetic characteristics recur in a fascinating adultery case from 1590s Cambridge, which gives definition to *Cymbeline*'s curiously unresolved hybrid of Britishness and Italianism. This duality, characterizing all the chapters in this first section, is encapsulated in Imogen's image of Britain's "tributary rivers" flowing into Rome's "emperious seas", which evokes an uneasy tension between a submissive payment of tax from a compromised sovereignty and an unbidden homage or act of compliment.

2 Eighteenth and Nineteenth Centuries: Translation and Collaboration

The early origins of Shakespeare's European reach are well attested. A Swiss tourist to London, Thomas Platter, attended a performance of *Julius Caesar* at the Globe (21 September 1599), commenting on the

14   *Chris Stamatakis*

localized cosmopolitanism of English theatre-goers: "the English pass their time, learning at the play what is happening abroad [...] since for the most part the English do not much use to travel, but prefer to learn of foreign matters and take their pleasures at home" (Platter 1937: 170). An adaptation of *Romeo and Juliet* was probably performed as early as 1603 on the continent, during a tour of Southern Germany by Robert Browne's English acting troupe (Oppitz-Trotman 2015). But it is not until the turn of the eighteenth century that Shakespeare appears in any meaningful way on Italian literary horizons. The eighteenth century witnesses Shakespeare's nascent reception by a matrix of Italian commentators, critics, translators, and adapters, in addition to, in the nineteenth century, a pantheon of actors, especially the *grandi attori* who exerted considerable sway in the versions of Shakespeare mediated to popular audiences. Chapters in this middle section of the volume consider how Shakespeare is repurposed for Italian audiences, adapted to new forms and metrical systems, and mediated through indirect routes. The networks and dialogues of the first section give way here to collaborations and go-betweens: intermediaries become instrumental in disseminating Shakespeare's dual literary status (split between page and stage), in adapting Shakespeare's language (often deemed untranslatable) to new forms, and in fashioning political, national, and cultural identities through successive rehandlings of his works. The tensions between a read and a performed Shakespeare sound a bass-note throughout this section.

"Until very recently", Hugh Grady recounts, "the story of Shakespeare's reception was almost always told as one in which the world gradually came to terms with Shakespeare's inherent and unchanging greatness" (Grady 2001: 265). This narrative of the emergent cult of Shakespeare, catalysed by Garrick's 1769 Stratford Jubilee, masks the fractious history of Shakespeare's accession to a European canon. For much of the eighteenth century, "Shakespeare" (a metonym less for his oeuvre itself than for the disembodied idea of a particular type of artist) was embroiled in a European literary-critical *querelle* that would spill over into the early years of the Ottocento in Italy too, between (broadly speaking) French critics who objected to his rough-hewn unruliness and a handful of Italian apologists who aligned him with a "tradition of the most prominent Italian literary figures (Dante, Petrarch, Ariosto)" and with an "*élite* of 'supra-national' [...] geniuses" (Locatelli 1999: 23). The process by which Shakespeare's works and iconicity were adopted as emblems of "a new transnational and transhistorical aesthetics in Italy" (Marrapodi 1999: 4) depended on multilateral interventions. The translator Michele Leoni, for instance, included translations of Nicholas Rowe's 1709 *Biography* and Samuel Johnson's 1765 *Preface to Shakespeare* as a paratextual filter of English literary criticism in the first volume of his 15-volume *Tragedie di Shakespeare* (1819–21).

Introduction   15

The first chapter in this section, Sandra Pietrini's "The Eighteenth-Century Reception of Shakespeare: Translations and Adaptations for Italian Audiences", recounts the slow, sporadic appearance of Shakespeare's drama in Italian literary circles over the eighteenth century, restricted in the first instance to isolated translations of his tragedies. Pietrini establishes the dominant context of French neoclassical paradigms, the role played by French intermediaries in disseminating Shakespeare's works to Italian audiences, the polemical squabbles between Italian and French critics over questions of aesthetic taste, and the linguistic impediments to translating Shakespeare's idiosyncratic lexis and turns of phrase. This fascinating history unfurls, variously, through the intervention of Anglo-Italian friendships and the movement of translators, patrons, and diplomats between the two countries, in a series of transnational collaborations that helped secure Shakespeare's critical bearings in a European literary pantheon. As Italian literary culture wrestled with convictions of native self-sufficiency and anxieties about a dependency on foreign vernacular literatures, Shakespeare's initially lukewarm reception is partly attributable to his linguistic obscurity and generic indecorum; his fluctuating status can be gauged by the recurrence of key terms ("error", "sublimity", "genius", "difficulty") used by critics and translators, opponents and apologists, alike.

Reconstructing the battle-lines between Shakespeare's eighteenth-century champions and detractors, Giovanna Buonanno devotes special attention to the Milanese translator Giulio Carcano in her chapter on Shakespeare's reception in nineteenth-century Italy. Carcano's ambitious project of translating Shakespeare's complete works into Italian verse is considered in relation to defences of translation, by Mme Germaine de Staël and Alessandro Manzoni, as a means of reinvigorating national vernaculars. Buonanno focuses on Carcano's *Macbeth* not least for its simmering political subtexts, all the more resonant in the context of Risorgimento Italy, Carcano's activities as part of the Milanese revolutionary movement, and his tussles with censors. Carcano's *Macbeth* furnishes evidence of his dual roles: first, as a punctilious, sensitive translator of Shakespeare's texts, and secondly as a collaborator, adapting his own translation for the stage, condensing an already brisk play to meet the whimsical demands of the *grande attore* Adelaide Ristori, who insisted on cuts to foreground her character, Lady Macbeth. Given these practical challenges—linguistic difficulties of translating Shakespeare into a new metrical idiom, and dramaturgical contingencies of reframing the action to satisfy its star performer—Carcano plays a potent role in disseminating both a literary, read Shakespeare, and a theatrical, staged Shakespeare.

Dwelling on a similar interplay of page and stage, René Weis considers the imaginative and political sway wielded by Shakespeare over

16 *Chris Stamatakis*

Verdi, focusing primarily on Verdi's *Macbeth* (1847) and *Otello* (1887). This chapter on "Verdi's Shakespeare" recounts how Verdi incorporated Shakespearean stage iconographies and political subtexts even in operas not primarily based on Shakespearean sources (*Rigoletto* invokes *King Lear*, *Nabucco* recalls *Macbeth*), and details the processes by which, through a kind of *contaminatio*, Verdi's *Otello* reaches beyond *Othello* to lift from *King Lear* (as Edmund feeds into Verdi's Iago) and from *The Tempest* (a possible model for unified action in a single location). Converting expansive Shakespearean tragedy into the syllabic "brevity" of the libretto, Verdi selectively excerpted Shakespeare's plays in a manner comparable to Shakespeare's own "telescoping" of source materials. For Verdi, Shakespeare was decidedly a *read* author, accessed via Rusconi's prose and Carcano's verse translations, yet Verdi carefully tailored material to specific personnel at his disposal, animating the dormant text by matching the vocal qualities of his singers to the idiolects of Shakespeare's characters.

In "Eleonora Duse as Juliet and Cleopatra", Anna Sica's intensely archival approach reconstructs Duse's acting philosophy in her Shakespearean roles. Duse offers a fascinating illustration of a key phase in the development of the Italian acting tradition known, through its various evolutionary stages, as *la drammatica*. In Duse's hands, this method is best evidenced by her interpretations of two Shakespearean roles: an early, mannerist, medievalist Juliet, and a more mature, nationalistically-inflected Cleopatra, indebted to Arrigo Boito's translation. This chapter compares Duse's annotations and prompt-books, uncovered from *The Murray Edwards Duse Collection* in Cambridge, to the practice adopted by other nineteenth-century Italian actors for accentuating particular syllables to heighten affective communicability with their audiences. Duse's annotations reveal some of the intricate procedures by which Shakespearean play-texts were converted by Italian actors into finely-calibrated subtleties of voice and gesture when those plays were performed, in Italian, for Italian and international audiences alike.

An intriguing example of transnational exchange conducted at two removes can be found in Shakespeare's representations of Italy as re-imagined through a Judaizing lens in the first full Hebrew translations of his works, produced in late nineteenth-century Eastern Europe. Several Italian-centric plays—*Othello* (Isaac Eduard Salkinson's 1874 איתיאל, or *iti'el*), *Romeo and Juliet* (Salkinson's 1878 רם ויעל, or *ram veya'el*), and *The Taming of the Shrew* (Jacob Elkind's 1892 מוסר סוררה, or *musar sorera*)—were translated as part of a wider project of Hebrew revernacularization, producing a set of texts for reading rather than performance. In this chapter, "Representations of Italy in the First Hebrew Translations of Shakespeare", Lily Kahn examines the domesticating strategies used to impart Jewish cultural references to texts that still retained something of their English, and Italian, foreignness. These

Introduction 17

translations construct an "obviously Jewish Italy" that is also clearly an "imagined Jewish Italy", underpinned by buried Biblical subtexts. A particularly inventive interplay, in the translation of *The Taming of the Shrew*, of Hebrew and Aramaic (to render Shakespeare's embedded Italian phrases) registers linguistic difference while striving to articulate a Jewish national or cultural identity.

In another trio of late nineteenth-century translations that reveal the lexical difficulties of transposing Shakespeare's language to a new literary system, Matteo Brera traces the Italian reception of Shakespeare's *Sonnets*. This chapter, "Through the Fickle Glass", focuses on the *Sonetti* translated by Angelo Olivieri (1890), Luigi De Marchi (1891), and Ettore Sanfelice (1898), dwelling especially on their struggles in Italianizing Shakespeare's language and prosody—what Giosuè Carducci called *fare alle braccia* [wrestling] with Shakespeare. Olivieri's prose translations sought, in their *mise-en-page*, to preserve the poetic structure of Shakespeare's sonnets; De Marchi's versions reveal the translator's anxieties in reconciling tradition and modernity; and Sanfelice, while dutifully respecting the Elizabethan sonnet's strophic divisions, sought to translate Shakespeare's poems as *sonetti italiani* [Italian sonnets], implying a return to either a Petrarchan model or Carducci's classicist poetics. Repeatedly, these translators favoured a collaborative *contaminatio* fusing Shakespeare's sonnets with earlier nineteenth-century literary traditions, interweaving words and phrases from their predecessors and contemporaries (Angiolo D'Elci, Giacomo Leopardi, Emilio Praga, Giosuè Carducci). The ground had been set for increasingly personalized, intertextually intricate responses to Shakespeare.

3 Twentieth Century to the Present: Originality and Ownership

"Shakespeare's special status in the literary canon", Douglas Lanier posits, "springs from a complex history of appropriation and reappropriation, through which his image and works have been repeatedly recast to speak to the purposes, fantasies, and anxieties of various historical moments" (Lanier 2002: 21). This third section of the book, devoted to Shakespeare's Italian afterlife in the twentieth century and beyond, moves away from the translations of the middle section to examine a series of appropriations and reappropriations by actors, novelists, poets, and directors that are simultaneously personalized and in dialogue with their broader historical moments. Chapters in this section address the constraints and opportunities afforded by adaptation to new settings or new media; consider how selections from Shakespeare are turned into something personal and original; and analyse the strategies of *contaminatio* by which a given Shakespearean play is melded with other Shakespearean plays (especially *The Tempest*) or independent Italian traditions

18   *Chris Stamatakis*

(often retaining their regional identity as Sicilian or Neapolitan). In these personalized visions and revisions, the processes of exchange are inflected in new ways, as Italian writers and artists often reach back to anterior Italian sources, some available to Shakespeare himself. These chapters, haunted by the spectres of an unburied past, confront questions of ownership and the paradoxes of originality—the simultaneous return to prior origins and the creation of new ones.

In the first chapter in this section, "Giovanni Grasso: The *Other* Othello in London", Enza De Francisci reconstructs the reception of the first Sicilian actor to perform Shakespeare in London by examining newspaper archives that record the critical responses to Giovanni Grasso's *Othello* (Lyric Theatre, 1910). Grasso and his Sicilian troupe enjoyed a reputation for naturalistic immediacy and impulsiveness readily associated with his Sicilian identity: early reviews ventured a romanticized, sentimental portrait of the Italian South (or Mezzogiorno), while simultaneously co-opting a condescending vocabulary of rustic primitivism and animalism—cultural stereotypes about Sicily's African and Arab heritage that Grasso both exploited and resisted. In the ethnographic context of late nineteenth-century Italian migration to Britain, and given Sicily's perceived "otherness" to mainland Italy, De Francisci argues that Grasso's Othello not only synthesized the multilateral cultural threads (Italian, African, "Turk") of the Jacobean *Othello* but also partnered this racial alterity with a new dramatic language of realism and immediacy.

In "Shakespeare, Vittorini, and the Anti-Fascist Struggle", another chapter devoted to Shakespeare's Sicilian afterlife, Enrica Maria Ferrara demonstrates how Elio Vittorini's novel *Conversazione in Sicilia* (1938–39) mythologizes Shakespeare as a cultural icon and accords his oeuvre undisputed cultural cachet across all levels of society. Moreover, Shakespeare (both as author and oeuvre) was conscripted by Vittorini for factional ends, as a paradigm of political "engagement" and an embodiment of an anti-Fascist ideology. Silvestro, Vittorini's protagonist and alter-ego, undergoes an Odyssean journey of regeneration—a return to Sicily and to a childhood infused with memories of his father's recitations of Shakespeare. Scenes of recollecting, rereading, and rewriting suffuse the novel, especially in Silvestro's visions of his "Shakespearean father", a resurgent father-figure who keeps activating memories of *Macbeth* and *Hamlet* like an importunate ghost dredging up the past. A second model, besides the "Shakespearean father", derives from Shakespeare's late romances, in the director-actor-author figure represented by Prospero. Where *Hamlet* and *Macbeth* resonate for Silvestro because of their buried memories and actorly metaphors, *The Tempest* and (briefly) *The Winter's Tale* animate Vittorini's novel because of their meta-narrativity and self-consciously fragile aesthetic illusions.

Introduction 19

Reprising these images of textual haunting, Giuseppe Stellardi traces Shakespeare's legacy on the malleable, shifting poetics of Carlo Emilio Gadda (1893–1973), arguing, in "Hamlet's Ghost", for the enduring importance of Shakespeare's works to the career of the Italian author, poet, and essayist. Gadda's fascination with Shakespeare manifests itself as both a lexical and stylistic indebtedness (part of a "heuristic" approach that unpacks meaning from his oeuvre), and a more personal, autobiographical identification, not with Shakespeare *per se* but with Hamlet. Hamlet is Gadda's doppelgänger and predecessor (as intimated in Gadda's 1952 essay *"Amleto* al Teatro Valle"), and a "model character" for Gonzalo Pirobutirro, the autobiographical protagonist of Gadda's *chef d'oeuvre*, his novel *La cognizione del dolore*. Yet despite Gonzalo's "Hamletic" qualities (to use Gadda's own literary-critical lexicon), Stellardi exposes points of resistance. Shakespeare is undoubtedly an inspiration perpetually haunting Gadda's literary style and thought, but this Shakespearean inheritance remains an incomplete pattern for Gadda's own writing: other traditions and influences (principally Alessandro Manzoni) jockey for attention, and Gadda must forfeit *Hamlet*'s ultimately cathartic, restorative conclusion which has no place in the unredeemed universe of *La cognizione*.

Resistance to Shakespeare also dominates Camilla Caporicci's chapter, "The rest which is *not* silence", discussing the multifaceted use of Shakespearean echoes in the writings of the Genoese poet, translator, and Nobel Prize-winner Eugenio Montale. Montale's characteristic lexis and colour symbolism reveal a range of intertextual methods that both align him with and distance him from Shakespeare: Montale's letters to his American muse, Irma Brandeis, betray a "casual intertextuality" that hints at Shakespeare's prestige and quotability; Gadda's poetry typically echoes *The Tempest* through "allusive" references (conspicuous excerpts meant to be recognised by readers as deliberate quotations); echoes from the *Sonnets*, by contrast, resemble "not allusive allusions" (impressionistic but autonomous references at one remove from Shakespeare). In his later poetry, Montale's allusivity becomes more explicit, parodic, and subversive, replacing his earlier reverence with something more resistant and interrogative—a poetics of negative citation and countermanding impulses that lifts phrases and images from their Shakespearean moorings and inverts them. Montale's various strategies—some paratextually explicit, others personalized and biographically-specific, still others abstrusely metatextual—excerpt and recontextualize Shakespeare in provocatively innovative ways.

The dialogue with Shakespeare becomes a vibrant, unresolved "dialectic" in Giorgio Strehler's *Il gioco dei potenti* [*The Game of the Powerful*], his magisterial adaptation of the *Henry VI* trilogy and the subject of Mace Perlman's chapter. Shakespeare's War-of-the-Roses

20   *Chris Stamatakis*

plays are reimagined by Strehler as a fusion of Brecht and earlier, native, pre-Shakespearean traditions (including the *commedia dell'arte*), staging political history as a play. In imposing his aesthetic stamp on the trilogy, Strehler expanded minor details; increasingly relinquished the text in order to embrace an all-pervading idea of theatricality; and interpolated new components, demonstrating what he himself termed the "courage to write on Shakespeare's behalf". Strehler's appropriative strategy for filling in the "terrible gaps" in Shakespeare's Italian reception reveals two related, but counterpointed, imperatives: a rigorous fidelity to the text, and a zest for creative adaptation. Strehler's legacy is hard to overstate: his portrait of an endlessly-replayed conflict of power, whose agents both perform roles and stand outside them as ironic commentators, possibly inspired La Compagnia del Collettivo's *Enrico IV* for the Teatro Due di Parma—part of another trilogy, with *Amleto* and *Macbeth* (1979–1982). This production iconoclastically harnessed diverse acting styles, from improvised street theatre to Noh, via musical interludes lifted from, *inter alia*, Brecht's *Threepenny Opera* (which Strehler had himself directed in 1956), conjuring an aura of an "emblematic cross-cultural montage of 'strange tongues'" (Hodgdon 1991: 183).

Gonzalo's utopian vision in *The Tempest* famously denied the conditions for commercial exchange ("no kind of traffic"), yet *The Tempest* itself remains one of Shakespeare's plays most subject to international reuse and recontextualisation. In this chapter, "Shakespeare behind Italian Bars", Mariangela Tempera examines two plays—*The Tempest* and *Julius Caesar*—chosen for performance by a company of inmate actors at Rebibbia prison on the outskirts of Rome. Fabio Cavalli selected Eduardo De Filippo's 1984 translation of *The Tempest* into seventeenth-century Neapolitan (in a curious return to early modernity) as his base text: under Cavalli's direction, *The Tempest* becomes a bricolage of Shakespeare, Neapolitan dialect, and anachronistic Italian popular culture that is (somehow) obliquely sanctioned by Shakespeare's play. In the Taviani brothers' handling, *Julius Caesar* undergoes a similar transformation: their 2012 film *Cesare deve morire*, recounting the rehearsal and performance of a Neapolitanized *Giulio Cesare* by the Rebibbia inmates, draws in places on *The Tempest*, not least in exposing the diaphanous boundary between performing actors and performed characters. Through several layers of translation—from English text to regional Italian dialects, from script to stage, from stage to film—Shakespeare's work and cultural cachet are co-opted for topical, social commentary.

The final chapter, "Shakespeare, Tradition, and the Avant-garde in Chiara Guidi's *Macbeth su Macbeth su Macbeth*", taking the form of a dialogue between Sonia Massai and director Chiara Guidi, examines how Italian avant-garde appropriations of Shakespeare negotiate what might be considered an authenticating point of Shakespearean origin.

Introduction 21

Guidi's *Macbeth su Macbeth su Macbeth* (2014), a self-consciously disruptive reinterpretation of *Macbeth*, incorporates echoes of *The Tempest* and privileges performance over textuality, and musicality and soundscape over words-as-signifiers. Conscious of the dramatic, critical, and editorial traditions surrounding Shakespeare's play, Guidi transforms *Macbeth* into a series of minimalist stage props and defamiliarizing, pun-laden phonemes: the burden of cultural heritage is emblematized on stage by a book that disintegrates in the opening scene, and by another piece of stage furniture, an imaginary "pietra d'inciampo" [stumbling block] that hints at Shakespeare's resistance to adaptation. Massai and Guidi consider *Macbeth*'s challenge to the idea of linear succession, and liken Macbeth's temporary illusion of fulfilment to the modern adapter's tentative (perhaps illusory) sense of ownership over Shakespeare. Macbeth's claim that "nothing is, but what is not" becomes a comment on the broader question of how avant-garde reinterpretations like Guidi's actualize something latent, dormant, and not-yet-in-being within Shakespeare.

The volume concludes with a brief afterword, "Shakespeare, an Infinite Stage". Surveying individual chapters and venturing fresh examples of exchange, Paolo Puppa teases out the volume's recurrent questions of ownership and appropriation; the idea of "accommodated resistance" between Shakespearean text and Italian reincarnation; the licence of actors and translators to adapt; and the endless opportunities to transplant Shakespeare and turn his works into something rich and strange.

Bibliography

Alonge, Roberto. 1988. *Teatro e spettacolo nel secondo Ottocento*. Rome.

Andrews, Richard. 2004. "Shakespeare and Italian Comedy". *Shakespeare and Renaissance Europe*, ed. by Andrew Hadfield and Paul Hammond. London. 123–49.

Ascham, Roger. 1570. *The Scholemaster*. London.

Bakhtin, Mikhail. 1968. *Rabelais and his World*, trans. by Hélène Iswolsky. Cambridge, MA.

Betteridge, Thomas. 2007. "Introduction: Border, Travel and Writing". *Borders and Travellers in Early Modern Europe*, ed. by Thomas Betteridge. Aldershot. 1–14.

Castellani, Arrigo. 1982. "Quanti erano gl'italofoni nel 1861?". *Studi linguistici italiani*, 8: 3–26.

Chapman, George. 1598. *Achilles shield* [...] *out of his eighteenth booke of Iliades*. London.

Clubb, Louise George. 1989. *Italian Drama in Shakespeare's Time*. New Haven, CT.

——— 2011. "How do we know when worlds meet?". *Shakespeare and Renaissance Literary Theories: Anglo-Italian Transactions*, ed. by Michele Marrapodi. Aldershot. 281–285.

22 Chris Stamatakis

Coldiron, Anne E. B. 2015. "Form[e]s of Transnationhood in the Case of John Wolfe's Trilingual *Courtier*". *Renaissance Studies*, 29.1. Special issue, "Translation and Print Culture in Early Modern Europe", ed. by Brenda M. Hosington. 103–24.

Derrida, Jacques. 1979. "Living On: Border Lines". *Deconstruction and Criticism*, ed. by Harold Bloom. New York. 75–176.

Elden, Stuart. 2013. *The Birth of Territory*. Chicago.

Florio, John. 1598. *A Worlde of Wordes, or Most copious, and exact Dictionarie in Italian and English, collected by Iohn Florio*. London.

—— 1603. *The Essayes [...] of Lo: Michaell de Montaigne*. London.

Grady, Hugh. 2001. "Shakespeare Criticism, 1600–1900". *The Cambridge Companion to Shakespeare*, ed. by Margreta De Grazia and Stanley Wells. Cambridge. 265–78.

Greenblatt, Stephen. 2010. "A mobility studies manifesto". *Cultural Mobility: A Manifesto, Stephen Greenblatt et al.* Cambridge. 250–253.

Hackett, Helen, ed. 2015. *Early Modern Exchanges: Dialogues Between Nations and Cultures, 1550–1750*. Farnham.

Henke, Robert. 1997. *Pastoral Transformations: Italian Tragicomedy and Shakespeare's Late Plays*. Newark.

—— 2008. "Introduction". *Transnational Exchange in Early Modern Theater*, ed. by Robert Henke and Eric Nicholson. Aldershot. 1–15.

Hoby, Thomas. 1561. *The courtyer of Count Baldessar Castilio*. London.

—— 1588. *The courtier of Count Baldessar Castilio deuided into foure bookes*. London.

Hodgdon, Barbara. 1991. *The End Crowns All: Closure and Contradiction in Shakesepare's History*. Princeton.

Hosington, Brenda M. 2015. "Translation as a Currency of Cultural Exchange in Early Modern England". In Hackett. 27–54.

Klein, Holger, and Michele Marrapodi, eds. 1999. *Shakespeare and Italy*. *Shakespeare Yearbook*, 10. Lewiston, NY.

Lanier, Douglas. 2002. *Shakespeare and Modern Popular Culture*. Oxford.

Lepschy, Anna Laura, and Giulio C. Lepschy. 1988. *The Italian Language Today*, 2nd edition. London.

Lethbridge, J. B. 1999. "Misrepresentation through porous borders: Italy and the conceit of England in Shakespeare". In Klein and Marrapodi. 317–32.

Locatelli, Angela. 1999. "Shakespeare in Italian Romanticism: Literary *Querelles*, Translations, and Interpretations". In Klein and Marrapodi. 19–37.

Loomba, Ania. 2002. *Shakespeare, Race, and Colonialism*. Oxford.

McEachern, Claire. 1996. *Poetics of English Nationhood, 1590–1612*. Cambridge.

Marrapodi, Michele. 1999. "Shakespeare and Italy: Past and Present". In Klein and Marrapodi. 1–18.

—— ed. 2004. *Shakespeare, Italy, and Intertextuality*. Manchester.

—— ed. 2007. *Italian Culture in the Drama of Shakespeare & his Contemporaries: Rewriting, Remaking, Refashioning*. Aldershot.

—— et al., eds. 1997. *Shakespeare's Italy: Functions of Italian Locations in Renaissance Drama*. Revised edition. Manchester.

Miola, Robert S. 2006. *Shakespeare's Reading*. Oxford.

OED Online. 2016. Oxford University Press.

Oppitz-Trotman, George. 2015. "Romeo and Juliet in German, 1603–1604". *Notes and Queries*, 62.1: 96–98.

Pfister, Manfred. 1997. "Shakespeare and Italy, or, The Law of Diminishing Returns". *Shakespeare's Italy: Functions of Italian Locations in Renaissance Drama*, ed. by Michele Marrapodi, A. J. Hoenselaars, Marcello Cappuzzo, and L. Falzon Santucci. Manchester. 295–303.

Platter, Thomas. 1937. *Thomas Platter's Travels in England*, trans. by Clare Williams. London.

Pratt, Mary Louise. 1991. "Arts of the Contact Zone". *Profession*. 33–40.

Rolli, Paolo. 1728. *Remarks upon M. Voltaire's Essay on the Epick Poetry of the European Nations*. London.

—— 1739. *Delle Ode di Anacreonte Teio*. London.

—— 1742. *Vita di Giovanni Milton. Il paradiso perduto [...] tradotto in verso sciolto dal signor Paolo Rolli*. Paris.

Samson, Alexander. 2015. "Epilogue: Exchanges: Time to Face the Strange". In Hackett. 243–50.

Sidney, Sir Philip. 1633. "A Letter to the same purpose". *Profitable Instructions [...] Robert, late Earle of Essex. Sir Philip Sidney, And, Secretary Davison*. London. 74–103.

Stierle, Karlheinz. 1996. "*Translatio Studii* and Renaissance: From Vertical to Horizontal Translation". *The Translatability of Cultures: Figurations of the Space Between*, ed. by Sanford Budick and Wolfgang Iser. Stanford. 55–67.

Tomita, Soko. 1999. "Elizabethan Dramatists and Italian Books: Henry Cheke's *Freewyl* and the Social Context". In Klein and Marrapodi. 97–121.

Woolfson, Jonathan. 1998. *Padua and the Tudors: English Students in Italy, 1485–1603*. Toronto.

Part I

Early Modern Period

Dialogues and Networks

Part 1

1 Shakespeare, Florio, and *Love's Labour's Lost*

Giulia Harding and Chris Stamatakis

Act 4 of *Love's Labour's Lost*, Shakespeare's comedy of frustrated courtship and "baroque poetics" (Elam 1984: 32) dating from the mid-1590s, contains an intriguing exchange between the constable Dull, the dim curate Sir Nathaniel, and the schoolmaster Holofernes. The dialogue is of interest not least because it soon fractures into a babel of confusion, willful mishearing, and misunderstanding—not unfitting for a play whose plot, such as it is, thrives on mistaken identity, misdirected letters, broken oaths, and punning ambiguity:

DULL	You two are bookmen: can you tell me by your wit What was a month old at Cain's birth, that's not five weeks old as yet?
HOLOFERNES	Dictynna, goodman Dull. Dictynna, goodman Dull.
DULL	What is Dictynna?
NATHANIEL	A title to Phoebe, to Luna, to the moon.
HOLOFERNES	The moon was a month old, when Adam was no more, And raught not to five weeks when he came to five-score. Th'allusion holds in the exchange.
DULL	'Tis true indeed: the collusion holds in the exchange.
HOLOFERNES	God comfort thy capacity! I say th'allusion holds in the exchange.
DULL	And I say the pollution holds in the exchange, for the moon is never but a month old; and I say beside that 'twas a pricket that the Princess killed.

(Love's Labour's Lost, 4.2.33–48)

This kind of conversation is not untypical of a play noted for its occasional "macaronic gabble" and "implausible hash of English, French, Greek, Latin, Italian, Spanish, and creative error" (Carroll 1976: 14)—a play that "delights in the use and abuse of language", is suffused with linguistic experiment and neologistic puns, and marked by a "verbal texture of repetition and allusion" in which words are "repeated, echoed, returned to and played with" (Woudhuysen 1998: 47–8). In the first instance, "allusion"—a term only ever used by Shakespeare in

28 Giulia Harding and Chris Stamatakis

this scene—here adverts to a local delight in word-play: the aptronymic Dull's riddle is answered by Holofernes' ponderous lexical gloss of "Dictynna" as another title for the moon. Equally, the term "exchange" here refers primarily to the transformation of "Cain" into "Adam", the moon's cyclical phases, and the verbal repartee between the interlocutors themselves. Yet the claim that "th'allusion holds in the exchange" enjoys a wider resonance: the line gets to the heart of the linguistic exchanges that underpin Shakespeare's text—a lexical, polyglottal interplay that characterizes the "great feast of languages" (5.1.35–6) on which the play's entourage dine with abandon.

In its intricate linguistic texture, the play embodies an ideal of lexical exchange—of Latinate, Italian, and French borrowings made English. The idea is perfectly encapsulated in Holofernes' adjective "peregrinate" (5.1.13), a "Shakespearean coinage" (Woudhuysen 1998: 225) denoting something that "affect[s] foreign styles or expressions", and a term whose etymology announces its connotations of interlingual travel and transnational journeying, something that has "travelled or sojourned abroad" (*OED*, "peregrinate, adj."). The dialogue between Holofernes and Dull shows the ready slippage of "allusion" into "collusion" (another unique usage in Shakespeare's oeuvre, here denoting a verbal or syllogistic ambiguity), and thence into "pollution" (a corruption or contamination). This threefold regression gestures to some of the dynamics of exchange that undergird Shakespeare's contact with foreign languages and literary cultures—the principles of substitution, transformation, conversation, and dialogic interaction. Extrapolating from this nexus of terms, a reader might note the ease with which a verbal *allusion*, whether a pun (*OED,* "allusion, n.", 3) or a passing literary reference (*OED*, 1), shades into a *corruption*, something approaching a *contaminatio*, or a blending of sources, plots, and genres. These principles of allusion, half-allusion, and admixture dominate the fabric of *Love's Labour's Lost*, and dictate the nature of its engagements with Italian language and literary culture.

It has become a commonplace of critical accounts of *Love's Labour's Lost* since the eighteenth century that Holofernes represents a cipher for John Florio. Florio was an Italian-language tutor (producing such parallel-text manuals as *Florio his Firste Fruites*, 1578, and *Second Frutes*, 1591), grammarian and lexicographer (whose monumental *A Worlde of Wordes*, 1598, comfortably surpassed the only previous Italian-English dictionary, William Thomas' *Principal rules of the Italian grammer* from 1550, before becoming yet more monumental in its revised, expanded form when Florio rebranded it as *Queen Anna's New World of Words* in 1611), and translator of Montaigne (*The Essayes*, 1603, from which Shakespeare may have borrowed phrases from the essay "Of the Cannibals" for *The Tempest*, 2.1). As Montini notes, "in his 1747 annotated edition of Shakespeare's works, William Warburton declared that 'by *Holofernes* is designed a particular character, a pedant

Shakespeare, Florio, and Love's Labour's Lost   29

and schoolmaster of our author's time, one *John Florio*, a teacher of the *Italian* tongue in *London*'" (Montini 2015: 109, citing Warburton and Pope, 2.227–8). Yet it is too simplistic to assume that Shakespeare modelled his "selfe-wise seeming Schoolemaister", to borrow a phrase from Sidney's *Defence of Poesie* (Sidney 1595: sig. I2^v), on the hapless John Florio. For one thing, other inspirations for Shakespeare's Holofernes include Sidney's Rombus from *The Lady of May* (Woudhuysen 1998: 2–3), and it seems unlikely that Shakespeare would have set out to ridicule Florio as a pedantic buffoon (Holofernes being routinely referred to in the speech-prefixes from the 1598 first Quarto as *"Ped."* or *"Peda."*, for *"Pedant"*, in a nod to stock types associated with the *commedia dell'arte* witnessed elsewhere in the prefixes and stage direction for Don Armado as *"Braggart"*). The distance between Holofernes and Florio is further suggested by the fact that Holofernes quotes unthinkingly from Florio's *Firste Fruites* a popular proverb about the beauty of Venice, as if, like the character in Florio's dialogue, he had visited the city himself, although clearly he has not and is merely being pretentious.

Notwithstanding the unlikelihood of an allusion to Florio in Holofernes, Shakespeare's play nevertheless shows a clear indebtedness to Florio and the world of Italian language-learning and literature to which he and his writings gave access. It is often remarked that the title of the play may derive from Florio's *Firste Fruites*: "We neede not speak so much of loue, al books are ful of loue, with so many authours, that it were labour lost to speake of Loue" (Florio 1578: sig. S3^r). In addition, there are some suggestions that *Love's Labour's Lost* responds to a skirmish between intellectual factions in the last years of the sixteenth century, whereby the play becomes a satirical attack on the so-called "School of Night", a secret English academy notionally involving both Florio and his Italian friend Giordano Bruno who was resident in England in the early 1580s (Feingold 2004). Whatever the grounds for these tantalizing connections between Shakespeare's play and Florio, several critics since Warburton's initial proposition, as Montini remarks, "have been haunted by a sort of 'magnificent obsession' to prove the existence of a liaison", whether biographical or linguistic or both, between Shakespeare and Florio, although she cautions that "no solid facts have been put forward" to cement a "possible, at best probable, acquaintanceship" between the two (Montini 2015: 109–110).

Whether Shakespeare's knowledge of Italian derived from direct, personal contact with Florio remains the subject of heated critical speculation. The debate has its roots at least as far back as Frances Yates (Yates 1934: 35–8, 334–6), and is periodically revived by such pronouncements as Jonathan Bate's that Florio was "the obvious person" to introduce Shakespeare to his Italian sources and would have subsequently exerted a formative role on Shakespeare's literary career (Bate 1997: 55). It is hard to resist the notion that Florio and Shakespeare must have been

30 *Giulia Harding and Chris Stamatakis*

close friends: the historical record and contemporary writings gesture to this relationship, which was commented on by their peers. To be sure, as Jason Lawrence cautions, by the early 1590s, it was quite possible for Shakespeare to have studied Italian independently of direct contact with Florio, relying simply on the aid of Florio's published works, chiefly the *Firste Fruites* and *Second Frutes*, the latter of this pair a collection of dialogues with a particular focus on Italian proverbs and their use in colloquial speech, bound with Florio's *Gardine of Recreation yeelding six thousand Italian prouerbs*, the most extensive list of proverbs to be published in the sixteenth century (Lawrence 2005: 11). Even more cautiously, Naseeb Shaheen asserts that "[n]othing certain is known" about Shakespeare's mode of access to his Italian sources, whether these texts were encountered directly or mediated through English or possibly French translations (Shaheen 1994: 161). Yet the testimony of Florio's contemporaries points to something potentially more tangible.

Intrigue remains around the possibility of some kind of personal acquaintance between Shakespeare and Florio not least since the latter was possessed of an invitingly capacious library of Italian books, subsequently bequeathed in his will to William Herbert, third Earl of Pembroke. The suggestion of Shakespeare's access to Florio's book collection dates back at least to Joseph Hunter's supposition from the mid-nineteenth century (Hunter 1845). To judge from the booklists (the "names of the Bookes and Auctors, that haue bin read of purpose, for the accomplishing of this Dictionarie") that precede both the 1598 *Worlde of Wordes* (detailing some seventy-two texts) and its expanded 1611 counterpart (drawing on over two hundred and fifty Italian texts), Florio's personal library could have supplied Shakespeare with his likely Italian sources from the late 1590s onwards, if not earlier too. Florio lists an interesting collection of both popular and rare Italian comedies in the bibliography to his 1598 dictionary, and Shakespeare seems to have drunk deeply from just such a well of literature for plots and characters in the composition of his own works: Sir Andrew Aguecheek, for instance, from the gender-bending farce of *Twelfth Night*, might take his origins from the Italian character "Malevolti" (literally, "sick cheeks" or "pox cheeks") to be found in the entertainment *Il Sacrificio* performed by the Accademia degli Intronati in the early 1530s along with *Gl'Ingannati*, recognised as a likely source for Shakespeare's *Twelfth Night* by modern editors and early witnesses alike. John Manningham, a law student at the Middle Temple, recounted in his diary a performance of *Twelfth Night* that took place at the Middle Temple in February 1602, remarking that the "play called 'Twelue Night, or What you Will'" was "much like the Commedy of Errores, or Menechmi in Plautus, but most like and neere to that in Italian called *Inganni*" (Bruce 1868: 18). There is evidence for Shakespeare's continuing recourse to Italian works that Florio himself drew on in compiling his dictionaries. As Lawrence remarks, certain key

Shakespeare, Florio, and Love's Labour's Lost   31

Italian texts resorted to by Shakespeare are "referred to only in Florio's second dictionary, and [...] were presumably acquired after completion of the first (by March 1596)". These include, importantly, Matteo Bandello's two-volume *Novelle* (1554), a subtext for *Much Ado about Nothing* (*c.* 1598) and for *Twelfth Night* (*c.* 1601); and Giambattista Giraldi Cinthio's *Gli Hecatommithi* (1565), a source for the plots of both *Measure for Measure* and *Othello* (both *c.* 1603–4), although of course French translations of both these collections were available to Shakespeare as well (Lawrence 2005: 127).

"Bilingued *Florio*", as he is styled in one of the commendations to him by "R. H. Gent." prefacing the *Firste Fruites* (Florio 1578: sig. **4^r), is of particular interest to any study of intercultural or transnational exchange between late sixteenth-century England and Italy. Not least among these reasons is his "liminal position—being neither an Italian nor an Englishman" (Costola and Saenger 2014: 153), as the son of an Italian Reformed minister in exile and an unidentified Englishwoman (O'Connor 2008). Given this bicultural, transnational heritage, Florio was, accordingly, obliged to "craft a persona that could ... appropriate and reflect both positive and negative stereotypes" of the Italian peninsular and its culture (Costola and Saenger 2014: 153). Exploiting this bilingual and intercultural untetheredness, Florio was celebrated by his contemporaries for his ability to obviate physical travel. In the prefatory verse "in prayse of Florio *his Labour*", another of the poems prefacing Florio's *Firste Fruites*, this time by the legendary and pioneering Elizabethan actor Richard Tarlton, this sense of linguistic journeying and labour is adverted to explicitly:

> IF we at home, by *Florios* paynes may win,
>   to know the things, that trauailes great would aske:
> By openyng that, which heretofore hath bin
>   a daungerous iourney, and a fearefull taske.
>   Why then ech Reader that his Booke doo see,
>   Geue *Florio* thankes, that tooke such paines for thee.
>   (Florio 1578: sig. ***1^v)

These "trauailes great", Florio's textual labours, mediate a foreign language and its culture to an English audience, substituting physical travel with a type of lexical travail or peregrination.

This deft polylinguality is likened, by less sympathetic contemporaries than Tarlton, to a kind of "intermeddling". When Thomas Nashe's friend Robert Greene brought out his play *Menaphon* (1589), Nashe contributed to it an epistle "To the Gentlemen Students *of both Uniuersities*", which amounted to an outburst against his rivals. One target in particular occupies his attention. This "idiote art-master" is described as intruding, as being among those "manie thred bare witts" who "emptie

32 *Giulia Harding and Chris Stamatakis*

their inuention of their Apish deuices, and talke most superficiallie of Pollicie, as those that neuer ware gowne in the Vniuersitie [as enrolled fellows]" (Greene 1589: sigs. **1ʳ, **2ʳ). Nashe's indictment continues, encompassing in general "some deepe read Grammarians, who hau[e] no more learning in their scull, than will serue to take vp a commoditie; nor Art in their brain" and specifically one who privately tutors an entourage of followers who "intermeddle with Italian Translations" (Greene 1589: sigs. **1ᵛ, **3ʳ). Here, Nashe's term "intermeddle" suggests not just the linguistic procedure of mixing together two languages through translation (*OED*, "intermeddle, v.", 1.a, transitive, "to intermingle") but also a more unwelcome type of intervention (*OED*, 3, intransitive, "to meddle, interfere; *esp.* to concern oneself with what is none of one's business"). To support his own salvo, Nashe, perhaps still resentful for being passed up preferment at Florio's hands, recalls the attack on the importation of Italian literature, manners, and morals published nearly twenty years earlier in Roger Ascham's *The Scholemaster*. In praising Robert Greene, Nashe contrasts him with "the Italionate pen, that of a packet of pilfries, affoordeth the presse a pamphlet or two in an age, and then in disguised arraie, vaunts Ouids and Plutarchs plumes as their owne" (sig. **1ᵛ), criticizing the expedient fluency and quick phrases or pithy sayings of which Florio was so fond.

Given these contemporary portraits of Florio as the English Italophile *par excellence* in Elizabethan England, the idea of some kind of proximity—biographical and personal, or more ambient and linguistic or intertextual—between Shakespeare and Florio becomes all the more provocative and enticing. First of all, Florio and Shakespeare can be located within shared professional networks. Early indications of Florio's contact with the theatrical world of Elizabethan England lie in 1575, during the Queen's visit to Kenilworth Castle, the stately Warwickshire home of Robert Dudley, Earl of Leicester, her lifelong friend and hopeful suitor. Florio may have been instrumental in teaching the Earl's company of theatrical players, "Leicester's Men", to perform Italian comedies for the delight of the queen and her guests. Dudley spoke Italian already, having been tutored, along with Lady Jane Grey and others of the Dudley faction, by John Florio's father, Michael Angelo Florio. The evidence for this Kenilworth scenario surfaces in the opening pages of Florio's earliest language-learning manual, *Firste Fruites*, which is dedicated to Leicester and even bears an imprint of the Earl's arms on the verso of its title-page. Florio addresses him, in both Italian and English prefatory epistles, as his lord and seeks his protection from critics as a novice scholar setting out on his career. Further clues come in the various commendatory verses from friends that precede the text. Four of them, grouped together, were penned by members of Leicester's troupe: Robert Wilson, "T. C." (Thomas Clarke), the aforementioned Richard Tarlton, and one "Iohn B.", who is most probably the actor John Bentley,

Shakespeare, Florio, and Love's Labour's Lost   33

famous for his tragic roles when a member of the Queen's Men in the 1580s. The confluence of Florio and these members of Leicester's Men makes for a compelling theatrical network that would in due course overlap with Shakespeare's.

Of these players in Leicester's Men, Robert Wilson stands out as a tantalizing intermediary. Of the men Florio is likely to have met during this period, it is the comic actor and playwright for The Queen's Men Robert Wilson whose career most clearly intertwines with both Florio and Shakespeare. The Queen's Men were hand-picked and financed by Francis Walsingham who poached at least half a dozen players from Leicester's Men, including Wilson and Tarlton. In his later years, Wilson reappears as one of Henslowe's so-called "stable" of playwrights where he organized writing partnerships and teams to produce an impressive collection of Jacobean city comedies: Henslowe's records reveal that Wilson was part of the writing team on sixteen plays over the course of just a couple of years (Henslowe-Alleyn: Manuscript 1, Articles 26, 31, 32). In the spring and summer of 1598 alone, Wilson collaborated on nearly a dozen plays for Henslowe, all now lost, and his reputation was such that he was listed among "the best for Comedy" by Francis Meres in *Palladis tamia* (Meres 1598: sig. Oo3^v; see Kathman 2004), the same phrase used a few leaves earlier to honour Shakespeare for his Plautine comedies (Meres 1598: sig. Oo2^r). While little remains of Wilson's collaborative work beyond a list of titles, the text of *The Three Ladies of London* (1581) does survive, an allegorical play involving a remarkable subplot in which the disreputable Italian merchant (fittingly called Mercadore) incurs debts to the Jewish Gerontus, a sympathetic character who may have served as a model for Shakespeare's Shylock (whose bond of 3,000 ducats over three months matches Gerontus' contract with Mercadore) (Kathman 2004). Moreover, beyond this ambient theatrical network, evidence for a likely acquaintance between Florio and Shakespeare specifically begins to emerge, given that both have been traced to the household of Henry Wriothesley, Earl of Southampton, at the time that Shakespeare dedicated his narrative poems, *Venus and Adonis* (1593) and *Lucrece* (1594), to the young earl. Florio acted as tutor in Italian to Southampton (as Florio reveals in the dedicatory epistle to, collectively, Southampton, the Earl of Rutland, and the Italophilic Lady Lucy, Countess of Bedford, that prefaces his 1598 *A Worlde of Wordes*). And in addition, Florio and Shakespeare may have enjoyed a shared publishing context too, in that Edward Blount, publisher of Shakespeare's first Folio, was also responsible for both Florio's dictionaries (1598 and 1611) and his translation of Montaigne's *Essais*.

Even if these common biographical traces and overlapping professional networks were discounted, a connection between Shakespeare and Florio can readily be established by locating them, as Montini does, within a "rich network of interdiscursive relations" yoking "Italian

34 Giulia Harding and Chris Stamatakis

humanistic language and culture" with early modern England and its literary culture (Montini 2015: 111–12). Strikingly, Shakespeare's borrowings from Florio, which pepper *The Taming of the Shrew* (*c.* 1592), predate the period of Southampton's patronage. Jason Lawrence has been foundational in establishing an interlingual field of reference joining Shakespeare and Florio, and persuasively argues for Shakespeare's increasingly competent reading of Italian, enabled in the first instance by close familiarity with Florio's works. From the "insistent parallel-text focus" of these bilingual dialogue books, Shakespeare derived a method for approaching his Italian sources, which he read "alongside English translations or adaptations" (Lawrence 2005: 11). Linguistic traces—that series of "lemmas, proverbs, or paraphrased concepts" identified by Montini (Montini 2015: 124)—are everywhere. The snippets of Italian dialogue found in *The Taming of the Shrew* probably derive directly from the opening chapters of Florio's *Firste Fruites*, while, over a decade later, Iago's indictment of women ("you are pictures out of door, | Bells in your parlours, wildcats in your kitchens, | Saints in your injuries; devils being offended, | Players in your housewifery, and hussies in your beds", 2.1) echoes the debate in Florio's *Second Frutes* between Silvestro and Pandulfo: "Women are in churches, Saints: abroad, Angels: at home, deuills: at windowes Syrens: at doores, pyes: and in gardens, Goates" (Florio 1591: sig. Z4^r).

These currents of intertextual, interdiscursive connection come together most obviously in *Love's Labour's Lost*, a play usually dated 1594 (Woudhuysen 1998: 61) and described by Jonathan Bate as "Florioesque" (Bate 2008: 12). This early comedy has routinely been favoured by critics as a potential trove of Florian influence and has duly been mined for borrowings from Florio's dialogue books. Not only can the play be located within a framework of Shakespeare's growing engagement with Italian proverbs over the 1590s (from *The Taming of the Shrew* (*c.* 1592) via *Richard III* (*c.* 1593) to *The Merchant of Venice* (*c.* 1596–7)) but, moreover, specific echoes include what Lawrence has labelled the "badly mangled proverb about Venice" ventured by Holofernes in Act 4 (which, in both the 1598 Quarto and 1623 first Folio, appears raggedly as "*Vemchie vencha, que non le unde, que non te perreche*"), deriving from the proverb "*Venetia, chi non ti vede, non ti pretia, ma chi ti vede, ben gli costa*" as found in both the *Firste Fruites* (Florio 1578: sig. 34^r) and *Second Frutes*, as well as one of Florio's own sources, James Sandford's *The Garden of Pleasure* (Sandford 1573: sig. P6^v; Lawrence 2005: 123).

The Italian trappings of the play become all the more intriguing if a third element, the heterodox firebrand Giordano Bruno, is introduced to bring Shakespeare and Florio into yet greater proximity, or more accurately to triangulate the writings of Shakespeare, Florio, and Sir Philip Sidney (Leicester's nephew, of course). Woudhuysen has demonstrated convincingly that Sidney is the "presiding spirit" of *Love's Labour's*

Shakespeare, Florio, and Love's Labour's Lost   35

Lost, and that the play is (as readers from Johnson and Coleridge have noted) steeped in Sidney's writings, developing "some of the literary and artistic problems which exercised him". Shakespeare, Woudhuysen provocatively intimates, had "mastered Sidney's writings ... turn[ing] the stuff out of which Sidney's life and art were made, or at least appeared to be made, into drama" (Woudhuysen 1998: 6). Sidney's Italian protégé Giordano Bruno arrived in England in 1583 bearing a royal letter of introduction from the French court, lived in the London house of the French ambassador Michel Castelnau de Mauvissière, and composed his *La cena delle ceneri* (1584) with a pointedly Sidneian setting, Fulke Greville's house, at which Sidney was probably present on 15 February 1584 for the Ash Wednesday meal alluded to in the title of Bruno's work (Woudhuysen 2004). Bruno's familiar proximity to Sidney is further attested by the publication of Bruno's works in London under the protection of Sidney as his patron.

Bruno's position in the same network as not just Sidney but Florio and Shakespeare is attested in a number of ways. From 1583 for two years, Florio served in the French embassy in London as tutor to the daughter (Katherine Marie) of the ambassador de Mauvissière, during which time he met Bruno, who befriended him and who would mention Florio directly as a companion in one of his six moral dialogues, the aforementioned *Cena delle ceneri*. In turn, Florio would later draw an affectionate picture of Bruno in one of the opening dialogues of *Second Frutes* portraying a character called "Nolano" (exclusively the sobriquet of Bruno, after his home village of Nola): Nolano is depicted lounging on a window-seat, leafing through a book and patiently waiting for his friend Torquato to get dressed, perusing his extensive wardrobe, and despairing that all his shirts are at the laundry. Later still, Florio would celebrate Bruno's remarks on translation in his prefatory address to the reader in his translation of Montaigne's *Essais*: "my olde fellow *Nolano* tolde me, and taught publikely, that from translation all Science had it's of-spring" (Florio 1603: sig. A5^r). Shakespeare's own literary network would overlap with Bruno's, in that Bruno's books were published by Thomas Vautrollier, whose printing business was later taken over by Shakespeare's Stratford friend, Richard Field, who published his narrative poems in 1593–4. And, no less importantly, Bruno's works are listed among the two hundred and fifty or so that Florio claimed to have consulted when compiling his revised Italian-English dictionary (1611), so Shakespeare may have had access to them directly in Florio's library, or at the very least in excerpted, commonplaced form in Florio's dictionary itself.

Given these biographical hints both of a literary and intellectual nexus connecting Florio and Shakespeare with Bruno and Sidney, and of an Anglo-Italian network underpinning *Love's Labour's Lost*, the next logical question to ask is whether it is possible to trace an Italian lexical

36   *Giulia Harding and Chris Stamatakis*

undercurrent in the play and, more specifically, whether Florio's linguistic signature can be seen to leave an impress on Shakespeare's language. It would be some years yet before Florio's first dictionary appeared in print, but he was already assembling the work at the time that Shakespeare was composing *Love's Labour's Lost*, and to Florio, or at least Florio's example, might be attributed the play of vocabularies and proverbial idiom found throughout *Love's Labour's Lost*—in, for instance, the series of variant spellings of "guerdon" or "remuneration" (in both Quarto and Folio texts), possibly reflecting a pointedly French pronunciation, which lies behind Costard's famous joke (3.1.165–8) that gained notoriety beyond the play's immediate reception (Woudhuysen 1998: 78). In *Love's Labour's Lost*, French and Italian puns are bandied with sophisticated ease: in the Princess' invitation to Boyet, "you can carve: I Break up this capon" (4.1.56–7) as she hands him a newly-arrived love letter, the word "capon" may signal an Italian pun, "pollicetta" [capon] sounding homophonically cognate with "polizetta"—a love letter, or surreptitious message, what Florio defines in his 1598 dictionary as "a little schedule, note, bill, or memorial in writing" (Florio 1598: sig. Aa4^r). The "capon" pun, obscure in English, appears to have come across in translation from an Italian source—a joke for the benefit of Italian speakers but not their monolingual English counterparts. The play is "particularly full" of "unfamiliar neologisms" (Woudhuysen 1998: 48), and Shakespeare, no less than Armado, seems a "man of fire-new words", a "mint of phrases in his brain" (1.1.176, 163). Words of Italian provenance bestrew the play. Where the *OED* credits Shakespeare with the first citation of "apostrophe" (to denote the punctuational mark of elision) in Holofernes' "You find not the apostrophus and so miss the accent" (4.2.119–20), closer inspection reveals an earlier usage, available to Shakespeare, in Florio's *First Fruites*: "I see that the *Apostraphes* are much vsed in the Italian ... wherby the Reader may knowe, where the vowel wanteth" (Florio 1578: sigs. Ff3^v–Gg1^r). Once again, Florio seems to be the foundational conduit through which Shakespeare's Italianate lexis is mediated, and, more generally, the case for personal contact of some sort between the two might be strengthened by the salutary reminder that Shakespeare's "Italian" source material existed not only in the emergent literary standard of Florentine (or Tuscan) but also regional dialects such as Neapolitan (Bruno), or Venetian, or Roman (Aretino), or Genoese (such as the Academy comedies), access to which would have been greatly facilitated by a speaker like Florio schooled in "the Venetian ... the Romane ... the Lombard ... the Neapolitane, ... so manie, and so much differing Dialects, and Idiomes, as be vsed and spoken in Italie, besides the Florentine" (Florio 1598: sig. a4^r).

To be sure, doubts will always remain over the precise nature of Shakespeare's familiarity with Florio the man. There is some evidence

Shakespeare, Florio, and Love's Labour's Lost   37

that Shakespeare may have accessed Italian material independently of Florio, since among the possible sources for *The Merchant of Venice* (1596–7) is Ser Giovanni Fiorentino's *Il Pecorone*, an Italian prose work composed in the fourteenth century, though unprinted until 1558, and ostensibly not one of the works consulted by Florio for either edition of his dictionary (Lawrence 2005: 127). Crucially, the work was not translated into English or even French, complicating the assumption that Florio was a necessary intermediary for Shakespeare's Italian materials: Miola argues that Shakespeare probably read the Italian original directly (Miola 2000: 81). By a similar logic, Shakespeare may have drawn upon Giovanni Battista Guarini's *Il pastor fido* (1590) for *All's Well that Ends Well* and *Measure for Measure*, according to G. K. Hunter who argues, from admittedly slender findings, that Shakespeare read not the 1602 translation of *Il Pastor Fido* but the original (Hunter 1973: 138–9). Contenders for Shakespeare's Italian intermediaries other than Florio include, in Katherine Duncan-Jones's reckoning, Shakespeare's fellow playwright, the "half-Italian" John Martson and the aforementioned Warwickshire printer Richard Field whose printing-house may have served as a "working library" for Shakespeare (Duncan-Jones 2001: 155, 114–15). For Robert Henke, Shakespeare's collaborator John Fletcher, rather than Marston, was the crucial intermediary responsible for furnishing Shakespeare with "the most important source of information about Guarinian tragicomedy"—a brand of Italian pastoral tragicomedy that, Henke contends, underpins both *Cymbeline* and *The Winter's Tale*, two late plays that can be considered "pastoral reformations" of the tragic paradigm encapsulated earlier in *Othello* (Henke 1997: 51, 103). So Florio might be part of a more extensive network of Italophile playwrights and printers at the turn of the century.

However, given that, as Lawrence notes, from the 1570s onwards language-learning activity in England was primarily a process "clearly predicated on the sustained use of parallel texts" (Lawrence 2005: 119), and given, moreover, that Shakespeare is, at the very least, evidently indebted to Florio's parallel-text dialogues, Florio's translational impress on Shakespeare's language and idiom cannot be doubted. The parallel-text method offers a useful analogy for the way in which intermediaries like Florio enabled two languages or literary cultures to be simultaneously present, and insistently demanding collation and continual comparison from their readers or listeners. This delicate duality of Italian and English vocabularies was expressly celebrated in the prefatory materials to Florio's *Firste Fruites*, in a series of horticultural analogies that would recur later in the prefatory sonnet (by Florio's anonymous friend "Phaeton") to *Second Frutes*, crediting Florio with a blossoming of English vernacular possibilities, a cornucopian flowering of England's linguistic foliage (Florio 1591: sig. *2ᵛ). In the *First Fruites*, especially

38 *Giulia Harding and Chris Stamatakis*

the commendatory poem by "R. H." to Florio, Florio's contemporaries and acolytes gracefully played off the floral, horticultural resonance of Florio's own name and the "fruites" alluded to in the work's title:

> an English Stocke, but an Italian Plant.
> The double graft did take a double roote,
> for ech of them supplies the others want.
>
> (Florio 1578: sig. **4^r)

The analogy here offers a model of a fine-tuned doubleness, reciprocity, and complementarity between the two languages. "The Graffer FLORIO", to use the terms of John Cowland's prefatory verse eulogizing Florio on the verso of this leaf (Florio 1578: sig. **4^v), ventures an endearing pun, on grafting and graphing (writing), from their shared etymological root (*graphein*), the same play (on "engraft") to be found in the final couplet of Shakespeare's Sonnet 15. Florio, in these prefatory encomia, is credited with a translation, a carrying over of a language and its literary culture—from "Italian soyle" to "our English fieldes", in Robert Wilson's terms (Florio 1578: sig. **4^v). It is to Florio we must look for this pioneering example of how to cultivate Italian linguistic culture in new English environs, domesticating the foreign yet preserving, in parallel, its indelible Italian character.

Bibliography

Bate, Jonathan. 1997. *The Genius of Shakespeare*. London.
——— 2008. *Soul of the Age: The Life, Mind and World of William Shakespeare*. London.
Bruce, John, ed. 1868. *Diary of John Manningham*. London.
Carroll, William C. 1976. *The Great Feast of Language in* Love's Labour's Lost. Princeton.
Costola, Sergio, and Michael Saenger. 2014. "Shylock's Venice and the Grammar of the Modern City". *Shakespeare and the Italian Renaissance. Appropriation, Transformation, Opposition*, ed. by Michele Marrapodi. Farnham. 147–62.
Duncan-Jones, Katherine. 2001. *Ungentle Shakespeare: Scenes from his Life*. London.
Elam, Keir. 1984. *Shakespeare's Universe of Discourse: Language-games in the Comedies*. Cambridge.
Feingold, Mordechai. 2004. "Giordano Bruno in England, Revisited". *Huntington Library Quarterly*, 67.3 (September 2004): 329–346.
Florio, John. 1578. *Florio his Firste Fruites which yeelde familiar speech, merie prouerbes, wittie sentences, and golden sayings*. London.
——— 1591. *Florios Second Frutes to be gathered of twelue trees, of diuers but delightsome tastes to the tongues of Italians and Englishmen*. London.
——— 1598. *A Worlde of Wordes, or Most copious, and exact Dictionarie in Italian and English, collected by Iohn Florio*. London.

Shakespeare, Florio, and Love's Labour's Lost   39

——— 1603. *The Essayes* [...] *of Lo: Michaell de Montaigne*. London.

——— 1611. *Queen Anna's New World of Words, or Dictionarie of the Italian and English Tongues*. London.

Greene, Robert. 1589. *Menaphon*. London.

Henke, Robert. 1997. *Pastoral Transformations: Italian Tragicomedy and Shakespeare's Late Plays*. Newark.

Henslowe-Alleyn Digitisation Project. *Letters and Papers relating to the English Drama and Stage during the life of Edward Alleyn and to the subsequent History of the Fortune Theatre, 1559–1662*. www.henslowe-alleyn.org.uk/.

Hunter, G. K. 1973. "Italian Tragicomedy on the English stage". *Renaissance Drama*, 6 (1973): 123–48.

Hunter, Joseph. 1845. *New Illustrations of the Life, Studies and Writings of Shakespeare*, 2 vols. London.

Kathman, David. 2004. "Wilson, Robert (d. 1600)". *Oxford Dictionary of National Biography*. Oxford University Press. www.oxforddnb.com/view/article/29682.

Lawrence, Jason. 2005. *"Who the devil taught thee so much Italian?" Italian Language Learning and Literary Imitation in Early Modern England*. Manchester.

Meres, Francis. 1598. *Palladis tamia. Wits treasury*. London.

Miola, Robert S. 2000. *Shakespeare's Reading*. Oxford.

Montini, Donatella. 2015. "John Florio and Shakespeare: Life and Language". *Memoria di Shakespeare. A Journal of Shakespearean Studies*, 2: 109–29.

O'Connor, Desmond. 2008. "Florio, John (1553–1625)". *Oxford Dictionary of National Biography*. Oxford University Press. www.oxforddnb.com/view/article/9758.

OED Online. 2016. Oxford University Press.

Sandford, James. 1573. *The Garden of Pleasure*. London.

Shaheen, Naseeb. 1994. "Shakespeare's knowledge of Italian". *Shakespeare Survey*, 47 (1994): 161–9.

Sidney, Sir Philip. 1595. *The Defence of Poesie*. London.

Warburton, William, and Alexander Pope, eds. 1747. *The Works of Shakespear*. London.

Woudhuysen, H. R., ed. 1998. *Love's Labour's Lost*. Arden Shakespeare. Walton-on-Thames.

——— 2004. "Sidney, Sir Philip (1554–1586)". *Oxford Dictionary of National Biography*. Oxford University Press. www.oxforddnb.com/view/article/25522.

Yates, Frances A. 1934. *John Florio: The Life of an Italian in Shakespeare's England*. Cambridge.

2 A Tale of Two Tamings
Reading the Early Modern *Shrew* Debate from a Feminist Transnationalist Perspective

Celia R. Caputi

> [A]s a woman, I have no country. As a woman, I want no country. As a woman, my country is the whole world.
> —Virginia Woolf, *Three Guineas*, 1938

> Oh, gentlemen, I know not where I am.
> —John Fletcher, *The Tamer Tamed, c.* 1609

Why read Shakespeare's *The Taming of the Shrew* and not John Fletcher's *The Tamer Tamed, or the Woman's Prize*? Fletcher's response to Shakespeare's controversial wife-taming "comedy" (1590) was a largely unknown entity twenty years ago; the individual play is now available in two paperback editions and at least three anthologies. Yet Fletcher's so-called sequel—which turns the tables on Petruchio and celebrates in its Epilogue "due equality" between the sexes—has yet to achieve the prominence it deserves in theatres or on course syllabi. This chapter aims to demonstrate the play's value not only for its delightful theatricality and more empowered female characters, but also for its refreshing contrast with Shakespearean approaches to foreign cultures.

Why read *The Taming of the Shrew*? One might answer, "Because it is set in Italy". The first lines of Act One emphasize the exotic setting, in Lucentio's statement:

> for the great desire I had
> To see fair Padua, nursery of arts;
> I am arrived at fruitful Lombardy,
> The pleasant garden of great Italy
>
> (Shakespeare 1996: 1.1.1–4)

This might seem like praise, but critics have pointed out the way in which Italy in this text and others by Shakespeare serves "as a primarily negative ideological model", for this "'pleasant garden' ... becomes an unpleasant garden of vices, a sort of Boschian inferno" (Elam 2004: 256). Lucentio's wording itself invites ambiguity: should we be surprised at the behaviour of the men of this play given that we find them in a *nursery?* Perhaps Petruchio's warning that he "woo[s] not like a babe" (2.1.137) is meant to set him apart for his Veronese origin, but the Verona of *Romeo and Juliet*—wherein a character by the same name makes a cameo appearance—is no "pleasant garden" either. After all, stereotypically Italian excess can make for tragedy or comedy.

Petruchio's ethnicity becomes significant when considered in the light of Shakespeare's sources. Unlike the Lucentio/Bianca material, which derives from Ariosto's *I suppositi* through (probably) the medium of George Gascoigne's English translation, *Supposes*, the Petruchio/Katharina plot was adapted by Shakespeare from the brutally misogynistic anonymous ballad, *A Merry Jest of a Shrewd and Curst Wife Lapped in Morel's Skin for her Good Behaviour* (c. 1550). It is as English as English can be. Whatever Shakespeare's motivation in "Italianizing" the ballad's un-named protagonist and naming him after a silent, servant character in Ariosto's play, the effect would have been to protect English cultural identity by exoticizing the hero's mistreatment of his bride. Shakespeare also sublimated the violence of the English source, wherein the husband tames his wife by beating her bloody and sewing her into the salted skin of a dead horse. In *Shrew*, Petruchio quells Katharina's will by way of isolation, sleep deprivation, starvation, indirect violence, and linguistic God-games—in other words, by brainwashing her (Detmer 1997). In sum, Petruchio's methods are more subtle—one might even say more *Machiavellian*—and thus make for better psychological drama. And what more fitting setting for a play that dramatizes the failure of female formal education (Wiesner 2000: 152–54) and the breakdown (among men) of Florian-style polite discourse than Padua (Elam 2007), that renowned centre for humanist learning?

Enter John Fletcher, and with him Petruchio's un-tameable and fiercely eloquent second wife, Maria—a "compelling" portrait of "women overcoming men through rhetorical skill" that "progressively challenges the notion of a male monopoly on intellectual debate" (Johnson 2011: 313). Surprisingly, given Fletcher's predilection for exotic settings (Spain, Italy, Moscow, Greece, France, Cyprus, and the Spice Islands), the play is set in London, and gives no rationale for the hero's deportation from Italy. Petruccio (Fletcher's spelling) is the only character identified in the *Dramatis Personae* as "Italian", though there is further overlap with *Shrew*, most notably in Bianca, identified as the heroine's "cousin" (then a casual marker of kinship) even while her function as feminist co-conspirator seems consistent with the latent "shrewishness" of Shakespeare's Bianca. To further complicate *Tamer Tamed*'s ethnography in relation to *Shrew*, Fletcher grants Maria's father a name from classical sources that links him to his son-in-law: Petronius, etymologically the large rock to Petruccio's little one. Most importantly, however, Petronius' misogyny is, if anything, more pronounced and more

42   *Celia R. Caputi*

violent than that of the play's foreign hero (Fletcher 2006: 21–22). In other words, in Fletcher's play, gender solidarity for both women and men (Bianca/Maria and Petruccio/Petronius) trumps divisions of national or ethnic identity. The first part of this chapter aims to reframe the ideological contrast between Shakespeare's *Shrew* and Fletcher's *Tamer Tamed* by elucidating a kind of proto-transnationalism or cosmopolitanism in Fletcher's play that reinforces its more progressive message about female mobility, speech, and learning. In this chapter, transnationalism and cosmopolitanism signal an attitude more accepting of cultural and ethnic difference than otherwise associated with early modern English political thought. The second part of the essay will critique a pair of recent readings of *Shrew* in relation to Italian sources, the goal being to underscore the subtle reinforcement of Shakespeare's misogyny *and* xenophobia that can arise from a *Shrew*-centric approach to early modern Anglo-Italian debates on gender and power.

In setting up a dialectic between Shakespeare and Fletcher on the grounds of ethnic stereotype or the fetishization of, in particular, *Italian* culture, I do not wish to suggest that the latter is incapable of cultural or ethnic bigotry: some studies have persuasively argued for Fletcher's anti-Spanish sentiment in plays such as *The Chances* (Boro 2013). Moreover, to call *The Tamer Tamed* cosmopolitanist is not to say it is untainted by ethnic stereotype or generally othering language, but when xenophobic or anti-Catholic rhetoric arises in this play, it is almost always a function of the speaker's misogyny. Maria's ethnicity turns out to be a moot point: as a woman (in Virginia Woolf's terms), she has "no country". Fletcher, to level the playing field, gives her both a husband who has left his own country behind, and the grit and smarts to re-map the marital landscape.

Other Countries, Other Women

Even a casual glance at Fletcher's play contrasted with Shakespeare's underscores the more fluid geography of the former and the obsessively Italianate—or, perhaps better, *Italianist*—texture of the latter. While "Italianism" may be construed as "an Italian practice, feature, or trait; esp. an Italian expression or idiom of language" or, alternatively, "sympathy with Italy" (*OED*, "Italianism, n."), I use the term to indicate a specifically English and generally Anglocentric fantasy about Italian culture or psychology. *Shrew* is peppered with Italian phrases and gratuitous references to not only its Paduan setting but to other Italian city-states (Pisa, Mantua, Florence, Verona, Rome, Venice, and Genoa). If anything, the lapses into English idiom only foreground the setting more powerfully: some of Petruchio's servants bear English names, and, in what may simply be a grab for easy laughs, Grumio misidentifies Italian as Latin (1.2.27). Though the Induction does seem to insert

A Tale of Two Tamings   43

Padua into an English setting, this (lop-sided) frame itself is Italianized in its allusion to Aretinean eroticism and in the beggar's strange, initial Latinizing of his given name. Both plays do share an interest in tropes of mobility and travel—Shakespeare's comic hero, too, has travelled to find a wife—and both plays apply naval and equestrian imagery to the notion of spouse-"taming". In addition to the well-noted misogynist tropes of horse-taming and "riding" in *Shrew* (Boose 1991; Hartwig 1982), Petruchio's references to "the swelling Adriatic seas" (1.2.69) and to "board[ing]" Katharina (1.2.89–90) reinforce the sense of mobility and adventure in his conquest of a bride. Fletcher's Petruccio does partake in the discourse as well, using, for instance, an extended metaphor of woman-as-vessel (3.5.105–114) and calling Maria his "colt" (5.4.88) even after *she* has tamed *him*, yet elsewhere in his play these tropes are inverted (Fletcher 2006: 19). Fletcher's resistance to the Italianism of his primary English source—his refusal to other Petruccio (or Bianca) *as Italian* in conjunction with his strategic and varied references to non-English cultures—makes for an entirely different atmosphere in this comedy.

Despite Petruccio's introduction as "an Italian gentleman" in the list of Fletcher's characters, the first reference to Italy does not associate it with Petruccio, but with Livia, Maria's sister, whose courtship by both young Roland and old Moroso constitutes the subplot—Moroso's name alludes to Ben Jonson's *Epicoene, or The Silent Woman* (1609), another "taming" play with an Italian source, as discussed below. "But shall [Moroso] have her?", one man asks another; "Yes, when I have Rome", is the sarcastic reply (1.1.12). The trope of woman-as-city-under-siege goes on to organize the first two acts of the play, a re-working of Aristophanes' *Lysistrata,* which also neatly inverts Petruccio's taming strategies with his first wife: Maria and her fellow female rebels lock themselves in the bridal chamber after stocking up on victuals and booze, in the hope that the bridegroom's sexual frustration will render him "easy as a child I And tame as fear" (1.2.115–16). The Roman theme is echoed by Livia's first speech, when she speaks of *sainting* her beloved, though she shortly after, interestingly, likens herself to a Jew, refusing to worship the "hog" of Moroso's money (1.2.6; 27), as well as in Maria's vow to reform Petruccio. "I'll do it," she declares, comparing herself (in a typically learned allusion) to the Roman hero Curtius: "To redeem my country have I I Leaped into this gulf of marriage" (1.2.67). The reference to a "country" here is puzzling. How is her marriage or her wedding-night protest patriotic? The ribald pun on "cunt" cannot be ruled out as operative: this nuance is underscored by the image of the "gulf of marriage", which subverts traditional masculinist tropes of the vagina as hell, even associating such a perilous pit with her husband. Livia attributes Maria's audacity to travel: "In what part of the world got she this spirit?" (128), she wonders. Not England, apparently.

44 *Celia R. Caputi*

Bianca envisions the women having to withstand "the power of the whole country" (1.3.130). The women's rebellion renders them outsiders within their own nation, even as they barricade themselves within the domestic sphere. Thus, while Bianca and Livia compare themselves to besieged Trojans and imagine founding (instead of Rome) a new Amazonia (2.1.38), men like Moroso call them "the most authentic rebels, next [to] | Tyrone" (1.3.213)—the leader of the Irish resistance to English occupation. This is but one in a slew of othering tropes: Petruccio compares Maria to a "Jewry" (1.3.253), an "Ethiope" (3.3.11), and a Jesuit (4.1.54), and one of her companions-in-arms is described as having both "the straits of Gibralter" and "all sunburnt Barbary" in her breeches (2.3.46–47). There are references to the Italian general Spinola (1.3.66), to the Amorites (the original, pagan occupants of Canaan, 3.2.20n), to "heathen whores" (21), to a Helen of Troy nicknamed (as if to emphasize her mobility) "Nell O' Greece" (2.3.17), and to a "nest of nuns" (4.4.74–75), the term "nun" connoting not just papacy but whoredom. The women even other themselves by occasionally speaking French or Italian (2.1.12; 2.5.65) and, indeed, the item "women to read French" (2.5.142) figures in the list of demands Petruccio must sign before Maria unbars her chamber door. What is curious about these linguistic patterns is their gendering. With the possible exception of the phrase "Petruccio Furius" (1.3.174, an allusion to Ariosto's *Orlando Furioso*), the women of the play make no reference to Petruccio's ethnicity.

The moment at which the "siege" ends is pivotal for the thematic focus on space, mobility, and power that underwrites what I am calling the cosmopolitanist rhetoric of the play. Far from declaring victory in having retained her maidenhead, humbled her husband, and marked out a room of her own, Maria goes on at this point to manoeuvre her bridegroom *into* the very kind of domestic incarceration that the "gulf of marriage" can represent for women. First, however, she proposes extensive changes to the marital estate, and in cosmopolitan terms—from new tapestries "of the civil wars of France" (3.5.58), to a new garden ("of the Italian fashion", 88), to the tearing down and rebuilding of the lodge—all in the same breath in which she orders "another suit of horses" (65) with which to ride off and "take [her] pleasure" (68). Her husband then compares her to a "whirlwind, that takes all | Within her compass" (150–51). The metaphor is significant given the slippery geography of the play: if "compass" refers to the literal instrument used in navigation (as opposed to merely meaning "vicinity"), Maria then becomes the reference-point for this text's cosmography. We will see this play out beautifully in the final scene, but before going there we must see what becomes of this house the men imagine "turned ... with the foundation upward" (3.2.18–19) thanks to Maria.

From Act Three onwards, Fletcher's Petruccio resorts to more desperate and effeminizing tactics. He feigns illness, only to have Maria

A Tale of Two Tamings   45

declare him infected with the plague—a claim that allows her to barricade him in the house and remove all the furnishings. He blows the door open with a musket, only to find himself abandoned, the others having fled the perceived threat of infection. In a perfect reversal of his own sun-is-the-moon word-games with Katharina in *Shrew*, he becomes victim of his second wife's manipulation of reality and social space. Finally, he announces his decision to travel:

> No, there be other countries [...] for me
> [...]   and other women,
> If I have need. "Here's money—there's your ware"
> (Which is fair dealing) [...] And the sun, they say,
> Shines as warm there as here.
>
> (4.4.7–11)

It is a curious speech from an ex-patriot: in the allusions to prostitution and warm climates, we glimpse a moment wherein Fletcher *might* indulge in Italianist stereotype, but then resists doing so. Indeed, the playwright goes on—seemingly—to have this "Italian gentleman" forget his pedigree: "None of my nation | Shall ever know me more" (15–16). None of *which* nation? This could be sloppy writing, or it could simply represent the apotheosis of Petruccio's domestication. In any case, though, Maria quickly calls his bluff, sparking his dry aside, "She'll ship me" (136). "Go far," she tells him, "too far you cannot; still the farther, | The more experience finds you" (160). The exchange is hilarious, but also significant for the attitude about educative, character-forming travel it conveys—an attitude consistent with the play's cosmopolitanism. In another demonstration of Maria's classical learning, she tells him to "Come home an aged man, as did Ulysses"; he interrupts her statement about being "glad Penelope" with the sarcastic retort, "with as many lovers as I languages" (172–74).

Petruccio's linkage of "language" and "lovers" pulls together a number of themes relevant to this argument. The line is easily misread as referring to Maria's theoretical language acquisition: Petruccio's "I" is almost lost in the alliterative leap between the nouns, and his wife has heretofore shown her interest in foreign languages—her last words in this scene are Italian (228). In fact, in Act 5, it is Maria who acquires multiple "tongues", in the misogynist invective of Petruccio's man-servants: the word "tongue" appears eleven times in five lines, modified by "lying", "lisping", "long", "lawless", and "liquorish", culminating in the statement that "More tongues, and many stranger tongues | Than ever Babel had ... | Were women raised withal, but never a true one" (5.2.35–40). The focus on a woman's troublesome tongue is borrowed from *Shrew*, but my reading of Fletcher's cosmopolitanism grants this masculinist tirade a different nuance from any complaint about Katharina's "scolding

46 Celia R. Caputi

tongue" (*Shrew*, 1.2.94), which, Shakespeare's play suggests, must be taught neither eloquence nor languages, but silence. The diatribe against Maria's "tongue" in *Tamer Tamed* is, however, patently risible: it amounts to a whole lot of angry babble directed at a woman who never resorts to the sort of invective Shakespeare puts in the mouth of the pre-tamed Katharina. Maria is far too clever for that.

At Petruccio's supposed funeral, Maria delivers her rhetorical *tour de force*: a 23-line mock-eulogy designed to denigrate, rather than honour, the departed. "'Tis true, I have cause to grieve ... But what's the cause? ... Not this man, | As he is dead ... but his life, | His poor unmanly wretched foolish life" (5.4.14–19). Her father now fumes: "Dost thou not shame?", and she responds, "I do ... to think what this man was, to think how simple, | How far below a man" (22–24). This seems a parody of Katharina's "I am ashamed that women are so simple | To offer war where they should kneel for peace" (*Shrew*, 5.2.165–66). Far be it for Maria to *kneel* to any husband, living or dead (never mind placing her hand below his foot); rather, she here *raises* Petruccio from his coffin by mortifying him out of his fake rigor mortis. She then, finally, capitulates: "I have done my worst ... | I have tamed thee, and now am vowed your servant. | ... Dare ye kiss me?" (44–46). He does so, thrice, then declares, "Oh, gentlemen, I know not where I am". He is told, "Get ye to bed then; there you'll quickly know, sir" (50–51). Such erotic disorientation is understandable in a man deprived of sex on his wedding-night, and he does locate himself geopolitically in his next speech. After describing himself as "born again", he declares: "Well, little England, when I see a husband | Of any other nation stern or jealous, | I'll wish him but a woman of thy breeding" (60–63). Maria becomes, here, his *compass*. Perhaps he has finally come home.

Aretino, Shakespeare, Jonson, Fletcher

Why read *The Taming of the Shrew?* Some people seem to find it sexy. Even women. Even feminists. "The submission of a woman like Kate", according to Germaine Greer, "is genuine and exciting because she has something to lay down, her virgin pride and individuality" (Greer 1970: 208). More nuanced defences of the play hold that it does not endorse male supremacy so much as satirize it (Kahn 1981; Patterson 1994), or that, paradoxically, Katharina's final speech, as performance, undercuts its content (Wayne 1985; Newman 1991). Yet much recent criticism continues to stress the play's potential for titillation. Along these lines, an illustration of acrobatic heterosexual copulation culled from the notorious volume of Italian Renaissance erotica, *I modi*, graces the cover of a 2014 anthology containing two chapters on *The Taming of the Shrew*, and each relates the play to that sexually graphic text (Marrapodi 2014). Although these readings invite a more complex understanding of the Italian

A Tale of Two Tamings   47

intertext of the *Shrew/Tamer* dialogue, their sugar-coating—indeed, eroticizing—of Shakespeare's misogyny gives pause, especially in light of the Fletcher/Shakespeare contrasts elaborated in the first part of this chapter. Beyond this, these two chapters perpetuate a brand of Italianism by arguing for the greater misogyny of Shakespeare's *Italian* sources, without mentioning his recourse to a violently misogynistic *English* source, the above-mentioned ballad of *Morel's Skin*. Moreover, both chapters leave out Fletcher's contribution to the early modern gender debates—and he plays a more pivotal role in the Anglo-Italian exchange than may at first appear.

First, a bit of background. Exhibit A: Pietro Aretino's scurrilous sonnets and the engravings by Marcantonio Raimondi that inspired them, together known as *I modi* [*The Positions*], a kind of satirical sex-manual, published in 1524 and immediately (and effectively) suppressed by order of the Pope. Exhibit B: Aretino's comedy, *Il Marescalco* [*The Stablemaster*], wherein a woman-hating sodomite is tricked into marrying a cross-dressed boy and when the truth is revealed the "victim" of the joke rejoices at his luck. Exhibit C: Ben Jonson's, *Epicoene, or The Silent Woman* (1609), an adaptation of the latter, which dramatizes the same practical joke but removes the sodomitical tendencies of its object and, thus, the surprise "happy ending".

Let us begin with the connection between Aretino's *I modi* and Shakespeare's *Shrew*. In his chapter "'Wanton pictures': The Baffling of Christopher Sly and the Visual-Verbal Intercourse of Early Modern Erotic Arts", Keir Elam makes an excellent case for Shakespeare's consciousness of the work known in England as "Aretine's Pictures" when crafting his Induction scene in *Shrew*, but he perhaps overstates the dichotomy between Aretinean and Shakespearean eroticism. Aretino's sonnets, according to Elam, "concede an apparently limitless sexual agency to women, who indeed seem to be the primary subjects rather than objects of hyperbolic desire", although, as he goes on to observe, these female characters "are, on closer inspection, thinly disguised projections of male pornographic desire ... [they] are essentially faceless and voiceless" (Elam 2014: 138). Of course, the charge of male ventriloquism would apply just as readily to female characters on the Elizabethan transvestite stage. If anything, since thirteen of the sixteen sonnets are in dialogic form, Aretino's *I modi* overall gives female voices close to equal time, in contradistinction to *Shrew*, wherein Katharina's voice is overwhelmed by Petruchio's, as Dolan remarks (Shakespeare 1996: 24–29).

Elam makes the transition from Aretino's *I modi* to his more obviously misogynistic *Il Marescalco* by way of the *culo*—the "arse, taile, fundament or bum", in Florio's definition (Florio 1598: sig. H5^r). "The disguising of homoerotic as heterosexual coupling, with particular reference to ... sodomy, is the central theme of Aretino's comic masterpiece" (Elam 2014: 139). Connecting *Shrew* to *Il Marescalco* in this

48   Celia R. Caputi

way complicates, even undermines, the dichotomy ventured between Aretino's and Shakespeare's eroticism in the case of Shakespeare's aforementioned contact with *I modi*. Elam briefly considers how the engagement with *Il Marescalco* implicates Shakespeare himself in misogyny:

> It may be, however, that the sexual ambiguities of Shakespeare's Induction, with its seductive boy actor Bartholomew, not only reflect its Italian source but in turn cast a somewhat problematic light on the main play, in which the somewhat misogynistic Petruccio is rewarded with an unruly lady played by a boy actor (possibly the same boy actor playing Bartholomew ...)
>
> (Elam 2014: 142)

A compelling point, but one that is glossed over too readily. Elam returns to the "wanton pictures" of the Induction, this time highlighting Shakespeare's references to Ovid: "The subject matter is erotic in the broad sense, but apparently innocuous compared to the crude physicality of the *Modi*". The term "innocuous" is ill-chosen: the Ovidian references are to rape and attempted rape. Typically, Shakespeare does not use the word "raped" but rather "beguiled and surprised", and he metonymizes the sexual violence in the "blood" of Daphne's thorn-scratched legs (*Shrew*, Ind.53; 58). As opposed to the "crude" Aretinean references to pricks, cunts and asses—in Italian, *cazzo, potta,* and *cul*, left untranslated in Lynn Lawner's edition to distinguish the sonnets from "pornographic exercises" (Romano 1988: ix)—and as opposed to the even cruder Raimondi artwork chosen for the cover of Marrapodi's volume, Shakespeare very prettily describes these assaults upon women. The attitude of Shakespeare's Induction, in other words, is in keeping with that of the play proper, which weaves comic material out of a forced marriage, a kind of rape: Petruchio marries Katharina against her will, as each character very plainly states (2.1.264; 3.2.8–9). The cumulative evidence frustrates attempts to counterpoint Aretino's and Shakespeare's eroticism, or to exonerate Shakespeare from an Italian misogynistic tradition.

Marrapodi's essay—"The Aretinean Intertext and the Heterodoxy of *The Taming of the Shrew*", the volume's final word on the play—also links *Shrew* to *Il Marescalco*, but equally glosses over the "somewhat problematic" correspondence (to return to Elam's terms) between the two endings. Marrapodi writes, "[i]n contrast to ... Aretino's misogynistic solution", Shakespeare celebrates "the heterosexual couple of Petruchio and Katherina, highlighting in them a rediscovered collaboration". The essay continues to argue for Shakespeare's "subverting" an Italian "misogynist tradition", extolling the "innovative, loving relationship" brought to being by the newlyweds' "vows of authentic feelings, genuine interests, and reciprocal needs and desires" (Marrapodi 2014: 254).

A Tale of Two Tamings   49

Yet there are no such vows in the final scene of Shakespeare's play. Moreover, if the contrast with the conclusion of *Il Marescalco* lies in the "heterosexual" nature of the union, what happens when we consider (as does Elam's reading, momentarily) the boy actor for whom Shakespeare scripted Katharina's role?

I have lingered on these two essays because, in yielding to the impulse to exonerate Shakespeare from misogyny, they imply that Shakespeare was *better* than his sources. Neither reading mentions Shakespeare's English source, wherein the misogyny is far more virulent, or question why he chose to touch *any* of this material with a ten-foot quill. Nor does either mention Fletcher's proto-feminist rebuttal: this text engaged not only with Shakespeare's *Shrew*, but with its reputed source, *Il Marescalco*, albeit, it seems, indirectly through Jonson's *Silent Woman*. Shifting the analytical focus to the Aretino-Jonson-Fletcher axis of influence richly complicates the assumptions and evaluations outlined above. Even if one accepts the suggestion that Shakespeare somehow improved upon Aretino's view of women, the fact that Jonson left in place—even, arguably, enhanced—the misogyny of *Il Marescalco* (Moulton 2000: 158–59), while also uncritically expanding upon the antifeminist "taming" rhetoric saturating *Shrew*, creates a guilt-by-association argument that tempers feminist enthusiasm for the latter. In other words, if *Shrew* is *not* antifeminist, both Jonson and Fletcher missed the point. It is therefore not surprising that Fletcher references Jonson's play ("I never will believe a silent woman. | When they break out they are bonfires", 1.3.110–11) and critiques its misogyny throughout *The Tamer Tamed* (Fletcher 2006: 11–13). In substituting Jonson's Morose with his own Moroso, in creating for the latter a young, sympathetic rival in Roland, and in removing the metatheatrical (and vicious) practical joke of the cross-dressed boy-bride, Fletcher in his sub-plot offers, in fact, the very sort of romantic "happy ending" Marrapodi sees in the final scene of *Shrew*. Indeed, Roland's underage status (1.4.54) might even be a conscious echo of Jonson and Aretino: rather than using a boy's body for a cruel joke (and, theoretically, inviting his pederastic abuse), Fletcher gives a virile and perhaps tractable young husband to the crafty (and implicitly more mature) Livia. *She* gets the "boy", and, like Aretino's stable-master, she delights in her "woman's prize".

Fletcher's exposure to *Il Marescalco* may have been solely through *Epicoene,* but he could not have been ignorant of Aretino's legacy in *I modi.* Despite the fascination with "Aretine's pictures" among early modern English playwrights which has been well-documented by Elam, Marrapodi, myself (Daileader 1998, 2006), and others, no allusion to it appears in *The Tamer Tamed* or any of Fletcher's solo-authored works set in Italy. Was there no temptation on the author's part to have Maria's plans for re-decorating the lodge call for "wanton pictures" instead of tapestries with a French military theme? Fletcher was by no means

50   *Celia R. Caputi*

squeamish of sexual topics: his comedy, in fact, was censored for profanity in 1633 (Fletcher 2006: 31–36). In choosing, in this play, to exploit neither an Italianist notion of the erotic, nor an exoticized brand of foreign misogyny, Fletcher reveals his cosmopolitanist leanings.

Conclusion

The Epilogue of *The Tamer Tamed* is a remarkable coda that still takes the breath away. There in plain "honest English" (4.3.33) was stated the author's intent: "to teach both sexes due equality" (Epilogue 97). Shakespeare's play has no Epilogue, but the conclusions of both the Folio edition and the disputed *Taming of a Shrew* are, like Fletcher's Epilogue, didactic: in the former, Katharina lectures her fellow wives on submission to their husbands and, in the latter, Christopher Sly, having learned how to tame his own shrew, goes off to do just that. Fletcher's play teaches both women and men how to learn from one another, where by contrast in Shakespeare's play women are to learn from women how to obey men and men are to learn from men how to make women obey. Which is as much to say—from a feminist point of view—that nobody learns anything.

Taming is not teaching. Animals are to be tamed: humans are to be taught. Interestingly, Shakespeare's most misogynistic play does imagine women having tutors, as opposed to nurses or bawds. On the other hand, neither "shrew" proves teachable: Katharina breaks her lute (on her teacher's head), and Bianca—the "ready scholar" according to Cecil C. Seronsy—turns "shrewish" herself, and must "go to school, to her sister ... to learn obedience" (quoted in Taylor and Bourus Forthcoming). In contrast, Maria is thrice described as "learned" in Fletcher's play (1.2.159, 2.2.112, 4.2.106), an appellation supported by her breadth of classical allusion and overall eloquence. Likewise, the *Dramatis Personae* list introduces her as "chaste" and "witty"—and Petruccio himself admits to marrying her for her "wit" (4.1.26). In one aside, a character named Sophocles for his wisdom calls Maria "an excellent woman to breed schoolmen" (*Tamer Tamed*, 4.4.154). Livia, on the other hand, proves herself wily enough in gaining her will (and young Roland) despite her lack of schooling. After her list of pranks against old Moroso, she brags: "All this ... did I; I, Livia, I alone, untaught" (5.1.95).

The moment is all the more comical for its Shakespearean echo. "O thou untaught!"—these are Montague's words at the news of his son's suicide in Act 5 of *Romeo and Juliet* (Shakespeare 1988: 5.3.212). Is Fletcher deliberately having fun with Shakespeare—and, perhaps, his Italianism as well—alluding to this moment of tragic pathos at the end of a cheeky mock-deathbed-confession like Livia's? Fletcher's irreverence toward his sometime-collaborator—along with the "indecency" of plays like *The Tamer Tamed*—was one factor in his decline in popularity in the Victorian Age, when Shakespeare's canonical preeminence was solidified. If Fletcher is yet to enjoy a comeback, it might be—ironically—due to these very same factors. Until then, "o thou untaught" will be an appropriate response to young scholars who assume Shakespeare had the last word in early modern debates about women—whether inside or outside "little England".

Bibliography

Boose, Lynda E. 1991. "Scolding Brides and Bridling Scolds: Taming the Woman's Unruly Member". *Shakespeare Quarterly*, 42.2: 179–213.

Boro, Joyce. 2013. "Blessed with a Baby or 'bum-fiddled with a bastard'? Maternity in Fletcher's *The Chances* and Cervantes' *Novela de la Senora Cornelia*". *The Creation and Re-creation of Cardenio: Performing Shakespeare, Transforming Cervantes*, ed. by Terri Borous and Gary Taylor. Basingstoke. 61–72.

Daileader, Celia R. 1998. *Eroticism and the Renaissance Stage: Transcendence, Desire, and the Limits of the Visible*. Cambridge.

―――― 2006. "Back-door Sex: Renaissance Gynosodomy, Aretino and the Exotic". *Straight Writ Queer: Non-Normative Expressions of Heterosexuality in Literature*, ed. by Richard Fantina. Jefferson, NC. 25–45.

Detmer, Emily. 1997. "Civilizing Subordination: Domestic Violence and *The Taming of the Shrew*". *Shakespeare Quarterly*, 48: 273–94.

Elam, Keir. 2004. "Afterword: Italy as Intertext". *Shakespeare, Italy, and Intertextuality*, ed. by Michele Marrapodi. Manchester. 253–58.

―――― 2007. "'At the Cubiculo': Shakespeare's Problems with Italian Language and Culture". *Italian Culture in the Drama of Shakespeare and His Contemporaries: Rewriting, Remaking, Refashioning*, ed. by Michele Marrapodi. Aldershot. 99–110.

―――― 2014. "'Wanton Pictures': The Baffling of Christopher Sly and the Visual-Verbal Intercourse of Early Modern Erotic Arts". *Shakespeare and the Italian Renaissance*, ed. by Michele Marrapodi. Farnham. 123–146.

Fletcher, John. 2006. *The Woman's Prize, or The Tamer Tamed*, ed. by Celia R. Daileader and Gary Taylor. Manchester.

Florio, John. 1598. *A Worlde of Wordes [...] collected by Iohn Florio*. London.

Greer, Germaine. 1970. *The Female Eunuch*. London.

Hartwig, Joan. 1982. "Horses and Women in *The Taming of the Shrew*". *Huntington Library Quarterly*, 45: 285–94.

Johnson, Sarah E. 2011. "'A Spirit to Resist' and Female Eloquence in *The Tamer Tamed*". *Shakespeare*, 7.3: 313–24.

Kahn, Coppélia. 1981. *Man's Estate: Masculine Identity in Shakespeare*. Berkeley.

Marrapodi, Michele, ed. 2014. *Shakespeare and the Italian Renaissance: Appropriation, Transformation, Opposition*. Farnham.

Moulton, Ian Frederick. 2000. *Before Pornography: Erotic Writing in Early Modern England*. Oxford.

Newman, Karen. 1991. *Fashioning Femininity and English Renaissance Drama*. Chicago.

OED Online. 2016. Oxford University Press.

52 Celia R. Caputi

Patterson, Annabel. 1994. "Framing the Taming". *Shakespeare and Cultural Traditions*, ed. by Tetsuo Kishi, Roger Pringle, and Stanley Wells. Newark. 304–313.

Romano, Giulio, et al. 1988. *I modi, the Sixteen Pleasures: An Erotic Album of the Italian Renaissance*, ed. and trans. by Lynne Lawner. London.

Shakespeare, William. 1988. *Romeo and Juliet. The Complete Works*, ed. by Stanley Wells and Gary Taylor. Oxford.

―――― 1996. *The Taming of the Shrew*, ed. by Frances Dolan. Boston.

Taylor, Gary, and Terri Bourus, eds. Forthcoming. *The New Oxford Shakespeare*. Oxford.

Wayne, Valerie. 1985. "Refashioning the Shrew". *Shakespeare Studies*, 17: 159–87.

Wiesner, Merry E. 2000. *Women and Gender in Early Modern Europe*, 2nd edition. Cambridge.

3 Shakespeare and the *Commedia dell'Arte*

Robert Henke

Did Shakespeare need the *commedia dell'arte*? Given that Shakespeare studied and probably acted the plays of Plautus and Terence at the Stratford Grammar school, Roman New Comedy provides a more fundamental source for his comedies than the Italian professional theatre. The *senex-iuvenis-servus* structure of New Comedy conditions the tripartite character hierarchy of Shakespeare's early comedies, and *The Comedy of Errors* directly reworks Plautus' *Menaechmi*. Relative to forms of Renaissance comedy, ancient Roman comedy must be considered the deep, common source for dramatists across Europe, one that underscores the *commedia dell'arte* itself, which absorbed it by one degree of separation via Cinquecento scripted plays such as those of Ariosto.

In any comparative study of Shakespeare and the *commedia dell'arte*, it is salutary to acknowledge where the Italian professional theatre is *not*: partisans for Italian influence in Shakespeare's plays do not help their cause by indiscriminate Pantalone and Zanni spotting. To call *Twelfth Night*'s Feste a "zanni" puts one in the undesirable camp of Malvolio, who disparages the clown as "no better than the fools' zanies" (Elam 2008: 1.5.85). As a despiser of "cakes and ale" and all that belongs to festive culture, Malvolio misses Feste's derivation from the tradition of English clowning from Tarlton to Kemp to Armin, itself partly based on the rich visual and verbal language of the Anglo-Germanic-Dutch folly tradition, and joins a widespread perception by many of Shakespeare's contemporaries that the comedy of Zannis and Pantaloons is a base, frivolous thing.

Other early modern European sources can also seem more immediate and closer to hand than the *commedia dell'arte*, such as the European novellas translated into English and French and ransacked for comic "theatergrams" (Clubb 1989), and the particular alchemy, in John Lyly's plays, of pastoral modalities and romantic situations without which plays like *A Midsummer Night's Dream* are unthinkable. Next to weighty comedic protagonists such as Benedict, Beatrice, Olivia, Orsino, Portia, and Bassanio, the "squirty, baudie comediens" of the Italian professional theatre, as Thomas Nashe uncharitably called them, seem worlds apart (McKerrow 1958: 1: 215). Does Shakespeare not, if we look at the big

54 Robert Henke

picture, show remarkably little interest in the comic gallery of the Arte, with its foolish old men, loquacious pedants, braggart soldiers, and servants who run the plot when their stingy masters are not starving them to death (Andrews 2014a: 38–39)?

If the *commedia dell'arte* was formative for Shakespeare, how do we allow for the fact that he may not have encountered any Arte actors in London during his lifetime? Although they travelled to the German-speaking regions, France, Spain, the Low Countries, Prague, and elsewhere, the *comici* seem to have found England rather inhospitable terrain: a challenging channel-crossing, a public hostile to female players, and an odd, non-Romance language to boot. Between 1573 and 1578, there was a modest string of visits by Italian players to England, but they abruptly stopped in 1578 (Chambers 1923: 2.261–65; Lea 1934: 2.352–58). And what need for actresses, when an English traveller such as Thomas Coryate could visit Italian theatres in Shakespeare's day, disparaging them for being less stately than the Globe and expressing his astonishment that Italian actresses could impersonate women as well as English boys: "I saw women acte, a thing I had never seen before [...] they performed it with as good a grace, action, and gesture, and whatsoever convenient for a Player, as ever I saw any masculine Actor" (Coryate 1611: 247)?

When early modern English writers cited the *commedia dell'arte*, it was often as a satirical tag meant to reinforce a sense of what is properly English—and not Papist. Protestant pamphleteers invoked the Italian actors' distinct use of masks as code for Italian, papal deception. In a 1625 tract by one Matthew Sutcliffe, the speaker accuses his Catholic adversary of being a "mountebank and a zanni", and "playing with a vizard" (Sutcliffe 1604: 319). Reflecting the fact that commedia-style actors actually did collaborate with mountebanks in Italian piazzas, Sutcliffe equates the two figures. To be a zanni is to bamboozle a credulous public with a charlatan's "boxes of drugs and serpents", and to be a mountebank is to engage in histrionic deceit: both figures achieve a virtuosic, and damnable, prowess in the art of "vizardry" (Sutcliffe 1604: 319). The theatre of masks will lead us all to the Antichrist.

Like Sutcliffe, Ben Jonson associates the *commedia dell'arte* with degraded forms of piazza entertainment. In his Venice play *Volpone*, the eponymous protagonist, in his quest to seduce the young Celia, impersonates the mountebank and actor Scoto of Mantua, an actual historical figure who had performed before Queen Elizabeth (Lea 1934: 2.360–61). Volpone/Scoto sets up his trestle stage under Celia's window in St. Mark's square, with the assistance of his dwarf, who for the nonce becomes Zan Fritata, the name of an actual zanni who performed and published cheap publications in the late sixteenth century (Henke 2016: 32–33). The ultimate horror of the pathologically jealous husband

Shakespeare and the Commedia dell'Arte   55

Corvino, after this attempt at seduction, is that he has been cast in—horror of horrors—a *commedia dell'arte* play:

> Come down! No house but mine to make your scene!
> Signor Flamineo, will you down, sir? Down!
> What, is my wife your Franceschina, sir?
> [...]
> Ere tomorrow, I shall be new christened,
> And called the Pantalone di Besogniosi
> About the town.
>
> (Watson 2003: 2.2.2–4, 7–9)

With transnational friends like this, who needs enemies? For the enraged Corvino, the wily mountebank Scoto has cast himself as the Arte lover Flaminio, who schemes to cast Corvino as the cuckolded Pantalone. Jonson suggests that the characters of his satiric drama are so venal and corrupt that they are no better than Italian actors: Nashe's "squirty, baudie comediens" or Malvolio's zanies.

But Jonson does not merely use the *commedia dell'arte* as a satirical tag; the characters and situational exchanges of *Volpone* are deeply and subtly shaped by the Italian *maschere* ["masks", the Arte's stylized characters], which Jonson knows as well as his Scotos and Zan Fritatas. As a Venetian "Magnifico", Volpone invokes the long Italian history of the Arte Pantalone, whose original designation as "Magnifico" evokes the possibility of urban gravitas and authority against which the comic notes of the flawed old man are played. Mosca, ambitious parasite and volatile servant, provides another Jonsonian example of an Arte character on steroids. The servant-master reversal typical of the *commedia dell'arte*—drawn, of course, from the Saturnalian instincts of Roman New Comedy—is ripped from its comic frame, as the fox and the fly go at each other's throats. The legacy hunters draw on the deep, mythopoetic source of zoomorphism, and perhaps more particularly on medieval bestiary than on anything else, but they certainly also recall the fundamental ties of Arte characters with animal forces, as discussed and enacted by Dario Fo.

Jonson's knowledge of the *commedia dell'arte* in *Volpone* is fairly precise, and he is not alone among English playwrights and writers. In addition to Nashe and Jonson, Gabriel Harvey, Thomas Heywood, Thomas Middleton, John Marston, John Day, Philip Massinger and others invoke the Italian characters, often specifically enough to suggest that they had seen them in performance: in the 1621 *Spanish Gipsy* (Middleton, Rowley, Dekker, Ford), a character about to play a father in a play-within-a-play is advised to "Play him up high: not like a Pantaloone" (2.4). Several decades earlier, Gabriel Harvey, in his libel *Speculum*

56 Robert Henke

Tuscanismi (1580), provides strikingly specific details on gesture, pose, attitude, and costume for Pantalone-Magnifico:

> For life Magnificoes, not a beck but glorious in shew,
> In deed most frivolous, not a looke but Tuscanishe allwayes.
> His cringing side necke, Eyes glancing, Fisnamie smirking,
> With forefinger kisse and brave embrace to the footewarde.
> Large-belled Kodpeasd Doublet, unkodpeased halfe hose
> Strait to the dock, like a shirte, and close to the britch, like a diveling.
> (Grosart 1884–85: 1.84)

Harvey concurs with the idea, expressed in the *Spanish Gipsy*, of a low centre of gravity for the old man ("brave embrace to the footewarde"). The degradation of his avian, glancing eyes and sideways-cringing neck plays against the "glorious [...] shew" of the Magnifico. As Kathleen Lea points out, Harvey here satirizes the Italianate Englishman, but still animates the figure with a lively and detailed stage "attitude" (Lea 1934: 2.378).

And so despite the relative infrequency of *commedia dell'arte* visits to England, early modern English writers can describe the Italian *maschere* with a detail and verve that suggests strong interest, even if they are using the Arte as a satiric device. The English, in fact, became aware of the *commedia dell'arte* almost as soon as the sustained version of the companies emerged in Mantua between 1566 and 1568, and the crucial intermediary at the beginning appears to be the French court (Henke 2014: 27, 30–31). A decisive event was the performance by Arte actors in France on 4 March 1571, in the context of entertainments celebrating the recent marriage of Charles IX to Elizabeth of Austria. Festivities honouring the French king and his Habsburgian bride were organized by the Duc de Nevers, who was none other than Luigi Gonzaga, the brother of the very Mantuan Duke (Vincentio) who had just begun to patronize the Italian players. In attendance at the performance, which probably included the famous actor Tabarino, was Thomas Sackville, Lord Buckhurst, who had been sent by Queen Elizabeth to the French court on a diplomatic mission. As coauthor, with Thomas Norton, of *Gorboduc*, which had been performed in the Inner Temple in 1561, Sackville may have been one of the first to tell fellow Englishmen of the Italian players, and there are two other records of English envoys viewing Italian professional actors in France between 1571 and 1572 (Henke 2008: 27–28; Baschet 1882: 16–18, 40–42). Word of this new theatrical phenomenon may have generated invitations to the Italian players, who were thwarted at public performance in France during the early part of the decade, to come to England (Baschet 1882: 18–24). Between 1573 and 1578 there was a flurry of visits by the Italian players, the most important of which involves a licence to the troupe of Drusiano Martinelli, the brother of the famous Arlecchino Tristano, to perform both within the city walls of London and without, in the Liberties, where James Burbage had constructed The Theatre in 1576. The fact that these visits appear not to have outlasted the 1570s can plausibly be ascribed to an aversion to female actors in a country where female roles were played by boys: a 1574 document complains about the "unchaste, shameless, and unnatural tomblings of the Italian women" (Lea 1934: 2.354).

But envoys were not the only Englishmen to report on Italian actors they had seen on the continent. In addition to Coryate in the previously-cited report on Venetian theatre, Fynes Moryson, George Whetstone, and others reported on performances of Italian players they had witnessed during their continental travels (Lea 1934: 2.342–50). Will Kemp, who had travelled to the continent with the Earl of Leicester's Men in 1586, went to Italy after leaving the Lord Chamberlain's Men and is figured in a 1607 play, *The Travels of the Three English Brothers*, as acting with an Italian Arlecchino. Travelling English companies would have had occasion to see and perhaps even act with Italian actors in Paris (Chambers 1923: 2.292–3), in the Low Countries, and even in Prague in 1627 (Schindler 2001: 73). Especially relevant for Shakespeare, at the beginning of his career, there appears to have been a pronounced *professional* interest on the part of English playwrights and actors in the *commedia dell'arte*, especially for its unique practice of improvisation. In the late 1580s, in Thomas Kyd's *The Spanish Tragedy*, Italian actors are admired for being

> so sharp of wit
> That in one hour's meditation
> They would perform anything in action.
>
> (Mulryne 1970: 4.1.164–66)

Just a few years later than *The Spanish Tragedy* can be dated several so-called "plots", or "plats", which bear some similarity to *commedia dell'arte* scenarios (Grewar 1993). These "plats", wooden tablets indicating characters and their entrances and exits, with holes so that they could be pegged backstage, were found in the library of Edward Alleyn and were used by several of Shakespeare's fellow actors and possibly Shakespeare himself to perform plays, some of which were governed by distinctly commedia-style plots. The theatergram of a young man cuckolding the young wife of an older man, as Jonson's Corvino thinks Scoto is doing to him, can be found in a "plat" entitled "The Dead Man's Fortune", dating from 1590–1592 and probably performed by a combination of the Lord Admiral's Men and the Lord Strange's Men, which included Richard Burbage and several other actors who would form the Lord Chamberlain's Men with Shakespeare in 1594. In the plat, the dashing young Validore, with the help of a servant, wins the heart of Asspida, the young wife of a character explicitly designated as "Pantaloon", along

58 Robert Henke

with the same designation for Gremio in the contemporary *Taming of the Shrew*, the earliest trace of the word in the English language.

Probably the most familiar reference to Pantaloon in Shakespeare's plays is Jaques' "lean and slippered pantaloon", sixth of seven stages on life's way in his famous speech in *As You Like It*. Here, Shakespeare is not invoking the Arte for a particular satiric target in the vein of Sutcliffe, Jonson, or Harvey, but enlisting the *commedia dell'arte* lover, Capitano, Dottore, and Pantalone as "universal" passages of life. It is difficult not to feel, at least in Pantalone's "shrunk shank" (2.7.162) that anticipates the endgame of "mere oblivion", a kind of pathos going well beyond the analytical sharpness of Jonson's satire. The lover, "sighing like furnace", is conventional enough, and a type easily available to Shakespeare without the *commedia dell'arte*. Still, the parody of the Petrarchan blazon ("woeful ballad | Made to his mistresses' eyebrow", 2.7.148–50) does recall the fact that it was the male and female Arte lover who most distinctly brought Petrarch to the early modern stage.

The soldier, Jaques' next age, might simply derive from the braggart of Roman New Comedy but for the specifically *fantastic* cast of his imagination, with "strange oaths" dedicated to the "bubble reputation" (2.7.150–53). The most famous Capitano text, the 1607 *Le bravure di Capitano Spavento*, was written by the great Arte Capitano Francesco Andreini. Partly based on actual stage routines, partly post-performance literary embellishment, the dialogues that it features between the *alazon* Spavento and his servant Trappolo as *eiron* are precisely characterized by their fantastic and hyperbolically mythopoetic imagination, magical speech-acts like oaths and curses and threats flung into the ether. The character was usually from Spain—the country that had taken over Naples, Milan, and other parts of Italy in the sixteenth century—so that there was some political satire here. Comically, this fantastic mythopoesis is nicely encapsulated in Don Adriano de Armado, "A Spanish knight and braggart" in *Love's Labour's Lost*, who goes well beyond the *miles gloriosus* in verbal imagination and virtuosity. Like a colossus, Armado bestrides the fantastic, auto-reflexive verbal universe that he creates for himself and that exists only for him, not altogether unlike Cervantes' knight of the mournful countenance: "Now, by the salt wave of the Mediterranean, a sweet touch, a quick venue of wit! Snip-snap, quick and home! It rejoiceth my intellect. True wit!" (Woudhuysen 1998: 5.1.54–56). Tragically, in the character of Othello, the Capitano may turn from the relatively safe mythopoetic world of the fantastic travel tales told to Desdemona, to engage in sudden, quick, and mortal quarrel with his perceived enemy Cassio, who has destroyed the bubble reputation of his once-chaste wife, falling to his knees to utter "strange oaths" with Iago, a kind of demonic Brighella.

Jaques' justice, the next stage of life, resembles the Dottore of the Arte much more specifically than anything English (or ancient Roman, for that

Shakespeare and the Commedia dell'Arte   59

matter), especially given the fact the Italian figure tended to be a justice rather than a professor. The "good capon" with which he "lines" his "fair round belly" (2.7.155) perfectly reflects the gastronomic obsessions of this *parte ridicolosa*: a character who artfully conflates food and knowledge, as we can see in the many "recipes" he both performed and printed— part of a popular "recipe" genre used by both the Dottore and Pantalone (Henke 2002: 141, 150–51). "Full of wise saws and modern instances" (2.7.157), the Dottore creates a formulaic repertoire of "secondary orality": he shores the fragments and shards of humanistic commonplace books against his ruin, as he carnivalizes language by the unfettered power of verbal association. From his inexhaustible verbal repertoire, Polonius spouts off a series of "wise saws" to Laertes, and his "tragedy, comedy, history, pastoral, pastoral-comical, historical-pastoral" speech can be seen as an improvisatory riff (discovered by one of Shakespeare's actors in performance?) that reflects the deeper practice of combinatory dramaturgy based on the building blocks of genre-based "theatergrams" employed in both Italian scenarios and English scripts.

The next age, that of the "lean and slippered pantaloon" (2.7.159), closely matches contemporary pictorial representations of the Magnifico, with his trademark slippers, hose, and closely-clutched money-bag; it is of a detail that recalls Harvey's minute description. But in a pathos well beyond what Harvey's or Jonson's satiric venom imagined, both Pantalone's body and his voice shrink towards death. With his whispering, piping voice "turning again towards childish treble" (2.7.163), Shakespeare's Pantaloon is less Jonson's ridiculous cuckold than an usher to second childhood, extreme old age, and death itself, of which Adam, whom legend reputes to have been played by Shakespeare himself, is also an image. For Shakespeare here, the non-English, the Italian, is used as a very window into the "strange eventful history" of human life itself (2.7.165). Although Shakespeare is certainly not above satirizing foreign stereotypes, sometimes the very evocation of the foreign can, in Susanne Wofford's words, "provide access into a kind of emotionality that would otherwise be unavailable in one's own culture" (Wofford 2008: 142).

The old man Gremio, explicitly designated as a Pantaloon by his successful rival Lucentio in *The Taming of the Shrew*, boasts to the merchant Battista, a kind of Pantalone figure, of the dowry that he can give the beautiful Bianca, younger than him by only about forty years. As he names his treasures, stuffed away in his chests and coffers, we can feel the weight of the Venetian empire crushing down his "shrunk shank". He is the obsessive hoarder, whose material accumulations have displaced, or become, his soul:

> First, as you know, my house within the city
> Is richly furnished with plate and gold,
> Basins and ewers to lave her dainty hands;

60 Robert Henke

My hangings all of Tyrian tapestry;
In ivory coffers have I stuff'd my crowns,
[...]
Myself am struck in years, I must confess,
And if I die tomorrow, this is hers,
If whilst I live she will be only mine.

(Hodgdon 2010: 2.1.350–54, 364–66)

If this skeletal wisp of a man does not get laughs gasping out the things (Mediterranean rapine secured by the Venetian empire) with which he has identified his being, something is wrong. But like Jaques' lean and slippered Pantaloon, Gremio hastens towards death, and it is not impossible to feel some pathos for the old man along with the laughter, as he leaves it all on the field for his new object of passion. Is this his last moment of straightening his back, looking up, and caring about something besides his things?

Space permits only a survey of how Shakespeare used the *commedia dell'arte* throughout his career. Generally, the most explicit Shakespearean references to the Arte tend to come in comedies written between 1592 to 1597—a time when the "plats" and references in *The Spanish Tragedy* and elsewhere suggest that the *commedia dell'arte* was "in the air" in London, as a new and innovative theatrical form that would have had a certain cachet. *The Comedy of Errors*, arguably Shakespeare's first comedy, can be played in commedia style, as it often has been, but it is resolutely Plautine. If the Drumios can be played like zanni, it is merely because both Shakespeare and the *commedia dell'arte*, in the latter case via the filter of the "commedia erudita" (humanist-inspired, scripted plays of the Italian Renaissance) were drawing on Roman New Comedy.

But *The Taming of the Shrew*, where we have already encountered a character explicitly designated as "Pantaloon" and much closer to the Venetian old man than the Roman *senex*, is a different story altogether, part of the play's embedment in Italian theatre (Henke 2014). The subplot of *Shrew*, of course, is lifted from George Gascoigne's *Supposes*, a 1566 translation of Ariosto's great commedia erudita *I suppositi*. That Ariosto's play was rather effortlessly turned into a *commedia dell'arte* scenario later performed by Venetian actors (Alberti 1996) demonstrates how close the relationship between the scripted and the improvised comedy was. With a feedback loop between scripts and scenarios, the *erudita* and the Arte were simply aspects of one overall system of Italian comedy: a system that Louise George Clubb has shown was hard-wired into Shakespeare, deeper than any single Italian-to-English play transmission can show, even though with *I suppositi* to *Shrew* we actually do have a one-to-one transmission (Clubb 1989).

More important than the single appearance of Gremio is the way the play is structured by a tripartite *vecchi-innamorati-servi*

Shakespeare and the Commedia dell'Arte   61

arrangement—with the active, inventive *innamorati* adding a romantic dimension not seen in Plautus and Terence. In addition to the aged Pantalone Gremio, we have the younger merchant-father Battista, and the hapless father of Lucentio who finally makes his way to Padua. Tranio plays the clever, Pedrolino-esque servant to Lucentio, performing the Ariostan reversal of servant and master that frequently occurred in the Arte itself. Grumio plays the beaten, harassed Arlecchino-esque servant of Petruchio. Katherina may be more English shrew than *innamorata*, although her witty exchanges with Petruchio certainly evoke *innamorati*; we are on firmer ground with Bianca as an *innamorata*, not without wit and spirit herself. The whole play is certainly about crossing borders, as the Pisans Lucentio and Tranio joyously do entering the Veneto at the beginning of the play, with the sense that something new and exciting will occur. And the play is also about *not* crossing borders: the whole fiction that Tranio invents for the bemused Mantuan traveller of mortal conflict between Italian states is taken from *I suppositi*, which is full of references to border-crossing travellers having trouble at customs frontiers. The play, with its incessant theatricality and role-playing, celebrates the mobility and capacity for reinvention typified by the itinerant Italian actors.

Love's Labour's Lost, where we have already met Don Adriano de Armado, features a bona fide Dottore in Holofernes. As with Don Armado for the originally classical role of braggart, Holofernes adds the elements of verbal copiousness, intended elegance, and farcical humanism practised by *commedia dell'arte* actors such as Lodovico dei Bianchi, who was among the first to alchemize the stock pedant role in the Arte Dottore. In a play that closely follows Italian character systems and comedic structures, despite its English setting, Doctor Caius in *The Merry Wives of Windsor* reaches these same linguistic heights—or depths—in combining aspects of both the Capitano and the Dottore. That Caius speaks with a heavy French accent rather than the Spanish accent of the Capitano or the Bolognese of the Dottore simply suggests Shakespeare's flexible use of *Arte* attributes and his understanding of the comic potential of accents and parodied forms of language, a principle thoroughly developed by the *commedia dell'arte*.

Like *The Taming of the Shrew*, *Two Gentlemen of Verona* points to both scripted play and improvised scenario as parts of a co-related system. In addition to Montemayor's 1559 *Diana*, Shakespeare draws from Luigi Pasqualigo's 1576 play *Fedele*, adapted into English by Antony Munday in 1584 as *Fedele and Fortunio*. Munday, interestingly, was said to have performed with *commedia dell'arte* actors in Italy, as did Will Kemp. The plot of Pasqualigo's play also appears in the Arte scenario "Flavio Tradito", published in Flaminio Scala's 1611 collection but cycling through the repertoire many years before that. Again, theatergrams flowed easily between scripts and scenarios.

62 Robert Henke

Certainly there are *commedia dell'arte* presences in the mature comedies, but it is to the scripted plays of the *commedia erudita* (systematically related, to be sure, to the Arte) that *Much Ado About Nothing* and *Twelfth Night* especially point us. It does appear that the vogue for the *commedia dell'arte* as a distinct calling card (*The Taming of the Shrew*, *Love's Labour's Lost*) seems to have passed by the turn of the century, and it is in the tragedies, in fact, that foolish old men, loquacious pedants, and plot-controlling servants oddly resurface. The *commedia dell'arte* is hardly at the centre of *Hamlet*, but it curiously informs, as Francis Barasch has demonstrated, the Polonius family of *vecchio* and his two children (Barasch 2011). We have briefly discussed Polonius as a Dottore. Laertes' hot-headedness meshes nicely with the tribe of Flavio and Flaminio, and Ophelia, as Eric Nicholson has shown, strikingly evokes the performing Italian actress in her "pazzia" or mad scene, a virtuosic set piece for Isabella and other Italian actresses (Nicholson 2008).

In *Othello*, as in *Shrew*, the overall character system is thoroughly, and centrally, shaped by the *commedia dell'arte* (Faherty 1991). As the obsessively blocking father of his daughter's love interests, the Venetian Brabantio evokes Pantalone. If he is also a figure of some gravitas, as occasional counsellor to the Senate, he claims Pantalone under the aspect of Magnifico, recalling Pier Maria Cecchini's injunction that Pantalone as a serious citizen of Venice should not be exclusively ridiculous. Roderigo, putty in Iago's hands, is a desperate and credulous *innamorato*. The Desdemona-Emilia pair, as Louise George Clubb has demonstrated, contrasts the amorous *innamorata* with the worldly-wise, street-smart Franceschina of Emilia (Clubb 1989). Othello, like Shakespeare's other great tragic protagonists, towers above type, but surely we can see in him a superb Capitano. And at the heart of it all, how about Iago as Brighella, the canny servant who has worked his way through the system and now (placed in a higher decorum, as were Jonson's Volpone and Mosca) seethes with the resentment of "injured merit".

> Three great ones of the city,
> In personal suit to make me his lieutenant,
> Off-capp'd to him: and, by the faith of man,
> I know my price, I am worth no worse a place:
> (Thompson and Honigmann 2016: 1.1.7–10)

Shakespeare's last word on the subject is not tragic but tragicomic in a pastoral arena: pastoral tragicomedy. The plot of the supposedly sourceless *Tempest*, as has long been recognized, is uncannily similar to a large group of what might be called "magical-pastoral" Arte scenarios published in 1618 but circulating well before that (Henke 2007; Andrews 2014b). In scenarios with titles such as "Arcadia Incantata", a petulant, irascible, but powerful *mago* lives on an island inhabited by spirits,

Shakespeare and the Commedia dell'Arte   63

satyrs, and shepherds, and causes a group of travellers to shipwreck on his island. The travellers, who are precisely the *commedia dell'arte* figures Pantalone, Dottore, Buratino, and Zanni, explore the island, but are vexed and thwarted by the spirits of the island and the *mago* himself, who at one point casts a spell that immobilizes them within a magic circle, until he agrees to forgive them and release them at the end of the play. In *The Tempest*, Stefano and Trinculo most distinctly evoke these shipwrecked buffoons and their *lazzi* [gags, witticisms, interludes], but some of the Italian theatergrams can be seen in the main court party as well: in one scenario, the famished buffoons prepare to eat a banquet of food that has miraculously appeared, only to have it snatched away. The figure of the satyr, distinctively evoked in Caliban, pervades these magical pastorals of the *commedia dell'arte*, which demonstrate how the Italian players, like Polonius's troupe, could play "pastoral" and "tragical" as well as "comical". No shepherds inhabit Prospero's island, but Ferdinand and Miranda certainly perform the *innamorati* function of the shepherds in the Arte pastorals. In sum, Shakespeare knew the *commedia dell'arte* well, both as the technique for his dramaturgical art and as figures, large enough for pathos, evoking the stages on life's way. He knew when to use the *commedia dell'arte*, when not to use it, and, best of all, he knew how to transform it and transpose it between different stages on his own dramaturgical way, between "comical", "tragical", and "pastoral".

Bibliography

Alberti, Carmelo, ed. 1996. *Gli scenari Correr: la commedia dell'arte a Venezia*. Rome.

Andrews, Richard. 2014a. "Resources in Common: Shakespeare and Flaminio Scala". In Henke and Nicholson 2014. 37–52.

———— 2014b. "*The Tempest* and Italian Improvised Theatre". *Revisiting the Tempest: The Capacity to Signify*, ed. by Silvia Bigliazzi and Lisanna Calvi. New York. 45–62.

Barasch, Francis. 2011. "Hamlet vs. the Commedia dell'Arte". *Shakespeare and Renaissance Literary Theories: Anglo-Italian Transactions*, ed. by Michele Marrapodi. Aldershot. 105–18.

Baschet, Armand. 1882. *Les Comédiens Italiens à la cour de France*. Paris.

Chambers, E. K. 1923. *The Elizabethan Stage*, 4 vols. Oxford.

Clubb, Louise George. 1989. *Italian Drama in Shakespeare's Time*. New Haven.

Coryate, Thomas. 1611. *Coryats Crudities; Hastily Gobled Up in Five Moneths Travells*. London.

Dusinberre, Juliet, ed. 2006. William Shakespeare, *As You Like It*. Arden Shakespeare. London.

Elam, Keir, ed. 2008. William Shakespeare, *Twelfth Night*. Arden Shakespeare. London.

Faherty, Theresa. 1991. "'Othello dell'Arte': The Presence of Commedia in Shakespeare's Tragedy". *Theatre Journal*, 43: 179–95.

64 *Robert Henke*

Grewar, Andrew. 1993. "Shakespeare and the Actors of the Commedia dell'Arte". *Studies in the Commedia dell'Arte*, ed. by David J. George and Christopher J. Gossip. Cardiff. 13–47.

Grosart, Alexander B., ed. 1884–85. *The Works of Gabriel Harvey*, 3 vols. London.

Henke, Robert. 2002. *Performance and Literature in the Commedia dell'Arte*. Cambridge.

———— 2007. "Transporting Tragicomedy: Shakespeare and the Magical Pastoral of the Commedia dell'Arte". *Early Modern Tragicomedy*, ed. by Subha Mukherji and Raphael Lyne. Woodbridge. 43–58.

———— 2008. "Border Crossing in the Commedia dell'Arte". In Henke and Nicholson 2008. 19–34.

———— 2014. "*The Taming of the Shrew*, Italian Intertexts, and Cultural Mobility". In Henke and Nicholson 2014. 23–36.

———— 2016. "Meeting at the Sign of the Queen: The Commedia dell'Arte, Cheap Print, and Piazza Performance". *Italian Studies*, 71.2: 22–34.

———— and Eric Nicholson, eds. 2008. *Transnational Exchange in Early Modern Theater*. Aldershot.

———— and Eric Nicholson, eds. 2014. *Transnational Mobilities in Early Modern Theater*. Aldershot.

Hodgdon, Barbara, ed. 2010. William Shakespeare, *The Taming of the Shrew*. Arden Shakespeare. London.

Lea, Kathleen. 1934. *Italian Popular Comedy: A Study in the Commedia dell'Arte, 1560–1620 with Special Reference to the English Stage*, 2 vols. Oxford.

McKerrow, Ronald B., ed. 1958. *The Works of Thomas Nashe*, 5 vols. Oxford.

Mulryne, J. R., ed. 1970. Thomas Kyd, *The Spanish Tragedy*. New York.

Nicholson, Eric. 2008. "Ophelia Sings Like a Prima Donna Innamorata: Ophelia's Mad Scene and the Italian Female Performer". In Henke and Nicholson 2008. 81–98.

Schindler, Otto. 2001. "'Englischer Pickelhering—gen Prag jubilierend'. Englische Komödianten als Wegbereiter des deutschen Theaters in Prag". *Deutschprachigen Theater in Prag: Begegnungen der Sprachen und Kulturen*, ed. by Alena Jakubcová, Jitka Ludvová, and Václav Maidl. Prague. 73–101.

Sutcliffe, Matthew. 1604. *A ful and round Ansvver to N.D. alias Robert Parsons*. London.

Taylor, Neil, and Ann Thompson, eds. 2006. William Shakespeare, *Hamlet*. Arden Shakespeare. London.

Thompson, Ayanna, and E. A. J. Honigmann, eds. 2016. William Shakespeare, *Othello*. Arden Shakespeare. London.

Watson, Robert N., ed. 2003. Ben Jonson, *Volpone*, 2nd edition. New York.

Wofford, Susanne. 2008. "Foreign Emotions on the Stage of *Twelfth Night*". In Henke and Nicholson 2008. 141–58.

Woudhuysen, H. R., ed. 1998. William Shakespeare, *Love's Labour's Lost*. Arden Shakespeare. London.

4 The Unfinished in Michelangelo and *Othello*

Rocco Coronato

"He that cummeth nighest"

Readers eager to detect evidence of the circulation of Neoplatonic lore in early modern England usually point to the celebrated praise of physical beauty as a ladder to the divine that concludes *Il Cortegiano*. Yet the work's beginning is even more revealing. In the preface, Castiglione affects *sprezzatura* towards those critics who claim that, being "so hard a matter and (in a manner) vnpossibile to finde out a man of such perfection [...] it is a vaine thing to teach that can not be learned". Castiglione rebuts that the impossibility of exactly matching that perfection does not entail that emulation is useless:

> I am content, to err with Plato, Xenophon, and M. Tullius, leauing apart the disputing of the intelligible world and of the Ideas or imagined fourmes: in which number, as [...] the Idea or figure conceyued in imagination of a perfect commune weale, and of a perfect king, and of a perfect Oratour are contened: so is it also of a perfect Courtier. To the image whereof if my power could not draw nigh in stile, so much the lesse peynes shall Courtiers haue to drawe nigh in effect to the ende and marke that I in writing haue set beefore them. And if with all this they can not compasse that perfection, [...] he that cummeth nighest shall be the most perfect.
>
> (Castiglione 1900: 22–23)

The doctrine of the Ideas was revived in England partly thanks to Henri Estienne II and Jean de Serres's new edition of Plato, which arrived in London in 1579. Despite the dominance of Aristotle at Oxford and Cambridge, references to Neoplatonism recur in Sidney and De Mornay; allusions to the theory of the Ideas, very fashionable in the 1590s, still emerge in Donne's poems between 1597 and 1603 (Jayne 1995); and Stephen Batman's theory of the symbol is based on the likeness between the visible and the invisible, so that "these things corporall may be coupled with things spirituall, and these things visibles maye be conioyned with things inuisibles" (Batman 1582: sig. ¶ʳ). Attention has been paid

66 *Rocco Coronato*

to the Neoplatonic legacy in Shakespeare's notion of beauty (Medcalf 1994), in poetry (Roe 1994) and in drama (Rowe 2010). However, Castiglione's preface evinces a further, less explored Neoplatonic thread.

"He that cummeth nighest shall be the most perfect": the imitation of the Idea implies a work of self-perfection that is often unfinished. This incremental process tries to impossibly reach that perfection, in Iago's malicious praise, "[w]hereto we see, in all things, nature tends" (*Othello* 3.3.236). It is an emulative task that intimately resembles artistic creation. Conversely, the artist's work turns into an ascent to Neoplatonic beauty through the diligent observation of nature and of the best works of art, until an Idea that perfects nature emerges in the artist's mind. The theory was widespread in Shakespeare's time. Conflating two distinctions found respectively in Plato (the one between *eikastiké* art, based on the making of likenesses, and *phantastické* art, which seems to be a likeness but is not really so, *Sophist* 235d, 236b) and in Aristotle (representing things as they are, as they are said and seem to be, or as they should be, *Poetics* 1460b), Sidney argues that in all imitation, poetry foremost, "the skill of ech Artificer standeth in that Idea, or fore conceit of the worke, and not in the worke it selfe"; the artist's task is that of improving nature, producing "things either better than nature bringeth forth, or quite anew, forms such as never were in nature" (Sidney 1980: 101). "Idea", albeit sparingly mentioned, means an image in Shakespeare (*Richard III* 3.7.12; *Much Ado About Nothing* 4.1.225–27; *Love's Labour's Lost* 4.2.66; in Shakespeare 2007).

The quest for ideal perfection responds to the question raised in *The Greater Hippias*: "not what is beautiful, but what the beautiful [*kalon*] is" (Plato 1996: 287e). As Socrates lists many possible definitions, Hippias vents his exasperation: "it is mere scrapings and shavings of a discourse, [...] divided up into bits" (304a). No less exasperated is Othello at Iago's half-formed, unfinished ejaculations, "these stops of thine", tragically mistaken for truthful revelations of his ideas, "close dilations, working from the heart | That passion cannot rule" (*Othello* 3.3.125, 128–29). Iago's fragmented words elicit that powerful sense of the unfinished that Eugène Delacroix divined in Michelangelo, Shakespeare, and Beethoven, opposed to the polished Mozart, Racine, and Cimarosa: in particular, Michelangelo inspires in us a feeling of trouble which is a kind of wonderment ("porte dans l'âme un sentiment de trouble qui est une manière d'admiration"; Delacroix 1950: 2.40).

I will first analyse the rise of the Idea from Plato to Italian art theory of the Cinquecento, its circulation in early modern England, and the light it may cast on Desdemona and Othello. I will then compare Michelangelo's *non finito* with the unfinished according to Iago. Of course, I do not mean to suggest any direct influence: that would be as foolhardy as implying any Neoplatonic osmosis between the two artists in the seven months they shared in 1564, Michelangelo as a

The Unfinished in Michelangelo and Othello   67

very old man and Shakespeare in his mother's womb. Michelangelo will instead serve as a foil to enhance the revolutionary quality of the unfinished in Iago.

The Idea from Plato to Italy and Shakespeare

Cognitive neurobiology has surmised that brain cells recognize objects in a view-invariant manner and thus form abstraction after just a brief exposure to several images (Zeki 2001). Long before the neurosciences, the ancient painter Zeuxis, commissioned to paint a portrait of Helen, anticipated the advent of Photoshop. Zeuxis selected the five most beautiful girls from Croton and virtually assembled in one image "all the lovely parts of those five to make one bodie of incomparable beautie" (Pliny 1601: 35.64, 534), "created | Of every creature's best" (*The Tempest* 3.1.46–7). As Braider (1993) and Di Stefano (2004) have shown, Zeuxis' anecdote circulated widely in the Renaissance as a memento for the artist to "always strive by [...] diligence and study to understand and express much loveliness" (Alberti 1966: 92) and to bring the work to "perfezione" (Ghiberti 1947: 21), showing through art in one body all that perfection of beauty that nature barely shows in a thousand (Dolce 1555: 176). According to Vasari, popularized in the north by the Flemish painter Karel Van Mander's *Het Schilder-Boeck* (1604) and a great influence on Wotton, Norgate and, later, Aglionby, Mantegna grounded the unrivalled beauty of ancient statues on the fact that the sculptors had extracted ("cavato") perfection from many living persons (Vasari 1991: 549–50; Gregory 2014).

Via a curious detour, Zeuxis' anecdote also came to inform the Neoplatonic justification of mimesis that Plato had excluded from his ideal city as being just an imitation of appearances (the world), not truth (the Ideas) (*Republic* 596e). Comparatively, two types of existence could be distinguished: one visible, and constantly in becoming, the other invisible and constantly the same (*Phaedo* 79a10), a gap reflected by the discrepancy between opinion and knowledge (*Republic* VI 509d1–5; Fronterotta 2001: 115–57). In Gombrich's recapitulation (1972: 147), this Platonic (and later Christian) doctrine implies that our world is just "an imperfect reflection of the intelligible world": Plato posits two modes of knowledge, discursive speech and vision, where the latter "becomes by virtue of its speed and immediacy a favoured symbol of higher knowledge". The good artist has then to create an ideal perfection, that internal image (ἔνδον εἶδος) posited by Plotinus in his *Enneades* (1989: 5.8.31), which is present both in the artist's mind and in the work. Cicero reconciles Zeuxis with Plato: the ruse of creating a silent image ("muta imago") of excellent female beauty is proposed as an inspiration for writers who also extract the best examples from other authors. Nature never polished something perfect in all its parts

(*De inventione* 2.1.1.4). The senses cannot provide the perfect beauty we embrace in our mind; therefore, the artist who creates a form is not imitating a real person but rather intuiting in his mind a certain species of excellent beauty (*Orator* 2.8, 9). To paraphrase Brabantio, "all things of sense", reasonable creatures, need to create an image that is "not gross in sense" (*Othello* 1.3.65, 73).

Thus legitimized, the Idea thrived in Italian Renaissance culture and flourished especially among Italian artists (Hankins 2004; Hedley and Hutton 2008). In his 1514 letter to Castiglione, Raphael admits that, in the absence of beautiful women and good judges, when he needs a model, he resorts to "una certa idea" [a certain idea] inside himself (Barocchi 1977: 2.1530). The Idea flourished in several art treatises. The artist Federigo Zuccaro, who visited England in 1574–75, defines the "disegno interno" [internal design] of an image as "una Idea, e forma" [an Idea and a form] that in our intellect expressly and distinctly represents the thing thereby meant (Zuccaro 1952: 154; Summers 1987). An attendant notion was that of *ingegno*, the acuity and sharpness of the artist's mind, rendered with the *disegno* [design] and the *schizzo* or *ghiribizzo* [etching] (Marr 2015). While "design" in Shakespeare usually means a secret plot or device (*Tempest* 1.2.164), "conceit" conveys many of the notions associated with the Idea, as when the raging Othello groans with a "strong conception" (5.2.60). Probably derived from Medieval French, "conceit" commonly means apprehension, understanding, opinion, judgement (*Hamlet* 2.1.557–58), a trifle or a humorous device. The proximity with the Idea is blatant in *The Rape of Lucrece*, where the "conceited painter" of the Fall of Troy has couched in his work a "conceit deceitful, so compact, so kind" to be discovered with "much imaginary work" (Shakespeare 2002, ll. 1371, 1422–23).

This Neoplatonic presence can even justify incompletion. In his hagiographic interpretation of Michelangelo's *non finito*, Vasari proposes the *disegno* as a clear expression and declaration of the concept inside the artist's mind. Never at a loss for rambunctious self-justification, Michelangelo himself (*Rime* 151.1–3) defined the best artist ("l'ottimo artista") as one who penetrates a block of marble until he gets to the *concetto* circumscribed by the superfluous ("circonscriva | Col suo superchio"; Buonarroti 1960: 161). The insight for probing deeper in search of what lies beneath, the *subjectum* that literally lies shrouded in matter, is proposed by the humanist Benedetto Varchi in his *Due Lezzioni* (1549) as an explanation of why Michelangelo's unfinished art seems "really alive" ("veramente vivissima") (Varchi 1549: 19; Jacobs 2005: 6; Schulz 1975). In Panofsky's summary, the Idea transcended Zeuxis' selection theory and morphed into the Ideal: beauty is not just "an external combination of separate parts" but "an inner vision that combines individual experiences into a new whole" (Panofsky 1968: 48, 64).

The Idea reached England via Italian art theory of the Cinquecento, which laid out the best artist's training process in "the diligent copying of the most graceful natural forms that are resident in the artist's mind", the result of "prolonged meditation on the beauties of nature and on the most perfect artistic representations of these beauties" (Semler 2004: 740). The most prominent Italian source was the Milanese painter Giovanni Paolo Lomazzo, author of both the *Idea del tempio della Pittura* (1590) and, crucially, the *Trattato dell'arte de Pittura, Scultura, et Architectura* (1585), translated by Richard Haydocke in 1598. The preface to the *Tracte containing the artes of curious paintinge caruinge building* defines, in conventional fashion, the Idea as the ultimate model of inspiration: if a painter and carver were instructed to take a particular king for their subject, they would begin with "the self same Idea, and similitude of him [...] [T]hey would delineate vpon paper, or some other matter, all that which they had first conceived in their minde: and so the draught expressing the Ideas of both these workmen, would agree in expressing the true resemblance, which is the essence of this arte: differing perchance accidentally only" (Lomazzo 1598: sig. A3^{rv}).

The same Neoplatonic ascent to the most perfect idea inside the artist's mind dominates much English art theory of the period. For Clement Edmondes, the skilful painter who has "his judgement habituated by knowledge, and perfected with the varieties of shapes and proportions" is one whose knowledge "guideth his eye, and his eye directeth his hand" (Edmondes 1609: 4). "Idea" is defined in Thomas' *Dictionarium linguae Latinae et Anglicanae* as the "figure conceiued in imagination, as it were ... a patterne of all other sort or kinde" (Thomas 1587: sig. Dd7^v), and is also alluded to in Robert Dallington's *Hypnerotomachia* (Dallington 1592: sig. 34^v). Nicholas Hilliard's *Arte of Limning* (c. 1598–1603, in manuscript form until 1912) also betrays the heavy influence of Lomazzo; according to John Harington, Hilliard "is so perfect" in drawing Queen Elizabeth's image "that he can set it downe by the Idea he hath without any patterne". Echoing a tradition already present in Vasari, Harington claims that the famously unfinished Leonardo was "so excellent in the Idea, or the conceived forme of his worke, that though he could finish but few workes, yet those he did, had great admiration" (Harington 1591: 278, 277). In *The Art of Drawing* (1606), a gentlemanly handbook of artistic instruction heavily based on Haydocke's translation of Lomazzo, Henry Peacham, who travelled to Italy at some time between 1595 and 1603, develops an incremental system of learning to draw, moving from simple objects to "mixed & uncertain" forms such as lions, guiding the pen by adhering to "that Idea you carrie in your minde", which, with the help of "strong imagination", "good memory", and "dailie practise", will propel the learned towards excellence (Peacham 1606: 15–16).

Debates on ideal beauty resonated later too. In the *Essay on Beauty* (1612), Francis Bacon criticizes Apelles because he would make a personage

70   Rocco Coronato

"by taking the best parts out of divers faces, to make one excellent", while beauty is the fruit of "a kind of felicity" beyond formulaic rules (Bacon 1890: 479). Writing in 1624, Henry Wotton condemned both Dürer and Michelangelo: "the German did too much expresse *that which was*, and the Italian, *that which should be*" (Wotton 1968: 11–12). As late as 1639, Franciscus Junius, the librarian of the Earl of Arundel, was still striving to reconcile Zeuxis' selection with the pursuit of the Idea: the artificer has to follow "the perfection of an inward image made up in his mind by a most earnest and assiduous observation of all such bodies as in their owne kind are most excelling" (Junius 1972: 13).

The Italian emphasis on the Idea as a creative process of painstaking rarefaction inside the artist's mind, so eloquently present in these contemporaries of Shakespeare's, may underlie the handling of the Neoplatonic theme of beauty in *Othello*, albeit with a distinctive application to the religious notion of inward refinement and especially to the characters of Desdemona and Othello. In a likely (perhaps parodic) echo of Sidney's Sonnet 71 from *Astrophil and Stella*, Shakespeare had already presented Adonis as the embodiment of "inward beauty" (Shakespeare 2002, l. 434). A brief, apparent detour will show how the English circulation of the Italian Idea might have helped Shakespeare adapt the "Song of Songs".

Amid the significant dearth of references to her physical traits, the "divine Desdemona", the "essential vesture of creation" (*Othello* 2.1.74, 65), embodies the Idea even at the point of death. Albeit negatively, she is still a "cunning'st pattern of excelling nature", elevated into an angel whose silent look will deny Othello any "possession of this heavenly sight" (5.2.285). Had this figure been true, she would have bested an ideal "world | Of one entire and perfect chrysolite" (5.2.151–52). In one of the play's many ironical displacements, the newcomer Othello also seems fixed near the centre of the old Neoplatonic belief, fully converted not only to Christianity but also to its philosophic jargon. Othello nearly petrifies flesh: the joy experienced as an absolute "content" (2.1.192) uncannily echoes the one experienced in Sidney's *Arcadia* by Pygmalion upon finding that the ideal beauty of stone, perfected by art, had turned to life, "while he found his beloved image was softer, and warmer in his folded armes, till at length it accomplished his gladness with a perfect womans shape (still beautified with the former perfections)" (Sidney 1977: 239). Yet there is a significant distinction: the process is the reverse, as Othello idealizes a living body into a statue "smooth as monumental alabaster" (5.2.5).

While the source for the chrysolite might have been Pliny (*Historia Naturalis*, 37.8), Boose (1981) proposed the Song of Solomon (Geneva Bible, 5:14), where the term seems to identify a white stone. It is widely known that the Song was read by Protestants (and Catholics) as an allegory of the mystical wedding between Christ and the Church. Black skin stood for ugliness, deformity, as well as unruly sexuality, "a mark

The Unfinished in Michelangelo and Othello   71

of a curse, an affliction, a weakness and a stain" (Korhonen 97), an allegory for "the re[m]nants of sinne, which make [the Church] *somewhat blacke*", scorched by "the strong beames of Gods sunne, and burning heat of his chastisements" (Fenner 1587: sig. B4ʳ). What is perhaps less known and more relevant is that Biblical commentators often resort to the Neoplatonic Idea. Blackness signifies "afflictions" that "diminish the outward beauty and glory of the Church" (Wilson 1612: sig. C6ᵛ). Inward and outward reflections are perplexing: this image is "oftentimes [hidden] vnder an exterior foulenesse, as that of a slubbered diamond"; the Churche "is browne, and yet faire; being blacke without, and burnt with afflictions, which notwithstanding blot not out her inward beautie" (De Moulin 1610: 115). The black bride may be "ill fauoured and deformed in eies of men; but inwardly, beautifull as the lilie" (Rogers 1603: 567).

It is by no means clear whether Shakespeare references the "Song of Songs" in this ironical fashion; what is less disputable is that Desdemona envisions the presence of inward beauty underneath Othello, seeing "Othello's visage in his mind" (*Othello* 1.3.252). And Othello complies with this belief in his self-interpretation: "My parts, my title and my perfect soul | Shall manifest me rightly" (1.2.31–2). His enterprises are set among "quarries, rocks and hills whose heads touch heaven" (1.3.140), the monumental, revengeful "marble heaven" (3.3.463) that recalls the vault of heaven whereto in Plato the chariots of the gods swiftly ride on their way to a banquet (*Phaedrus*, 247a, 247c).

Intelligent *disegno* does exist, then, at least in the Renaissance, with its discontents. The emergence of the Idea mutually assumes its manifestation, as beauty tautologically confirms virtue: "inward beauty" and "outward grace" were given to the Jewish heroine Esther "that so she might be fitter for that honor" (Cooper 1609: 109); and outward beauty "argues th'*inward* beauty of the *Minde*; | For *goodnes* is th'*effect*, *Beauty* the *Cause*, | And both togither commonly we finde" (Davies 1603: 164). A fallacy in fact undermines the belief in inward beauty, even in such virtuous cases: physiognomy might fail to recognize Sappho's "most rare gifts of minde" underneath her defective "outward lineaments" (Walkington 1607: sig. 17ᵛ); conversely, despite her mutilation, Lavinia still offers "a pattern, president, and lively warrant" (*Titus Andronicus* 5.3.44). The hoped-for imbrication between outward and inward beauty was indeed a thorny issue. Sometimes the argument unravels even in the same sentence. Pierre de la Primaudaye first advocates beauty, "a floure of goodness, that is the seed", as "a witnesse and testimony of the beauty in the soule"; then he hastens to warn that often we see "the cleane contrary", as "ordinarily the goodliest men & such are best furnished with the gifts of nature, in the disposition of their body, are most wicked and vicious; and more beautifull women are strumpets, then foule women" (De la Primaudaye 1618: 48). With his *mezza voce* cynicism, Iago (whose physical beauty or ugliness remains unspecified) exposes this manifold

72   Rocco Coronato

conundrum of the Idea: "[m]en should be what they seem, | Or those that be not, would they might seem none" (3.3.131–32). Michelangelo's unfinished rendition of an Ovidian theme casts a mutually illuminating light on Iago.

Non finito, Michelangelo, Iago

Ideally, the Idea should correspond to its outward signs, but their presence (or absence) does not prove its presence (or absence). In *Othello* the Neoplatonic terminology lingers on, though channelled by Iago towards the inexpressible. The Idea shrinks into mere reputation, "the immediate jewel" of the soul (3.3.159). And the depths from which the Idea supposedly emerges now enhance its invisibility, like Desdemona's honour, "an essence that's not seen" (4.1.16). Iago's "hearted" cause (1.3.367), embedded in an invisible heart (3.3.165–66), is no longer the source of inward beauty but the closely-patrolled precinct of interiority, where we determine and confine our invisible essence: "'tis in ourselves that we are thus, or thus" (1.3.320–22). Iago refuses to demonstrate with his "outward action [...] | The native act and figure of my heart in complement extern" (1.1.60, 61–2), in a masterly plunge into the deliberately unfinished, the obverse side of the Idea.

The Neoplatonic Idea was in fact uneasily attended by the unspoken, "the ineffable, diaphanous 'charm' or grace of beautiful things" (Lobsien 2010: 10). In its fragmentation, the *non finito* still conveys the greatness of the artist's enterprise. Such is the importance of the original Idea that perhaps by definition every work is "inachevée" (Dresden 1976: 459). It is a positive absence, enhanced by interruption: in his jocular despair, the exiled Ovid invites a friend of his not to trust the golden effigy he had had made but rather the "maior imago" to be found in the *Metamorphoses*, although the escape of their author had interrupted the work ("fuga rupit opus", *Tristia* 1.7, 11, 13, 14).

This reading probably rested on Aristotle's distinction between virtual and actual and the subsequent definition of art as the form of a still potential thing, existing in the artificer's soul (*Metaphysics* VII.7, 1032^b), what Desdemona calls the "discourse of thought" in opposition to the "actual deed" (4.2.155). The primacy of the *non finito* also rested on such famously unfinished works as the *Aeneid*, as well as on the finding of ancient remains like the Belvedere Torso (allegedly depicting Hercules), often interpreted as wilfully unfinished rather than fragmentary works. In a seminal passage of the *Historia Naturalis*, Pliny advocates that the unfinished paintings (*imperfectasque tabulas*) left by ancient artists were more admirable because in their remaining lines (*liniamenta*) they better showed the thoughts (*cogitationes*) of their artists, foreshortened by their deaths and the ravages of time (Pliny 1601: 35.145).

The Unfinished in Michelangelo and Othello   73

This defence was extended to the many statues left unfinished by Michelangelo. Vasari offers a practical reason for the *non finito*: it allows the artist to take away marble ("levando del marmo") and to reserve further room to draw away ("ritrarre") and change something ("mutare qualcosa") if needed (Vasari 1964: 378). Modern scholars have proposed a whole set of explanations, ranging from the knowledge of Pliny to the long quarrel between Michelangelo and the Duke of Urbino regarding the tomb of Pope Julius II (Brunius 1967: 51), or pointed to the similar technique of *sfumato* (softened, hazy outlines) in his painting and the inchoate form of much of his poetry (Wallace 2015: 5, 19). In Vasari's *Vita di Michelangelo*, especially in the 1568 edition of the *Vite*, after the artist's death, the very imperfection of the sketch ("imperfezione della bozza") demonstrates the perfection of the work ("la perfezione dell'opera") (Vasari 1964: 410). The point had already been made in 1553 by Ascanio Condivi, a pupil of Michelangelo's and a biographer bitterly opposed by Vasari: for Condivi, although none of the Medici tombs had received finishing touches ("l'ultima mano"), they still showed perfect beauty (Vitaletti 1930: 83). Likewise for Vasari, Michelangelo had searched only for the perfection of art; so refined was his judgment that he (unlike Othello, one might add) could never be content with anything he did (Vasari 1964: 427, 451).

A list of apologists, spearheaded by Vasari, reckoned the unfinished a sign not of artistic failure but of the overwhelming greatness of the *concetto*. Michelangelo's *non finito* features in formally unfinished works (the Florentine and the Rondanini *Pietà*), in works that only imitate this status (his *Battle of the Lapiths and Centaurs*), and in works where highly finished parts coexist with rough-hewn ones (his *Night*). Of special relevance are the Prisoners (*Prigioni*), where the *concetto* of liberating the figure from the stone recalls the Neoplatonic struggle to escape from the earthly prison of the body (Barolsky 1998: 457–63). The emergence from the stone, redolent of the Ovidian myth of Deucalyon and Pyrrha, and intimated by Othello's "stones in heaven" (5.2.241), also recalls the myth of Pygmalion as the artist who extracts the *concetto* from matter. The Florentine *Pietà* thus becomes for Vasari a miracle that shows, again implicitly referring to Zeuxis, how a formless stone was reduced to that perfection ("ridotto a quella perfezzione") that nature is at pains to create in the flesh. Fuelled probably by Cicero (*De divinatione* 1.13, 23) and Pliny (*Historia naturalis*, 36: 4), Vasari claims that Michelangelo also extracted ("cavare") the "reasonable shape" ("ragionevole figura") of his David from a block botched by a previous artist (Vasari 1964: 374, 371). As Michelangelo himself wrote in a 1549 letter to Varchi, sculpture is produced "by means of taking away" ("per forza di levare"), rather than, as in painting, by adding (Barocchi 1960–1962: 82).

74 Rocco Coronato

It is perhaps another Ovidian influence that explains why Michelangelo was haunted by the Belvedere Torso (Barkan 1999: 205–7). As Lomazzo contends in his *Idea del Tempio della Pittura* (1590), Michelangelo could never add anything to that fragment, no matter how relentlessly he pursued it; Michelangelo also studied an ancient torso of Marsyas (the satyr flayed by Apollo), in the Medici garden, whose polished, detailed rendition of the anatomy made it, despite its fragmentariness, "cosa vivissima" [a most living thing] (Lomazzo 1973: 2.381). In Francesco Bocchi's *Eccellenza della statua del San Giorgio di Donatello* (1571), the Ovidian episode of Marsyas (*Metamorphoses* 6.382–400) is symbolically interpreted in the wake of Dante's *Paradiso* 1.19–21 as the artist who gets refined and polished by the god of poetry; it also echoes the extraction of the *concetto* shrouded in matter by way of "penetration" (*penetrare*) and "flaying" (*scorzare*), peeling away the layers of matter to unveil the concept (Barocchi 1960–1962: 3.166). Ovid uses the verb *concepi* to convey how the earth absorbed Marsyas' tears before dispersing them as a river in Phrygia: the verb connotes physical absorption, as well as catching fire, conceiving, and creating through art (Jacobs 2002: 433). This interpretation of *Marsyas religatus* (now often proposed as the actual subject of the Belvedere Torso) echoed Zeuxis as an extraction of the best from esteemed works of art or from life, the *imitare* that, differing from simple reproduction (*ritrarre*), creates the thing not as it is but as it should be in order to be perfect, as argued by Vincenzo Danti's *Trattato delle perfette proporzioni* (Barocchi 1960–1962: 2.1575–76; Mansfield 2007).

In this Ovidian vein, Michelangelo's adaptation of both the Neoplatonic Idea and the unfinished offers a novel perspective on Iago. Both in art and poetry, Michelangelo often professed to wielding a rough hammer ("rozzo Martello"), its roughness (*rozzezza*) deriving from *rudis* (raw, rough), the opposite of *polito* (polished, polite) (Barolsky 1998: 463). The stance might have appealed to the "rude" Othello (1.3.81) and his ironically unpolished speech, the "round unvarnished tale" (1.3.90). Prodigiously skilled in conversation, Iago collapses the drunken quarrel into an indistinct coacervate: "I remember a mass of things, but nothing distinctly; a quarrel, but nothing wherefore" (2.3.281–2), remembering nothing before, either – "I cannot speak | Any beginning to this peevish odds" (2.3.177–78). Half-heartedly extracting matter from the inflated shroud of matter, from what Othello, with a metaphor of inflationary supererogation, had called "the exsufflicate and blown surmises" (3.3.186), Iago exfoliates his own persona as one who, because of his "scattering and unsure observance", cannot make the *concetto* emerge, being one that "imperfectly conceits" (3.3.156, 154).

Iago's deliberate *non finito* is ominously clear in the temptation scene. That passion could stop the flow of words was a commonplace, but Iago fashions his interruptions into the metamorphic figure of Echo, hiding

The Unfinished in Michelangelo and Othello   75

a still invisible monster far crueller than the conventionally reassuring green-eyed jealousy: "thou echo'st me | As if there were some monster in thy thought | Too hideous to be shown" (3.3.110–12). His speaking "so startingly and rash" (3.4.79) and his contracted face conjure up the inaccessibility of a closely-pent design, "[a]s if thou then hadst shut up in thy brain | Some horrible conceit" (3.3.119). Iago is probably recalling a long tradition of *aposiopesis* as the best way to say things through silence (*Rhetorica Ad Herennium*, 4.30.41; Quintilian, 9.2.54; Longinus, 33.2). Yet he is also intimating a new inwardness, no longer the shrine of internal beauty but something recognised as inviolable. Yearning for the Idea and consciously echoing Sidney, Samuel Daniel's *Musophilus* claims that poetry shows "the speaking picture of the mind, | The extract of the soule that laboured how | To leaue the image of her selfe behind" (Daniel 1965: 74). *Othello* often voices this hopeful, perhaps irrecoverable, nostalgia for the extraction of the Idea: the charmer who "could almost read | The thoughts of people" (3.4.57–8), the prayers drawn from Desdemona's heart (1.3.151), Iago's own jealousy, whose thought "[d]oth like a poisonous mineral gnaw my inwards" (2.1.296). In a psycho-physiological metaphor (Deutermann 2013), the once-shining *concetto* turns into the deep metamorphic poison of "[d]angerous conceits" burning like "the mines of sulphur" (3.3.330, 333).

Iago and Indistinction

According to Vasari, Michelangelo's *non finito* showed "l'infinito del fine"—the infinite, unattainable nature of all ends and aims in art (Vasari 1964: 881). Iago performs a dizzying plunge into both himself and the other characters, turning "the wrong side out" (2.3.48) and extracting from Desdemona's goodness not the Idea but a net (2.3.352). Here, Ovidian metamorphosis fosters not a simultaneous coincidence of the bestial and the human, but introversion, "a monster | Begot upon itself, born on itself" (3.4.158–59). Iago had warned against "preposterous conclusions" (1.3.329), perhaps with a deliberately artificial sense in mind, as his openings ironically emerge as intimations of deep, "close dilations" (3.3.128).

Castiglione's preface offered a numinous example of that "increased self-consciousness about the fashioning of human identity as a manipulable, artful process" that Greenblatt defined as self-fashioning, achieved in relation to a "threatening Other [that] must be discovered or invented in order to be attacked or destroyed" (Greenblatt 1980: 2, 9). Iago's unfinished mischievously gestures to a mixture of manipulation and wilful obscurity. Iago expresses the gigantic, resentful depths where the mind imprisons itself, drawing away from the light and virtue of the Idea. What before precariously testified to the existence and agency of the Idea (its emergence either as glorious manifestation or as an unfinished

76   Rocco Coronato

state that enhanced the *concetto*), now only asserts its unfathomable darkness. Shakespeare transcends the hailing hopes of both the Idea of Italian art theory and the *non finito* into a third realm: an unknowable, obscure introversion that through denial renders inwardness. This darkness evinces not the shining virtue, the "delighted beauty" (1.3.289) punningly divined by the Duke in Othello, but the unknowability of what lingers there, all but indifferent to extraction.

In this sense, perhaps, the gloriously unfinished Iago remains silent. There is no conceit inside his heart, and the question of whether we can know if there is something inside it remains undecidable. And it is from this deliberately narrowed perspective that Iago, now taking on Aristotle's principle of non-contradiction and the Bible's Tetragram, undermines identity by simply slipping in a word: "I am not what I am" (1.1.65). Adding another interpretation of this celebrated expression of Iago's duplicity would perhaps be a sin unredeemed by inward beauty—yet how to resist the temptation to see there the end of the symbol, the full exposure of the duplicity of Othello's unwittingly Platonic Idea, amazingly similar, in its atemporality, to the Freudian unconscious, devoid of that "dilatory time" (2.3.363) that not only Iago's plot but also life itself needs? It took Iago, the ensign, to expose the frail Neoplatonic inward beauty and the Mannerist *non finito* and to flag up the word as "indeed but sign" (1.1.159).

Bibliography

Alberti, Leon Battista. 1966 [1956]. *On Painting (Della pittura)*, trans. by John R. Spencer. New Haven.

Bacon, Francis. 1890. *Bacon's essays including his moral and historical works.* London.

Barkan, Leonard. 1999. *Unearthing the Past: Archaeology and Aesthetics in the Making of Renaissance Culture.* New Haven.

Barocchi, Paola, ed. 1960–1962. *Trattati d'arte del Cinquecento: fra Manierismo e Controriforma*, 3 vols. Bari.

———— 1977. *Scritti d'arte del Cinquecento*, 3 vols. Milan.

Barolsky, Paul. 1998. "As in Ovid, So in Renaissance Art". *Renaissance Quarterly*, 51.2: 451–74.

Batman, Stephen. 1582. *Batman vppon Bartholome, His Booke De Proprietatibus Rerum.* London.

Boose, Lynda. 1981. "Othello's 'Chrysolite' and the Song of Songs Tradition". *Philological Quarterly*, 60: 427–37.

Braider, Christopher. 1993. *Refiguring the Real: Picture and Modernity in Word and Image, 1400–1700.* Princeton.

Brunius, Teddy. 1967. "Michelangelo's non finito". *Contributions to the History and Theory of Art.* Uppsala. 29–67.

Buonarroti, Michelangelo. 1960. *Rime*, ed. by E. N. Girardi. Bari.

Castiglione, Baldessar. 1900 [1561]. *The Book of the Courtier*, trans. by Thomas Hoby. London.

The Unfinished in Michelangelo and Othello   77

Cooper, Thomas. 1609. *The Churches deliuerance contayning meditations and short notes vppon the booke of Hester*. London.

Dallington, Sir Robert. 1592. *Hypnerotomachia*. London.

Daniel, Samuel. 1965. *Musophilus*. In *Poems and a Defence of Ryme*, ed. by Arthur Colby Sprague. London.

Davies, John. 1603. *Microcosmos. The Discovery of the little world, with the gouernment thereof*. London.

Delacroix, Eugène. 1950. *Journal d'Eugène Delacroix*, ed. by André Joubin. Paris.

De la Primaudaye, Pierre. 1618. *The French Academie Fully discoursed and finished in foure bookes*. London.

De Moulin, Pierre. 1610. *Theophilus, or Loue diuine*. London.

Deutermann, Allison K. 2013. "Hearing Iago's withheld confession". *Shakespearean Sensations. Experiencing Literature in Early Modern England*, ed. by Katharine A. Craik and Tanya Pollard. Cambridge. 47–63.

Di Stefano, Elisabetta. 2004. "Zeusi e la bellezza di Elena". *FIERI: Annali del Dipartimento di Filosofia, Storia e Critica dei Saperi*. University of Palermo. 77–84.

Dolce, Lodovico. 1555. *Dialogo della pittura intitolato l'Aretino*. Venice.

Dresden, Sem. 1976. "Platonisme et conceptions humanistes du 'Non-finito'". *Platon et Aristote à la Renaissance*. Paris. 453–68.

Edmondes, Clement. 1609. *Observations upon Caesar's Commentaries*. London.

Fenner, Dudley. 1587. *Paraphrases. The song of Songs [...] translated out of the Hebrue and into English meeter*. Middleburgh.

Fronterotta, Francesco. 2001. *ΜΕΘΕΞΙΣ. La teoria platonica delle idee e la partecipazione delle cose empiriche*. Pisa.

Ghiberti, Lorenzo. 1947. *I commentari*, ed. by Ottavio Morisani. Naples.

Gombrich, E. H. 1972. "*Icones Symbolicae*: Philosophies of Symbolism and their Bearing on Art". *Symbolic Images: Studies in the Art of the Renaissance*. London. 123–95.

Greenblatt, Stephen. 1980. *Renaissance Self-fashioning. From More To Shakespeare*. Chicago.

Gregory, Sharon. 2014. "Vasari on Imitation". *The Ashgate Research Companion to Vasari*, ed. by David J. Cast. Farnham. 223–44.

Hankins, James. 2004. *Humanism and Platonism in the Italian Renaissance*, 2 vols. Rome. Vol. 2, *Platonism*.

Harington, John. 1591. *Orlando Furioso*. London.

Hedley, Douglas, and Sarah Hutton, eds. 2008. *Platonism at the Origins of Modernity. Studies on Platonism and Early Modern Philosophy*. Dordrecht.

Jacobs, Fredrika H. 2002. "(Dis)assembling: Marsyas, Michelangelo, and the Accademia del Disegno". *The Art Bulletin*, 84.3: 426–48.

—— 2005. *The Living Image in Renaissance Art*. Cambridge.

Jayne, Sears. 1995. *Plato in Renaissance England*. Dordrecht. 115–33.

Junius, Franciscus. 1972. *The Painting of the Ancients – De pictura veterum, according to the English translation* (1638), ed. by Keith Aldrich, Philipp Fehl, and Raina Fehl. Berkeley.

Korhonen, Anu. 2005. "Washing the Ethiopian white: conceptualising black skin in Renaissance England". *Black Africans in Renaissance Europe*, ed. by T. F. Earle and K. J. P. Lowe. Cambridge. 94–113.

78 Rocco Coronato

Lobsien, Verena Olejniczak. 2010. *Transparency and Dissimulation: Configurations of Neoplatonism in Early Modern English Literature*. Berlin.

Lomazzo, Francesco. 1598 [1585]. *Tracte containing the artes of curious paintinge caruinge building*, trans. by Richard Haydocke. Oxford.

—— 1973. *Idea del Tempio della Pittura* [1590]. *Scritti sulle arti*, ed. by Roberto Paolo Ciardi. Florence.

Mansfield, Elizabeth C. 2007. "Myth and Mimesis in the Renaissance". *Too Beautiful to Picture: Zeuxis, Myth, and Mimesis*. Minneapolis. 39–53.

Marr, Alexander. 2015. "Pregnant Wit: *ingegno* in Renaissance England". *British Art Studies*, 1, http://dx.doi.org/10.17658/issn.2058-5462/issue-01/amarr.

Medcalf, Stephen. 1994. "Shakespeare on beauty, truth and transcendence". *Platonism and the English Imagination*, ed. by Anne Baldwin and Sarah Hatton. Cambridge. 117–125.

Panofsky, Erwin. 1968. *Idea. A Concept in Art Theory*, trans. by Joseph J. S. Peake. Columbia.

Peacham, Henry. 1606. *The Art of Drawing with the pen, and limming in water colours*. London.

Plato. 1996. *Cratylus, Parmenides, Greater Hippias, Lesser Hippias*, trans. by H. N. Fowler. Revised reprint. Cambridge, MA.

Pliny. 1601. *Historia Naturalis*, trans. by Philemon Holland, *The Historie of the World*. London.

Plotinus. 1989 [1966]. *Plotinus*, trans. by A. H. Armstrong, 7 vols. Cambridge, MA.

Roe, John. 1994. "Italian Neoplatonism and the poetry of Sidney, Shakespeare, Chapman and Donne". *Platonism and the English Imagination*, ed. by Anna Baldwin and Sarah Hutton. Cambridge. 100–116.

Rogers, Richard. 1603. *Seuen treatises containing such direction as is gathered out of the Holie Scriptures*. London.

Rowe, M. W. 2010. "Iago's Elenchus: Shakespeare, *Othello*, and the Platonic Inheritance". *A Companion to the Philosophy of Literature*, ed. by Garry L. Hagberg and Walter Jost. Chichester. 174–92.

Schulz, Juergen. 1975. "Michelangelo's Unfinished Works". *The Art Bulletin*, 57.3: 366–73.

Semler, L. E. 2004. "Breaking the Ice to Invention: Henry Peacham's *The Art of Drawing* (1606)". *The Sixteenth Century Journal*, 35.3: 735–50.

Shakespeare, William. 2002. *The Complete Sonnets and Poems*, ed. by Colin Burrow, Oxford.

—— 2007. *The Oxford Shakespeare*, ed. by John Jowett, William Montgomery, Gary Taylor, and Stanley Wells. Oxford.

Sidney, Philip. 1977. *The Countess of Pembroke's Arcadia*, ed. by Maurice Evans. Harmondsworth.

—— 1980. *An Apology for Poetry*, ed. by Geoffrey Shepherd. Manchester.

Summers, David. 1987. "The Idea of Federigo Zuccaro". *The Judgement of Sense: Renaissance Naturalism and the Rise of Aesthetics*. New York. 283–308.

Thomas, Thomas. 1587. *Dictionarium linguae Latinae et Anglicanae*. Cambridge.

Varchi, Benedetto. 1549. *Due Lezzioni di M. Benedetto Varchi*. Florence.

Vasari, Giorgio. 1964. *Vita di Michelangelo*. In *Vite scelte*, ed. by Anna Maria Brizio. Turin.

―――― 1991. *Vita di Mantegna*. In *Le vite de' più eccellenti architetti, pittori, et scultori italiani, da Cimbaue insino a' tempi nostri*, ed. by Luciano Bellosi and Aldo Rossi. Turin.

Vitaletti, Guido. 1930. *Michelangelo: Lettere e Rime*. Turin.

Walkington, Thomas. 1607. *The optick glasse of humours*. London.

Wallace, William E. 2015. "The 2014 Josephine Waters Bennett Lecture: 'Certain of Death': Michelangelo's Late Life and Art". *Renaissance Quarterly*, 68.1: 1–32.

Wilson, Thomas. 1612. *A Christian Dictionarie Opening the signification of the chiefe words dispersed generally through Holy Scriptures of the Old and New Testament*. London.

Wotton, Henry. 1968. *The Elements of Architecture*, ed. Frederick Hard. Charlottesville.

Zeki, Semir. 2001. "Artistic Creativity and the Brain". *Science*, 293.5527: 51–52.

Zuccaro, Federigo. 1952. *L'idea de' pittori, scultori e architetti* [1607]. *Scritti d'arte di Federico Zuccaro*, ed. by D. Heikampf. Florence.

5 Shakespeare and Italian Republicanism

John Drakakis

At the beginning of *The Elizabethan World Picture*, E. M. W. Tillyard insisted that Elizabethan culture inherited a "world picture" in which "everything had to be included and everything had to be made to fit and connect". He acknowledged the presence of secular writers like Machiavelli, "to whom the idea of a universe divinely ordered throughout was repugnant" (Tillyard 1943: 5), but his emphasis upon a theocentric universe obscured some of the more pressing political, and implicitly juridical, issues involving the organisation of society and the state that had begun to emerge at the end of the sixteenth century. A reader of Aristotle's *The Politics*, published in a new English translation in 1598, would have encountered the following:

> Hereby knowe wee how it is contrarie to the nature of a Cittie, that it should bee so vnited as some men set downe: and how that which they vphold for the greatest welfare of Cities, dooth ouerthrowe them: for euerie thing is preserued by the goodnesse thereof. Also there is another reason to prooue, that it is not best to procure the vniting of a Cittie too much: for a house hath more sufficiencie than a man, and a Cittie than a house. And then commonly doe men thinke there is a Cittie properly, when it hath there within a sufficient companie of Inhabitants: Wherefore, if the most sufficient is most to bee wished: then is that which is least one, to bee preferred before that which is most one.
>
> (Aristotle 1598: sig. I3^r)

Of course, Aristotle was writing out of the experience of the Athenian republic, but the tensions that he pinpointed were to be re-articulated in Machiavelli's *Discourses* (1517), providing a detailed gloss on Livy's *History of Rome*. Shakespeare himself had recourse to the shape of ancient Roman history in his four Roman plays that opportunistically sampled various moments: the fall of Rome at the hands of the Goths (*Titus Andronicus*); the tension between "republican" and "imperial" Rome (*Julius Caesar* and *Antony and Cleopatra*); and the internal divisions within republican Rome (*Coriolanus*). These four

Shakespeare and Italian Republicanism   81

plays do not comprise a chronological tetralogy, but taken together they offer representations of particular historical conjunctures in the long history of Rome. They are also augmented by a tyrannical pre-history in Shakespeare's long narrative poem *The Rape of Lucrece*. But, of course, Rome was not the only part of Italy that attracted the attention of Elizabethan and Jacobean dramatists and political commentators. *Romeo and Juliet* (*c.* 1594) is set in Verona, while *The Merchant of Venice* (1596) and *Othello* (*c.* 1603–4) focus critically on Venice; there are mentions of other Italian locations, although in *The Merchant of Venice* Shakespeare's carelessness in identifying Doctor Bellario's location first in Mantua (3.4.49) and then in Padua, widely regarded as a centre of civil law (4.1.118), may suggest an uncertain sense of Italian geography.

My concern is not with the long history of Rome that contains examples of all forms of political organisation, or with Shakespeare's occasional mention of other Italian locations, but with the two plays that Shakespeare sets in Venice, a geographical location that, as John Gillies points out, "was a glorious—yet unsettling—contradiction". Gillies suggests that there was a contradiction between Venice "as the constitutional heir of the ancient city-state" and the "idea of Venice as an open or cosmopolitan city whose citizens mingled promiscuously with the peoples of the world" (Gillies 1994: 123). He focuses on Venice as an exemplary instance of the themes of "exorbitance" and "intrusion", arguing that "Shakespeare's Venice invites barbarous intrusion through the sheer 'exorbitance' of its maritime trading empire" (Gillies 1994: 125). But in addition to its well-documented exotic appeal to Elizabethan and Jacobean travellers, Venice presented another kind of threat, that of an open and thriving "republic", suggesting another kind of link with the Athenian city-state but also raising certain political anxieties for English commentators. The physical "artificiality" of Venice as a city constructed on water was a commonplace, and its reputation as a trading rather than a military republic had been observed by William Thomas in *The History of Italy* (1549 and 1561) (Shakespeare 2010: 3–7). But it was Richard Bancroft, Bishop of London, who contended in his *Survey of the Pretended Holy Discipline* (1593) that in libertarian Venice "[t]hey haue no Earles, no Barons, no Noblemen of whom their Gentlemen stand in awe" (Bancroft 1593: 8), and that such liberties as the republic afforded were a threat to the fabric of social order.

The term "republic" seems to have been semantically ambiguous for Elizabethans. Sir Thomas Smith's account of the "realme" of England was entitled *De Republica Anglorum* (1583), and despite having a number of details in common with Aristotle's *The Politics*, Smith was clearly describing a monarchy and not a republic in the technical sense, although historian Patrick Collinson describes the realm as a "monarchical republic" (Collinson 1987: 395). Indeed, as with other political commentators of the period, Smith begins his analysis by rehearsing the various types

82 John Drakakis

of political organisation ranging from monarchy through oligarchy to democracy, all of which he labels "commonwealths or gouernment". Political order is ensured by law, which is a system of regulation that underpins hierarchy; for example, when discussing the operation of justice and what happens to any deviants from the law's regulative demands, he claims,

> [A]s there is profitable and likelyhoode of profite, so there is right and likelyhoode of right. And aswell may the ruling and Soueraigne part commaund that which is not his profite, as the iust man may offend (notwithstanding his iust and true meaning) when he would amend that which is amisse, and helpe the common wealth, and doe good unto it. For in asmuch as he attempteth to doe contrarie to the Lawe which is already put, he therefore by the lawe is iustly to be condemned [...]
>
> (Smith 1583: 2)

The patriarchal "family" is the foundation of the social order and of law, and the metaphor Smith uses is a sumptuary one: "when to ech partie or espece and kinde of the people that is applied which best agreeth like a garme[n]t to the bodie or shoe to the foote, then the bodie politique is in quiet, & findeth ease, pleasure and profite". When the body politic is not appropriately ordered (and indeed clothed) then hierarchy is disrupted and disorder follows:

> [I]f a contrary forme be giuen to a contrary maner of people, and when the shoe is too little or too great for the foote, it doth hurt and encomber the conuenient use thereof, so the free people of nature tyrannized or ruled by one against their willes, were he neuer so good, either faile of corage and were seruile, or neuer rest until they either destroie their king and them that would subdue them, or be destroyed themselues. And againe another sort there is which without being ruled by one prince, but set at libertie cannot tell what they shoulde doe, but either through insolencie, pride, and idleness will fall to robbery and all mischiefe, and to scatter and dissolue themselues, or with foolish ambition and priuate strife consume one another and bring themselues to nothing.
>
> (Smith 1583: 17–18)

Smith anticipates the kind of criticism of the "republican" sentiment that Bancroft levelled specifically against Venice, even though, as Lewis Lewkenor's translation of Gasparo Contarini's *The Commonwealth and Gouernment of Venice* (1599) made very clear, Venice was governed by a series of very complex political procedures. As J. G. A. Pocock observed, those who in Italy promulgated the "myth" of Venice did so

Shakespeare and Italian Republicanism 83

not because they believed that "the only return to order lay through the union of the intellect with the cosmos, a dramatic restoration of the unity of the intelligible world", but because they "proposed to restore the world through citizenship and political order, and the image of Venice was merely the vehicle through which they conveyed once more the categories of Aristotelian politics" (Pocock 1975: 102).

While there are elements of the dialectic between the "toleration" and "exorbitance" that Gillies identifies in Shakespeare's two Venetian plays, the nature of the recurrent political debate surrounding the concept of "republicanism", as Pocock's more general remarks imply, indicates something much more specifically *political*. Both plays involve "outsiders", whom Venice officially welcomed. But in both *The Merchant of Venice* and *Othello,* the issue revolves around how these "strangers" are *accommodated* and the tensions that result from those accommodations. Or, put a little differently, what we have are late Elizabethan and early Jacobean readings of an Italian phenomenon that was both a political threat (even though at this time the historical influence of Venice was waning), and an example of how the very potential for disequilibrium that Sir Thomas Smith identified within the "republican" type of democracy could produce tension that required comedy to alleviate, or, in the later play, led to tragedy. Both plays focus on tensions not far beneath the surface of a society that visitors found seductively attractive, and which from a partisan "English" position provided an international screen onto which domestic anxieties could be projected.

The Merchant of Venice was performed around 1596–97 and was, in part, a continuation of a dialogue with the late Christopher Marlowe's *The Jew of Malta* (*c.* 1590), which had been regularly performed after Marlowe's death in 1593, and on some eight occasions in the first half of 1596 alone. The Prologue of Marlowe's play personified what had become for the Elizabethans something of a demonic figure, Machevil; this was the English caricature of Machiavelli, whose writings were not published in English until well into the seventeenth century but whose influence on political life was already being felt during the latter part of the sixteenth century. It was "Machiavel" who became a distinctively Italianate figure of political intrigue and duplicity, and Machiavelli who effectively rewrote the manual on how to secure and maintain political power. But *The Merchant of Venice* is also preoccupied with the topic of the circulation of money that was at the centre of Venetian trading activities. Marlowe's Machevil provided a *curriculum vitae* of his practices, which included the misanthropic observation "And let them know that I am Machevil, | And weigh not men, and therefore not men's words" (Marlowe 1978: 63, ll. 7–8); and the Jew, Barabas, is presented as someone "Who smiles to see how full his bags are crammed, | Which money was not got without my means" (Marlowe 1978: 67, ll. 31–2). Shakespeare's Jew, Shylock, extends this tradition and in *The Merchant*

84 John Drakakis

of Venice becomes, among other things, the device whereby Venice's own internal political and social tensions are subjected to critical analysis.

Scholarly criticism has occasionally concerned itself with trying to decide who is the "merchant" of the title. The title-page of the first quarto of 1600 makes it abundantly clear that the "merchant" is Antonio, and that it is "the extreame crueltie of *Shylocke* the Iewe" towards him that establishes the latter's Machiavellian credentials. The question that Portia asks when she enters the Venetian court disguised as the lawyer Balthazar, "Which is the merchant here, and which the Jew?" (4.1.170), may be superfluous since Shylock's own attire is referred to earlier as a distinctive "gaberdine" (1.3.108) that would make him instantly recognisable. On the other hand, both Antonio and Shylock are alike in sharing a common interest in "money", although Antonio makes it clear that his request to the Jew for a loan arises out of an embarrassing necessity:

> Shylock, albeit I neither lend nor borrow
> By taking nor by giving of excess,
> Yet to supply the ripe wants of my friend.
> I'll break a custom.
>
> (1.3.57–60)

This early exchange raises a fundamental question about Venice's "hospitality" to "strangers", and points to a distinction between two kinds of lending: one, between friends, that incurs no financial penalty, and the other, usury proper, that allows money to "breed". The homily that Shylock advances to justify his own fiscal practice is undermined by Antonio's question that establishes him as a mercantilist rather than a full-blown capitalist: "Was this inserted to make interest good? | Or is your gold and silver ewes and rams?", to which Shylock replies, "I cannot tell, I make it breed as fast" (1.3.90–92). Clearly two different *readings* of Shylock's homiletic biblical narrative are at issue here, one allegorical, the other analogical. The point is that the issue of the sterile breeding of money, which has its roots in Aristotle, is established from the outset as a mark of distinction between creditor and debtor that threatens to undermine the entire moral and ethical fabric of the "state". The instrument of that undermining is the very stranger who is both an "insider" (Shylock's name has a Christian, English etymology meaning "fair haired", not a colour with which the Jew is identified in Shakespeare's play) and an "outsider", a resident of Venice yet one treated inhospitably. This further challenges the Venetian claim to be hospitable to "strangers" and suggests that, as elsewhere in Shakespeare, the enemy is both within and outside the boundaries of the state.

From the very outset, Venice in this play is not at ease with itself. Antonio is "sad", though he admits "I know not why I am so sad" (1.1.1); Portia laments that her "little body is aweary of this great world" (1.2.1–2); and Shylock, after his enforced conversion to Christianity,

Shakespeare and Italian Republicanism 85

asks permission to leave the court, adding "I am not well" (4.1.391–2). At the very heart of Venetian social life there is a malaise about which the play is not always clear or explicit. Antonio's sadness appears to have no recognisable cause, and so is the subject of speculation that in modern productions often descends into innuendo. Portia's "weariness" is the result of the continued exertion of patriarchal control by her dead father, while Shylock's "illness" is more than the manifest result of his being stripped of all that would define him theatrically as a "Jew"; indeed, far from being fully "accommodated" into Venetian society, the shabby destruction of his own "family" condemns him to a fate that brings into existence the potential for a Machiavellian splitting of subjectivity that will result in precisely the kind of duplicity that Marlowe's Machevil had extolled, and that had been the substance of Bassanio's earlier strictures against Shylock's motives:

> ANTONIO   Hie thee, gentle Jew.
>   The Hebrew will turn Christian, he grows kind.
> BASSANIO
>   I like not fair terms and a villain's mind.
>   (1.3.173–75)

Antonio's possibly ironic play upon the words "gentle" (gentile) and "kind" (kindness but also "kind" in the anthropological sense of "kindred") arrogates to itself a generosity that smacks of self-congratulation to the extent that it advertises its own superiority and reinforces an internal division between Christian and Jew that is constitutive of the Venetian republic *and* that threatens to undermine its inclusive sentiments (Adelman 2008: 11–12).[1] But it also renders Antonio open to criticism as a specifically Venetian Christian.

This is only the most extreme example of internal divisions within the fabric of Shakespeare's representation of Venetian society. The prose narrative that contains the basic elements of the plot of *The Merchant of Venice*, Ser Giovanni Fiorentino's *Il Pecorone* (1558), involves a relationship between one of three sons of a rich Florentine merchant (Gianetto), his father (Bindo), and his wealthy Venetian godfather (Antonio). In Shakespeare's version of the narrative, Antonio is a Venetian merchant and a "kinsman" of Bassanio who is himself a "lord" who habitually lives beyond his means. The Jew attaches the epithet "prodigal" (2.5.15) to his Christian Venetian adversaries in general, but, long before that, Bassanio reveals his aristocratic financial predicament:

> 'Tis not unknown to you, Antonio,
> How much I have disabled mine estate
> By something showing a more swelling port
> Than my faint means would grant continuance.
>   (1.1.122–25)

86   John Drakakis

Moreover, Bassanio denies to Antonio an anxiety that he might expect to derive from his loss of aristocratic kudos: "Nor do I now make moan to be abridged | From such a noble rate" (1.1.126–7). This is as much an "English" dilemma as it is a Venetian one, and suggests a displacement of a recognisably domestic tension onto Shakespeare's Venetian canvas. Bassanio is Antonio's "most noble kinsman" (1.1.57), but he is also indebted to him. From the very outset, then, there are, despite Venice's claims to a republican democratic ethos, internal divisions and anxieties within the hierarchically-divided indigenous community that force a merchant such as Antonio, who does not always have access to liquid capital, to seek financial assistance from the "stranger" Shylock. The seemingly unitary republican ethos of Venice is shown to be internally fractured, and along some of the lines with which an English audience might identify. Or, put another way, the English perspective on Venice mixes together historical differences *and* similarities insofar as they become meaningful through a recognizably "English" perspective. This does not, of course, invite us to "read" Venice as though it were a thinly disguised representation of Elizabethan London, but it does offer certain points of contact for the spectator. Venice is the same but it is also different.

The entry of Shylock "the Jew" into the equation complicates the picture even further. Officially there were no Jews in England during this period, although a number of attempts have been made to identify covert Jewish communities. (For a useful catalogue of the evidence for small communities of Jews in England during this period, see Adelman 2008: 4–6). But as Joshua Trachtenberg and Debra Strickland have observed, the "history" of the myth of the demonized Jew extends back into the medieval period (Trachtenberg 1983; Strickland 2003); as a "usurer" he becomes a necessary evil in an environment with a pressing need for liquid capital but without ready access to money except by borrowing (Shakespeare 2010: 14; Christians were even identified as "usurers", Caesar 1579: sig. 4^v). Arguably, the Jewish presence in Venice was meant primarily to fulfil that need; the incredulous claim that Venice preserved cordial social relations was something about which an English audience might have been sceptical. A Venice that was the perfect, ordered republic, full of sensual delights, where indigenous inhabitants and "strangers" lived harmoniously together, is exposed in Shakespeare's play as a myth.

In the light of the play's serious elements we need to remind ourselves that the title-page of the 1600 quarto advertises it as "The Most Excellent Historie of the *Merchant of Venice*", although in the 1623 Folio the play is classified as one of the "Comedies". As a comedy, the play contains two instantly recognisable comic components: tension between the generations in relation to the securing of marriage partners, and obstacles that are required to be overcome so that an ordered, happy conclusion might be reached. For some time, critics tended to view the play as a

Shakespeare and Italian Republicanism 87

"problem" play because of the seriousness of some of its concerns: the Jew turns out to be a villain who has to be overcome; the merchant, Antonio, is brought almost to the point of a death that threatens to re-play in miniature the death of Christ; the Jew's daughter, Jessica, elopes with a Christian (Lorenzo); and Portia, constrained by the "law" of her dead father, betrays a quasi-racist revulsion for her "foreign" suitors, especially the Moor, Morocco. There is no doubt that some of these tensions would have been familiar to a metropolitan English audience, since the presence of Moors and Jews openly in London was exceptional rather than the norm. And as Janet Adelman has pointed out, the con-verted Shylock would become a "converso", a figure familiar in England (Adelman 2008: 11).

The tension between parents and children frequently generates ele-ments of plot in Shakespeare's comedies. That tension is exacerbated in *The Merchant of Venice* by the presence of two plots—one in which the daughter (Portia) obeys her father's "law" and marries the Venetian Bassanio, the other in which the Jew's daughter (Jessica) disobeys her father and elopes to marry Lorenzo. The latter is handled in an unusual way, since Jessica's marriage affirms the means whereby her father is converted to Christianity, and elicits a degree of approval that in *Oth-ello* becomes the foundation for tragedy. The issue here is not the *fact* of what we might recognise as prejudice, with which an Elizabethan audience might have had common cause, but the fact that this tension surfaces within a republic noted for its democratic processes and pro-cedures. Ideologically, the play steers away from miscegenation, most notably in Portia's comment after the failure of Morocco:

A gentle riddance. Draw the curtains, go.
Let all of his complexion choose me so.

(2.7.77–78)

In the previous scene, Gratiano transforms Jessica with the comment, "Now, by my hood, a gentle and no Jew" (2.6.52). In both cases, the "stranger" is not welcomed but marginalized. Portia's dismissive com-ment, however, is authorized by her dead father, whose provision for her is shown, in the event, to harmonize with Bassanio's choice. But there is another feature of Venice that has occasioned little comment.

It has become a critical commonplace that Portia directs Bassanio to the correct casket through the rhyme in the song that accompanies his deliberations. For his part, Bassanio's musings begin with a statement about the difference between "reality" and outward appearance:

So may the outward shows be least themselves,
The world is still deceived with ornament.
In law, what plea so tainted and corrupt,

88   *John Drakakis*

But, being seasoned with a gracious voice,
Obscures the show of evil. In religion,
What damned error but some sober brow
Will bless it and approve it with a text,
Hiding the grossness with fair ornament.

(3.2.73–80)

These sentiments echo through the play but, as Harry Berger Jr. has recently observed, "the overt knavery of Lorenzo and Jessica becomes a proleptic parody of what transpires more slowly and more deviously at Belmont" (Berger 2013: 62). That deviousness extends even further when Bassanio turns his attention to "beauty", ostensibly in the abstract, but having as a target Portia herself:

Look on beauty,
And you shall see 'tis purchased by the weight,
Which therein works a miracle in nature,
Making them lightest that wear most of it:
So are those crisped snaky golden locks,
Which maketh such wanton gambols with the wind
Upon supposed fairness, often known
To be the dowry of a second head,
The skull that bred them in the sepulchre.
Thus ornament is but the guiled shore
To a most dangerous sea; the beauteous scarf
Veiling an Indian beauty; in a word,
The seeming truth, which cunning times put on
To entrap the wisest.

(3.2.88–101)

Bassanio, is, of course, addressing the caskets, but his humanizing of "beauty" extends his frame of reference to the real object of his attentions, Portia. Bassanio's doubts fall away in the successful choice of the leaden casket but, within the larger context of Venice, his questioning of the physical manifestations of beauty's veracity creates a tension between the pleasures of "appearance" and the death that it disguises. However, if his analysis of "beauty" is to have any credence at all, when he discovers "Fair Portia's counterfeit" in the leaden casket (3.2.115), he may well have uncovered the counterfeit of a counterfeit. It is this that takes us closer to Venice and to the Machiavellian duplicity that at every level informs its daily life. The picture that Bassanio draws is that of a Venetian courtesan who will, in the later play, be transformed into that figure in Iago's mythography, a "Venetian huswife". And it is that myth that hovers over the play when Bassanio's and Gratiano's alleged infidelities are used by Portia and Nerissa to undermine their patriarchal authority. The play leaves us in no doubt of Portia's and Nerissa's fidelity to their husbands, but this

Shakespeare and Italian Republicanism 89

does not quite abolish the masculine suspicion that is the darker and potentially more dangerous other side of Venetian patriarchy. *The Merchant of Venice* thereby allows its English audience to feel superior when confronted with a republic that is not what it seems. Not only is Venice geographically "artificial", but its institutions ranging from domestic to public life do not square with the publicity that lauded the republic as a harmonious society that welcomed "strangers" (Shakespeare 2010: 5).

The Merchant of Venice negotiates its way through the differences and similarities between English and Venetian mores, casting a critical eye on the latter's republican claims. The play's nervousness about miscegenation has been frequently noted, and it could be argued that Shylock, despite his English name, may have been doubled with Morocco in original performance. The villain speaks, but like the satanic archetype that he resembles he can offer a critique of Christian Venice that is unflattering. Between this play and *Othello*, Shakespeare himself may have been involved in the performance of Ben Jonson's *Every Man in His Humour* (1598), first printed in quarto in 1601, and set in Florence, since it was mounted under the auspices of the Chamberlain's Men (Jonson 2000: 11). The play's most recent editor, Robert Miola, has argued persuasively that Jonson's play was fully attuned to contemporary events in London, and that the Italianate setting was designed to protect Jonson from the unwelcome attention of the authorities (Jonson 2000: 25ff.). Moreover, he suggests that Shakespeare remembered the play when he came to write *Othello*, since Jonson's comic sub-plot contains a pathologically jealous merchant Thorello, whose wife's name is, tellingly, Bianca (Jonson 2000: 65). The possible metathesis that produced the name "Othello", coupled with the ascription of a comic jealousy that teeters on the brink of a potentially murderous pathology, provides one of the strands, linked with others from *The Merchant of Venice*, that Shakespeare fashioned into *Othello*.

Whereas in the earlier play miscegenation was dismissively touched upon, or, in the case of the Jessica-Lorenzo marriage, fudged, in the later play, it is confronted head-on in the elopement of Desdemona and Othello. It is as though Shakespeare, having firmly resisted what may have been a momentary temptation in *The Merchant*, resurrected a thought that he had earlier dismissed, and imagined a marriage between Portia and Morocco. No doubt an early Jacobean audience would have been scandalised by such a union, but Shakespeare adds an important ingredient to the relationship by setting it in Venice and making Othello both a "stranger" *and* the guardian of Venetian institutions. Those who reduce the play to the level of a domestic tragedy miss the intrinsic connection between Othello's domestic affairs and the manner in which Venice's republican interests are both articulated and protected (Nuttall 1983: 133–4). Indeed, it is the Venetian setting that produces in a modern critical sensibility the tension between the terms "domestic" and "tragedy". For an early Jacobean audience, for whom the political continuity between household and wider community was axiomatic—traced back

90 *John Drakakis*

explicitly to Aristotle's *Politics* and the lesser-known but nonetheless influential *Oeconimica*, and thence forward to Sir Thomas Smith's carefully-integrated model of the household as a mini-polity—the distinction would not have been so clear-cut. In addition, Shakespeare's play, stimulated perhaps by laws governing racial difference at home, probes, in a revision of the cultural register of *The Merchant*, the problems to which the assimilation of "strangers" led. Indeed, in her observation of the Freudian coupling of *Heimlich/Unheimlich*, and the suggestion that in the *unheimlich* "the familiar and intimate are reversed into their opposites" (Kristeva 1991: 182), Julia Kristeva describes a situation that bears a close resemblance to the predicament of the "stranger" in *Othello*:

> that which *is* strangely uncanny would be that which *was* (the past tense is important) familiar, and, under certain conditions (which ones?) emerges. A first step was taken that removed the uncanny strangeness from the outside, where fright had anchored it, to locate it inside, not inside the familiar considered as one's own and proper, but the familiar tainted with strangeness and referred (beyond its imaginative origin) to an improper past. The other is my ("own and proper") unconscious.
>
> (Kristeva 1991: 183)

The question is: what is there in the democratic republic of Venice of the Jacobean imagination that resides at the heart of its "unconscious" and that under "certain conditions (which ones?) emerges"?

There are at least three entry points into the "unconscious" of Venice in *Othello*, beginning with the "dream" of Brabantio, and including the lurid fantasy hatched by Iago that requires "Hell and night" to "bring this monstrous birth to the world's light" (1.3.401–2), along with the recounting of Michael Cassio's "dream" in which he is alleged to reveal his innermost thoughts in sleep:

> There are a kind of men
> So loose of soul that in their sleeps will mutter
> Their affairs – one of this kind is Cassio.
> In sleep I heard him say "Sweet Desdemona,
> Let us be wary, let us hide our loves,"
> And then, sir, would he gripe and wring my hand,
> Cry "O sweet creature!" and then kiss me hard
> As if he plucked up kisses by the roots
> That grew upon my lips, lay his leg o'er my thigh,
> And sigh, and kiss, and then cry "Cursed fate
> That gave thee to the Moor!"
>
> (3.3.418–28)

Shakespeare and Italian Republicanism 91

Each of these dreams is accorded its particular psychological geography through the prism of Iago's perversity, and their collective effect is to catapult Othello into a lurid nightmare in which physical "blackness" and nobility of mind wage war against each other. Having secured the commitment of the dupe Roderigo, Iago proceeds to tutor Brabantio in the matter of his own unconscious patriarchal fears, to the point where even the empirical evidence of Desdemona's absence from her father's house allows him to draw a prefabricated conclusion. Iago's crudely offensive image of "your daughter covered with a Barbary horse", and claim that Barabantio will "have your nephews neigh to you, you'll have coursers for cousins and gennets for germans" (1.1.110–13), only slightly ameliorated in Roderigo's more decorous but explicit account, lead the victim of deception to conclude "It is too true and evil, gone she is, | And what's to come of my despised time | Is nought but bitterness" (1.1.158–60).

Clearly, the underbelly of republican freedom and ethnic harmony is the demotion of the "stranger" as a representative of what Contarini calls "the wonderful concourse of strange and forein people, yea of the farthest and remotest nations" to the status of a demonic beast (Lewkenor 1599: sig. B1ʳ). Iago's allegation that "Even now, now, very now, an old black ram | Is tupping your white ewe!" transforms the ill-fated Desdemona into a sub-human stranger (a "iewe" that reminds us of Jessica in the earlier play) and, from the point of view of a cynical mal-contented Iago, reduces the defender of Venice to a beast. Venice is, indeed, troubled by the discrepancy between its "appearances" and by its own subterranean anxieties, by its own freedoms and the tensions that are secreted in its collective unconscious where they are encouraged to breed like a deadly virus. Indeed, the complex language of the play, oscillating as it does uncomfortably between Othello's denial of sexual potency ("the young affects | In me defunct", 1.3.264–5) and its reduction of sexual intimacy to the metaphor of fiscal exchange ("Come, my dear love, | The purchase made, the fruits are to ensue: | The profit's yet to come 'tween me and you", 2.3.8–10), shows that it is contaminated by Venice's "mythical" identity as a republic that is both a fiscal centre *and* a centre for physical pleasure (Shakespeare 2010: 4; Shakespeare 2006: 9; Shakespeare 2016: 23). Othello and Iago carry this image with them to Cyprus, and it is on the corrosive ambiguity that sustains the myth that the latter preys. In short, Cyprus is both the external and the internal embodiment of a Venetian psychological landscape that is anything but "serene" or paradisal, and directs our attention as much to the "barbarian" ("Turk") within as to an external enemy.

The sentiment of Marlowe's Machevil, "I am Machevil, | And weigh not men and therefore not men's words", reverberates throughout Shakespeare's play, and is encapsulated from the outset in Iago's sinister disclosure that "I am not what I am" (1.1.64). As his title "ensign" suggests, he "must show out a flag and sign of love, | Which is indeed but sign"

92 John Drakakis

(1.1.154–5), indicating that he is an embodiment of the fraught process of representation that in the treatment of Brabantio will function structurally as the curtain-raiser for the onslaught against Othello. Indeed, the repetitions in this play simply expand the subterranean tensions that show Venice to be riven with the kind of anxiety that had been comically contained at the end of *The Merchant of Venice*.

The Othello who can arm himself against an irate father-in-law with the assertion that "My parts, my title and my perfect soul | Shall manifest me rightly" (1.2.31–32) is what Julia Kristeva, following Freud, would call "the archaic, narcissistic self not yet demarcated by the outside world" (Kristeva 1991: 183). In both *Othello* and earlier in *The Merchant of Venice*, the "stranger" is the locus of projection of what is, in Kristeva's terms, "dangerous or unpleasant in itself, making of it an alien *double*, uncanny and demoniacal", but is also the distillation of the experience of "otherness" that must either be co-opted into the republic (as in the case of Shylock) or expelled in a psychomachic struggle (as in the case of Othello). In both cases, that which is "strange" in Venice "appears as a defense put up by a distraught self: it protects itself by substituting for the image of a benevolent double that used to be enough to shelter it the image of a malevolent double into which it expels the share of destruction it cannot contain" (Kristeva 1991: 183–84). The strategy that is adopted in *The Merchant of Venice* offers the Jew no introspection beyond an awareness of his own capacity to "mime" Christian sentiments, with the result that he is pressed into the service of the Venetian republic and will always resent his subjugation. The play's comic displacement of this tension onto the anxieties that beset the tension between male-male and patriarchal male-female relations in the play (the substance of the final scene) translates the problems of republican Venice into a register that reflects some of the archetypal concerns of an Elizabethan audience. The Jew is a divided subject, resentful but economically necessary, and the comedy offers a provisional conclusion to an issue that simply will not go away.

When Shakespeare returned to this problem in *Othello*, he embedded the tragic hero in a network of "[m]agical practices" and "animism" that result "in a weakening of the value of signs as such and of their specific logic" (Kristeva 1991: 186). In the tragedy, the "black" stranger is encouraged to enter a world of fantasy, for which the language that describes material reality is shown to be inadequate. At the moment of his murder of Desdemona, Othello cannot "name" what he is about to do:

> It is the cause, it is the cause, my soul!
> Let me not name it to you, you chaste stars,
> It is the cause. Yet I'll not shed her blood
> Nor scar that whiter skin of hers than snow

Shakespeare and Italian Republicanism 93

And smooth as monumental alabaster:
Yet she must die, else she'll betray more men.

(5.2.1–6)

And when he articulates the "cause" it is found ultimately to be false. At this stage the "black" Othello hovers over the sleeping body of the "white" Desdemona, and the act he plans is nothing less than a violation of the "justice" in whose name he carries it out. Here the feminized representative of Venice, regarded doubly by the audience as innocent but by her husband earlier as "the cunning whore of Venice" (4.2.91), is at the mercy of the stranger who for a moment *is* what he represents. But that is not where the play leaves the matter.

After the waiting-woman Aemilia (who knows a thing or two about Venice's masculine determination of female subjectivity) discloses the *truth* of Iago's scheme, the stable demonic image that is the result of Othello's having been made the deed's creature bifurcates in an act of justice that he perpetrates upon himself. In this play, the linguistic sign is never allowed to remain stable for long, and Othello's allegorisation of his own suicide offers a tableau of one of the republic's constitutive difficulties. Elements of the narcissistic Othello return, but now only as a prelude to a deadly assault on the archaic self:

I pray you in your letters,
When you shall these unlucky deeds relate,
Speak of me as I am. Nothing extenuate,
Nor set down aught in malice. Then must you speak
Of one that loved not wisely, but too well;
Of one not easily jealous, but, being wrought,
Perplexed in the extreme; of one whose hand,
Like the base Judean,[2] threw a pearl away
Richer than all his tribe; of one whose subdued eyes,
Albeit unused to the melting mood,
Drops tears as fast as the Arabian trees
Their medicinable gums. Set you down this,
And say besides that in Aleppo once,
Where a malignant and a turbaned Turk
Beat a Venetian and traduced the state,
I took by th' throat the circumcised dog
And smote him – thus!   *He stabs himself.*

(5.2.336–54)

This is also the moment that Othello draws back from the "psychic reality" into which he has fallen (Kristeva 1991: 186, although for Kristeva the "fantasy" expresses "infantile desires or fears", not deep-seated

94 John Drakakis

cultural anxieties), and which follows what Michael Neill has shown is Othello's own "blackness" "not merely as the badge of his own damnable savagery, but as the analogical proof of Desdemona's hidden (but now, to *his* jealous eye, shockingly visible) adultery" (Neill 1998: 147). In his edition of *Antony and Cleopatra*, Neill goes on to contrast the botched suicide of Antony with "the self-immolation of Othello ... that compels the Venetian Moor to figure his death as the annihilation of a 'malicious' and barbarous Other" (Shakespeare 1994: 107–8). What Othello's allegorical representation replays is the war between the republican "Venetian" and the barbarous "Turk", an enemy that is both external and internal, that arises from the military necessities of a "state" that requires external forces to defend its interests. What has been in recent years the legitimate emphasis upon post-colonial discourse to unpick the problems of this tragedy has inadvertently neglected the critique of republicanism that both Venetian plays contain. As the noble Moor charged with representing Venetian interests on a frontier (Cyprus), Othello encounters the "Turk" that resides at the heart of the Venetian state, and the consequences are devastating.

At the end of the tragedy the "noble" Moor, acting on behalf of Venice, kills the "Turk" within, but not before the barbaric Other has wreaked havoc in the domestic sphere. The villain Iago remains alive, as indeed do his prejudices that the threatened loosening of his tongue will once more release into the republic. In *The Merchant of Venice,* the converted Jew is forced to live the life of a split subject. Both, along with the tragedy of the "noble" Moor, point towards the difficulties endemic in the Venetian state that welcomes strangers but that cannot contain the Otherness that exposes the corrosive fissures in its domestic and military life.

Notes

1 Of the "converted" Shylock, who is "already a Venetian alien", Adelman asks, "after his conversion, what would he be – a Christian Jewish Venetian alien?", and wonders "what if the Jew was there in the Christian, not through some inadmissible excess or residue but constitutively, at the heart of Christianity?".

2 Although I follow in the main the text of Honigmann's edition of the play (Shakespeare 2006), I see no reason to depart from the Folio's "Iudean" here. The link between the Moor and the Jew goes back to *The Merchant of Venice,* and establishes both as "outsiders" in Venice.

Bibliography

Adelman, Janet. 2008. *Blood Relations: Christian and Jew in* The Merchant of Venice. Chicago.

Aristotle. 1598. *Aristotles politiques, or Discourses of gouernment*, trans. by John Dee. London.

Bancroft, Richard. 1593. *A suruay of the pretended holy discipline*. London.

Berger Jr., Harry. 2013. *A Fury in the Words: Love and Embarrassment in Shakespeare's Venice.* New York.

Caesar, Philip. 1579. *General Discourse Against the Damnable Sect of Usurers.* London.

Collinson, Patrick, 1987. "The Monarchical Republic of Queen Elizabeth I". *Bulletin of the John Rylands Library*, 69.2: 394–424.

Freud, Sigmund. 1985. *Art and Literature*, ed. by Albert Dickson. Harmondsworth.

Gillies, John. 1994. *Shakespeare and the Geography of Difference.* Cambridge.

Jonson, Ben. 2000. *Every Man in His Humour*, ed. by Robert S. Miola. Manchester.

Kristeva, Julia. 1991. *Strangers to Ourselves*, trans. by Leon S. Roudiez. New York.

Lewkenor, Lewis. 1599. *The Commonwealth and Gouernment of Venice. Written by the Cardinall Gasper Contareno.* London.

Marlowe, Christopher. 1978. *The Jew of Malta*, ed. by N. W. Bawcutt. Manchester.

Neill, Michael. 1998. *Issues of Death: Mortality and Identity in English Renaissance Tragedy.* Oxford.

Nuttall, A. D. 1983. *A New Mimesis: Shakespeare and the Representation of Reality.* London.

Parker, Patricia. 2008. "Cutting Both Ways: Bloodletting, Castration/Circumcision, and the 'Lancelet' of *The Merchant of Venice*", *Alternative Shakespeares 3*, ed. by Diana Henderson. New York. 95–118.

Pocock, J. G. A. 1975. *The Machiavellian Moment: Florentine Political Thought and the Atlantic Republican Tradition.* Princeton.

Shakespeare, William. 1994. *Antony and Cleopatra*, ed. by Michael Neill. Oxford.

——— 2006. *Othello*, ed. by E. A. J. Honigmann. Arden Shakespeare. London.

——— 2010. *The Merchant of Venice*, ed. by John Drakakis. Arden Shakespeare. London.

——— 2016. *Othello*, ed. by Ayanna Thompson and E. A. J. Honigmann. Arden Shakespeare. London.

Smith, Sir Thomas. 1583. *De Republica Anglorum.* London.

Strickland, Debra Higgs. 2003. *Saracens, Demons, and Jews: Making Monsters in Medieval Art.* Princeton, NJ.

Tillyard, E. M. W. 1943. *The Elizabethan World Picture.* London.

Trachtenberg, Joshua. 1983. *The Devil and the Jews.* Philadelphia.

6 "A kind of conquest"

The Erotics and Aesthetics of Italy in *Cymbeline*

Subha Mukherji

The Vice Chancellor's Court records in the holdings of Cambridge University Library turn up a set of extraordinary documents, including a list of objections to a witness, written in the hand of a female defendant in an adultery case from 1596 (Cambridge University Library, V.C.Court. III.5.61–70, 72; III.6.36, 49; see Figure 6.1). This is Bridget Edmunds, wife of John Edmunds, an "employee of Peterhouse", accused of adultery with William Covell, Fellow of Queens' College. No precise information survives about her education, but the love-letters between her and Covell, and exhibits such as this, give us some idea. What we do know is that she turned witness for the prosecution alongside her husband, after briefly protesting innocence. By the time the case was transferred to the Vice Chancellor's Court in the University, she was giving evidence to prove that the affair had indeed taken place, despite Covell's protestations of innocence (Cambridge University Library, V.C.Court.III.5.63, detailing the circumstances and background to the case).

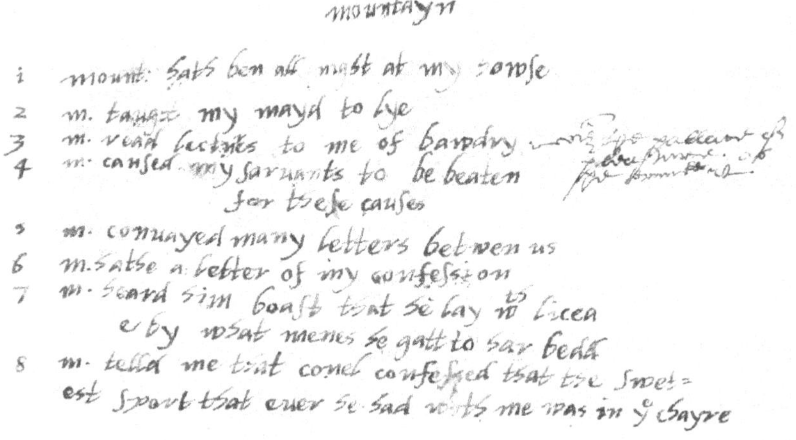
mountayn

1 mount: hath ben all night at my howse
2 m. taught my mayd to lye
3 m. read lectures to me of bawdry
4 m. caused my sarvants to be beaten
for these causes
5 m. conuayed many letters betwen us
6 m. hathe a letter of my confession
7 m. heard him boast that he lay wth Licea
& by what menes he gatt to har bedd
8 m. tolld me that conel confessed that the swet=
est sport that euer he had with me was in ye chayre

Figure 6.1 Bridget Edmunds' objections, 3 September 1596; Cambridge University Library, V.C.Court.III.5.69. Reproduced by permission of the Syndics of the University Library of Cambridge.

"A kind of conquest" 97

The objections in this court exhibit are to Roger Mountain—the "mountayn" of the heading—a witness for Covell, presented to discredit his reliability as a witness. Of immediate relevance is point 3:

m. read lectures to me of bawdry

and the marginal annotation, presumably added by the court clerk,

viz. the pallace of pleasure as she termeth it.

This became a detail of some contention in court. Mountain protests that he read out "Bocchas [Boccaccio] in Frenche", where "there was noe bawdry at all"—several pre-1596 French editions of the *Decameron* were available in the Cambridge libraries. Bridget, however, insists "that she meanethe ... an englishe booke ... the Palace of pleasure" (*Ibid.*, I.3, 117). This is very probably William Painter's *Palace of Pleasure* (enlarged second edition, 1575), a series of adaptations of *novelle* and histories, including many by Boccaccio, Bandello, Cinthio, and Straparola, alongside histories by classical writers such as Plutarch and Livy; or it *could* be George Pettie's *Petite Pallace of Pettie his Pleasure, containing many pretie histories* (1576), modelled on Painter. Both were collections of prose tales, mainly from Italy. On occasion, they provided plots for early modern tragic drama (Webster's *Appius and Virginia* and *The Duchess of Malfi*, Shirley's *Love's Cruelty*, not to mention Shakespeare's *Romeo and Juliet*), and were framed as moral *exempla*. Yet their most persistent association in the cultural imagination was with witty, amorous stories: as several scholars have noted, their very inventiveness, narrative vividness, rhetorical skill, and copious ornamental style could pull against the ostensible moral purpose of the tales in the actual reading experience (Kirkpatrick 1995: 250; Pressler 2014). Painter, in particular, was a mediator of narrative sources for numerous Elizabethan plays, often providing the basis both for plots of erotic intrigue and for Italian settings. Shakespeare's *Romeo and Juliet*, *All's Well that Ends Well*, *Timon of Athens*, and *The Rape of Lucrece* are all indebted to Painter. Pettie copied Painter but also included tales from Ovid, such as "Tereus and Progne". *Cymbeline*, the subject of this chapter, draws on the ninth novella of the second day in Boccaccio's *Decameron*. This particular tale about a wager is not translated by Painter, but belongs unmistakably to the same genre of *novelle* as Painter's and Pettie's stories, and exists in an English variant on Boccaccio's story as *Frederyke of Jennen* (first published in 1518 and reprinted in 1560).

That Mountain insists that Boccaccio in French is somehow more respectable than Boccaccio (or his peers) translated or adapted alongside a bunch of *novelle* is telling. Painter's *Palace of Pleasure* had translations of Marguerite de Navarre too, but was associated mainly with Italianate stories. Bridget's subtext is clear: the man who read Italian "tales of bawdry" to her and who told her that Covell had "confessed that the swetest sport that euer he had with [her] was in the chayre" (Figure 6.1, point 8), could not be trusted to give sober, sexually disinterested evidence. Can a compelling, seductive, persuasive reporter-narrator be a reliable witness? Yet the first of the three love letters Covell sent to Bridget through go-between "widow Towlson" (Cambridge University

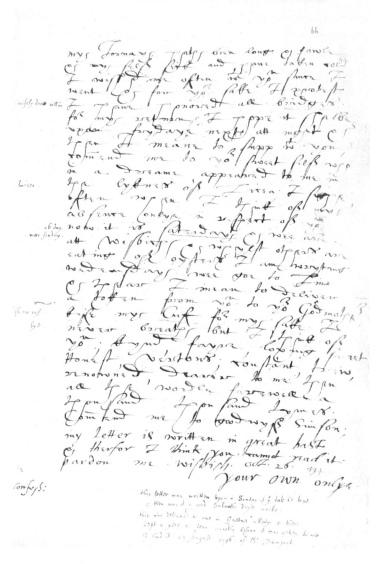

Figure 6.2 Letter from Covell to Bridget, 26 October 1594, exhibited 30 August 1596, Cambridge University Library, V.C.Court.III.5.66. Reproduced by permission of the Syndics of the University Library of Cambridge.

"A kind of conquest"   99

Library, V.C.Court.III.5.66, 67a, 68), intercepted by her husband John and presented by him to be "openly read" in court, suggests a slightly different literary association with Italy.

Covell's love-talk enmeshes with a very particular literary register early on. "Commend me to your sweet self who in a dreame appeared to me in the lykness of Licea" (Figure 6.2, lines 9–11). "Licea", a reference John spots and notes in the margins, alludes to the unattainable mistress in Giles Fletcher's sonnet sequence *Licia* (1593), a reference attested by the clear echo of his prefatory sonnet in the address that follows in the letter: "kynd, fayre, loving, sweet, Honest, Vertous, constant, trew, renowned, dearer to me then all the worlde" (lines 22–25).

Covell made rather a habit of writing about the idealized mistresses of Elizabethan love-sonnet sequences as if they were the *dramatis personae* of his life. Writing in praise of Samuel Daniel in his book *Polimanteia* (published 1595, a year before the adultery case began), Covell claims that, unless he errs, "deluded by dearlie beloued *Delia*, and fortunatelie fortunate *Cleopatra*", Oxford may "extoll" her "*Daniell*, whose sweete refined muse ... were sufficient amongst men, to gaine pardon of the sinne to *Rosemond*, pittie to distressed *Cleopatra*, and euerliuing praise to her louing *Delia*". He also notes his admiration of Shakespeare in the margins of this section on the excellence of native poetry, as well as, more specifically, of his epyllion *Venus and Adonis*: "All praiseworthy. Lucrecia Sweet Shakspeare. Eloquent Gaueston. Wanton Adonis. Watsons heyre" (Covell 1595: sigs. R2^v–R3^r). His epithet "wanton" reflects the contemporary notion of the epyllion as an erotic Ovidian verse narrative. *Venus and Adonis*, prefaced by a familiar quotation from Ovid's *Amores*, and dedicated to the "first heir of [his] invention", sees Shakespeare looking for his own poetic myth of origin in an Ovidian tradition, even though he both claims and outgrows this legacy (Mukherji 2013; all quotations from Shakespeare refer to Shakespeare 2011). Ovid was the newly-discovered inventive writer who somehow managed to combine erotic appeal with respectability through an association with classical values and sophistication—distinct in specifics from, but curiously mapping on to, a larger duality in early modern England's preoccupation with Italy.

Covell was immersed in literary traditions influenced by Italian precedents, both Renaissance and classical. Love sonnets seem to have been a particular favourite, and both *Licia* and *Delia* were heavily influenced by Petrarch in content, although Daniel was formally more indebted to Sidney and Shakespeare. In between the two amorous-poetic allusions, Covell packs in a brief but self-delighting and *enargeic* report on how he is writing to her from Wisbech "whylst others are eating of oysters" (Figure 6.2, lines 15–16). Here, then, is an example, from an unwonted domain, of Italianate sonnet sequences shaping the verbal practices of adulterous love, and not just in literature: Roger Ascham would have loved this. But Covell was a Fellow in Divinity at Queens' College, Cambridge, and ended up full of pomp and honour as Prebend of Lincoln

100 *Subha Mukherji*

Cathedral. The tone of this letter is romantic, refined, literary, and lyrical, distinct from the "bawdy tales" Mountain allegedly told Bridget. Keir Elam's enormously suggestive notion of "Italy as intertext" takes on unprecedented immediacy and an unusual form in these legal remains (Elam 2014). Yet Covell spends three pages putting down "*Italies* of-spring, who of long time hath carried herself with excessiue pride" before he praises Daniel's semi-Petrarchan sonnets and Shakespeare's Ovidian poem, to emphasize the superiority of English literary writing: "that *Italian Ariosto* did but shadowe the meanest part of thy muse, that *Tassos Godfrey* is not worthie to make compare with your truelie eternizing Elizas stile" (Covell 1595: sigs. R1^v–R2^v).

The early modern English stereotype of Italy as a hothouse of lust, or even the association of Italian literature with amorous enticements, is pervasive and widely attested; indeed, it becomes at times an object of parody itself: in *Volpone* (1605), Jonson's Corvino remarks on the "hot Tuscan blood | That had read Aretine" and "knew every quirk in lust's labyrinth" (Jonson 1984: 3.2.258–60). What interests me about this glimpse of Italian literary texts in a real-life narrative of illicit love in a middle-class context in a quasi-academic community is its paradoxical place in cultural perception: at once a ground for loss of credit, and part of the texture of the language of sophisticated epistolary romance used by a Cambridge academic in the early, fervent stages of courtship. I want to connect this paradox to the ambiguity in the relationship between Britain and Rome in *Cymbeline*, as embodied in the figure of Iachimo, and more specifically the proto-rape scene in the British princess Imogen's bedroom. This may seem to be a leap. But this chapter will suggest that the specific form that erotic energy takes in this play has everything to do with the uneasy co-existence of political reconciliation between Rome and Britain and their unresolved competition in the realm of poetics, aesthetics, and intertextuality. In this regard, the not-quite-rape is an equivalent to the pointed irresolution of both war and peace in this play.

The political and historical underpinnings of this ambivalence have been charted extensively. Perhaps the most nuanced and compelling account is John Kerrigan's unpacking of the geopolitics of England, Scotland, and Wales in Jacobean drama, and what "Rome" had to do with it (Kerrigan 2008). As Kerrigan points out, despite Polydore Vergil's revisionist critique in *Anglia Historia* (1534), Geoffrey of Monmouth's myth, in *Historia Regnum Britanniae* (1136), of Britain's Roman origins (via Aeneas' descendant Brutus) still had sufficient hold on the cultural imagination in Shakespeare's time. To the classically educated, the narrative of Roman origin lent early modern Britain the dignity and legitimacy of a classical civilisation; the primitivism of early Britons as conjured up by Camden's *Britannia*, for instance, found a welcome counter-stereotype in the claim to Roman civility, while ancient

"A kind of conquest" 101

Rome's imperialism proved a handy expansionist model. Yet Geoffrey, in a more complex way, also rewrote available histories (such as Bede and Nennius) to ascribe a valiant and clever resistance to the original Britons in response to Caesar's second invasion. Spenser's treatment of Boadicea's uprising against the Romans in *The Ruines of Time* (as in *The Faerie Queene*) is heroic, yet set against a lament for the razing of Roman Verulamium. On the one hand, then, any antagonism between Britain and Rome always had the potential to be shadowed by affiliation and imagined affinity. On the other, there was a strand in the cultural imaginary in which Roman decadence was a corrupting influence on a noble indigenous simplicity. Wales, partial setting for *Cymbeline*, came to be an imagined embodiment of the latter and of the essence of proud Britishness, as in Holinshed's *Chronicles* (Holinshed 1587: 9). As Kerrigan brilliantly demonstrates, "Wales became a site of authentic Britishness", a "taproot into Galfridian antiquity", as the Jacobean theatre negotiated the "braided histories" of the British Isles and contemporary politics (Kerrigan 2008: 117–19, 2). Its religious history also fed into an identification of the Welsh with resistance to both the Catholicism and the (earlier) paganism of Rome.

Cymbeline, however, differs from Holinshed, and falls in with other contemporary plays about the same geopolitical terrain, ending with a reunion of Britain and Rome. The Brexiteers of the play are the wicked Queen and her son Cloten, who is at once a buffoon and a villain: "Britain's a world by itself" is Cloten's sentiment (3.1.13). Even Caesar's historical conquest is qualified in the Queen's grudging reference as she asserts Britain's insular impregnability to Caius Lucius: "A kind of conquest | Caesar made here, but made not here his brag | Of 'Came, and saw, and overcame'" (3.1.23–25). Her words, however, touch on an ambiguity that was pregnant at the time. The play can be seen as a consolatory romance, staged freshly against the background of the rejection of James I's proposal for political incorporation with Scotland in the English Parliament in 1607. Even the unease of the play's final reconciliation can be—and has been—read in the light of the fragility of the Union project (Marcus 1988: 118–48 (146)). At any rate, it signals "understood relations"—to borrow Macbeth's phrase (3.4.123)— among his audience which Shakespeare is tapping into. The case for the imbrication of the play's geopolitical plot with the politics of the Stuart court, and of national and ethnic identities of Britain, is convincing. But there is another layer to its ambiguous integration of Britain and Italy (and, more specifically, Rome), even if the intra-British transactions can be explained through a Stuart-political reading: the aesthetic texture of this equivocal engagement. This chapter's primary quarry is a literary idea that emerges from national types and stereotypes, but feeds into an intertextual dynamic that fails, with curious precision, to map on to the geopolitical interrelation underpinning the play's plot. As

102 *Subha Mukherji*

such, the Italian source material—often narrative texts—and Italianate generic affiliations will prove to be at least as important as the notion of Italy as a place or nation.

The virtual rape scene in Imogen's bedroom is a pointer to this play's placement of "Italy" in the story. Does it take Shakespeare's audience into the world of the "bawdry" that Bridget cites as grounds for suspicion and discredit? Or does it lure them into a world of narrative sophistication, bravura performance, and a specifically "Italianate" artifice? For while Shakespeare's Italy was, in part, the "Italy" of the early modern English imagination, it was also a distillation of something implicit in general perception, and which emerges as a distinctive Shakespearean vision in his late works: Italy as an aesthetic impulse, with its particular predilections—both ethical and generic. Subtle Iachimo, the "Italian fiend" (5.5.210) who at once fascinates and repels, is its embodiment. But it is in relational terms that the treatment of this impulse is worked out. Kerrigan astutely points out the cultural infiltration and colonial penetration figured by rape, threatened or virtual, in Jacobean plays dealing with Rome; how lust is always connected with Rome; and how these plays nonetheless end in union rather than hostility. I contend that in *Cymbeline*, the erotic energy is *displaced* into narrative *jouissance*; that the particular frisson and perversity of that transference is more specific and more literary than the range of rapes in the other plays. Until we grasp its underpinnings, we cannot wholly comprehend the peculiar sense of intertextual and inter-aesthetic irresolution at the end, despite the Roman and the British ensigns "[waving] | Friendly together" (5.5.481–82).

The wager scene in Rome which triggers Iachimo's plot to invade Britain and its chaste princess is a competition between nationalities which slides from patriotic and sexual rivalry into a narratological competition that eventually percolates through the play: a Frenchman, a Dutchman, a Spaniard, Posthumus the Briton, and Iachimo the "Italian" (2.1.37, 48) vie with each other to prove their country-women the most unassailable. Like Tarquin in Livy and Shakespeare's *Lucrece*, Iachimo is provoked by the confident husband's eloquent praise, as Posthumus extols Imogen as a paragon of virtue: "You must not so far prefer her 'fore ours of Italy" (1.5.65–66). But "[h]e spoke of her, as Dian had hot dreams, | And she alone were cold", Iachimo recounts, till "his description | Prov'd us unspeaking sots" (5.5.180–81, 177–78). Narrative discomfiture incites sexual challenge. The wager comes from Boccaccio's *Decameron*, where it happens in Paris, and where the focus narrows to a rivalry between the Genovese Bernabò who brags of his wife Zinevra, and the Venetian Ambrogiuolo who travels to Genoa and, finding Zinevra untemptable, steals into her bedroom to collect corporeal tokens to prove his false claim that he has made her yield. The focus in Shakespeare's play shifts pointedly to a tussle between the Briton and the Italian. But

"A kind of conquest" 103

by the time the bedroom episode, absent in *Frederyke of Jennen*, goes straight into *Cymbeline*, Ambrogiuolo's observation of "a small wart upon her left pappe, with some few hairs growing thereon, appearing to be as yellow as gold" (Boccaccio's *Decameron*, quoted in Bullough 1975: 8.55–6) morphs subtly but significantly: "On her left breast | A mole cinque-spotted: like the crimson drops | I'th' bottom of a cowslip" (2.2.37–9). As Iachimo studies the sleeping Imogen by items which he stores "t'enrich [his] inventory" (2.2.30), his language transforms this scene of virtual rape into one of an art connoisseur lovingly collecting priceless miniatures: her lips, "rubies unparagon'd", like the mole, are translated into the same order of preciousness as the bracelet he slips off her arm (2.2.17).

This fluently metamorphic image-making evokes a distinct aesthetic, one that the young Shakespeare virtuosically displayed at the start of his first poem, *Venus and Adonis*, the epyllion Covell admires. For though Iachimo-in-Imogen's-bedchamber comes out of Boccaccio's story, the most vivid Italian source this scene both figuratively and materially inscribes is the Augustan Roman poet Ovid. Like Ovid, who wrote about rape after rape with effortless elegance and turned violence and death into perennial and beautiful forms, the narrator of *Venus and Adonis*—partly through Venus' rhetoric, but initially sharing her habit—repeatedly converts the grotesque into the dainty, the morbid into the exquisite. So Adonis' sweaty breath becomes "heavenly moisture" (64, 542); the tears in Venus' affrighted eyes are "like pearls in glass" (980); the gored Adonis, in his final possession by Venus, turns into a pretty trinket, a diminutive flower cradled in her bosom, white and purple as the blood trickling down his fair flank. Ovid is, of course, materially present in Imogen's bedroom: for she has been reading the "tale of Tereus" in bed, leaving the pages "turn'd down | Where Philomel gave up" (2.2.45–46). Shakespeare would no doubt have been familiar with this story via Painter's *Palace of Pleasure*—the offending book in the Edmunds case—or indeed Pettie's *Petite Pallace*. But his association of it, and of rape and representation, with Ovid's *Metamorphoses*—named and hurled on the stage in *Titus Andronicus* (4.1.42), his early and intricate elaboration on the Philomel myth, along with *Lucrece*—surely suggests that Imogen has been reading Ovid, the source of this rape-story, in this intimate scene teeming with rapacious possibilities.

And who should leap out of it—as it were—but Iachimo, the moment Imogen sinks into sleep? Physically, he emerges "from the Trunke" (Folio stage direction). The only other thing suggestively half-open in the room is Imogen's book, generating the lure of what Gaston Bachelard might have called objects that may be opened, not unlike the tease of unfolding narratives. Iachimo claims his own Italian legacy as he steps out: "Our Tarquin thus | Did

104 *Subha Mukherji*

softly press the rushes, ere he waken'd | The chastity he wounded" (2.2.12–14). Imogen being one of the earliest staged readers of Ovid, following on from young Lucius and Lavinia in *Titus*, this moment has the feel of a joke not only about the chaste English princess' bedtime pleasure in Ovidian rape-stories, but about the erotics of Italy—"our Tarquin—in the aesthetic imagination of English readers. Less straightforwardly, the mediation by the arch-narrator and image-maker Iachimo makes it a scene about the male voyeuristic imagining of an eroticized female reader's closet-reading of Ovidian literature (Mukherji 2013). With his initial longing for touch and a kiss, however, all the expectation is aroused for Roman lust in action. But this only sharpens the diversion of erotic energy from sexual action to aesthetic narration. The sleeping British princess' chastity is not wounded by this descendant of the Roman Tarquin; ravishment is replaced with ravishing description, both of her body and her classicized surroundings, all feeding into his "inventory", "the contents o'th' story" (2.2.27). And that is where the peculiar unease of the scene lies, and its perverse *frisson*.

A comparison with a play set in Venice and aware of Anglo-Italian literary dynamics, though less centrally focused on the relation between Italy and Britain, highlights the currency of the Ovidian affiliation of such displacement. Jonson's Volpone lusts after the virtuous Celia, and goes to great lengths to connive to be locked in a room alone with her. But once there, instead of pouncing on her, he spouts metamorphic poetry and fantasies of dizzying fluidity of form:

> In varying figures I would have contended
> With the blue Proteus, or the horned flood.
> [...]
> While we in changed shapes, act Ovid's tales:
> Thou like Europa now and I like Jove,
> Then I like Mars and thou like Erycine;
> [...]
> And I will meet thee in as many shapes,
> Where we may, so, transfuse our wandering souls
> Out at our lips, and score up the sum of pleasures
> (Jonson 1984: 3.2.351–53, 419–21, 431–33)

Between these visions of transformation, Volpone sings and spins out a self-delighting poetry of sensual magnificence, with the quaking Celia's brief, sporadic interjections the only reminder of her presence in the play-text, though in performance her presence could be turned to affective use. "Why should we defer our joys?", he sings (3.2.372), before deferring them some more, as he creates infinite riches in a little room through sheer rhetorical felicity, impervious to Celia's subjectivity.

"A kind of conquest" 105

When, at the end of this long, weirdly-suspended scene he makes a notional move, he does so by reflecting on the fact that he has failed to do so for too long:

I do degenerate and abuse my nation
To play with opportunity thus long.
I should have done the act, and then parleyed.

(3.2.461–64)

The cruder stereotype of the lustful Italian is played off here against the subtler notion of a poetic of deferral and an idea of aesthetic self-enjoyment that were emerging as recognisably Italianate, inasmuch as Ovid was associated with self-delighting transformative poetry in the face of atrocity, fear, and danger. The Ovid of the 1590s, who drip-fed into the drama of a whole decade, mediated through a predominantly amoral and eroticized reading and through the associations of the love elegies and the *Metamorphoses*, stood for narrative self-consciousness, aesthetic smoothness, and pleasure on the edge of risk. The effect of deferral in Imogen's bedroom is, in part, reminiscent of the withholding of sexual fulfilment in *Venus and Adonis*, a self-proclaimed epyllion that arouses specific sexual expectations in its readers but then teasingly frustrates them by not delivering. But while, in that early poem, the narrative voice works its way out of a complicity with a "sick-thoughted" aesthetic (*Venus and Adonis*, l. 5), *Cymbeline* "places" the Ovidianism of the young Shakespeare in the character of a designated aesthete.

Deferral and dilation, however, can also be a propensity of inset narratives in drama; their ethical and affective impact depends on the generic context. The suspense of the bedroom scene is not unrelated to the suspension of time as we circle around the vulnerable, sleeping Imogen's body with Iachimo's words describing the scene in exquisite detail; or as Lavinia was stelled into a speaking picture by Marcus' forty-seven-line address, arresting her flight with "Cousin, a word" (*Titus Andronicus*, 2.4.12). Once Iachimo is done, the clock strikes again: "One, two, three: time, time"; and back he goes into his material source—trunk or book. The Ovidianism of Marcus' narrative in the earlier play is replaced, here, with an additional affiliation, also Italianate in the early modern English imagination. For in the late plays, self-conscious and self-pleasuring artifice is specifically connected to tragicomedy. The influential Renaissance theorist of tragicomedy, Giovanni Battista Guarini—whose *Il Pastor Fido* was Englished in 1602 by John Dymoke and whose ideas were variously transmitted to Shakespeare's England (via, for instance, Fletcher's imitative homage, *The faithfull shepheardesse*, 1610)—defines the genre's characteristic affect as *"il pericolo, non la morte"*. For Guarini—one of the stereotypically popular Italian authors from whom, according to *Volpone*'s Lady Politic Would-be, "All our English writers ... Will deign to

106 *Subha Mukherji*

steal" (Jonson 1984: 3.2.109–119)—tragicomedy deploys the danger, but not the death, of tragedy; it licenses a prolongation of pain and suspense at the cost of subjective feelings, since the artificer, be it the playwright or an inscribed dramaturge or artist, knows that all will be well at the end and that the end is in hand (Guarini 1962: 511). Indeed, Guarini suggests that the sense of marvel at the final untying of knots is directly proportional to the degree of danger packed into the plot, the intensity of pain. But this aesthetically productive strategy makes for a peculiar asymmetry of knowledge within the fiction, and sometimes across the fourth wall of the theatre. So Imogen can wake up and speak the most surreally anguished lament over what she thinks is her dead husband's body, while the audience titter to see that it is really Posthumus' gross double, Cloten, whom she has derided in physical comparison to him (4.2.296–332). So also in the final recognition scene, Iachimo's relishing retardation of his disclosure holds up the urgency of the action while protracting other people's anguish and ignorance.

Such cognitive dissonance is a typical affective component of tragicomedy, which works through "rassomiglianza del terribile" [a passing resemblance of true terror] (Guarini 1737–38: 3.418)—the fictive terror of someone else. But it is a simulacrum only to the plot-maker; to the characters affected, the terror is far from unreal. It is in the final recognition scene that Iachimo's pleasure in the exquisite culminates in a zestful, erotic recounting of the act of stealth he repents, which has cost Imogen all her pain. Professedly a confession, it becomes really an exercise in aesthetic self-congratulation—"O cunning, how I got it!"—a bravura performance in an Italianate, sensationalist, almost operatic style. Not unlike Painter's tales, but more flamboyantly, the vividness and energy of the narrative pull against the guilt and repentance that it is meant to express. "Glad to be constrain'd to utter that | Which torments me to conceal" (5.5.141–42), he makes the most of this opportunity to *be* the narrator. This is not a man in a hurry to relieve his audience of their anxious uncertainty about where their loved ones are, and indeed who they might be now; the crafted balance of his syntax belies his professed longing to bring clarity and knowledge: "Thou'lt torture me to leave unspoken that | Which, to be spoke, would torture thee" (5.5.139–40). "Give me leave; I faint" (5.5.149), he exclaims, minutes after starting to speak, but recovers promptly enough to self-consciously set about building up an ekphrastic cadenza: "Upon a time, unhappy was the clock ..." (5.5.153–209).

This dilatory disclosure generates the sense of a scene of narration being staged: the impatience it elicits from other characters conveys the element of perversity that can be involved in the narrative moment trying to enter, take over, and arrest the movement of the drama: "I stand on fire. | Come to the matter", Cymbeline urges (5.5.168–69). The association of Iachimo's narrative with the erotic element in the story can obscure as well as help locate the real origins of his pleasure—in the pleasure of the text, in narrative *jouissance*. We remember an earlier moment when Iachimo puts Imogen through an agonizing first meeting as he insinuates (through ellipses, aposiopeses, and suggestive phrases such as "the Briton reveller") but does not reveal some distressing truth about her husband's way of life in Italy that makes him take pity on her (1.7.31–92 (61)). Driven nearly to distraction, the perceptive Imogen challenges him:

> You do seem to know
> Something of me, or what concerns me; pray you,
> Since doubting things go ill often hurts more
> Than to be sure they do—for certainties
> Either are past remedies; or timely knowing,
> The remedy then born—discover to me
> What both you spur and stop.
>
> (1.7.93–99)

Narrative's power of suspension works precisely through spurring and stopping. But the danger of this technique, which Imogen articulates with affective clarity, is the risk that is disacknowledged by tragicomic theory, and by this play's physician Cornelius who almost translates Guarini when he prepares the false poison—that classic tragicomic ingredient—to placate the wicked Queen but save Imogen's life by numbing her senses for a while: "there is | No danger in what show of death it makes" (1.6.39–40). Imogen, though, will not let the emotional cost of salutary plotting go unnoticed: when Posthumus, failing to recognise her in the guise of a page, strikes her in the final scene ("There lie thy part"), the tragicomic habit of flirting with danger could have been allowed a safe arena; the theatrical wit of the moment—inhering in a character unwittingly commenting on a boy playing the "part" of a girl playing the "part" of a page—could have absorbed the theatre audience and deflected the potential for subjective anguish in the human situation. But it is rebuked as she comes back at her husband and demands:

> Why did you throw your wedded lady from you?
> Think that you are upon a rock, and now
> Throw me again.
>
> (5.5.261–63)

The play's inscription of the price of tragicomic suspense and self-enjoyment is of a kind with such moments as these. The real menace of Italianate aestheticism manifests, in the final scene, in a formal tension between the dramatic and the narrative modes. In narrative romances such as Heliodorus' *Aethiopica*—a major channel of romance plots and a precursor of English tragicomedy—the language of the theatre

108 *Subha Mukherji*

valorizes the text. But in *Cymbeline*, the narrative urge surfaces like a guilty thing, the libidinous "id" of this "British" play, dragging in with it its Italianate hinterland of sources, precepts, and analogues, its impulses and temptations.

The commercial contest between narrative and drama in Shakespeare's England takes a curiously intertextual form in this play, and remains unresolved. The Britons have their own narrative competitions too: Guiderius cuts Pisanio's report short with a brusque, non-Latinate, and stereotypically Welsh (and, by extension, essentially ancient British) rustic directness: "Let me end the story: | I slew him there. [...] I cut off's head, | And am right glad he is not standing here | To tell this tale of mine" (5.5.286–87; 295–97). But they cannot compete with the Italian. Posthumus, for all his fateful rhetorical prowess in the wager scene, erupts into vulgarity and violence when Iachimo presents him with supposed proof of his wife's infidelity: "Perchance he spoke not, but | Like a full-acorn'd boar, a German one, | Cried 'O!' and mounted" (2.4.167–69). He may swear by Jove and dream of the Roman God, but *in extremis* his rhetoric has nothing of Rome in it; it shares more with Cloten's sexual language. His gullibility and lack of discernment are what Iachimo's interracial contrast is premised on:

> mine Italian brain
> Gan in your duller Britain operate
> Most vilely [...]

> (5.5.196–98)

Between subtle Italian aestheticism and dull British rage and credulity, the difference is wide; wide enough, just, to lend perverse resonance to what Iachimo says he was taught by the chaste British princess: "the wide difference | 'Twixt amorous and villainous" (194–95).

And this brings us back close to where we began: the question of the credibility and credit of a witness immersed in Italianate modes of speaking and plotting. After all, Iachimo's collection of details of the bedroom is done with an evidentiary purport. When, back in Rome with Posthumus, he recounts the scene we have already witnessed in the private inner sanctum of the British royal house, what we watch is a dangerously successful testimony. A Renaissance Italian hovering in Roman Britain and drifting back and forth across the two countries, Iachimo telescopes literary and aesthetic legacies in parallel to the telescoping of historical time in early modern "archipelagic" plays. He channels, through compelling, *enargeic* narrative, the rhetorical precepts of Roman rhetoricians such as Quintilian and Cicero (as familiar to the classicist curriculum of early modern English grammar schools as Ovid was), persuading Posthumus of Imogen's alleged sexual laxity. To any grammar-school boy, the association of *enargeia* with *evidentia* would be familiar from the rhetorical textbooks in the humanist curriculum. Yet this is one of several instances in Shakespeare's theatre when the assumed correlation between the two is shown to be rife with the potential for error. *Enargeic* narrative, which brings the unseen and off-scene before one's eyes, has the power to procure conviction of both the right and the wrong kinds. Rhetorical temptation can both overtake and obscure legal necessity, and its founts are deeply classical, indeed Roman, in early modern culture. Iachimo is an unreliable witness, not because of his expertise in "tales of bawdry", like Roger Mountain's; but because of his rhetorical sophistication, narrative artistry, and generic affiliation, all of which have roots in "Italy" as imagined by Shakespeare's England. Shakespeare's own literary roots, sources, and techniques share too much of all of these for comfort, but he turns the unease to dramatic advantage. Stereotypes are placed, but paradox is embodied as well as wielded by the play.

Surprised by the kindness of the seemingly savage youths in Belarius' cave, Imogen exclaims:

> Experience, O, thou disprov'st report!
> Th'emperious seas breed monsters; for the dish
> Poor tributary rivers as sweet fish.
>
> (4.2.34–36)

Her immediate meaning is that poor tributary rivers breed fish as sweet as the emperious seas that can, contrary to expectation, breed monsters. But the resonance is wider. For while Cymbeline's and Britain's "tributary rivers" flow into "Th'emperious seas" of (imperial) Rome which "breeds monsters", the doubleness of the final reconciliation is inscribed in the implicit contronymy of "tribute": both a monetary act premised on antagonism, and an act of compliment, potentially encompassing desire and, therefore, unresolved competition. Whichever way one looks at it, it is only "a kind of conquest", as long as we remember to factor in the literary alongside the political transactions between Shakespeare's England and his Italy, however synecdochic our sample may be.

Note

The research for this essay has received funding from the European Research Council under the European Union's Seventh Framework Programme (FP7/2007–2013)/ERC.

Bibliography

Bullough, Geoffrey. 1975. *Narrative and Dramatic Sources of Shakespeare*, 8 vols. London.

Covell, William. 1595. *Polimanteia*. Cambridge and London.

110   *Subha Mukherji*

Elam, Keir. 2014. "Afterword: Italy as intertext". *Shakespeare, Italy, and Intertextuality*, ed. by Michele Marrapodi. Manchester. 253–58.

Guarini, Giovanni Battista. 1737–1738. "Compendio della poesia tragicomica". *Delle opere del cavalier Battista Guarini*, 4 vols. Verona. 4.389–469.

———— 1962. "A Compendium of Tragicomic Poetry". *Literary Criticism: Plato to Dryden*, ed. by Allan Gilbert. Detroit. 504–33.

Holinshed, Raphael. 1587 [1577]. *Chronicles of England, Scotland and Ireland*. London.

Jonson, Ben. 1984 [1962]. *Volpone*, ed. by David Cook. London.

Kerrigan, John. 2008. "The Romans in Britain: Wales and Jacobean Drama". *Archipelagic English: Literature, History and Politics 1603–1707*. Oxford. 115–40.

Kirkpatrick, Robin. 1995. *English and Italian Literature from Dante to Shakespeare: A Study of Source, Analogue and Divergence*. London.

Marcus, Leah. 1988. *Puzzling Shakespeare: Local Reading and its Discontents*. Berkeley.

Mukherji, Subha. 2013. "Outgrowing Adonis, Outgrowing Ovid: The Disorienting Narrative of *Venus and Adonis*". *The Oxford Handbook of Shakespeare's Poetry*, ed. Jonathan Post. Oxford. 396–412.

Pressler, Charlotte. 2014. "Intertextual transformations: The *Novella* as mediator between Italian and English Renaissance drama". *Shakespeare, Italy, and Intertextuality*, ed. by Michele Marrapodi. Manchester. 107–16.

Shakespeare, William. 2011. *The Arden Shakespeare: Complete Works*, ed. by Richard Proudfoot, Ann Thompson, and David Scott Kastan. London.

Part II

Eighteenth and Nineteenth Centuries

Translation and Collaboration

7 The Eighteenth-Century Reception of Shakespeare

Translations and Adaptations for Italian Audiences

Sandra Pietrini

From the first studies of the fate of Shakespeare's plays in Italy (Graf 1911; Collison-Morley 1916; Nulli 1918), scholars have been drawn to the processes by which Shakespeare's works spread into various Italian contexts, often clashing en route with a well-established neoclassical heritage. The conservative nature of Italian tragedy, based on the audacious deeds of noble heroes and composed in high-sounding verse, was an obvious impediment to an appreciation of the astonishing variety of action, style, and character contained in Shakespeare's plays. Nevertheless, a fascination with his rich world of imagination, simultaneously suggestive and concrete, moved some open-minded Italian intellectuals, who found in wider European literary traditions an avenue for national cultural renewal, to contribute to the spread of his masterpieces on the Italian peninsular. Before the nineteenth-century tradition of the *grandi attori* came into its own as a medium for disseminating Shakespeare on stage, early translations of his plays, examined more or less chronologically in this chapter, were no less crucial in establishing the cultural canonicity of Shakespeare, as were the critical salvos that formed part of a wider polemic among European literati about the criteria for judging the merits of vernacular literary cultures and about Shakespeare's place in the history of English (and indeed European) theatre.

The first engagements with Shakespeare take the form, unsurprisingly, of occasional critical asides—limited bursts of intrigued admiration or passing curiosity—rather than full-blown dramatic adaptations. In 1705, the composer Francesco Gasparini had proposed an *Ambleto* with a libretto by Apostolo Zeno and Pietro Pariati, but the inspiration here came from Saxo Grammaticus' *Historia Danica* and François de Belleforest's *Histoires Tragiques* (1570)—Shakespeare's own sources, of course—rather than Shakespeare's *Hamlet* itself, which very probably remained unknown to them. In these early decades of the eighteenth century, the Italian critic and scientist Antonio Conti (1677–1749) showed an incipient interest in Shakespeare, having come into contact with English literature in London, where he had settled in 1715 in the hope of making the acquaintance of a renowned

114 *Sandra Pietrini*

colleague, Isaac Newton. In a prefatory letter to his play *Il Cesare* (1726), possibly based on Shakespeare's *Julius Caesar* or the adaptation of that play by John Sheffield, Duke of Buckingham (Crinò 1950: 35–36), Conti refers to "Sasper" in the context of European theatre, in what constitutes the earliest formal discussion in print of Shakespeare in Italian. Conti's "Sasper" forms part of a series of mispronunciations and misspellings among early Italian commentators, ranging from "Sachespar" to "Jhakespeare", "Sakespir", and Abate Gaetano Golt's superlative "Seckpaire" (Bassi 2016), perhaps an unwitting homage to the orthographic fluidity of Shakespeare's name in early modern English. Conti christens this "Sasper" England's Corneille:

> Sasper è il Cornelio degli Inglesi ma molto più irregolare del Cornelio, sebbene al pari di lui ripieno di grandi idee e di nobili sentimenti.
> (Nulli 1918: 10)

> [Sasper is the English Corneille, but much more irregular than Corneille; even though equally full of grand ideas and noble feelings]

The verdict is typical of the lukewarm reception of Shakespeare— routinely read through French and German intermediary translations (for instance, Pierre-Antoine de La Place's loose French versions in *Théâtre Anglois*, 1746–1749, or Christoph Martin Wieland's equally incomplete German renditions, 1762–1766), rather than the English original—whereby strictures against his "irregularity", especially his disregard of classical unities, tend to dominate. This evaluation, based on a prejudicial approach shared by other mid-century commentators, would be repeated in various quarters by, *inter alia*, Francisco Quadrio, who objected to the "farse mostruose che si chiaman tragedie" [monstrous farces that are called tragedies] (Nulli 1918: 11), a judgement indebted to Voltaire's bias and strictures against Shakespeare's liberal handling of generic divisions. The position is perhaps best exemplified by the concise formula used in a 1735 letter to Abbot Franchini by Francesco Algarotti, who referred to "errori innumerabili e pensieri inimitabili" [innumerable faults and inimitable thoughts] in Shakespeare's oeuvre (Algarotti 1794: 9.6). This sort of oxymoron reveals a dual consciousness in the critical portrait of Shakespeare, as an undisciplined author marred by a questionable literary style but capable of considerable depth of thought—thoughts perhaps made "inimitable" (usually a term of praise in an author's literary afterlife, a celebration of a predecessor's unrepeatable greatness) *because* of his stylistic infelicities. Praising Voltaire's imitations of Shakespeare's plays, and specifically *La mort de César*, Algarotti implied that only the kind of intervention offered by Voltaire could bring out the value of Shakespeare's literary creations as mirrors of eloquence (Algarotti 1794: 9.8).

The Eighteenth-Century Reception of Shakespeare 115

This assumption about Shakespeare's unpolished craftsmanship had a currency even in his own country, his untutored "genius" requiring refinement at the hands of more learned, neoclassically-attuned editors and commentators (Dobson 1992).

In 1739, the Italian librettist and poet Paolo Rolli, acquainted with English theatre thanks to his experience as a teacher of Italian language at the English court and his activity as a librettist at the Royal Academy in London, produced the first printed Italian translation of any passage from Shakespeare, in this instance Hamlet's "To be or not to be" speech ("Essere o no, la gran questione è questa"; Rolli 1739: 97–99), although an earlier unpublished translation of Hamlet's speech survives, dated to *c.* 1700 and attributed to Lorenzo Magalotti (Magalotti 1984). Rolli published his largely faithful translation of the speech together with other poetic works of his own devising, and included an adversarial swipe at what he considered Voltaire's misunderstanding of Shakespeare's plays. Voltaire's engagements with Shakespeare's oeuvre "deviò da' Sentimenti e dallo Stile di quell'originalmente sublime Poeta" [deviated from the Sentiments and the Style of that originally sublime Poet] (Rolli 1739: 96). Beyond the mere fact that Shakespeare is here being spoken of, remarkably, as a "Poeta" (presumably connoting an author of elevated and enduring works) rather than an ephemeral, crowd-pleasing playwright, Rolli's assessment suggests that it is not only Shakespeare's thematic and intellectual content that deserves praise but also his distinctive stylistic fingerprint, an idiosyncratic idiom accorded the epithet "sublime"—a term of critical merit only newly being used to personalize literary "genius".

Yet for the best part of the century, the Italian critical landscape was dominated by Voltaire's faint praise and vociferous critique, articulated formally in his 1733 *Lettres Philosophiques*. By discussing the merits and (more extensively) the faults of Shakespeare's plays, Voltaire helped to secure Shakespeare's place in pan-European debates about literary excellence. Indeed, Shakespeare's early reception in Italy is most obviously as a pawn in wider literary-critical dialogues between neoclassical and modern (or proto-romantic) apologists. Voltaire acknowledges the force of Shakespeare's literary imagination, but laments the absence of even "la moindre étincelle de bon goût et [...] la moindre connaissance des règles" [the tiniest portion of good taste and the most basic understanding of the rules] (Voltaire 1964a: Letter XVIII, 120). In observations accompanying his *La mort de César*, partly inspired by Shakespeare's *Julius Caesar*, he averred that, in Shakespeare's play,

> il y a beaucoup de naturel; ce naturel est souvent bas, grossier et barbare. Ce ne sont pas des Romains qui parlent; ce sont des campagnards des siècles passés qui conspirent dans un cabaret.
>
> (Voltaire 1964b: 190–91)

116 *Sandra Pietrini*

[there is much that is natural; [but] this natural element is often coarse, vulgar, and barbarous. These are not Romans talking; they are peasants from a past era, conspiring in a tavern]

The terminology—a lexis of admiration for what is natural in Shakespeare's writing that soon shades into disparagement of the low and indecorous qualities—acknowledges Shakespeare's sublimity (the "traits sublimes" that shine out at moments like diamonds "répandus sur de la fange" [sprinkled in the mud]) but continually modifies any approbation with censure of a roughness, unruliness, and lack of formal polish.

In the wake of Rolli's burst of translation from *Hamlet*, Domenico Valentini, clergyman and Professor of Church History at the University of Siena, produced the first translation of a Shakespeare play in Italian in 1756, namely *Julius Caesar* (perhaps inspired by Conti and Voltaire), in Tuscan, the literary standard (Valentini 1756). Astonishingly, he completed this feat without knowing English, but nonetheless managed to follow the Shakespearean text fairly faithfully, albeit with some omissions and additions. Justifying the enterprise, he explained to his readers that "cavalieri di quella illustre Nazione che perfettamente intendono la Lingua Toscana, hanno avuto la bontà e la pazienza di spiegarmi questa Tragedia" [gentlemen of that illustrious Nation who understand the Tuscan Tongue perfectly, have had the kindness and patience to explain this Tragedy to me]. Through this indirect approach to literary translation, English intermediaries played a collaborative role in helping to disseminate Shakespeare's oeuvre and reputation. This paradigm recurs in the literary friendship between the British consul in Venice between 1744 and 1760, Joseph Smith (1673/4–1770), an Italophilic patron of the arts and book collector, and the Venetian playwright and librettist Carlo Goldoni (1707–1793), whose 1754 comedy *I malcontenti* gestures—in its prefatory address—to a reading of Shakespeare informed by John Murray, another English resident in Venice and associate of Smith's. On this evidence, Shakespeare's works, and his emerging authorial iconicity, formed the centre-piece of a cross-cultural exchange between English and Italian men of letters engaged in an interlingual dialogue on the cultural status of the author and his oeuvre.

I malcontenti encapsulates two divergent responses to Shakespeare, split between the play proper and its prefatory address to John Murray, written two years later, as carefully detailed by Marvin Carlson's brilliant account of Goldoni's project (Carlson 1985: 13–14). In the play, Shakespeare is parodied in the character of Grisologo (a thinly-veiled cipher for Goldoni's rival Pietro Chiari, a portrait so slanderous that the play was banned in Venice); Grisologo, from his impoverished study of "lo stile di Sachespir, celebre autor inglese" [the style of Sachespir, the celebrated English author], has tried to imitate him but managed only to produce a "ridicola caricatura" [ridiculous caricature] of the English playwright

The Eighteenth-Century Reception of Shakespeare 117

(Goldoni 1935: 1019–20). Grisologo aspires to a style characterized by the "forza di dire vibrato, ampolloso, sonoro, pieno di metafore, di sentenze, di similitudini" [power to speak in a vibrant, ample, sonorous way, full of metaphors, sententiae, similes], unshackled from the "dura legge dell'unità" [strict laws of the unities], combining "il tragico ed il comico" [the tragic and comic modes], surrendering himself to "furore poetico" [a poetic frenzy] (Goldoni 1935: 1059). Yet the same terminology that goes into the stylistic make-up of Grisologo as an irregular, overblown poetaster recurs in the preface itself, in which Shakespeare is now prized as a model, reverently held up by Goldoni, for playwrights seeking to escape the strictures of Aristotelian and Horatian unities, or to reconcile "la Tragica e la Comica facoltà" [the Faculties of the Tragic and the Comic]. This bivalent appraisal of Shakespeare in Goldoni's work harnesses the partisan discourses in which Shakespeare's status is debated in these formative middle decades of the eighteenth century. Shakespeare is both "Il vostro celebre *Shakespeare*" [your famous Shakespeare], a Shakespeare still inalienably English and the property of Goldoni's addressee Murray, and also an exemplar "presso le nazioni estere ancora" [among foreign nations too] of a laudable generic hybridity and untroubled freedom from Aristotelian fetters (Goldoni 1935: 1019–20).

More sustained critical interest in Shakespeare's plays, and a riposte to Voltaire's dominant reading, began to emerge in the 1770s. Giuseppe Baretti, who had spent ten years in England, arriving in London in 1751, published his *Discours sur Shakespeare et sur monsieur de Voltaire* in 1777, which voiced critical opposition to neoclassical conventions and what he considered the uninspired, servile imitation of French theatrical models and rules associated with those conventions (Carlson 1985: 14). It was, unashamedly, a provocative rejoinder to another *Discours*—a violent attack on English literature delivered by Voltaire to the French Academy. In the journal *Frusta letteraria* [*The Literary Scourge*], founded by Baretti, Shakespeare's transgression of the rules is once again praised: "Shakespeare, come l'Ariosto, è uno di que' trascendenti poeti *Whose Genius soars beyond the reach of Art*" [Shakespeare, like Ariosto, is one of those transcendent poets...] (Baretti 1830: 270), an aptly interlingual eulogy to Shakespeare whereby the English playwright, now named along with Ariosto, has formally become a denizened author of Italian literary culture, and whose international status is secured through a recognisable echo of the phrase "And snatch a grace beyond the reach of art" from Pope's 1711 *Essay on Criticism*. Baretti's role in recuperating Shakespeare's standing from rule-bound opprobrium is hard to overstate, although he nonetheless expressed caution about the enterprise of translating Shakespeare into Italian, given the polyglossal nature of Shakespeare's English (fusing a romance lexis with words of Anglo-Saxon provenance), hard to render in any language derived from Latin: "cette poésie qu'on ne saurait rendre dans aucune langue derivée

118   *Sandra Pietrini*

du latin" (Kennan and Tempera 1996: 131). Despite these reservations, and despite reactionary disquiet to his defence of Shakespeare's generic and tonal licence, Baretti forms an indispensable lynchpin in establishing Shakespeare's place in Italian literary culture. The *Discours sur Shakespeare et sur monsieur de Voltaire* shows a cross-fertilisation with English criticism (already hinted at in the aforementioned echo from Pope), in the impress left in Baretti's defence by the Shakepearean prefaces of Samuel Johnson, whom Baretti befriended in England. Recalling Johnson's praise for Shakespeare's "just representations of general nature", Baretti offers a critical portrait of Shakespeare's affinity for the natural, the organic, privileged over generic prescriptivism and aesthetic artifice. Baretti's "Discours" remains the first substantial essay by an Italian critic to offer an apologia for Shakespeare and to refute Volatire's objections, locating Shakespeare in a European theatrical tradition of artistic freedom (including luminaries of Spanish theatre) and inaugurating some of the terms (transgression of rules, innovative handling of genre, designed irregularity) that would undergird later Romantic defences of Shakespeare's poetics.

Shakespeare provided a stimulating challenge to Italian intellectuals sufficiently adventurous to look beyond the narrow confines of a national literature. An emergent literary cosmopolitanism triggered forms of Anglomania (Conti translated Pope, Rolli translated Milton), promoted interest in Shakespeare *per se*, and fostered the conditions for internationalizing and rejuvenating Italian literary culture—a trend manifested by the blossoming of Italian translations of what came to be considered the masterpieces of European literature. Translations of Shakespeare's tragedies, in the first instance, began to pepper the later decades of the eighteenth century: versions of *Othello* and *Hamlet* were completed by Alessandro Verri in 1777, and prose translations of *Othello*, *Macbeth*, and *Coriolanus* by the Venetian noblewoman Giustina Renier Michiel (1755–1832) were published between 1798 and 1800 (and republished at Florence in 1801). The emerging pattern was of texts to be read, rather than performed: strictly speaking, Verri's *Hamlet* was, like Valentini's *Il Giulio Cesare*, never performed (indeed, it was never even published), and the translations by Renier Michiel (who hailed from a prestigious family and was introduced to the study of literature by the prominent scholar, poet, playwright, and translator Vincenzo Monti) were treated as works to be read by a literary and aristocratic elite, rather than performed for a general audience. Little wonder, then, that these last decades of the century were marked by only sporadic attempts at staging Shakespeare—a version of *Hamlet* was staged by Antonio Morrocchesi (1791), and another by Francesco Menichelli (1795).

These final decades of the eighteenth century, then, might be characterized by an effort to establish Shakespeare's canonicity on philological, linguistic grounds. The question of his literary excellence (and,

The Eighteenth-Century Reception of Shakespeare   119

concomitantly, the question of cultural taste) is intricately tied to the question of his translatability into Italian. A parallel movement in England might be cited in the efforts of Edmond Malone (an acquaintance of Baretti's), in many ways the culmination of an eighteenth-century tradition of critically-annotated editions of Shakespeare starting with Nicholas Rowe's in 1709, to establish an accurate, authentic Shakespearean text. In a letter to his brother Pietro (from Rome, 9 August 1769), Alessandro Verri, the aforementioned translator of *Hamlet* and *Othello*, lamented Voltaire's failure to appreciate the linguistic subtleties and contours of Shakespeare's texts (Colognesi 1963: 183–216; Iacobelli 2006: 205–228). Voltaire, he claimed, either "non sa bene questa lingua o ha voluto, a tutt'i conti, mettere in ridicolo Shakespeare" [does not know the language well, or had wanted, in every respect, to make Shakespeare ridiculous] (Novati and Greppi 1911: 17). Recounting the difficulties of his labours to his brother, Verri took pride in having published "l'unica traduzione letterale che vi sia di quest'autore" [to date the only literal translation of this author] and, reaffirming his fidelity to the original text, declared that "[l]a traduzione è precisamente una parola dopo l'altra, come il testo" [the translation is precisely in keeping with the text, word for word] (Novati and Greppi 1911: 18), invoking an ideal of *verbum e verbo* accuracy. Verri, pointedly and ostentatiously, did not draw from intermediary French adaptations, translations, and rewritings that continued to proliferate in these decades—in Jean-François Ducis' adaptations (1769 onwards), and Pierre Le Tourneur's lavishly-produced translations (1776–83)—and voiced an impassioned rationale for a return *ad fontes*. Not only does Verri—evidently a connoisseur of Shakespeare's language, which litters Verri's tragedies in *Tentativi Drammatici* (1779) and his novel *Notti romane al sepolcro degli Scipioni* (1792, 1804) in the form of nods and allusions (Petrone Fresco 1993: 112)—mark a crucial waymark in the shift from a French Shakespeare to an English one. The additional implication, from his private correspondence with his brother, is that the interest to Italian literary audiences lay not just in the raw materials (narrative incident or character development) of the Hamlet story, but specifically in some unique, praiseworthy property of Shakespeare's language that he considered deserving of a faithful rendition into another tongue.

Notably, Verri's translation stands apart from contemporary translations and adaptations of Shakespeare into European vernaculars. Ducis' French adaptation of *Hamlet*, for which he whole-heartily dipped into Pierre-Antoine de La Place's translation (he was yet another translator who did not know English), was clearly a version conceived for performance, rather than for reading (Golder 1992). *Hamlet, tragédie imitée de l'anglois* extensively rewrites the original plot for the purpose of satisfying the tastes of contemporary theatre audiences: Ducis eliminates the action's encompassing historico-political context, centring the tragedy

120   Sandra Pietrini

instead on Hamlet's personal, interpersonal crisis—his conflicted relationship with his mother and intermittent love for Ophelia. Ducis rewrote his adaptation several times, in 1803 printing a version that was staged by the actor François-Joseph Talma, who had substantively contributed to the adaptation in a kind of precursor to the interventionist role of later nineteenth-century *grandi attori* who would wilfully, even wantonly, insist on the omission of scenes, the reduction of non-essential supporting characters, the diminishing of roles by fellow cast members (reduced to *pertichini*, crutches for leaning upon), all for the purpose of heightening the histrionic, affective centrality of the protagonist in the audience's field of vision. Ducis' substantial transformations of Shakespeare's play had an enormous influence on later nineteenth-century European versions, many of which were inspired by his rewriting: not coincidentally, the first operatic performance of *Hamlet* in Venice had been based on this version. At the turn of the nineteenth century, librettists such as Giuseppe Foppa and Felice Romani availed themselves of Ducis' adaptation; only Angelo Zanardini endeavoured to find a compromise between the French rewriting and the original (Melchiori 2006), in an asymmetrical triangulation between Shakespearean source, French adaptation, and the commercial tastes of Italian audiences accustomed to neoclassical codes and conventions.

Before the dominance of this tradition of a staged Shakespeare, Verri seems to have considered Shakespeare's cultural iconicity one of a literary figure whose medium was the page rather than the (popular) stage. Verri's ideal of a translation faithful to the original text, circumventing French accretions and distortions, was an ambitious one, and tallied with his convictions that Italian was a vernacular better suited than French for translating Shakespeare (Petrone Fresco 1993: 118). Verri did not manage complete fidelity when transposing parts of the texts into Italian, and the meaning of some words and phrases continued to elude him. One reason for these lacunae is perhaps the absence of a sufficiently advanced system of critical and editorial machinery around Shakespeare's plays in Italy. Of course, even some English editors and commentators were unclear about the meaning of the obscurer reaches of Shakespeare's lexis. Verri's appreciation of Shakespeare was fundamentally a linguistic one, based on a recognition of Shakespeare's ingenuity, expressive force, and freedom from rules. In the aforementioned letter to his brother Pietro, and perhaps as a strategy for announcing his own skills as a translator more openly, Verri grumbles about Shakespeare's unusual and occasionally abstruse language, at least as difficult to understand as Dante's verses are for Italian readers:

> Quest'autore è tanto difficile, che neppure la metà degl'inglesi lo intendono bene, come pochi italiani intendono Dante. E questo nasce dall'esser quello inglese ripieno di frasi antiquate e di voci inusitate

The Eighteenth-Century Reception of Shakespeare 121

e, talvolta, composte da lui di sbalzo; di più, vi si trovano molte parole prese dall'antico anglosassone.

(Novati and Greppi 1911: 16)

[This author is so difficult, that not even half his English readers understand him properly, just as few Italians understand Dante. And this comes from using a variety of English full of antiquated phrases and unusual words and, at times, phrases that are jerkily written; moreover, many words are taken from Old English.]

The disquiet about the Anglo-Saxon provenance of some of Shakespeare's linguistic palette recalls Baretti's anxieties about the very project of carrying over Shakespeare's texts into a different linguistic system. Verri refers to Baretti's *Dictionary of the English and Italian Languages* published in London in two volumes in 1760, to which he seems to have had recourse during his translational labours (Baretti 1760). These points of lexical obscurity and resistance notwithstanding, Verri's frustrations also gesture, paradoxically, to the ways in which Shakespeare's linguistic difficulty might even be one of the constituent criteria of literary value or cultural status (perhaps recalling Algarotti). Lexical obfuscation thwarts the translator, but becomes a measure of authorial canonicity—a benchmark by which Shakespeare might be elevated to the prestigious position of a Dante.

Despite Verri's linguistic attentiveness and efforts at precision, his *Hamlet* was, in Leonardo Bragaglia's judgement, "badly translated and badly turned in [...] halting lines" (Bragaglia 2005: 18). Yet this was the first complete and relatively faithful translation of the tragedy into Italian, not in verse but in prose. And it clearly reveals all the difficulties of translation, appropriation, and reception of Shakespeare in an Italian context. Verri was perfectly aware of the specific function of the alternation between verse and prose in the works of Shakespeare. In another letter to his brother Pietro (7 May 1777), he notes the tonal variety of an author "il quale fa parlare in verso i caratteri nobili ed in prosa i plebei, e, posto che mescola gli uni e gli altri nelle tragedie, aveva ragione di fare differenza nel loro stile" (Iacobelli 2006: 208) [who makes noble characters speak in verse and common people in prose, and, since he mixed both kinds of character in his tragedies, rightly gave them different styles]. Nevertheless, he dispensed with verse in the interests of adhering more closely to the sense (if not necessarily the register) of the original. Any omissions are, consequently, the result of his scruples as a translator, or gaps in the era's comprehension of English, rather than a desire to censor or standardize the Shakespearean base text.

Conceived as texts for reading, and not commissioned by an actor as a script for performance, Verri's translations seem quite removed from the stage. When *Hamlet* was adapted for the stage in 1783, at the Borgo

122 *Sandra Pietrini*

Ognissanti Theatre in Florence, Antonio Morrocchesi played the role of the protagonist and personally contributed to rewriting the play for the stage, with numerous alterations to the original. Probably fearing commercial failure, the actor used a pseudonym during his performances and soon abandoned Shakespeare to return to his familiar repertoire of Vittorio Alfieri's heroic tragedies. Morrocchesi's interpretation of Hamlet was largely ignored by contemporary critics, and later historiography too: his original audience seemed ill-prepared for even a sugar-coated version of a Shakespeare play, because of its intricate plotting, stylistic discontinuity, and the perceived vulgarity of many characters and scenes. Sustained theatrical interest in Shakespeare would take root only later, with the advent of the *grandi attori* in the mid-nineteenth century. Moreover, the influence of French culture and dramatic taste dominated theatrical productions of Shakespeare's tragedies. The version of *Hamlet* staged in Venice in 1774 took the form of a musical performance drawn from Ducis' French adaptation, translated into Italian by Francesco Gritti: its title, *Amleto tragedia di M. Ducis ad imitazione della inglese di Shakespeare*, gave authorial priority to Ducis, relegating Shakespeare to a distant object of "imitation". The version was revived at Bologna in the summer of 1795, with Francesco Menichelli in the role of the protagonist (Cioni 1966). The paucity of these stagings, not to mention their limited commercial success, further suggests that Shakespeare's canonization as a cultural landmark was limited to an academic, readerly sphere in Italy, and that mainstream, popular audiences were still enthralled to a watered-down, simplified French brand of drama.

Even without mainstream approval, these early translations of Shakespeare's plays into Italian helped secure Shakespeare's literary cachet, which would be further strengthened in the early decades of the nineteenth century by the critical efforts of Alessandro Manzoni. A sentence mischievously and sardonically employed by Manzoni in Chapter 7 of his masterpiece, his 1827 novel *I promessi sposi [The Betrothed]*—"un barbaro che non era privo d'ingegno" [a barbarian not devoid of wit]— was misconstrued as condemnation rather than as a mocking quotation that alluded to Voltaire's well-established critique of Shakespeare. Even in the early nineteenth century then, the critical animosity between acolytes of Voltaire and apologists for Shakespeare continued to announce itself, and to announce itself in a bivalent critical discourse in which the loading of the terms was unclear: terms of censure and rebuttal were still indistinct from terms used to celebrate and canonize. Manzoni's defence of Shakespeare was clearly articulated, in around 1817, in his *Traccia del Discorso sulla Moralità delle Opere Drammatiche*:

> Le obbjezioni contro il dramma si risolvono in questa: / Che si eccitano le passioni—e che non si può esser poeta drammatico altrimenti. / Questo giudizio è nato dal non esaminare che drammatici

The Eighteenth-Century Reception of Shakespeare 123

francesi. / Essi sono tali; ma si può e si deve interessare altrimenti. / Essi fanno simpatizzare il lettore con le passioni dei personaggi, e lo fanno complice. / Si può farlo sentire separatamente dai personaggi e dei personaggi, e farlo giudice. / Esempio insigne Shakespeare.

(Manzoni 1991: 55)

[Arguments against drama can be summarised in this way: / That passions are aroused—and it is not possible to be a playwright otherwise. / This judgement originated from taking into consideration only French playwrights. / They are of that sort; but one could and should engage the audience otherwise. / They make the reader empathise with the passions of the characters, and they make him an accomplice. / One can make him feel in ways separate from the characters, and make him a judge. / An eminent example is Shakespeare.]

Manzoni's observation overthrows well-rooted principles of dramatic identification as the chief means of audience engagement with a dramatic work. It pre-empts a Brechtian model of distanced judgement, though for the purposes of exercising the audience's moral discretion. A keen reader of Schlegel's *Vorlesungen über dramatische Kunst und Literatur* [*A Course of Lectures on Dramatic Art and Literature*], Manzoni made licit an appreciation of Shakespeare for the psychological complexity of his portraits, and for his "ingegno" (wit, genius), rather than as a playwright whose oeuvre required shoehorning into an alien, French template of unity and decorum.

Bibliography

Algarotti, Francesco. 1794. *Opere del conte Algarotti. Edizione novissima*, 17 vols. Venice.

Baretti, Giuseppe. 1760. *A Dictionary of the English and Italian languages. By Joseph Baretti [...] To which is added, an Italian and English grammar*, 2 vols. London.

――― 1777. *Discours sur Shakespeare et sur monsieur de Voltaire*. London and Paris.

――― 1830 [1761]. "Discorso sopra le vicende della letteratura di Carlo Denina". *La frusta letteraria [...] di Giuseppe Baretti*, 3 vols. Venice. 1.265–271.

Bassi, Shaul. 2016. "The Tragedies in Italy". *The Oxford Handbook of Shakespearean Tragedy*, ed. by Michael Neill and David Schalkwyk. Oxford. 691–705.

Bragaglia, Leonardo. 2005. *Shakespeare in Italia. Personaggi e interpreti. Fortuna scenica del teatro di Shakespeare in Italia. 1792–2005*. Bologna.

Carlson, Marvin. 1985. *The Italian Shakespearians: Performances by Ristori, Salvini, and Rossi in England and America*. Washington.

Cioni, Ferdinando. 1966. *Le maschere di Amleto*. Modena.

Collison-Morley, Lacy. 1916. *Shakespeare in Italy*. Stratford-upon-Avon.

124 *Sandra Pietrini*

Colognesi, Silvana. 1963. "Shakespeare e Alessandro Verri". *Acme*, 16: 183–216.

Crinò, Anna Maria. 1950. *Le traduzioni di Shakespeare in Italia nel Settecento*. Rome.

Dobson, Michael. 1992. *The Making of the National Poet: Shakespeare, Adaptation and Authorship, 1660–1769*. Oxford.

Golder, John. 1992. *Shakespeare for the Age of Reason: The Earliest Stage Adaptations of Jean-François Ducis. 1769–1792*. Oxford.

Goldoni, Carlo. 1935. *I malcontenti. Tutte le opere di Carlo Goldoni*, ed. by Giuseppe Ortolani, 14 vols. Milan. Vol. 5.

Graf, Arturo. 1911. *L'anglomania e l'influsso inglese in Italia nel secolo XVIII*. Turin.

Iacobelli, Alessandra. 2006. "Alessandro Verri traduttore e interprete di Shakespeare: i manoscritti inediti dell'*Othello*". *Traduzioni letterarie e rinnovamento del gusto: dal Neoclassicismo al primo Romanticismo*, ed. by G. Coluccia and B. Stasi. Congedo. 205–228.

Kennan, Patricia, and Mariangela Tempera, eds. 1996. *International Shakespeare: the tragedies*. Bologna.

Magalotti, Lorenzo. 1984 [1700]. "An Unknown *Verso Sciolto* Translation of Hamlet's Soliloquy *To be or not to Be* in the Archivio Magalotti". *Shakespeare Today: Directions and Methods of Research*, ed. by Keir Elam. Florence. 215–220.

Manzoni, Alessandro. 1991. "Traccia del Discorso sulla moralità delle opere drammatiche". *Scritti linguistici e letterari*, ed. by C. Riccardi and B. Tavi, 2 vols. Milan. 1: 51–72.

Melchiori, Giorgio. 2006. *Shakespeare all'opera. I drammi nella librettistica italiana*. Rome.

Novati, Francesco, and Emanuele Greppi, eds. 1911. *Carteggio di Pietro e di Alessandro Verri dal 1766 al 1797*. Milan.

Nulli, Siro Attilio. 1918. *Shakespeare in Italia*. Milan.

Petrone Fresco, Gaby. 1993. "An Unpublished Pre-Romantic 'Hamlet' in Eighteenth-Century Italy". *European Shakespeares: Translating Shakespeare in the Romantic Age*, ed. by Dirk Delabastita and Lieven D'Hulst. Amsterdam. 111–28.

Rolli, Paolo. 1739. *Delle Ode di Anacreonte Teio*. London.

Valentini, Domenico. 1756. *Il Giulio Cesare, Tragedia Istorica di G. Shakespeare tradotta dall'Inglese in Lingua Toscana*. Siena.

Voltaire. 1964a. *Lettres Philosophiques*. Paris.

—— 1964b. "Observations sur le Jules César de Shakespeare". *La mort de César*, ed. by A. M. Rousseau. Paris. 189–197.

8 Shakespeare's Reception in Nineteenth-Century Italy
Giulio Carcano's Translation of *Macbeth*

Giovanna Buonanno

The early history of Shakespeare's reception in Italy stands out as one of both acceptance and resistance. From the first scanty references to the "English bard" in reports of Italian travellers to England and men of letters between the late-seventeenth and early-eighteenth century, to the ambitious translations of his complete works in the nineteenth century, the debate on Shakespeare steadily grew to become central within Italian literary circles. "Shakspier" is mentioned for the first time in the travel reports of the Florentine writer Lorenzo Magalotti in 1668, who includes in his account of his journey to England a two-page list of "Poeti inglesi", placing Shakespeare between Drayton and the more famous Jonson (Magalotti 1968: 134). The poet and translator Paolo Rolli refers to Shakespeare's work in his "Vita di Giovanni Milton", which accompanies his translation of Milton's *Paradise Lost*. Rolli praises Shakespeare's "prodigioso ingegno" [extraordinary genius] and fully acknowledges his importance to English vernacular culture and, especially, English theatre, which, thanks to his tragedies, is said to have "reached heights which can never be surpassed" ["elevò il Teatro Inglese ad insuperabile sublimità"]. Rolli also draws attention to Shakespeare's debts to Italian writers, pointing out that material for *Il Moro di Venezia* (*Othello*) had actually been found in Giraldi Cinthio's stories and that the choice of blank verse had been borrowed from Trissino (Rolli 1742: 11–12). Given these reflections, he even ventures that Shakespeare must have had a good knowledge of Italian. Rolli's critical remarks arguably mark the dawn of Shakespeare criticism in Italy.

This chapter traces the progressive strengthening of Shakespeare's fame in Italy thanks to the production of a sizeable corpus of translated works in the nineteenth century, which effectively contributed to securing Shakespeare's place within the Italian literary canon. It finds its theoretical framework in the field of translation studies, which since its formal genesis in the mid-1970s has placed great emphasis on translated literary texts as mediations, potentially able to "influence the development of the receiving culture" (Lefevere 1978: 235). The focus of my analysis will be the Milanese writer and translator Giulio Carcano (1812–84), a major figure in the growing process of assimilation of Shakespeare's works in

126   *Giovanna Buonanno*

Italy, who over the central decades of the century set himself the task of producing the first verse translation of Shakespeare's complete works and played a decisive role in introducing Shakespeare to the Italian literary world. His translation of *Macbeth* (1848), which is discussed here, offers a valuable example of the significant role played by translated works in the nineteenth-century Italian reception of Shakespeare. Thanks to Carcano's work, which in addition provided the blueprint for the stage adaptations of the Italian *grandi attori* who presented Shakespearean roles to Italian and international audiences, Shakespeare began to circulate widely in Italy, both in print and on stage. Of chief interest in this chapter is Carcano's translation both as a literary work in itself and a playtext for the tragedienne Adelaide Ristori, in her landmark performance of Lady Macbeth.

Shakespeare's Early Reception in Italy

Several ambitious endeavours to translate Shakespeare were undertaken throughout the nineteenth century. Michele Leoni published his translation of *Giulio Cesare* as early as 1811, followed in the next decade by his verse adaptation of *Othello* for the stage ("ridotta per la scena italiana" [reduced for the Italian stage]), a play which had a special appeal for Italian scholars and translators on account of its Italian setting. In his preface to *Otello*, Leoni claims to have been particularly drawn to this "insigne dramma" [distinguished play] by the "più insigne fra Tragici inglesi" [most distinguished among English tragic authors] (Leoni 1825: 5). The *Opere di Guglielmo Shakespeare*, translated by Giunio Bazzoni and Giacomo Sormani, appeared in three volumes in 1830—not a complete works of Shakespeare in Italian, but nonetheless a significant step towards a more extensive circulation of his drama in Italy, as the range of Shakespeare plays in translation was beginning to expand beyond the canonical tragedies.

The two main achievements in the nineteenth century were undoubtedly Carlo Rusconi's prose translation of Shakespeare's complete works (1838), which enjoyed several editions well into the twentieth century, and Giulio Carcano's complete translations, published between 1875 and 1882. The work of Carcano as a translator extended over a period of forty years, during which he constantly revised his translations. The history of Shakespeare's early reception in Italy is far from straightforward, ranging between the two extremes of pure "bardolatry" on the one hand and quite overt disparagement on the other. The most striking illustration of the former phenomenon came in the nineteenth-century vogue for ballets and operas based on Shakespeare (Graf 1911). The latter response has its roots in the widely-acknowledged role played by Voltaire in bringing Shakespeare to the attention of Italian literary culture: his *Lettres philosophiques* (1734) are considered a landmark in the

Shakespeare's Reception in Nineteenth-Century Italy 127

history of Shakespeare criticism in France and Italy. Voltaire's reflections on Shakespeare are presented in the eighteenth letter *Sur la tragédie* in which he maintains that Shakespeare had essentially "created" ["créa"] theatre in England by fully expressing his powerful, abundant, natural, and sublime genius ["un génie plein de force et de fécondité, de naturel et de sublime"], yet contended that his oeuvre was entirely lacking in good taste and failed to conform to accepted conventions. Voltaire's Shakespeare, a portrait in part uncritically accepted by the Italian literary world, was an undisciplined, uncouth writer albeit one powerfully endowed with creative genius. According to Voltaire, Shakespeare's works abounded in momentous scenes, but, on the whole, were to be regarded as "farces monstrueuses" [monstrous farces], full of "idées bizarres et gigantesques" [bizarre and gigantic conceptions]. These "monstres brilliants" [brilliant monsters] (1986: 124–128) exerted a pernicious influence on the English stage by hampering and delaying the rise of a classical dramatic tradition, in Voltaire's opinion the only feasible, critically worthy one.

In response, some eminent Italian men of letters countered Voltaire's harsh censures. The critic and lexicographer Giuseppe Baretti, one of Voltaire's strongest opponents, in his *Discours sur Shakespeare et sur monsieur de Voltaire* (1777), attacked Voltaire's criticism for its insufficient understanding of Shakespeare's poetic world, mainly due to his inadequate knowledge of the English language. By means of a close analysis of Shakespeare's language, Baretti offered a new, philologically-sensitive appreciation of Shakespeare's work as the expression of a free, unspoilt creativity set against classical restraint. The turning point in Shakespeare's stage history in Italy came not only with the rise of a new acting tradition around the middle of the century, centred on the *grande attore*, but also with the new revolutionary political context of these middle decades, as the Risorgimento gave impulse to a rediscovery of Shakespeare's versatile political appeal.

A new appreciation of Shakespeare in keeping with Romantic aesthetics was fostered by the writer, literary critic, and intellectual luminary Mme Germaine de Staël who, in her article "Sulla maniera e l'utilità delle traduzioni" ["On the Manner and Usefulness of Translations"] (de Staël 1816a), published in Italy, lamented the state of contemporary Italian literature and recommended that, in order to renew and reinvigorate vernacular literary culture, Italian writers should find inspiration in foreign literatures. In a letter to the editors of *Biblioteca Italiana*, published a few months after her essay on translation, de Staël expressed her surprise at the lack of Italian translations of Shakespeare: she mentions the work of one "Florentine literary man" (Michele Leoni) as the sole example of engagement with Shakespeare's oeuvre, citing his thorough study of English literature and his commitment to translating Shakespeare (de Staël 1816b).

128   *Giovanna Buonanno*

Given these twin responses, broadly speaking, to Shakespeare's reception, and at times reprising Voltaire's early judgement on Shakespeare, critics and commentators were split between praising his "Beauties" (his reserves of powerful images, fascinating subject-matter, extraordinary characters) and rejecting his "Faults" (his uncultivated style, his indecorous mixture of verse and prose), so much so that even Leoni, in the preface to his translations, felt himself compelled repeatedly to point out the good that could be drawn from Shakespeare's plays, by way of an extensive apologia for his stylistic virtues. Following in the footsteps of de Staël, the next major voice in the Shakespearean debate was undoubtedly the author Alessandro Manzoni, who acted as a catalyst in speeding up the process of Shakespeare's assimilation by Italian culture. Manzoni had read Shakespeare in Le Tourneur's French versions and the influence of the English poet can be found in his two historical tragedies, *Il Conte di Carmagnola* (1820) and *Adelchi* (1822). In *Il Conte di Carmagnola*, Manzoni rejected the Aristotelian unities and loosely followed Shakespeare's history plays, finding in Shakespeare a precedent for his project of founding a new dramatic tradition that questioned an adherence to both French models and classic unities.

Manzoni's opinions are clearly expressed in his prose writings where references to Shakespeare abound, not least his *Lettre à Monsieur Chauvet* (1823), a manifesto of Manzoni's own poetics and of a newly-born Italian Romanticism. In this essay, Manzoni praises the dramatic structure of Shakespeare's plays, free as they are from the constraints of the unities, and contrasts them favourably with French models. The letter reads as a persuasive attempt to counter criticism levelled against *Il Conte di Carmagnola*, on account mainly of Manzoni's rejection of the received models for tragedy. Manzoni argues that the three unities severely restrict action to a given time and space. As part of his argument, Manzoni discusses Shakespeare's *Macbeth* and argues for the impossibility of unfolding this tragedy within the frame of conventional rules, unless one chooses to highlight only Macbeth's remorse and doom, failing consequently to render the beauty and intrigue of the previous stages of the story leading up to the dénouement. Later in the essay, Shakespeare himself is invited to speak in defence of his dramaturgy against classicist "purism" by claiming that his plays owe their loose structure to the chronicles of historians such as Holinshed, who provided him with "one simple and yet great and varied action" ["l'idée d'une action simple et grande, une et variée"] (Manzoni 1961: 359–60). The *Lettre à Monsieur Chauvet*, arguably the most resounding defence of Shakespeare in nineteenth-century Italian literary culture, privileged Shakespeare's superiority over the French classicists and praised his style and dramatic technique over the constraints of Aristotelian unities. Manzoni opened up a new perspective in criticism on Shakespeare, linking Shakespeare's reception to the need for both literary and political renewal urged by

Shakespeare's Reception in Nineteenth-Century Italy 129

Romanticism and the Risorgimento, so much so that, as Collison-Morley points out, "[b]y the time Manzoni's tragedies and Leoni's translations appeared, the battle was really won" (Collison-Morley 1916: 122).

Carcano's Translations

Manzoni's legacy in the arena of Shakespeare's reception was taken over by Giulio Carcano, who produced the first complete Italian verse translation of Shakespeare's works. A disciple of Manzoni, Carcano started his literary career as a writer of short stories, poems, and novels. These early writings, characterized by their domestic setting, are already shot through with the author's concern for social and political commentary, a major feature of his later dramatic output. As early as 1834, his poem *Ida della Torre* was censored by the Italian authorities for its provocative political content. As a playwright, following Manzoni's model and that of other contemporary playwrights such as Giovanni Niccolini and Paolo Giacometti, his historical tragedies came under attack from Italian censors and could not be published until the 1860s. Yet, despite his rich literary output, Carcano's fame among his contemporaries rested first and foremost on his work as translator of Shakespeare, rather than on his own literary endeavours.

His first translations were a selection of scenes from *King Lear*, published in 1841 in his first volume of poems, *Prime poesie*, the first complete translation of *King Lear* appearing in 1843 to warm critical acclaim. Carcano's privileging of Shakespeare's tragedies was in keeping with the early nineteenth-century reception of the dramatist in Italy and arguably reflected Carcano's own interest in plays that dealt with issues of power, usurpation, succession, and revenge that would resonate with and speak to an unstable political climate on the Italian peninsular. The 1843 *Re Lear* was prefaced by a critical introduction in which Carcano gave his reasons for translating Shakespeare and his critical stance towards the English playwright and the state of modern theatre. Echoing Manzoni's *Lettre à Monsieur Chauvet*, he briefly traces a history of Shakespeare's fortunes in Europe and points out how his "barbarian" genius was now widely appreciated (Carcano 1914: 1). Then, akin to de Staël, he asserts the importance of emulating Shakespeare—whom he considers, in grandiloquent terms, the poetic spokesperson for modern Europe—in order to renew both European and Italian dramatic traditions. Cautiously, he seems to hint that this act of literary and dramatic appropriation would imply a breach in Italian culture, still heavily imbued with classicist models and only slowly and quite controversially reforming under the impact of social and political pressures exerted by the Risorgimento in the early decades of the century (Carcano 1914: 2). Carcano seemed to be aware of the potential influence that a substantial body of Shakespeare's works in Italian translation might have on the Italian literary system and,

130 *Giovanna Buonanno*

shortly after *King Lear,* translated four more tragedies over the politically tense years 1843–1848: *Amleto, Giulio Cesare, Romeo e Giulietta,* and *Macbetto* (the last of these published only a few days before the "five days of Milan" insurrection against the Austrian regime).

In the 1830s and 1840s, dissatisfaction with the French-based model of theatre and its undisputed representatives, Corneille and Racine, along with the rejection of the Aristotelian unities, seemed to find a political counterpart in the fight against Austrian rule. Carcano himself was a politically-committed writer who took an active part in the Milanese revolutionary movement in 1848. As a consequence, he lost his job as a librarian in Brera and was sent into exile to Switzerland for two years, where he continued to work on his translations of Shakespeare. When approaching Shakespeare's texts, Carcano was inspired above all by the need for philological accuracy. According to Carcano, even the most recent attempts to translate Shakespeare were somehow inadequate, and, in the aforementioned "Introduction" to *Re Lear,* he referred favourably only to the translations by Bazzoni and Sormani, failing to mention Rusconi's inaugural translations of the complete works.

Like Rusconi before him, Carcano used as a source text the English original rather than a French intermediary, but rendered this base text into Italian verse rather than prose, despite an evident awareness of the difficulties of this type of metaphrase. In a letter to his friend Ruggero Bonghi, he stressed the importance of using a plain, simple form in order to preserve what he deemed to be the naturalness of Shakespeare's style (Carcano 1887: 178). Giovanni Rizzi, in his preface to an edition of Carcano's letters, remarks on the difficulty of translating Shakespeare's poetic idiom that seemed alien to the criteria of elegance and controlled inspiration of which Italian translators, more familiar with the classics, were so fond. Not all his translations can be considered successful, by Rizzi's assessment, since Carcano was still committed to "measured expressions", the imprint left by his literary education based on the imitation of classical writers.

Despite these apparent shortcomings, Rizzi concurred with Carcano's choice of a plainer style and with his attempt at following Shakespeare closely, so that the more he advanced with his translations, the more familiar he would become with his author's idiom (Carcano 1887: xix). On the whole, Carcano's translations, when first published, were regarded as far superior to any earlier attempts: Collison-Morley praises his blank verse that "owes a little to his master" (namely, Manzoni) and argues that he is not only

> far more accurate than Leoni, but his lines often catch something of a Shakespearean ring [...] and he is at great pains in choosing his Italian equivalents.
>
> (Collison-Morley 1916: 137)

Shakespeare's Reception in Nineteenth-Century Italy 131

Carcano's translations can be said to rely on three main principles. First, he aimed at rendering the text in its entirety, rejecting any abridgement or bowdlerization. His argument with the celebrated actress Adelaide Ristori concerning the adaptation of *Macbeth* sheds light on this point. When Ristori decided to stage the play, she asked the translator to alter her final scene so that her character could die on stage and even suggested that the title be changed to *Lady Macbeth* to reflect the primacy she believed her character wielded as protagonist in this version, a not untypical demand from a nineteenth-century *grande attore*. Carcano consented to write the stage adaptation for Ristori but refused to make the "sacrilegious" changes suggested by the actress (Duranti 1979: 107). Secondly, he chose unrhymed hendecasyllables since they were the recognized medium for tragic poetry, allowed great flexibility, and were suitable to the rhythm of Shakespeare's blank verse. In Carcano's opinion, only a verse translation, inherently more suited to dramatic purposes, could adequately render the power and variety of Shakespeare's image clusters. Thirdly, departing from his Shakespearean sources, he deliberately avoided mixing verse and prose as this mixture was considered unsuitable for the Italian ear. Although he argued that the shift between verse and prose was an "admirable artifice", he felt unable to dispense with this still in-vogue unity of style. In this way, however, the register shifts so peculiar to Shakespeare were lost, the striking *energeia* of his images was to a certain extent diminished, and the use of an elevated verse idiom produced a general effect of artificial "embellishment" not found in Shakespeare's plays themselves. As Duranti argues, Carcano's strategy imbued his Shakespearean source texts with a kind of literary dignity and regularity, effacing the "rough" poetic power that instilled both admiration and disquiet in his Italian audiences.

Another important aspect of his work as a translator is connected to the stage adaptations he was commissioned to produce by the first three Italian *grandi attori*—Adelaide Ristori (1822–1906), Ernesto Rossi (1827–1896), and Tommaso Salvini (1829–1915)—who, around the middle of the century, began to discover Shakespeare and demand translations of his plays that would later become mainstays of their international repertoires. The closest collaboration was established with Tommaso Salvini. Starting with *Othello*, which would furnish the actor's greatest role, Carcano adapted at least six of his translations for Salvini. His relationship with Ristori was more controversial and did not go beyond the adaptation of *Macbeth*. These stage adaptations are perhaps the most important result of Carcano's ambitious cultural undertaking due to the striking popularity these plays enjoyed in Italy and abroad. However, due to censorship on the one hand and the peculiar features of the dramaturgical interpretations of Italian actors on the other, which tended to stress the psychological aspects of Shakespeare's characters, the political

132 *Giovanna Buonanno*

subtexts and possibilities of Shakespeare's plays that Carcano had managed to preserve and even foreground in his translations were rather overshadowed in performance. A rupture between text and performance, between political page and depoliticized stage, was beginning to emerge.

Carcano's *Macbetto*, between Page and Stage

In Carcano's *Macbetto,* the general principles outlined above pertain. The original text is followed quite closely and only few alterations were made. Carcano's translation finds its frame of reference in an Italian Romantic aesthetic and the wider context of the early nineteenth-century reception of Shakespeare, which provides a model for understanding the stylistic features of the text. His *Macbetto* can be considered a highly refined experiment in which the need to render the source text as closely as possible becomes the guiding principle, though another major concern is to produce a text deeply rooted in the target culture, alert to the aesthetic tastes and political sensibilities of his readers. Among the stylistic features that characterize Carcano's *Macbetto*, his tendency to resort to high dramatic language stands out, especially given the treatment of prose passages that, in verse, lose the function they ostensibly had within the whole texture of the play. When Carcano adapted his translation of *Macbeth* for Adelaide Ristori, the original text underwent several cuts and was even readapted by an English editor, "Mr Clark" (probably the Shakespeare scholar Charles Cowden Clarke), who reworked the translated text in order to make it more suitable for the stage. In the leap from the page to the stage, the translator, who had not originally meant his work for performance, had to address several problems in order to render his literary translations stageable, while taking into account the different modes of reception between readers and theatre audiences. Carcano's adaptation for the stage seems to have directly responded to the criteria of "speakability" and "performability" that have been identified as central concerns in the translation of theatre texts (Snell-Hornby 1984; Bassnett 1998).

Carcano's main concern when adapting his translations for the stage was, however, to cater for the individual demands of the actors who often required a tailor-made adaptation that would emphasize their roles at the expense of the overall structure; accordingly, texts were often reduced in length with whole scenes, even whole acts, omitted. This was certainly the case with Ristori's *Macbetto,* which constitutes a clear attempt to give priority to the female protagonist. Ristori's *Macbetto* reduces the play to four acts to give primacy to Lady Macbeth. In general, Italian actors of the nineteenth century tended to use the play-text as a kind of libretto, freely adapting the base text at their disposal, with an eye for making any alterations they considered necessary in order to

Shakespeare's Reception in Nineteenth-Century Italy   133

produce particular climactic effects. Carcano's adaptation was printed in the countries where Ristori performed, circulating as libretti (most likely on sale before the beginning of the performance) as an aid for the audience following the play in Italian: they partner Carcano's Italian with a translation into the local national vernacular (English, Spanish, Portuguese, German, French), several of them surviving in the British Library, London, and in the Civico Museo Biblioteca dell'Attore, Genoa. The Italian text is the same in every edition, all published between 1857 and 1858 at the time of Ristori's first international tours. At first glance, the translations, probably done in haste, do not seem particularly accurate, and only roughly follow Carcano's Italian. Marvin Carlson argues that a possible explanation for the massive reduction of this play, as well as of other Shakespearean translations reworked for *grandi attori*, lies in a difference in taste between foreign audiences (who expected plays to last no more than two and a half hours) and Italian theatregoers, who were used to longer performances, so when the Italian actors began their international tours they had to stage reduced versions of Shakespeare's plays (Carlson 1985). Furthermore, in this particular case, most of the cuts were made in order to emphasize Ristori's centrality. Ristori carefully studied the role of Lady Macbeth and modelled her interpretation on other distinguished tragic actresses such as Sarah Siddons and Charlotte Cushman. As a key tragic role in her international repertoire, Lady Macbeth became a staple of Ristori's long career (Buonanno 2013). The principal allure for international audiences was the actress, rather than the text or the accuracy of its translation to a new tongue (Carlson 1985).

In Carcano's adaptation for Ristori, the play starts at 1.3 in Shakespeare's text, the first two scenes having been cut completely. The fourth scene of this first act was also cut, thereby heightening the implicit connection between Macbeth's and Banquo's encounter with the witches and Lady Macbeth's reading of the letter. In the second act, the "Porter scene" (2.3) is omitted almost in its entirety, and 2.4 is also excised so that the curtain falls at the moment of Lady Macbeth's apparent fainting. In Act 3, the opening scene is considerably shortened, and 3.3 (the murder of Banquo), 3.5 (Hecate and the witches), and 3.6 (Lennox and Gentleman) are culled so that the act is almost entirely focused on the banquet in 3.4, which became one of the key points in the production, not least due to Lady Macbeth's prominent role. The following act is subject to similar pruning: 4.1 (the cauldron scene) and 4.2 (the murder of Lady Macduff and her son) are omitted so that the act starts with the dialogue (itself heavily compressed) between Malcolm and Macduff before a precipitate shift to the subsequent appearance of Lady Macbeth in the sleepwalking scene, the climax of the act, culminating in the line "A letto, a letto!" [To bed, to bed!] and the exit of Ristori, after which the play speedily comes to an end with the hailing of Malcolm as future

134 *Giovanna Buonanno*

king. The stage version aimed at focusing the whole action on the main plot and on Macbeth and Lady Macbeth, denuding the text of its parallelisms between main plot and subplots, and indeed all but writing out the original's political reflections on the causes of and responses to tyranny, regicide, a succession crisis, and the forms of government appropriate to an unstable polity undergoing self-redefinition.

The text used by Ristori is commented on in reviews of her first performance of *Macbetto* in England in July 1857. It is quite surprising that some commentators remark that even greater abridgement would have been "judicious", and that "[m]any of the immaterial scenes in which Ristori does not appear might well be omitted" (unidentified cutting, 5 July 1857, held in the Ristori archive, Civico Museo Biblioteca dell' Attore, Genoa). Just the day before, *The Lady's Newspaper* had pointed out that Carcano's adaptation succeeded in making Lady Macbeth the prominent character with (in an astonishing verdict) the "least possible alteration of the original text, and without detriment to the intelligibility of the story", and even that "Shakespeare is more closely followed in the second act than by the ordinary conventions of our stage", as if Carcano's version were somehow more authentically Shakespearean. A similar comment appeared in *The Standard* on the same day:

> The alterations in the acting copy were far less than imagined [...] Neither the public nor the critics would have regretted any amount of abridgement or compression in the scenes or the dialogue, as long as it did not interfere with Lady Macbeth.

However, the critical responses were far from uniform. *The London Atlas* lamented that "[e]verything has been sacrificed to the part of Lady Macbeth. We protest against this heresy", regretting in particular the omission of 1.2, especially its historico-political premise and background details on the eponymous character, because it "deforms the character altogether and turns the heroic soldier into a vulgar timid assassin" (*London Atlas*, 11 July 1857). Other critics fustily opined that "Shakespeare's language cannot be reflected in a translation" (unidentified cutting, 5 July 1857) and, in another disparaging remark, that staging Shakespeare in languages other than English risked ridicule since "Macbetto and Macduffo sound oddly" (unidentified cutting, 11 July 1857). However, such comments on the treatment of this specific version of the text and on Shakespeare in translation more broadly are few in number.

Carcano's role in Ristori's success on her European tours is acknowledged by the actress herself, who would even send the translator newspaper cuttings that praised his translation. While he seemed, publicly, to be pleased at his success, he nonetheless commented quite sardonically on the critical response to his rendition of Shakespeare's language. For

Shakespeare's Reception in Nineteenth-Century Italy   135

instance, in the postscript to a letter written to his wife (2 August 1857), he states that the difficulty of his task as a translator registered by some theatre critics was of very little consequence compared to more pressing political matters (the Indian Rebellion of 1857):

> Vuoi ridere, mia cara? Lessi ora un articolo nel *Courier Franco-Italien*, che parla del *Macbeth*. [...] Quanto alla traduzione (dice) "che non era facile trasportare nel dolce ritmo italiano il verso âpre et aceré [*sic*] di Shakespeare["]. [...] Figurati, coll'India in fuoco e fiamme! Che affar serio!
>
> (Quoted in Duranti 1979: 107)

> [Would you like to hear something funny, my dear? I have just read an article talking about *Macbeth* in the *Courier Franco-Italien* [...] As for my translation, it says "that it was not easy to carry Shakespeare's rugged and jagged verse across into the sweet rhythms of Italian". [...] Just think of it – and this whilst India burns! Such a weighty matter!]

These qualms about the preoccupations of critics notwithstanding, Carcano was perhaps also ill at ease about his role as stage adapter of translations that he had been working on so conscientiously for years—translations that were now subject to the narcissistic whims of megalomaniac, all-pervasive *grandi attori*. The stage versions of his translations form part of Carcano's double role of "mediator", as suggested by Duranti, as he facilitated the circulation of Shakespeare's works in Italian translation not only in print but also on the stage. Carcano's role as a translator, acquainting mid-nineteenth-century Italian readers with Italian texts of Shakespeare's complete works, is paralleled by his extensive activity as adapter of those works for stage renditions by leading Italian actors. These twin activities helped both to strengthen the position of Shakespeare in Italy as a canonical, literary author worthy of study, and to secure Shakespeare's place within the emerging Italian *grande attore* tradition of theatre in the crucial, formative decades between Romanticism and Risorgimento.

Bibliography

Baretti, Giuseppe. 1911 [1777]. *Discours sur Shakespeare et sur monsieur de Voltaire*. Lanciano.

Bassnett, Susan. 1998. "Still Trapped in the Labyrinth: Further Reflections on Translation and Theatre". *Constructing Cultures: Essays on Literary Translation*, ed. by Susan Bassnett and André Lefevere. Clevedon. 90–108.

Buonanno, Giovanna. 2013. "Shakespeare and the Nineteenth-century Italian International Actress: Adelaide Ristori as Lady Macbeth". *"No other but a woman's reason": Women on Shakespeare. Towards Commemorating the 450th Anniversary of Shakespeare's Birth*, ed. by K. Kujawinska-Courtney, I. Penier, and K. Kwapisz-Williams. Frankfurt. 77–86.

136 *Giovanna Buonanno*

Carcano, Giulio. 1854. *Macbetto. Teatro di Shakespeare, scelto e tradotto in versi da Giulio Carcano.* Naples.

—— 1887. *Lettere alla famiglia e agli amici (1827–1884),* ed. by Giovanni Rizzi. Milan. 1887.

—— 1914. *Introduzione a King Lear. Teatro di Shakespeare, scelto e tradotto da Giulio Carcano.* Naples.

Carlson, Marvin. 1985. *The Italian Shakespearians: Performances by Ristori, Salvini, and Rossi in England and America.* Washington.

Chambers, David Laurence. 1903. *The Metre of Macbeth.* Princeton.

Collison-Morley, Lacy. 1916. *Shakespeare in Italy.* Stratford-upon-Avon.

de Staël, Madame. 1816a. "Sulla maniera e l'utilità delle traduzioni". *Biblioteca Italiana,* 1.1: 9–18.

—— 1816b. "Lettera di Madama la Baronessa di Stael Holstein ai compilatori della Biblioteca Italiana", *Biblioteca Italiana,* 2.1: 417–422.

Duranti, Riccardo. 1979. "La doppia mediazione di Carcano". *Il teatro del personaggio: Shakespeare sulla scena italiana dell'800,* ed. by L. Caretti. Rome. 81–111.

Graf, Arturo. 1911. *L'anglomania e l'influsso inglese in Italia nel secolo XVIII.* Turin.

Guerrieri, Gerardo. 1955. "Sasper, Sachespar, Shakespear". *Cinquant'anni di teatro in Italia,* ed. by Centro di Ricerche Teatrali. Rome. 71–86.

Lefevere, André. 1978. "Translation Studies: The Goal of the Discipline". *Literature and Translation,* ed. by James Holmes, José Lambert, and Raymond Van den Broeck. Leuven. 234–235.

—— ed. 1992. *Translation/History/Culture: A Sourcebook.* London.

Leoni, Michele. 1825. *Otello o il moro di Venezia, Tragedia di G. Shakespeare, Ridotta per la scena italiana da Michele Leoni.* Naples.

Magalotti, Lorenzo. 1968 [1668]. *Relazioni di viaggio in Inghilterra, Francia e Svezia,* ed. by Walter Moretti. Bari.

Manzoni, Alessandro. 1961 [1823]. "Lettre à M. Chauvet". *Opere,* ed. by G. Bezzola, 3 vols. Milan. 3: 281–424.

Ristori, Adelaide. 1858. *Répertoire de Mme A. Ristori. Macbeth Tragedie de Shakespeare, reduite en quatre actes pour la Compagnie Italienne par un auteur Anglais Traduite en vers Italiens par Giulio Carcano,* trans. by P. Raymond-Signouret. Paris.

Rolli, Paolo. 1742. "Vita di Giovanni Milton". *Il paradiso perduto, poema inglese di Giovanni Milton [...] tradotto in verso sciolto dal signor Paolo Rolli.* Paris. 1–14.

Shakespeare, William. 2015. *Macbeth,* ed. by Sandra Clark and Pamela Mason. Arden Shakespeare. London.

Snell-Hornby, Mary. 1984. "Sprechbare Sprache-Spielbarer Text. Zur Problematik der Bühnenübersetzung". *Modes of Interpretation,* ed. by R. J. Watts and U. Weidman. Tübingen. 101–116.

Voltaire. 1986 [1730]. "Sur la tragédie". *Lettres Philosophiques,* ed. by Frédéric Deloffre. Paris. 124–128.

9 Verdi's Shakespeare
Musical Translations and Authenticity

René Weis

Verdi and Shakespeare share much common ground as professional men of the stage. The nineteenth-century maestro was writing for the opera houses of Europe and their stars just as the Elizabethan actor-dramatist was for the Curtain, Globe, and Blackfriars. Shakespeare knew the strengths of his company, the Lord Chamberlain's Men (later the King's Men), intimately. His star, Richard Burbage, premièred a number of his most famous parts, including Richard III, Hamlet, and Othello, while other members of the company such as Will Kemp played Falstaff, with the musical Robert Armin probably cast in the roles of Touchstone and Feste in *As You Like It* and *Twelfth Night*, two comedies studded with songs (Gurr 2011: 232, 218). Shakespeare clearly wrote some roles with the specific talents of his company in mind. To that extent, his creative energies were partly controlled by contingent factors such as the personnel of the company as well as, to a lesser degree, by the theatrical spaces in which they performed.

Unlike Shakespeare, Verdi was never embedded in a company as such, but he was intensely fastidious about what he expected of his performers. He cared about their appearance, notoriously so in the case of Violetta in *La Traviata*, and their vocal ranges, notably with regard to Lady Macbeth whose voice he wanted to lie in the "ugly" registers of the soprano vocal range. As Verdi writes in a letter to Salvatore Cammarano of 23 November 1848:

> [Eugenia] Tadolini has a wonderful voice, clear, flexible, strong, while Lady Macbeth's voice should be hard, stifled and dark. Tadolini's voice is angelic; I want Lady Macbeth's to be diabolic.
>
> (Osborne 1971: 59)

Verdi was keen to preserve the authenticity, as he saw it, of Shakespeare's unsexed "lady" who, as David Kimbell notes, is "a much more obviously operatic figure than Macbeth himself and certainly loses less in the adaptation" (Kimbell 1981: 539). Verdi was relentless when it came to matching singers to new parts. In 1886, on the eve of his penultimate opera *Otello*, he wrote to his publisher Giulio Ricordi, noting that

138 *René Weis*

while the great heroic tenor Francesco Tamagno possessed considerable qualities, in the part of Otello "there are some broad, extended, legato phrases where the words are produced *mezza voce*, a thing impossible for him". On Desdemona's willow song, Verdi commented that this was very demanding and that "the performing artist ... like the Holy Trinity, must produce three voices, one for Desdemona, another for Barbara (the maid) and a third voice for the 'Salce, salce, salce'" (Weaver and Chusid 1979: 158, 159–60). Hamlet's instructions to the players in Act 3 of *Hamlet* come to mind: "Speak the speech, I pray you, as I pronounced it to you, trippingly on the tongue, but if you mouth it, as many of our players do, I had as lief the town-crier spoke my lines" (Shakespeare 1997: *Hamlet*, 3.2.1–4). This injunction is probably not that different from the ones Shakespeare issued to his fellow actors when new plays of his were rehearsed for the first time, that crucial moment when the play moves from text on the page to performance on the stage.

Such professional affinities between Verdi and Shakespeare, as drama-tists of one kind or another, belong of course primarily to the perspective of later generations. Verdi probably never quite knew the extent to which he and Shakespeare were fellow craftsmen since, for Verdi, Shakespeare was primarily a *read* author. He first saw a fully-fledged Shakespeare play, *Macbeth* as it happens, in London in 1847, *after* composing his own *Macbeth*. Even then his exposure to Shakespeare on the stage would have been a limited, mostly visual, experience as Verdi, unlike his eventual life's companion Giuseppina Strepponi, did not speak or read English.

Verdi's love of Shakespeare verged on idolatry and although he based more operas on Schiller in the end (*Giovanna d'Arco* (1845), *I Masnadieri* (1847), *Luisa Miller* (1849), and *Don Carlo* (1867)), it was Shakespeare who commanded his lifelong artistic loyalty. In a letter to Léon Escudier, the director of the Italian opera in the Salle Ventadour and Verdi's publisher and champion in Paris, Verdi claims to have had Shakespeare "in my hands from earliest youth", and that he read and reread Shakespeare all the time (Marvin 2011: 35). The impact of Italian translations of Shakespeare has been discussed by David Kimbell, among others (Kimbell 1981: 522–23). As it is, Verdi owned the complete prose Italian translation by Carlo Rusconi (1838) and the verse translations by Giulio Carcano (published 1843–53), the latter a close friend of Verdi's who sent his translations to the composer as he went along, thus expos-ing Verdi to a continuous diet of Shakespeare (Phillips-Matz 1993: 134). We know that he shared his translation of *King Lear* with Verdi in 1843. Also, Carcano may have read Verdi his translation of *Macbeth* in 1846 when they were both staying as guests in a friend's villa; rumours even circulated that Carcano was to be credited with parts of the *Macbeth* libretto (Phillips-Matz 2011: 11).

Verdi, unable to read a single line by Shakespeare in English, never-theless thought that, of all the plays, *King Lear* was the most powerful.

He shared Keats's reverence for Shakespeare's apocalyptic tragedy. In a letter of 21 December 1817, Keats famously remarked that the "excellence of every Art is its intensity, capable of making all disagreeables evaporate, from their being in close relationship with Beauty & Truth— Examine King Lear & you will find this examplified throughout" (Gittings 1975: 42). The awesome scale of *King Lear* and its challenge to a composer are acknowledged by Verdi in a letter of 28 February 1850 to Salvatore Cammarano: "Il *Re Lear* si presenta a prima vista così vasto, così intrecciato che sembra impossibile cavarne un melodramma" [*King Lear* seems at first sight so vast, so interwoven that it seems impossible to quarry a melodrama out of it] (Cesari and Luzio 1913: 478).

Cammarano had been the librettist of Gaetano Donizetti's *bel canto* classic *Lucia di Lammermoor* (1835), based on Sir Walter Scott's novel *The Bride of Lammermoor*. He had produced Verdi's *Macbeth* in Naples and had provided the libretto for Verdi's seminal opera *Luisa Miller* (1849), the pinnacle of the composer's lyrical achievement before the great melodic trilogy of *Rigoletto*, *Il Trovatore* (for which Cammarano provided the first draft of the libretto), and *La Traviata*. Was Cammarano's experience as a librettist working from Scott's novel the reason why Verdi approached him in connection with his own British subject matter? Or did he turn to Cammarano because he had done a good job on Schiller's *Kabale und Liebe*, the drama Verdi set to music in *Luisa Miller*? Verdi evidently esteemed Cammarano highly enough to want to entrust him with his most ambitious project to date. But in July 1852, before the idea of a *King Lear* opera could be explored at length by both librettist and composer, Cammarano died.

It had been little over a year since the triumphant première in Venice of *Rigoletto*. In its aftermath, Verdi returned to *King Lear*, prompted perhaps by the fact, among others, that the first ever Rigoletto, the baritone Felice Varesi, had earlier sung the part of Macbeth: with Varesi so successful in one major Shakespeare role, might he not undertake another? Verdi commissioned a libretto for a *King Lear* opera from the playwright Antonio Somma. Somma obliged but his two versions of the *Lear* libretto, from 1853 and 1855, never made it on to the stage. Many years later, Verdi confessed to being overawed by the scale of Shakespeare's grand tragedy.

Among Verdi's operas, *Rigoletto* probably has the deepest affinities with the unrealised *King Lear*. Like Shakespeare's masterpiece, the opera involves a father and a self-sacrificing daughter, and the play and opera each set a key moment in a spectacular storm. Act 3, Scene 2 of *King Lear* opens with the King's desperate defiance of the elements – "Blow, winds, and crack your cheeks! Rage ..." (3.2.1) – while the murder of Gilda happens in the thick of a storm that drowns out all sense and ethical being. In *King Lear,* nature and humankind form an uneasy organic whole and the "unkindness" of the storm refracts the violation of the

140   *René Weis*

"bias of nature" (1.2.111) in the royal household and its male shadow, the Gloucester family. For Shakespeare and his audience, the scene on the heath marks the external manifestation of the moral cataclysm that is engulfing the country: even nature mourns the collapse of values in the kingdom and the rain is as wet and uncomforting as the scalding tears of a king reduced to rags.

King Lear reflects an early seventeenth-century anatomy of the world that suffuses external and material nature with moral meaning. Two and a half centuries later, Verdi's storm in *Rigoletto* is the heir of the Romantic tempests of Scott and Byron; it has more in common with the sound and fury of *Wuthering Heights*, its contemporary, than with a pre-Enlightenment political theology that erased the boundaries of human, divine, and cosmic. Verdi's storm acts as a mood-setter. It functions as both prelude and background music to a horrible calculus by Sparafucile and his sister who agree to trade murders, the Duke of Mantua's death for Rigoletto's daughter Gilda. Like Cordelia, Gilda is motherless, but whereas Lear's daughter dies off-stage never to waken again, Gilda revives briefly in her father's arms. Rigoletto is granted the supreme melodramatic reward of communing with his dying daughter, a consolation that Shakespeare resolutely withholds from Lear, much though the two final father-daughter scenes resemble each other visually in their on-stage pietà iconographies. Cordelia's silence in *King Lear* translates into Gilda's hope that soon she will join her mother in heaven, the kind-hearted woman who loved her father in spite of his hunch-back appearance, just as Desdemona fell in love with Othello because she saw his "visage in his mind" (1.3.252). *Lear* was on Verdi's mind at the time of *Rigoletto* and it is not difficult to pick up a subliminal Shakespearean trace history in the opera, which is based on a sombre play by Victor Hugo, *Le roi s'amuse* (1832).

Perhaps the most immediate question posed by the synchronicity of Verdi's interest in *King Lear* and *Rigoletto* is whether an opera like *Rigoletto* could have been based on Shakespeare's masterpiece. After all, *Lear* would seem to be fundamentally different from the other Shakespeare plays Verdi adapted with such felicitous ease, mostly perhaps by the sheer scale of its philosophical questioning and its profound desolation. While the play lends itself perfectly to a dialogue with the Beckett of *Endgame* and of *Waiting for Godot* too, works which share its concern with pervasive *aporia* and a world without moral compass, Italian Romantic opera needs more licence to be creatively frivolous. For Verdi, the character of the strutting Duke of Mantua (originally François I of France before the censor intervened) was a gift: no one can resist the maverick chanticleer of the opera whose glorious singing lifts him above good and evil, not a moral luxury that *King Lear* possesses.

Verdi's instincts were right: *King Lear* would never be compatible with his particular blend of dramatic power and mellifluous *bel canto* genius. While Verdi readily tackled complex and epic subjects, in *Nabucco*

Verdi's Shakespeare 141

(early) and *Aïda* (late), the structure of the play, its characters, and the depth of its suffering may lie beyond the reach of singing. In 1896, the 83-year-old Verdi, then himself, like Lear, "fourscore and upwards", confided in the composer Pietro Mascagni that he could not set *Lear* to music because the scene of Lear on the heath left him traumatized ("terrorizzato") (Abbiati 1959: 598). The only operatic composer in the nineteenth century who might have created a successful *King Lear* opera in the manner of Shakespeare was Verdi's great rival Richard Wagner, the architect of the concept of *Gesamtkunstwerk* (literally "total work of art"), with *Lear* being a *Götterdämmerung* of sorts.

King Lear proved to be Verdi's unclimbed Everest even if, as the letter to Mascagni demonstrates, he never quite gave up hope. Three years after *Falstaff*, his failure to write a *Lear* opera still haunted him. Perhaps it was the success of *Falstaff* that prompted this renewed expression of regret, but then *Falstaff* is an *opera buffa* with a larger-than-life rogue in it, another character instantly lending himself to the cock-of-the-walk musical treatment meted out to the Duke of Mantua. Indeed, Falstaff and the Duke of Mantua share more than a love of song, women, and wine. The Falstaff of Shakespeare's comedy is at best a comedic, emasculated version of the monstrous Duke, and the moral issues in *Falstaff* are as tame as they are in Shakespeare's original, *The Merry Wives of Windsor* (c. 1597), which is commonly seen as Shakespeare's most innocent play. Only a few months earlier, in the two *Henry IV* plays, the same Falstaff had been portrayed as a corrupt predator (he compares himself to an old pike in a pond stocked with gulls), notably when recruiting in Gloucestershire in *Henry IV, Part 2* where he is aided and abetted by his former compadre Shallow in allowing recruits to buy themselves out of the king's press.

Verdi first saw *Macbeth* on the London stage when he was in the city to conduct the première of *I Masnadieri* at Her Majesty's Theatre on 22 July 1847. The play is in many respects the most Aristotelian and satisfying of the tragedies inasmuch as it follows a curve of temptation, crime, atonement, and retribution. The horror of its actions may just be mitigated by the portrayal of the two leading characters, who never quite forego our sympathy, not least because their relationship as a couple is affectionate and intimate. The chief triumphs of *Macbeth* are traditionally thought to reside in its psychological explorations of the build-up to the regicide as conveyed through the intimate relationship of Macbeth and his wife, a childless (or is it?) marriage that resonates in every corner of the work's metaphorical texture. The imaginative core of Shakespeare's *Macbeth* therefore seems to lie in the psychomachic first half of the play, while the political and historical fall-out of the usurpation, particularly the scene in England with Malcolm and Macduff, feels at times like an imaginative falling-off. Shakespeare, it seems, was more interested in the agony of individuals than in the suffering of nations.

142 *René Weis*

While there is some truth in this, Shakespeare's *Macbeth* also engages the politics of the first decade of the seventeenth century, to such an extent that one of its most famous scenes, the Porter's (2.2), was probably censored during early performances. When Simon Forman saw *Macbeth* at the Globe Theatre in April 1611, the Porter's scene was conspicuous by its absence. The only conceivable reason for the omission is the presence in this scene of allusions to the Powder Plot of 1605, through the references to the "farmer that hanged himself on th'expectation of plenty" and the Jesuits' "equivocations" at their trials (opening of 2.3), "farmer" being the undercover name of the Jesuits' chief-of-staff in London at the time, Father Henry Garnett. It so happens that the Porter does not figure in Verdi's *Macbeth* either. That Verdi and his librettist Piave knew much about the particular political context of Shakespeare's play is doubtful. Apart from the specific historic moment of 1606 when the Scottish play was written, a mere three years after King James's accession to the English throne, internally the play clearly involves the two separate kingdoms of Scotland and England and shows them to be organically linked in the long English scene. The army of "English epicures" who converge on Dunsinane with loyal Scots to free Scotland from the tyranny of Macbeth are a British force intent on restoring harmony. It is this political part of the play that struck a chord with Verdi. It provided a direct link back to his own seminal *Nabucco*, which features a dispossessed, enslaved nation, whose citizens sit on the banks, as the psalmist has it, and long for their lost homeland. They are the so-called Hebrew slaves, hence the name for the Chorus for *Va pensiero sull'ali dorate*, or "Fly, thought, on wings of gold ... Greet the banks of the Jordan ... Oh, my country, so beautiful and lost! | Oh, remembrance, so dear and so fatal!". The words, by the Italian librettist Temistocle Solera, were inspired by Psalm 137, which, in the Authorised Version, starts with "By the rivers of Babylon, there we sat down, yea, we wept, when we remembered Zion" (Carroll and Prickett 1997: 716).

As a child of the Italian Risorgimento, Verdi grasped the opportunity of the exile scene in *Macbeth* once more to sing for all of Italy just as he had done with the chorus of the Hebrew slaves. The result is the glorious chorus "Patria oppressa, il dolce nome? | No di madre aver non puoi | Or che tutta a figli tuoi | Sei conversa in un avel" [Oppressed homeland of ours! You cannot have the sweet name of mother now that you have become a tomb for your sons]. This closely echoes Ross's lines from Shakespeare: "Alas, poor country, | Almost afraid to know itself. It cannot | Be call'd our mother, but our grave" (4.3.164–66). Verdi and Piave here closely follow Shakespeare as is their wont at key moments in the opera, notably in the dagger soliloquy.

If the turbulent political landscape of 1840s Italy drew Verdi and his librettist to Act 4 of *Macbeth*, the murder of Macduff's family may have struck an even deeper, more intimate note. In the Jacobean tragedy, news of his family's murder elicits from Macduff three of the most powerful lines in Shakespeare: "I cannot but remember such things were, | That were most precious to me. Did heaven look on, | And would not take their part?" (4.3.222–24). If only Verdi could have felt the resonance of those words on his pulse; if only his ear, that of one of the greatest musicians of the nineteenth century, could have heard the original music of Shakespeare here. As it is, Verdi and Piave rewrote the lines occurring immediately before the ones quoted just now with "O figli, o figli miei! da quel tiranno | Tutti uccisi voi foste, e insieme con voi | La madre sventurata" [Oh children, oh my children! You were all killed by that tyrant, and together with you your most unfortunate mother!].

The death of a mother and her children would haunt Verdi most of his life because, between August 1838 and June 1840, he lost his two infant sons and his wife Margherita, the daughter of his benefactor Antonio Barezzi. He was still only 26 at the time of their deaths. The repercussion of this bereavement reached into everything he composed, including the death scene of Violetta in *La Traviata*, another Piave libretto, and of course into *Macbeth*. It is quite possible that Macduff's lines in the opera are one of the reasons why Verdi was so keen for the Barezzi family to be present at the première of *Macbeth* at the Teatro della Pergola in Florence on 14 March 1847, and why he dedicated the score of *Macbeth* to Barezzi, noting that it was his favourite among all his operas and one worthy to be presented to Barezzi:

> Now here is this *Macbeth*, which I love more than my other operas and thus believe is more worthy of being presented to you. The heart offers it; may the heart accept it, and may it be a witness to the eternal memory, the gratitude, and the love felt for you by your affectionate G. Verdi.

Barezzi was profoundly moved. In his reply to Verdi he assured him that

> your recognition of me will always remain engraved in my heart. Deign to receive in exchange the hot tears of love that I shed for you, the only tribute that I can offer you. Love me, O my adored son of my heart, as I love you; and receive a thousand kisses. Addio! Your Antonio Barezzi.
>
> (Phillips-Matz 1993: 208)

Such was Verdi's esteem for Shakespeare that he interfered with the libretto to an unprecedented degree. Not only would he write out in prose specific passages for Piave to dramatize, only to insist on countless revisions, but he would even stipulate the number of syllables needed from the librettist for particular lines. Above all he wanted "brevity" and "sublimity" from Piave and repeatedly berated him for not delivering on

144 *René Weis*

his brief of "*poche parole ... poche parole ... stile conciso*" [few words ...
few words ... be concise].

The maestro's conception of his Shakespeare opera was not to turn
a literary masterpiece into an opera but to mould Italian opera into a
vehicle for a major musical drama worthy of Shakespeare. The result
is, in the words of one writer on Verdi, "the first Italian opera that is
Shakespearian in any meaningful sense of the word" (Kimbell 1981:
524). Verdi was adamant that he had the *tinta* of *Macbeth* in his mind's
eye from the start, the *tinta* being the quintessential mood music of the
piece, its primal imaginative coloration. Verdi's use of *tinta* almost always signalled, as Piave would learn quickly, that the core musical and
dramatic vision was already fixed in Verdi's imagination. Not only did
he rarely deviate from it, but it would prompt him to sketch out dialogue
ahead of libretto and musical composition, as he did with the famous
abbozzi (sketches) for *La Traviata,* where everything flowed from the
original *tinta* that allegedly came to him during a production of Dumas'
La dame aux camélias.

Verdi's craving for authenticity is reflected both in the opera's occasionally literal adherences to the Shakespearean text, as in the dagger soliloquy, and in its lavish recreations of scenes from the play, notably the
banquet scene. In a letter of 22 December 1846 to Alessandro Lanari,
the director of La Pergola in Florence where *Macbeth* premièred, Verdi
urged the impresario to ensure that Banquo's ghost entered "from underground", that he must "wear an ash-coloured veil", and that his various wounds should be visible on his neck: "All these ideas I've got from
London where they've been playing *Macbeth* continuously over the last
two hundred years". Later, when he was revising *Macbeth* for Paris, he
told his correspondent Léon Escudier that the opera contained only three
main characters: "Macbeth, Lady Macbeth, and the chorus of witches.
The witches dominate the drama; everything stems from them—rude and
gossipy in Act I, exalted and prophetic in Act III. They make up a real
character and one of the greatest importance" (Budden 1973: 1.272, 278).

Macbeth was a triumph at its première. Verdi's revisions in 1865 nevertheless were at first prompted by the demands of his Paris impresario Léon Escudier for the maestro to add a ballet. In his response of
24 October 1864, Verdi noted,

> I have glanced through *Macbeth* in order to do the ballet music, but
> alas! I have found a few things in it that must be changed. In short,
> there are certain numbers which are weak, or even worse, lacking
> in character.
>
> (Osborne 1971: 134–35)

He would therefore need to revise it rather more extensively. The scale
of his revisions to score and libretto is revealed in two further, detailed

Verdi's Shakespeare 145

letters to Escudier, of January and 3 February 1865, in which Verdi ranges from instructions about Hecate's mime ("this *adagio* must be played by the *clarone* or bass clarinet as is indicated, so that in unison with cello and bassoon it will produce a dark, hollow, and severe tone in keeping with the situation") to revisiting the staging of the banquet scene and the apparition of Banquo's ghost (Osborne 1971: 136–38). He does not specifically mention the most striking differences between the two versions—a new aria for Lady Macbeth (*La luce langue*, "the light is fading") and making Macbeth die offstage, as in Shakespeare, rather than in full view of the audience as he did in the 1847 version. Verdi was a very different composer in the 1865 version and the new *Macbeth* opera for Paris was wedged between *La forza del destino* (1862) and *Don Carlos* (1867).

Given the success of *Macbeth* in 1847, Verdi's zest for revising it in 1865, and a lifelong love affair with Shakespeare, it is surprising that it took forty years before another Shakespeare opera by Verdi, *Otello*, would be staged, this time in the temple of opera itself, La Scala in Milan. Perhaps the shadow of the unattempted *King Lear* hovered over Verdi and stopped him from requesting a further Shakespeare libretto in case he again failed to set it to music. Or did he sense that Wagner was after all better suited for scoring a Shakespeare opera? It is tempting to think that Wagner's death in 1883 set Verdi free to return to Shakespeare, the more so since *Otello* is the most Wagnerian of Verdi's operas, self-consciously so to the point where it deliberately echoes *Tristan und Isolde* (as discussed later in this chapter).

By the time *Otello* premièred in Milan, Verdi had been unofficially "retired" for sixteen years, although his *Requiem* for Manzoni of 1874 ranks among his major achievements. His last opera before *Otello* had been *Aïda* (1871). He was at last coaxed back to opera by his long-time publisher Giulio Ricordi and the director of the Scala, after 1871, the conductor and composer Franco Faccio, who shrewdly played on Verdi's friendship with Arrigo Boito, a talented composer and librettist who had revised the libretto for Verdi's *Simon Boccanegra* for an 1881 revival of the opera. Also, Boito had already completed a Shakespeare libretto for an opera called *Amleto*, which premièred in Genoa in 1865, the same year as Verdi's revised *Macbeth* in Paris. The composer of *Amleto* was none other than Faccio himself. If the fashion in Italy was gradually turning away from the grand mythic operas of the past, as part of the forward march of *verismo* that would culminate in Puccini's opera *La Bohème* in 1896, three years after Verdi's *Falstaff*, Verdi and Boito would prove that audiences could still enjoy the grandest of nineteenth-century operas.

The gestation of *Otello* stretched over at least seven years. The setting of the tragedy in Venice—its full title in the 1623 Folio is *The Tragedie of Othello, the Moore of Venice*—may have added to its attraction for

146 *René Weis*

Verdi. Venice was a city that he knew very well from countless rehearsals and premières of his own works. Also, the story on which Shakespeare based *Othello* is an Italian novella in Giraldi Cinthio's *Gli Hecatommithi*. For once, an Italian librettist and composer could synchronize the genesis of a Shakespeare opera with researches into Italy as seen by their hero. Whereas to most British audiences the quintessential Italian Shakespeare play is *Romeo and Juliet*, *Othello*, like its Venetian cousin *The Merchant of Venice*, is more specifically anchored in a familiar and historically recognizable location.

What more than anything though drew Verdi to the play was its villain, Iago. In a letter of early February 1880, to the painter Domenico Morelli, Verdi enthused that "Questo Iago è Shakespeare, è l'umanità, cioè una parte dell'umanità, il brutto" [This Iago is Shakespeare, is humanity, that's to say a part of humanity, the ugly part] (Osborne 1971: 212). Such was his fascination with Shakespeare's most morally opaque villain that for a while he intended to call the opera *Iago*. In the critical literature, Iago as arch-schemer is not infrequently compared to the playwright himself, for his sheer manipulative intelligence and delight in creating scenarios that above all else serve to entertain him. It was Coleridge who coined the now famous phrase of "motiveless malignity" to render Iago's irrational wickedness; senseless in that his course of action quickly transcends his original reason of thwarted ambition that the cashiering of his rival Michael Cassio was meant to avenge. In the course of the play, the purpose of Iago's existence becomes the destruction of Othello and everything the Moor has and loves, particularly Desdemona.

Verdi was curiously untroubled by the racial tensions in the play, despite the fact that Italy's first colonial settlements in Eritrea were beginning to be established in 1882, preferring to view the play's colour-coded plot in terms of metaphor. To the extent that he referred to his new opera as "il progetto di cioccolata" [the chocolate venture], the maestro was evidently largely impervious to tensions that are undoubtedly present in Shakespeare's play, which probes the literal and metaphorical meanings of "black" and "white" throughout, such that even Michael Cassio's paramour (he is, moreover, "a fellow almost damned in a fair wife", 1.1.21) is called "Bianca". Her name matters because Shakespeare invented all the names in the play except one. Boito too was struck by this. In his sketch about *Otello*, "The Characters' Traits", he commented on the tale's lack of names, remarking that Cinthio introduces Iago by character, as "un alfiero di bellissima presenza, ma della più scellerata natura che mai fosse uomo del mondo" [an ensign of a splendiferous presence but of the most wicked character that ever man possessed] (Boito 2012: 31–2).

The only character Cinthio names is "Disdemona", blaming her father for giving her "a name of unlucky augury", because Disdemona in

Verdi's Shakespeare 147

Greek translates as "unfortunate". Othello on the other hand is only known as "il capitano moro". While modern studies of *Othello* have become obsessed with the play's racial interest, Verdi was dismissive of Othello's appearance in the play, preferring to concentrate on Iago in another letter to Morelli who was providing him with sketches for *Otello*:

> Nothing could be better than to have Iago dressed in black, just as his soul is black. But I don't understand why you should dress Othello as a Venetian! ... You can hardly have Otello dressed as a Turk, but why not have him dressed as an Ethiopian, without the usual turban. The question of Iago's type of figure is more serious ... if I were an actor, and had to play Iago, I would rather have a long, thin, face, thin lips [...]
>
> (Osborne 1971: 216–17)

In the same letter, after a lengthy explanation on how best to imagine Iago's physical appearance as arch-deceiver, Verdi proceeds to dismiss both Iago's and Otello's looks as ultimately irrelevant. His librettist Boito independently concurred in his sketch in which he notes that, while Othello is jealousy, "Iago is Envy. Iago is a scoundrel. Iago is a critic" (Boito 2012: 31). Boito was very conscious of the age difference between the two characters. Quoting Othello's "Haply, for I am black ... declined | Into the vale of years" (3.3.263–66), he compares Othello, who "is over forty years old", with Iago's "mere twenty-eight years". Iago is one of the few Shakespeare characters whose age is given in the plays, with King Lear over eighty at the other end of the spectrum. Why does Shakespeare turn Iago, who is a father in Cinthio, into a sterile young man? Presumably to isolate Othello further from his young wife and other Venetians. In the play, as the line quoted by Boito suggests, the source of Otello's anxiety is both racial and connected to his age: Iago is young and Venetian, like Desdemona, as he intimates to Othello when he remarks

> I know our country's disposition well;
> In Venice they do let heaven see the pranks
> They dare not show their husbands [...]
> She that, so young, could give out such a seeming,
> To seal her father's eyes up, close as oak,
> He thought 'twas witchcraft –
>
> (3.3.201–11)

Librettist and composer were emphatic in their belief that Iago's wickedness was not something supernatural, a "motiveless", unfathomable, moral alienation, but profoundly human. It comes as a surprise then that the most

148 *René Weis*

famous passage in the opera, Iago's Manichaean prayer, should be cast in metaphysical terms. It starts with "Credo in un Dio crudel che m'ha creato | simile a sé" [I believe in a cruel God who created me in his image]. Iago then continues with "Son scellerato | perché son uomo" [I am wicked because I am human], a perverse distortion of Descartes' *Cogito ergo sum*.

> E credo l'uom gioco d'iniqua sorte
> dal germe della culla
> al verme dell'avel.
> Vien dopo tanta irrision la Morte.
> E poi?—La Morte è il Nulla.
> e vecchia fola il Ciel.

> And I believe man to be the toy of an unjust fate
> from the seed of the cradle
> to the worms of the grave.
> After so much mockery comes Death.
> And then? Death is nothingness,
> and Heaven an old fable.

The hands of Boito and Verdi are equally manifest in this defiant musical soliloquy that challenges the Deity and the myths of established religion just as surely as Darwin. Verdi had lost none of his anti-clerical fire and here uses Iago to voice his own agnostic challenge. Iago's creed in *Otello* bears the imprint of another Shakespeare soliloquy, Edmund the Bastard's paean to a predatory nature, which starts the second scene of *King Lear* with "Thou, nature, art my goddess". In spite of this, it may well be the case, as Frank Kermode has remarked, that "as literature, [Boito's] libretto is ... a doctored Victorian *Othello*", a derivative toning down of the original that Kermode attributes in part to the librettist's use of a French translation of Shakespeare by François Victor Hugo (Kermode 2003: 364). Certainly, much of the steamy eroticism of Shakespeare's play is missing from the opera, some of it undoubtedly lost in translation as in the case of sexual images embedded in the play's metaphors and similes— for example in "I had rather be a toad | And live upon the vapour of a dungeon | Than keep a corner in the thing I love | For others' uses" (3.3.270–73), echoed in another suggestive image in the next act, "The fountain from the which my current runs | Or else dries up: to be discarded thence! | Or keep it as a cistern for foul toads | To knot and gender in!" (4.2.59–62). Other more explicit references such as Iago's "dream" of sharing a bed with Michael Cassio, or the voyeurism of his suggestive talk about a Desdemona "full of game" (2.3.19) consummating her marriage, would simply not have been possible on the nineteenth-century opera stage.

Nevertheless, Kermode concedes that

> despite this dependence on the French translation, and despite the loss of so much material that seems central to the theme, I believe the opera to be almost as potent a pathological study as the play, and the question must be asked how this was achieved when so much of the play wasn't directly available.
>
> (Kermode 2003: 367)

In his use of sources, Shakespeare was singularly adept at telescoping his materials, at filleting long prose texts to the needs of drama, homing in on essentials, making them his own by a process of cutting and reshaping. Verdi did much the same with *Othello*, just as he had done with *Macbeth*, by reducing the cast and expanding those scenes that seemed essential to his vision of the opera. In the end, the libretto of *Otello* contains 800 lines, whereas Shakespeare's play runs to 3,500. The most striking departure from Shakespeare's play is the opera's excision of its entire first act and consequent starting in Cyprus, chiming with Dr Johnson's stricture about Shakespeare's play, that "had the scene opened in Cyprus and the preceding incidents been occasionally related, there had been little wanting to a drama of the most exact and scrupulous regularity" (Woudhuysen 1989: 248). Maybe so, but Shakespeare rarely heeded "regularity" except for *The Tempest*, his only fully-fledged neo-classical play. In fact, Verdi's *Otello*, all of which plays in Cyprus, opens in a manner instantly reminiscent of *The Tempest*, with a thunderous storm, the same storm that in Shakespeare ominously separates Othello and Desdemona at sea. As for Johnson's "occasionally related" retrospective, this holds no interest for Verdi and Boito as the first act of Shakespeare's text largely sets up the racial dynamic that haunts the play but not the opera.

Otello is as close as Verdi ever got to a Wagnerian *Gesamtkunstwerk*. It is an opera of dark psychological and philosophical probings. It does not allow its characters the luxury of soaring arias with the exception of the uncompromising baritone *Credo* by Iago, which is not really an operatic number at all. Such is its complexity and radical defiance that the musical line refuses to be assimilated to a comforting melody. It is as dramatic and total in its expressive purchase on the text as anything in Wagner, which may be why the great German composer is lyrically evoked in the scene of the lovers' final parting. When Otello asks for "un bacio ... ancora un bacio", the music swells to a Wagnerian climax with unmistakable, ominous echoes of the *Liebestod* of *Tristan und Isolde* (1865). It is entirely fitting that at the Royal Opera House's famous 1980 production of *Otello,* the great baritone Renato Bruson's Iago should be partnered by Jon Vickers, a legendary "Heldentenor" whose spell-binding Tristan enthralled audiences all over the world.

150   *René Weis*

In the words of the distinguished Shakespeare scholar Stanley Wells reviewing the Royal Opera House's 1987 production of *Otello*, by Elijah Moshinsky, "Verdi's *Otello* is a rare instance of one masterpiece engendered by another" (Wells 2012). The same would apply to *Macbeth* and also to *Falstaff*, Verdi's last opera. That the maestro of Busseto would finish his career with a *buffa* Shakespeare opera, one moreover entirely designed on his own terms, seems especially appropriate. He may be the only imitator of Shakespeare to have rivalled the master's creations in each of his three attempts at capturing his works' genius.

Why was Verdi so attracted to Shakespeare? Perhaps the anarchic energy of Shakespeare's drama, the sheer musical pulse of it (even in translation), its brilliant transgressions (fools and madmen talking to kings and kings becoming them), the compulsive chaos that is Falstaff, the countless happy violations of decorum—these are some of the glories of Shakespeare that drew Verdi to him, in addition to the complex moral passions that beat their drum below the surface of the works. Shakespeare is the most anarchic and creative among dramatists, his works a gift for the most Romantic and compassionate of nineteenth-century composers.

Bibliography

Abbiati, Franco. 1959. *Giuseppe Verdi*, 4 vols. Milan.
Boito, Arrigo. 2012. "The Characters' Traits". *Otello*. Royal Opera House programme.
Budden, Julian. 1973. *The Operas of Verdi*, 3 vols. London.
Carroll, Robert, and Stephen Prickett, eds. 1997 [1611]. *The King James Bible*. Oxford.
Cesari, Gaetano, and Alessandro Luzio, eds. 1913. *I copialettere di Giuseppe Verdi*. Milan.
Gittings, Robert, ed. 1975. *Letters of John Keats*. Oxford.
Gurr, Andrew. 2011. *The Shakespeare Company, 1594–1642*. Cambridge.
Kermode, Frank. 2003. *Pieces of my Mind: Writings 1958–2002*. London.
Kimbell, David R. B. 1981. *Verdi in the Age of Italian Romanticism*. Cambridge.
———— 2002. *Italian Opera*. Cambridge.
Marvin, Roberta Montemorra. 2011. "Verdi and Shakespeare". *Macbeth*. Royal Opera House programme.
Osborne, Charles, ed. 1971. *Letters of Giuseppe Verdi*. London.
Phillips-Matz, Mary Jane. 1993. *Verdi: A Biography*. Oxford.
———— 2011. "*Macbeth*: the composer as artist". *Macbeth*. Royal Opera House programme.
Shakespeare, William. 1997. *The Riverside Shakespeare*, 2nd edition, ed. by G. B. Evans and J. J. M. Tobin. Boston.
Weaver, William, and Martin Chusid, eds. 1979. *The Verdi Companion*. New York.
Wells, Stanley. 2012. *Blogging Shakespeare*. http://bloggingshakespeare.com/year-of-shakespeare-verdis-otello, accessed June 2014.
Woudhuysen, H. R., ed. 1989. *Samuel Johnson on Shakespeare*. London.

10 Eleonora Duse as Juliet and Cleopatra

Anna Sica

From her debut as Juliet in 1872 onwards, the career of Eleonora Duse (1858–1924) is marked by an evolving, changeable approach to her Shakespearean roles. In different ways and under diverse circumstances, each of her Shakespearean parts represented something of a turning-point in her cursus. Scholars have argued that life and art, emotional instinct and theatrical performance, coalesced seamlessly throughout her Shakespearean repertoire, and in particular in her interpretation of Cleopatra (Puppa 2009). Yet while this theory that she acted out her own personal life, and that her characters' feelings coincided with her own, is an attractive one, it is also reductive. New evidence—the discovery of her personal library, housed in Cambridge and now known as the *Murray Edwards Duse Collection* (MEDC)—and an appreciation of the declamatory theatrical code of *la drammatica* (Sica 2013) reveal Duse's intensely erudite work in preparing for these Shakespearean roles. The MEDC offers the clearest record that, first, her literary education began—or became active—around 1886; secondly, that it assumed an ideological character in the early 1890s; and, finally, that the development of her thinking informed her acting. So pronounced was her artistic and literary prowess that she was considered one of the foremost Italian aesthetes of her time, and the reconstruction of the MEDC has helped to reshape our understanding of her intellectual profile, shedding fresh light on the art of her acting (Sica 2012). The two principal subjects of analysis to be discussed in this chapter are, first, Duse's early mannerist medievalism, which can be traced to her performance of Juliet, and secondly her variegated, contradictory interpretation of Cleopatra, a cornerstone of her repertoire that led to her being immortalized as "absorbingly interesting" (Symons 1903: 55–56) and an "exquisitely sympathetic actress" (Shaw 1952: 38).

Duse's Shakespearean roles need to be understood in the context of the Italian acting method of the *drammatica*, as primarily theorized by Luigi Riccoboni (1676–1753) in the early eighteenth century, most famously in his 1728 treatise *Dell'arte rappresentativa* [*On the Art of the Rappresentativa* (=Acting, Performance)]. It is just as important to recognise that the Italian actors, and Duse specifically, used the *drammatica*

152   *Anna Sica*

when enacting tragic Shakespearean roles as it is to register the different translations of Shakespeare's tragedies into Italian, translations that were themselves often heavily influenced by the *drammatica*'s principles and rules. By the nineteenth century, Gustavo Modena (1803–1861) and some of the members of the Reale Compagnia Sarda acting company had developed Riccoboni's principles and formulated a method that was known as the second period of the *rappresentativa*: it is datable to between 1821 and 1859, and, going once again by the name of *la drammatica*, designated a new style of acting. By 1870, Italian actors had promoted yet another revision of the *drammatica*, one that may be considered the final phase of the tradition. By the early decades of the twentieth century, the method had been completely deconstructed by the Italian academies of theatrical arts. In its *longue durée*, the *drammatica* was called, variously, "classical" (*la classica*) in the eighteenth century, "romantic" (*la romantica*) in the first half of the nineteenth century, and "neoclassical" (*la neoclassica*) in the second half of the century, in what might be considered an era of naturalism.

The "classical" method, also referred to as *l'antica rappresentativa* and theorized by Riccoboni, consisted of combining mime and declamation (Sica 2013), and dominated the period that saw the publication of Riccoboni's *Dell'arte rappresentativa* and the establishment of the first Italian theatre company (the aforementioned Reale Compagnia Sarda) in 1821. The "romantic" method has been branded a *novo stile* or *nuova rappresentativa* or *drammatica* (Sica 2013), and a departure from its predecessor: the classical style was reinvented, transformed by Gustavo Modena into the romantic style, in such a way as to prioritize tone, voice pitch, and rhythmical delivery. From the evidence of the prompt-books used by the actors and actresses who most clearly represented the three different styles of the *drammatica*, the "classical" style embraced by Adelaide Ristori (1822–1906) was "shouted" or declaimed, the "romantic" style by Tommaso Salvini (1829–1915) was delivered in a more rhythmical way, and the "neoclassical" style of Eleonora Duse privileged a yet more clearly modulated kind of acting. Duse's acting did not boast great volume or tonal range, nor did it suggest a rhythmical style; rather, it was consciously modulated, the result of combining a hexameter with a hendecasyllabic line. Using the metrical variance of hexameters and hendecasyllables as found in Giosuè Carducci's prosodically innovative *Odi barbare* (1873–93), a masterclass of varying line length and vocal modulation, Duse managed to give the impression of acting out real life, although her performances were always carefully orchestrated and governed by rules of artifice. Evidence for this conscientious strategy in her performances is to be found in the declamatory, elocutionary symbols inscribed in her Shakespearean prompt-books, as well as in her prompt-books for other authors (including Gabriele D'Annunzio's 1896 *La città morta* [*The Dead City*] and Tommaso Gallarati Scotti's 1922 *Così sia* [*So Be It*]).

Eleonora Duse as Juliet and Cleopatra   153

Close attention to this acting code of the *drammatica* reveals the crucial role played by the declamatory master Gaetano Gattinelli (1806–1886) in reinvigorating Duse's Shakespearean roles. Gattinelli, who had played in the Reale Compagnia Sarda (which was dismantled in 1859, just before the unification of Italy), became Duse's elocution teacher in 1883–1884, and from 1870 onwards was the director of the theatrical academy in Florence (Reale Accademia de' Fidenti), which was later renamed Reale Accademia di Recitazione and run by Luigi Rasi. In 1850, he produced one of the foundational treatises on the *drammatica*, namely *Dell'arte rappresentativa in Italia: Studi riformativi* [*On the Art of the* Rappresentativa *in Italy: Studies towards Reform*], in which he also gave attention to the role played by patriotic sentiment in the method (Sica 2013; Antona-Traversi 1926; Fusero 1971). New elements, such as broken speech or modulation of tone and voice, were incorporated into Duse's acting, and beyond that into the nineteenth-century Italian acting tradition more widely, through the influence of the *drammatica*, with crucial consequences for the nineteenth-century reception of Shakespeare (Carlson 1985). Major actors who performed in Shakespeare's plays included Adelaide Ristori, Ernesto Rossi (1827–1896), and Tommaso Salvini, the last of whom debuted in 1875 as Hamlet and Othello at the Drury Lane Theatre in London. During his tour of England, Salvini probably drew upon a less rhythmical brand of declamation that enabled him to transform the characters of Hamlet and Othello into two inwardly-suffering men, rather than extravagantly "sensual and violent tigers" (Fortis 1878). Having seen Henry Irving (1838–1905) in the role of Hamlet at the Lyceum, and judging his acting to be baroque and mannerist, especially in scenes that required more vehemence and emotional reach, Salvini worked on reducing the force, tone, and grade of his own voice. In a few cases, Salvini's prompt-book of *Amleto* (1860) retains the same metre as the original, and his notations correspond at times exactly to the equivalent accentuation of the original text, suggesting some degree of close correspondence between the phrasing and accentuation of Shakespeare's English and Salvini's Italian. The following is from Salvini's prompt-book of *Amleto* (from 1.2), the opening performance of which took place in 1860 at the Teatro dei Fiorentini in Naples:

AMLETO   *Ascolta, ascolta, Se tuo padre amasti*
[HAMLET   O list, o list, if thou didst ever thy dear father love]

The "S" of "*Se*" appears in bold in Salvini's prompt-book, a conventional device used in the early nineteenth century to mark out syllables for particular accentuation. This common phonetic practice adopted by nineteenth-century Italian actors enabled them to communicate with international audiences in Paris, Berlin, Moscow, London, Australia, and the Americas, even as they recited their lines in Italian. In this tradition,

154 *Anna Sica*

we need to place Duse's Shakespearean roles, heavily steeped in the distinctive intonations and gestures of the *drammatica*, in order to understand her "glorious and unique intuition" (Stanislavsky 1924), especially notable in her performances of Juliet and Cleopatra.

An Ageless Juliet

When Duse first performed the role of Juliet in her formative years, she was a teenager like Shakespeare's character herself (Signorelli 1955). The date was 1872, and she appeared with the young Carlo Rosaspina (1854–1929), five years her junior, as Romeo, both of them hailing from renowned acting families. Carlo was the son of Cesare Rosaspina, whose repertory company merged with that of Duse's father Alessandro. The two young actors performed an Italian version of Shakespeare's play, translated and adapted by the Veronese librettist Giuseppe Daldò (Cuppone 2009). A year later, Duse once again performed the role of Juliet with Libero Pilotto (1824–1900) as Romeo. D'Annunzio (1863–1938), in his autobiographical novel *Il fuoco* [*The Flame*] (1900), memorably portrays Duse's debut in the role of Juliet. He recounts what the actress herself had told him: in the early afternoon of the day she was to perform, the young Duse took a long walk; in the Piazza delle Erbe, she bought a bunch of roses, later used as a prop in her interpretation of the role. D'Annunzio's Duse recollects that she

> entered Verona one evening in the month of May through the gate of the Palio. Anxiety suffocated me. I held the copy-book, where I had copied out the part of Juliet with my own hand, tightly against my heart, and constantly repeated to myself the words of my first entrance: "How now! Who calls? I am here. What is your will?" A strange coincidence had excited my imagination: I was fourteen years old on that very day,—the age of Juliet! [...] One Sunday in May, in the immense arena in the ancient amphitheatre under the open sky, I have been Juliet before a popular multitude that had breathed in the legend of love and death. [...] I had bought a great bunch of roses with my little savings, in the Piazza delle Erbe, under the fountain of Madonna Verona. The roses were my only ornament. I mingled them with my words, with my gesture, with each attitude of mine. I let one fall at the feet of Romeo when we first met; I strewed the leaves of another on his head from the balcony; and I covered his body with the whole of them in the tomb. The air, the light, and their perfume ravished me.
>
> (D'Annunzio 1914: 319–21)

Approximately twenty years later, Olga Signorelli reported that, at the Theatre Malij, the opening performance of *Romeo and Juliet* on 22 April 1891 astonished its Russian audience (see Figure 10.1).

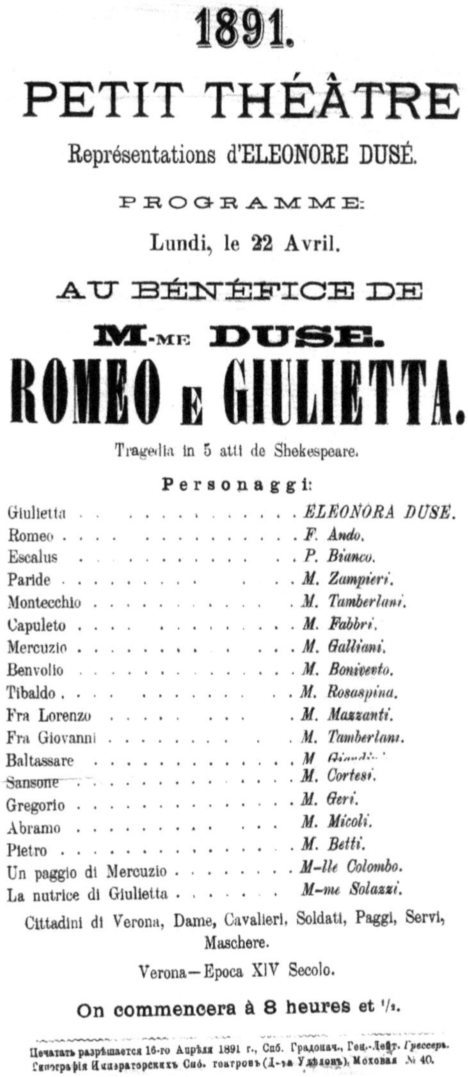

1891.
PETIT THÉÂTRE

Représentations d'ELEONORE DUSÉ.

PROGRAMME:

Lundi, le 22 Avril.

AU BÉNÉFICE DE
M-ᴍᴇ DUSE.
ROMEO ᴇ GIULIETTA.

Tragedia in 5 atti de Shekespeare.

Personaggi:

Giulietta	*ELEONORA DUSE.*
Romeo	*F. Ando.*
Escalus	*P. Bianco.*
Paride	*M. Zampieri.*
Montecchio	*M. Tamberlani.*
Capuleto	*M. Fabbri.*
Mercuzio	*M. Galliani.*
Benvolio	*M. Bonivento.*
Tibaldo	*M. Rosaspina.*
Fra Lorenzo	*M. Mazzanti.*
Fra Giovanni	*M. Tamberlani.*
Baltassare	*M. Giandi...*
Sansone	*M. Cortesi.*
Gregorio	*M. Geri.*
Abramo	*M. Micoli.*
Pietro	*M. Betti.*
Un paggio di Mercuzio	*M-lle Colombo.*
La nutrice di Giulietta	*M-me Solazzi.*

Cittadini di Verona, Dame, Cavalieri, Soldati, Paggi, Servi, Maschere.

Verona—Epoca XIV Secolo.

On commencera à 8 heures et ½.

Печатать разрѣшается 16-го Апрѣля 1891 г., Спб. Градонач., Ген.-Лейт. Грессеръ. Типографія Импараторскихъ Спб. театровъ (Д-за Ухвъловъ), Моховая № 40.

Figure 10.1 Eleonora Duse's St Petersburg production of *Romeo and Juliet*, 1891. Courtesy of the Giorgio Cini Foundation, Venice.

Duse still looked like a teenager, as she had that evening in Verona: though she did not have a childish face, her movements, gestures, and the roses had an unforgettable power; she moved with surprise as a teenager does.

Sophie Clary Und Aldringen (2009) has traced how the painter Alexandre Volkoff (1844–1928) acquainted Duse with mannerist compositional

156 Anna Sica

tensions when she was preparing the role of Juliet for her Russian tour in the early 1890s. Duse shared Volkoff's views and, having committed to adopting a medieval style, managed to transpose Juliet into an ageless icon. In so doing, she moulded herself, a woman now over thirty years old, into the guise of the young Juliet. Volkoff argued against characters dictating the terms of presentation, contending instead that stage appearances should be guided by the actress' features and physiognomy. The painter's suggestion was for her to wear a gown in a colour that suited her—a dress of the same hue as her under-dress, insisting that, if she were to select a shade of sky-blue, she should find the exact shade among the fifty or so variations available to her. In the end, rather than blue, they collectively decided on a yellowish-brown colour in their efforts to invoke a medieval aura (Clary Und Aldringen 2009: 23–28).

Giovanni Pontiero records that Volkoff urged Duse for some time "to spread her wings and conquer new audiences" (Pontiero 1986: 88), and that Volkoff himself set about investigating the possibility of obtaining engagements for the actress in his native Russia. Duse debuted at the Theatre Korš in Moscow, appearing elsewhere at the Theatre Malij in St Petersburg, the Theatre Dramatičeskij in Kharkov, the Theatre Setov in Kiev, and the Theatre Ruskij in Odessa. On 13 March 1891, she opened in St Petersburg as Margherita Gautier in *La dame aux camélias*. It was at this point that, according to Pontiero, Alexey Suvorin wrote in *Novoie Vremya* that Duse had, unexpectedly, overtaken her rival Sarah Bernhardt, displaying extraordinary accomplishment in combining gesture and voice, and that he had never seen such an authentic Margherita before. Yet Duse's real triumph came in her interpretation of the Shakespearean roles of Juliet and Cleopatra. The Russian tour was so successful that the most renowned Russian critics, writers, and artists of the time testified to the unrivalled performances of this great Italian tragedienne. Anton Chekhov wrote to his sister on 16 March of that year, expressing his plaudits for the actress:

> I have just seen the Italian actress Duse in Shakespeare's *Cleopatra*. I don't know Italian, but she acted so well that it seemed to me I understood every word. A remarkable actress! I have never seen anything like it before.
>
> (Chekhov 1920: 233–34)

The playwright was so inspired by Duse's acting that he praised her in his 1896 masterpiece *The Seagull* (Act 1, Scene 2), and other admirers of her acting would include Stanislavsky, who was moved by Duse's example to lay down rules for training his actors to reach the kind of spontaneity that the Italian actress displayed on stage. As recorded in his *My Life in Art*, first published in 1924, Stanislavsky confessed that he was in debt to Duse for the acting system that he formed, whose aim was

Eleonora Duse as Juliet and Cleopatra   157

to match her spontaneous methods. Stanislavsky was most profoundly attracted by her air of simplicity on the stage. The same was true of Suvorin, who noted the unaffectedness of the actress but at the same time remarked that every gesture of hers was precisely delineated, and every vocal inflection articulated with such perfection that a sense of complete harmony was established between the character's inner soul and Duse's outer appearance and gestures.

Nevertheless, Duse's acting was not simply the product of a natural, instinctive approach or attitude, as has often been assumed. The Italian philosopher Benedetto Croce (1866–1952) noted that the aesthetes of the journal *Convito*, a key agent promoting a new decadent taste and an English brand of aestheticism in the last years of the nineteenth century (1895–96), under the auspices of Gabriele D'Annunzio, were heavily indebted to Duse's art (Croce 1973). In addition, Croce remarked that, from the aesthetes' circle, it was she who was most acquainted with the contemporary artistic, philosophical, and literary environment, and she who was best-positioned to embody the philosophical and literary Italian programme christened by Croce himself as *Il programma della pura bellezza* [*The Programme of Pure Beauty*] (Sica 2010). Croce's opinion that Duse had a remarkable intellectual profile before she began her relationship with D'Annunzio is reflected in what remains of her personal library and in what Volkoff's letters reveal. It seems that Duse's early introduction to Volkoff's mannerism enabled her to emancipate herself completely from naturalistic concepts and move along the pathway of neoclassicism and pre-Raphaelite art. Later, James Huneker (1910) would number Duse and D'Annunzio among the iconoclasts. Yet the roots of Duse's medieval style are readily identifiable in her reworking of an ageless Juliet.

A Wagnerian Cleopatra

Arrigo Boito (1842–1918) exerts sizable influence over Duse's Shakespearean reworkings. This indebtedness, related in part to the clandestine affair they conducted between 1887 and 1894, becomes clear when exploring the Duse collection in Cambridge. The holding includes a set of works that I have named "Cleopatra's Books", and I have identified some others belonging to this grouping from the Duse Collection in the Actresses' House Library in Rome, and yet more in the Asolo Arch House Duse Collection (Sica 2012). Specifically, they reveal the roots of her much-discussed role of Cleopatra. According to Pontiero, she first performed the role on 22 November 1888 at the Teatro Manzoni in Milan. The play was produced by the repertory company run by Duse herself, La Drammatica Compagnia della Città di Roma.

"Cleopatra's Books" reveal how Boito managed to create a kind of Italian theatrical, literary environment in his translation of *Antony and*

158 *Anna Sica*

Cleopatra. A number of Italian works about the Egyptian queen influenced him more than Shakespeare's tragedy, including Giraldi Cinthio's *Cleopatra* (1583), Giovanni Delfino's *La Cleopatra* (1660), and Vittorio Alfieri's *Antonio e Cleopatra* (1774). It is evident that Duse was helped by Boito's translation when it came to piecing together Cleopatra's historical profile. Moulded by Boito, the actress subtly implied in her portrait of Cleopatra that nationalist feelings held sway over the suicide of a woman who had been betrayed and humiliated: D'Annunzio labelled Duse a "Wagnerian" artist (D'Annunzio 1914: 201), one who both embodied the figure of a national heroine and forged a distinctive, neoclassical brand of the *drammatica*. Clearly, Duse did not overlook the historical context in which the two lovers lived, but undoubtedly went to great lengths to construct an archetypal Cleopatra at the same time. And Boito, who in part aimed to reproduce philological equivalents to Shakespeare's language, offered Duse a refurbished play for the Italian stage (Sica 2010), one downplaying Antony's presence so as to accord greater prominence to Cleopatra, and of course Duse herself. He had met the young Duse in Milan in May 1884 (Nardi 1942), during which time she was working with Cesare Rossi's repertory company and had started attending *drammatica* classes given by Gaetano Gattinelli. She had separated from her husband, the actor Tebaldo Checchi, and had given birth to their daughter Enrichetta Angelica in 1882. This was the time that she herself considered an "[é]poque si fine de ma vie" [such a delicate time in my life] (Sica 2012). Her love affair with Boito began later, in 1887, the same year Boito produced his translation of *Antony and Cleopatra* and his libretto for Verdi's *Otello*. Boito had already written the libretto *Amleto* (1860) for the composer Franco Faccio, and in 1892, probably almost simultaneously, he both wrote the libretto for *Falstaff* and prepared his translation of *Macbeth* for his beloved actress. Dante and Shakespeare greatly inspired Boito's literary landscape, and he helped to school Duse in a more mature, erudite familiarisation with Shakespeare's plays.

Traces of Duse's annotations are still legible in "Cleopatra's Books", as are her declamatory symbols for the neoclassical *drammatica* in her prompt-book for Shakespeare's tragedy. Duse's prompt-books for *Antony and Cleopatra* (1888), *Macbeth* (1892–93), and *Adriana Lecouvreur* (1898), all part of the Sister Mary Mark bequest, are housed at the Giorgio Cini Foundation, Venice, and each retains traces of Duse's annotations. Some of these annotations shed light on why the actress was much criticized for her interpretation of the Egyptian queen. William Archer (1894), who otherwise enthusiastically applauded Duse's acting, expressed his disapproval of her Cleopatra, lamenting the depiction of the queen as a woman and heroine rather than a lover, and concluded that her version was not Shakespeare's. What Duse had found in Boito's translation was a queen with a powerful sense of nationalism—a

Eleonora Duse as Juliet and Cleopatra   159

nationalism that spoke, in many ways, to prevailing nineteenth-century Italian ideologies and philosophies. The critic Addison McLeod (1912) pointed out that Duse was considered to be ultra-modern in the role of Cleopatra. Repeatedly, he affirmed that modern music, drama, and the decorative arts could be tested against the touchstone of novelty and perfection offered by Duse. He reported the observation of the Italian critic Giulio Piccini (writing under the pseudonym Jarro) about her persistent, arguably excessive, tendency in the part of Cleopatra to break up her sentences with pauses or breathing points—pauses that were, Jarro observed, introduced by her in order to disrupt her phrasing (McLeod 1912). Duse's Shakespearean roles were undoubtedly much inspired by Boito's literary and political environment. But further evidence proves that the role of Cleopatra should rightfully be considered a watershed in Duse's career because it casts light on how she applied the declamatory code-system of Italian acting to new ends. Duse's *Antony and Cleopatra* is one of the earliest plays that was prepared by the actress according to the rules of the *drammatica* which she had been taught by Gattinelli. He, like most of the actors and actresses of the Reale Compagnia Sarda (1821–1855) (Costetti 1893), had learned the romantic style of the *drammatica* from the actor Gustavo Modena. Gattinelli improved on Modena's principles by reforming the romantic style, and Duse—one of the last of Gattinelli's disciples—improved on and remade the neoclassical style in turn.

Proof of the young Duse's emancipation from a romantic style is to be found in her portrayal of Cleopatra. Her prompt-books for Cleopatra, preserved at the Giorgio Cini Foundation in Venice, are crucial to understanding how she developed her application of annotative symbols and how she was instrumental in renovating a romantic style into a neoclassical one. For the role of Cleopatra, Duse pointedly did *not* use notations to mark the accentuation of vowels, a declamatory norm that Italian actors generally adopted when reciting foreign plays in their own language. Normally, Duse followed this system when preparing her French roles, as she did in Eugène Scribe and Ernest Legouvé's *Adriana Lecouvreur* (for which she debuted in the role of Adriana in 1893), as revealed by her 1898 prompt-book showing declamatory symbols for emphasis, double emphasis, and vocal complexion. This annotative system for nuancing vocal complexion in the tradition of the *drammatica* is designed to draw out a character's inner emotions. The reason why, in the case of her Cleopatra, Duse did not use the vocal system seems to have its roots in the nature of Boito's prosody, based on an Italian stylistic tradition rather than on Shakespeare's verse line. This discrepancy perhaps explains some of Archer's criticism of a Cleopatra who showed a different kind of emotion from the Shakespearean Cleopatra with which he was familiar, even though Duse's Cleopatra had been a noted triumph in Moscow (see Figure 10.2).

Figure 10.2 Eleonora Duse in the role of Cleopatra at the Malij Teatr, St Petersburg (1891). Courtesy of the Giorgio Cini Foundation, Venice.

In the early 1920s, Duse was planning to come back to the role of Cleopatra for *une seule soirée* [one night only], as the actress herself noted on the front page of a letter assumed to be dated to between 1921 and 1922 (and which now forms part of the Sister Mary Mark Bequest at the Giorgio Cini Foundation, Venice). Duse did not intend to stage the play in its entirety, but to present excerpts, drawing on previous productions: her purpose, to judge from the surviving evidence, was to group together those scenes in which Boito's Cleopatra was represented as a distinctly tragic heroine. In a letter (see Figure 10.3) referring to one of her Shakespearean prompt-books housed in Asolo, she lists these

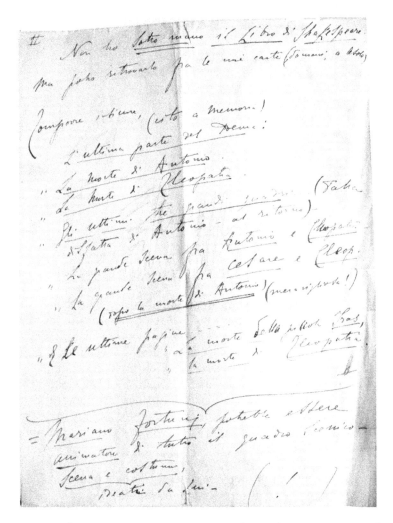

Figure 10.3 Eleonora Duse's note on scenes involving Cleopatra (*c.* 1921). Photo by Anna Sica. Courtesy of the Giorgio Cini Foundation, Venice.]

final scenes from *Antony and Cleopatra*, noting that they would be well served by the attentions of Mariano Fortuny, the Spanish fashion designer who lived in Venice and who created dresses for Duse's roles in D'Annunzio and Ibsen:

Non ho <u>sotto mano</u> <u>il Libro di Shakespeare</u>
ma posso ritrovarlo fra le mie carte (domani, a Asolo)
Comporre insieme,
                    (cito a memoria)

162　*Anna Sica*

L'ultima parte del Poema:
"La morte di Antonio.
"La morte di Cleopatra.
"Gli ultimi tre grandi quadri ... (dalla
disfatta di Antonio—al ritorno [da Azio])—
"La grande scena fra Antonio e Cleopatra—
"La grande scena fra Cesare e Cleop.
　　　(dopo la morte di Antonio) (meravigliosa!)
"E le ultime pagine ...
　　　"La morte della piccola Iras,
　　　"la morte di Cleopatra.

Mariano Fortuny, potrebbe essere
animatore di tutto il quadro scenico—
scena e costumi,
　　　creati da lui (!)
　　　　　(Letter, *c.* 1921, Sister Mary Mark Bequest, Giorgio Cini
　　　　　　　　　　　　　　　　Foundation, Venice)

[I do not have the Shakespeare prompt-book to hand but I can find
it among my papers (tomorrow, in Asolo). Let's try to put together
(I'm quoting [my prompt-book] from memory) the final scenes of the
poem: "Antony's death". "Cleopatra's death". "The final three great
scenes ... (from Antony's defeat—to the return [from Actium])"—"The
great scene between Antony and Cleopatra"—"The great scene between Caesar and Cleop., after Antony's death (wonderful!)". "And
the final pages ... 'The death of the young Iras'. 'Cleopatra's death'".
Mariano Fortuny could oversee all the scenography—sets and costumes, created by him(!)]

In this letter, whose addressee remains frustratingly indecipherable (the
likeliest recipient being Ettore Mazzanti, the director of Duse's company), Duse seems to have listed these scenes from the end of the play
with considerable care and precision, presumably because they allowed
her to bring out a more fully nationalist dimension in her portrayal of
the Egyptian queen's final moments—a queen finally closer in conception to Boito's Cleopatra than Shakespeare's.

Other Shakespearean Roles

The last Shakespearean work that Boito translated for Duse was *Macbeth*, but she never staged the play. Her prompt-book for *Macbeth*,
which is housed in the Giorgio Cini Foundation, is in Boito's handwrit-
ing and includes some declamatory symbols. In particular, there are

Eleonora Duse as Juliet and Cleopatra   163

some annotations for emphasis and double emphasis relating to Lady Macbeth's entrance. This system of declamatory emphasis was also used by Adelaide Ristori, and it is surprising to find it applied here to the role of Lady Macbeth because the symbols for emphasis and double emphasis imply that the intonation should be volubly projected rather than delivered in a more naturally rhythmic way. Ristori, a leading exponent of the classical style of the *drammatica*, had met with great success in Europe, and particularly in England, as Lady Macbeth (Carlson 1985). Duse may well have avoided a role already championed by Ristori, and there is further evidence for Duse's resistance to taking on the part of Lady Macbeth: Ristori's acting was closer to the declamatory intonation of the classical style than the modulated tone and volume of the neo-classical style; and, moreover, Duse's annotative symbols in her prompt-book of *Macbeth* suggest that she envisaged a Lady Macbeth who could only be presented in the classical style of the *drammatica* (a mode closely associated with Ristori), a stilted, declamatory rendition of the part that would not have accorded with her own characteristic methods.

In the 1878–79 season, Duse also acted as Ophelia and Desdemona for Giacinta Pezzana's repertory company (1841–1919) at the Teatro dei Fiorentini in Naples, reprising the part of Desdemona once more in 1887 (Vecchioni 1975). Describing her rendition of Ophelia, Giuseppe Napoleone Primoli wrote:

> Pour jouer les rôles de force, la Duse [n]'abandonna pas les rôles de grâce et, avant de quitter Naples, elle apparaît encore dans Ophélie. Ce ne fut pas ici comme dans Electre et, pour se trouver dans la verité, elle n'eut qu'à s'abandonner au flot shakespearien, comme le corps de l'amante d'Hamlet s'abandonner au torrent qui l'emporte à la mer. La Duse eut la joie de se sentir comprise: un article surtout qui lui tomba sous les yeux lui alla au cœur. Au lieu des banals coups d'encensoir ou des perfides louanges à deux tranchants, il se terminent par ces simples mots: "Elle fut Ophélie".
>
> (Primoli 1897: 491)

[For all her playing of strong characters, Duse did not relinquish graceful roles, and, before leaving Naples, she appeared once again in the role of Ophelia. This time, things did not go as they had with Electra and, in order to embody the truth of the character, she had only to surrender to the Shakespearean flow, just as the body of Hamlet's lover surrenders to the current that carries her to the sea. Duse experienced the joy of feeling herself understood: a particular article that she came to see touched her deeply. Instead of banal flattery or perfidiously double-edged praise, the review concluded by stating simply that "She was Ophelia".]

164   *Anna Sica*

This kind of account gets to the heart of Duse's method. Her complex acting code seems to have eluded Archer, who failed to perceive that Duse's spontaneity, immediacy, and authenticity on stage were not the result of an intuitive approach but rather the outcome of the skillful, careful, and deliberate calibration of vocal emphasis, depth, and tone—in short, the modulated intonation of the neoclassical style of the *drammatica*, a system enabling Duse to inject fresh life into Shakespeare's heroines, both eponymous females like Juliet and Cleopatra, and those unnamed in the titles of their respective tragedies like Desdemona and Ophelia.

Bibliography

Antona-Traversi, Camillo. 1926. *Eleonora Duse*. Pisa.

Archer, William. 1894. "Eleonora Duse". *The Theatrical "World" 1893*. London. 144–155.

Calderon, George, ed. 1912. *Two Plays of Tchekhof: The Seagull, The Cherry Orchard*. London.

Camilli, Lorenzo. 1835. *Istituzioni sulla Rappresentativa fondate ne' classici autori antichi e moderni e ridotte a sistema teorico-pratico universale*. Aquila.

Carlson, Marvin. 1985. *The Italian Shakespearians: Performances by Ristori, Salvini and Rossi in England and America*. Washington.

Chekhov, Anton. 1920. *Letters of Anton Tchehov to his Family and Friends*, trans. by Constance Garnett. New York.

Clary Und Aldringen, Sophie. 2009. *Eleonora Duse—Briefe als kulturhistorische Quelle*. Unpublished Thesis. University of Vienna.

Costetti, Giuseppe. 1893. *La compagnia reale Sarda e il teatro italiano dal 1821 al 1855*. Milan.

Croce, Benedetto. 1973. "Adolfo De Bosis (1911)". *La Letteratura della nuova Italia*, 6 vols. Bari. 4: 133–147.

Cuppone, Roberto. 2009. "'Io fui Giulietta'. La prima volta di Eleonora". *Voci e Anime, Corpi e Scritture*. Rome, ed. by Maria Ida Biggi and Paolo Puppa. Rome. 21–38.

D'Annunzio, Gabriele. 1914. *The Flame of Life* [*Il fuoco*, 1900], trans. by Kassandra Vivaria. Boston.

Delgado, Maria M. 2015. "Margarita Xirgu". *The Cambridge Encyclopedia of Stage Actors and Acting*, ed. by Simon Williams. Cambridge. 628–29.

Fortis, Leone. 1878. "Conversazione". *Illustrazione Italiana*, 5.6, 10: 82–86.

Fusero, Clemente. 1971. *Eleonora Duse*. Milan.

Gattinelli, Gaetano. 1850. *Dell'arte rappresentativa in Italia: Studi riformativi: onde richiamare il teatro drammatico al primitivo suo scopo di educare il popolo*. Turin.

——— 1879. *Dell'arte rappresentativa. Manuale ad uso degli studiosi della drammatica e del canto*. Rome.

Huneker, James. 1910. "Duse and D'Annunzio". *Iconoclasts: A Book of Dramatists*. New York. 343–48.

McLeod, Addison. 1912. *Plays and Players in Modern Italy*. London. 176–177.

Nardi, Piero. 1942. *Vita di Arrigo Boito*. Milan.

Eleonora Duse as Juliet and Cleopatra 165

Pontiero, Giovanni. 1986. *Eleonora Duse: In Art and Life*. Frankfurt am Main.
Primoli, Giuseppe. 1897. "La Duse". *La revue de Paris*. Verona. 491.
Puppa, Paolo. 2009. "La Cleopatra di Eleonora". *Voci e Anime, Corpi e Scrit-*
ture, ed. by Maria Ida Biggi and Paolo Puppa. Rome. 279–300.
Riccoboni, Luigi. 1820–29. *Dell'arte rappresentativa* [1728]. *Lettere intorno*
alla mimica (*Ideen zur einer Mimik*), ed. by Johann Jacob Engel with Giovanni
Rasori, 2 vols. Milan.
Shaw, George Bernard. 1952. "Duse and Bernhardt". *Plays and Players: Essays*
on the Theatre, ed. by Alfred Charles Ward. Oxford. 33–41.
Sheehy, Helen. 2003. *Eleonora Duse: A Biography*. New York.
Sica, Anna. 2009. "Eleonora Duse tragica Sapiente". *Voci e Anime, Corpi e*
Scritture, ed. by Maria Ida Bigi and Paolo Puppa. Rome. 389–403.
——— 2010. "Eleonora Duse's Library: The Disclosure of Aesthetic Value in
Real Acting". *Nineteenth Century Theatre and Film*, 37.2: 66–85.
——— 2013. *La drammatica metodo italiano: trattati normativi e trattati te-*
orici. Milan.
——— 2014. "La drammatica". *The Italian Method of La Drammatica: Its*
Legacy and Reception, ed. by Anna Sica. Milan. 19–54.
——— and Alison Wilson. 2012. *The Murray Edwards Duse Collection*. Milan.
Signorelli, Olga. 1955 [1938]. *Eleonora Duse*. Rome.
Stanislavsky, Constantin. 1980 [1924]. *My Life in Art*. London.
Symons, Arthur. 1903. "Duse in some of her Parts". *Plays, Acting, and Music*.
London. 55–56.
Vecchioni, Mario. 1975. *Eleonora Duse*. Pescara.

11 Representations of Italy in the First Hebrew Translations of Shakespeare

Lily Kahn

The first Hebrew translations of complete Shakespeare plays appeared in Central and Eastern Europe in the final quarter of the nineteenth century, although Jewish authors had expressed admiration for the English playwright as far back as the first few decades of the Haskalah (Jewish Enlightenment) in the late 1700s and early 1800s (Almagor 1975; Toury 2012: 145–7, 171–2). This small group of six late nineteenth-century translations was produced by adherents of the Haskalah and comprised part of a singular drive to establish a modern European literature in Hebrew imbued with Jewish national consciousness (Patterson 1964: 1988; Abramson and Parfitt 1985; and Pelli 2006). The authors' selection of Hebrew as the vehicle of this new literary enterprise was a highly conscious and ideologically motivated decision, given that in the eighteenth and nineteenth centuries the language was almost solely a written rather than a spoken medium, just on the cusp of its large-scale revernacularization in Palestine at the end of the nineteenth and early twentieth centuries (Harshav 1993: 81–180, and Sáenz-Badillos 1993: 267–72). As such, the translated plays were intended primarily for private reading rather than performance; indeed, there was no established Hebrew-language theatre at the time, the first organized attempts at such an initiative emerging only in 1909 (Zer-Zion 2010). Five of the six Hebrew renditions that appeared during this period (including the three to be examined in this chapter) were translated directly from the English, though it is not known which editions of Shakespeare were employed in these endeavours.

As part of this intensely ideological endeavour, Maskilic (Jewish Enlightenment) writers typically employed a highly domesticating translation strategy with the aim of producing target texts reflecting Jewish culture. This translatorial philosophy was not a new development, but one rooted in a long tradition of dechristianizing and Judaizing Hebrew adaptations of European literary works dating back to the medieval and early modern periods, including the thirteenth-century Hebrew version of the legend of King Arthur (see Leviant 2003; Rovang 2009; Valles 2013: 38–76), the *Bovo-bukh*, a sixteenth-century Yiddish adaptation of the English romance *Bevis of Hampton* via its Italian version *Buovo*

Representations of Italy   167

d'Antona (Shmeruk 1988: 150–52; Baumgarten 2005: 176–77, 183–84; Valles 2013: 152–209), and Sephardic Jewish versions of Spanish ballads (Armistead and Silverman 1965). This domesticating approach manifests itself in many areas of the Hebrew Shakespeare translations, with common techniques including the deletion or Judaization of references to Christianity and classical mythology, the insertion of biblical fragments into the target text, the addition of Jewish religious and cultural elements, and the Hebraization of Latin and French linguistic features appearing in the source text (Kahn 2017 and Forthcoming (a) and (b)).

A particularly fascinating aspect of the Maskilic Shakespeare translators' approach concerns their treatment of Italy. Of the six plays translated into Hebrew in the late nineteenth century, three have a wholly or partially Italian setting: Isaac Eduard Salkinson's איתיאל *iti'el* (*Othello*, 1874) and רם ויעל *ram veya'el* (*Romeo and Juliet*, 1878) and Jacob Elkind's מוסר סוררה *musar sorera* (*The Taming of the Shrew*, 1892). The translators' selection of these particular plays as opposed to other well-known Shakespearean works set in Italy such as *The Merchant of Venice* or *Much Ado about Nothing* is unclear. While the perceived anti-Jewish subject matter of *The Merchant of Venice* may have been a factor in their avoidance of that play, Maskilic authors did not shy away from it entirely: Hebrew translations of various small fragments of the work, including Shylock's "I am a Jew" set-piece, appeared during the last quarter of the nineteenth century (Almagor 1975: 739). In the case of *Othello*, *Romeo and Juliet*, and *The Taming of the Shrew*, the translators' familiarity with the rich cultural legacy of Jewish Italy merged with their domesticating tendencies to shape the translations in remarkable ways, as explored in detail in this chapter.

The Jews' relationship with Italy is a long and vibrant one dating back to the first groups of Judean captives brought to Rome, traceable to as early as the first century BCE (Noy 2000: 47). Jewish communities spread throughout the south of the country over the course of the next thousand years, leading to the emergence of a thriving cultural life by the end of the millennium that took the form of Talmudic academies as well as significant literary and scholarly activity which continued to flourish over the medieval period (Milano et al. 2007: 798–99). These communities produced major works on subjects ranging from Jewish philosophy and biblical commentary to science and medicine, some of which continued to be studied by Jews throughout Europe until the modern period; prominent examples include *Josippon*, a popular tenth-century adaptation of Josephus' *Jewish War*; the *Arukh*, an eleventh-century lexicon of the Talmud and midrashim composed by Nathan ben Jehiel of Rome; and the writings of the tenth-century physician Shabbetai Donnolo. Over the subsequent centuries, significant Jewish settlements were established in the central and northern parts of the country as well. Italian Jews continued to produce significant literary and scholarly contributions in the late

168   *Lily Kahn*

medieval period; noteworthy examples include Obadiah of Bertinoro (*c.* 1450–*c.*1516), author of the standard commentary on the Mishnah; Elijah Levitas (1468/69–1549), a grammarian, lexicographer, and author of the previously mentioned Yiddish adaptation *Bovo-bukh*; and the extremely prominent biblical exegetes Isaac Abarbanel (1437–1508) and Obadiah Sforno (*c.* 1470–*c.* 1550). By this period there were important Jewish centres in the major locations mentioned in *Othello*, *Romeo and Juliet*, and *The Taming of the Shrew*—Venice, Padua, Mantua, and Verona (Milano et al. 2007: 801).

Moreover, following the arrival of the printing press in Italy in the mid-fifteenth century, the country became the centre of Hebrew publishing in Europe, a position it retained until the eighteenth century (Zilberberg and Breger 2007: 531; Hacker and Shear 2011: 7–10). David Bomberg's printing house in Venice was a particularly prominent early hub of such activity, producing editions of the Hebrew Bible with commentaries, the Talmud, and numerous other essential Jewish texts (Nielsen 2011). As such, Italy played a key role in literary production and dissemination not only for local Jews, but also for their Central and Eastern European counterparts, as trade links between the Jewish communities in Italy and those in Germany and Poland-Lithuania ensured the widespread circulation of Hebrew books published in these Italian centres (Hacker and Shear 2011: 10).

This type of knowledge transfer continued into the eighteenth and nineteenth centuries, with the writings of Italian Jewish authors being widely circulated among their contemporaries in Central and Eastern Europe. Noteworthy examples of this trend include Moses Chaim Luzzatto (1707–46), a kabbalist from Padua whose ethical writings came to be held in extremely high esteem among Eastern European Jews (Dan and Hansel 2007: 284); Samuel Aaron Romanelli (1757–1817), a Maskilic author from Mantua who wrote poetry, drama, and a well-known travelogue and who lived in Vienna for several years (Klausner 1952–58: 1.307–19); Isaac Samuel Reggio (1784–1855), a rabbi from Gorizia who wrote widely on various aspects of Jewish religion (Klausner 1952–58: 4.10–37; Malkiel 2000: 276–303); and Samuel David Luzzatto (1800–65), a prominent biblical commentator, philosopher, translator, and philologist from Trieste (Tobias 2007).

Salkinson and Elkind were almost certainly familiar with this long-established Jewish presence and cultural productivity in Italy, given the prominence of medieval Italian-based exegetes and commentators such as Obadiah of Bertinoro, Isaac Abarbanel, and Obadiah Sforno, whom they would undoubtedly have studied in the course of a traditional Jewish education. Moreover, they are likely to have regarded Italy as a thriving centre of Hebrew literary production thanks to the activity of Maskilic and other eighteenth- and nineteenth-century authors and thinkers such as Romanelli, Reggio, and Luzzatto. This perception is corroborated by

Representations of Italy 169

their unusual translatorial approach to the Shakespearean source texts set in Venice, Verona, and Mantua: Salkinson's and Elkind's awareness of Italy as a Jewish space is reflected in their decision to preserve the Italian geographical labels appearing in the English originals while infusing their translations with domesticating cultural and linguistic elements, including the Hebraization of personal names, the removal of Christian references, and numerous allusions to Jewish religious and folk-cultural concepts. These techniques serve to transform Italy from the somewhat exotic foreign location of Shakespeare's source texts into an unmistakably Jewish realm that serves as a plausible setting for the thoroughly domesticated Hebrew target texts.

Maskilic translators systematically retain the Italian geographical labels appearing in the original plays, rather than replacing them with either biblical or Eastern-European locations. This practice contrasts starkly with the otherwise overwhelming tendency towards domestication seen throughout the translations. This seeming anomaly is likely rooted in the authors' aforementioned perception of Italy as the home of a long-established and distinguished Jewish population, with important communities in the locations mentioned in the plays, and as a centre of Jewish literary production. As such, this choice is likely not an exception to the translators' general domesticating principles, but rather an intentional decision to retain the original settings by transforming them into components of an obviously Jewish Italy. This practice of preserving Italian geographical designations (while Judaizing the names of the characters that inhabit them) can be seen by comparing the full title of the English *Othello* with the one that Salkinson gave to his translation:

*Othello, the Moor of **Venice***

איתיאל, הכושי מווינעציה

iti'el, hakkuši mivvineṣia [Ithiel, the Moor of **Venice**]

Similarly, both Salkinson and Elkind retain the other place names appearing in the source texts. Thus, Verona is the setting of *Romeo and Juliet* in both the English and Hebrew versions: "With all the admired beauties of **Verona**" (1.2.85) becomes "בֵּין בְּנוֹת וֵירוֹנָה הַיְּקָרוֹת" (*ben benot **verona** hayyeqarot* [Among the precious girls of **Verona**]) (Salkinson 1878: 20). Likewise, Padua remains the setting of the play-within-the-play in Elkind's version of *The Taming of the Shrew* although, notably, the framing story is set in "Sharon", the northern coastal plain of Israel, a decision that conforms with the tendency to employ romantic motifs from the Book of Ruth and Song of Songs throughout the translation (Kahn Forthcoming (a)). Petruccio's "I come to wife it wealthily in **Padua**" (1.2.74) finds a natural equivalent in the Hebrew "אֶרְאֶה אִתָּה בְּפַדֻּבָּה חַיֵּי עֹשֶׁר" (*ere ittah befaddubba ḥayye ošer* [I shall see a life of wealth with her in **Padua**]) (Elkind 1892: 41), and in comparable fashion, Salkinson preserves the

170   *Lily Kahn*

other Italian geographical epithets and markers for Florence and Mantua in, respectively, *Othello* and *Romeo and Juliet*: Michael Cassio, "a **Florentine**" (1.1.19), remains "פְּלָארעֶנְץ" (*florens* [a native of the city of **Florence**]) (Salkinson 1874: 2), and the Nurse's reminiscence, "My lord and you were then at **Mantua**" (1.3.29), is easily rendered in a direct equivalent, "וְאַתְּ גְּבִרְתִּי, הָיִית עִם אֲדֹנִי אָז בְּמַנְטוּבָה" (*ve'at, gevirti, hayit im adoni az bemanṭuva* [And you, my mistress, were then with my lord in **Mantua**]) (Salkinson 1878: 22).

Similarly, Elkind preserves Italian place names in a comparable gesture of fidelity to the geographical setting of the original texts. Lucentio's expositional "I am arrived for fruitful **Lombardy**" (1.1.3) becomes the near-identical "וּבָאתִי הֲלוֹם, לְלָמְבַּרְדִיָה הַפּוֹרִיָּה" (*uvati halom, lelombardya happoriyya* [And I came here, to fruitful **Lombardy**]) (Elkind 1892: 23), and his ruse later in the scene to rebrand himself as a "meaner man of **Pisa**" (1.1.204) finds a ready equivalent in Elkind's phrase "בֶּן־בְּלִי־שֵׁם מִפִּיצָה" (*ven-beli-šem mippizza* [a nameless man from **Pisa**]) (Elkind 1892: 34). Elkind also retains an explicit mention of Italy near the beginning of this opening scene, in the gloss on "fruitful Lombardy":

The pleasant garden of **great Italy**

(1.1.4)

הֲלֹא הִיא גַּנָּה שֶׁל **אִיטַלְיָה הַבְּרוּכָה**
(*halo hi gannah šel iṭalya habberuḵa* [Of course it is the garden of
blessed Italy])
(Elkind 1892: 23)

It is noteworthy that Elkind chose to translate "great" with בְּרוּכָה (*beruḵa* [blessed]), as this alteration is quite undermotivated. This adjective has strong Jewish religious connotations, featuring regularly in the liturgy, including numerous appearances in the daily prayers, an association that Hebrew-reading audiences would likely have made. This translation decision thus effectively recasts Italy as a location of Jewish religious culture, a rebranding which may be attributable to the tradition of mystical, philosophical, and ethical writings composed by Italian Jews delineated previously.

In contrast to their treatment of the Italian geographical labels appearing in Shakespeare's works, Salkinson and Elkind routinely replace the Italian names of the source texts with biblical substitutes that would have been familiar to Maskilic readers. The names of the three plays' eponymous characters illustrate this convention. Thus, Othello becomes אִיתִיאֵל (*iti'el* [Ithiel]), meaning "God is with me", a name derived from Proverbs 30:1 and Nehemiah 11:7; similarly, Romeo is reinvented as רָם (*ram* [Ram]), which appears in Ruth 4:19, while Juliet becomes יָעֵל (*ya'el*

Representations of Italy 171

[Jael]), based on Judges 4:18–22. Italian or Italianate names of other major and minor characters appearing in the original plays are altered in similar ways: Petruccio is renamed פֶּרֶץ (*pereṣ* [Peretz]), a common Jewish name based on the biblical character mentioned in Genesis 38 and Ruth 4:18, while Katherina is called חָגְלָה (*ḥogla* [Hoglah]), a name deriving from Numbers 26:33. Mercutio and Benvolio are named מְרָיוֹת (*merayot* [Meraioth]) and בְּנָיָה (*benayya* [Benaia]), both mentioned on various occasions in Ezra and Chronicles. Iago becomes דּוֹאֵג (*do'eg* [Doeg]), based on a character first mentioned in 1 Samuel 21:7, while Desdemona is transformed into אָסְנַת (*asnat* [Asenath]), the namesake of Joseph's wife (first appearing in Genesis 41:45).

As these examples illustrate, Salkinson and Elkind often selected their Hebrew names on the basis of phonological correspondences with the English originals. In addition, there were sometimes symbolic factors motivating their choices, as the biblical names in question had unmistakable associations with certain qualities relevant to the characters bearing them. For example, Hoglah (for Katherina) is one of the daughters of Zelophehad whose story is related in Numbers 27:1–11; in Jewish tradition, she and her sisters are highly regarded as strong, independent women who dared to argue for equal inheritance rights alongside their male counterparts (as in the Babylonian Talmud *Bava Batra*, 119b), and as such this name can be considered an appropriate equivalent for Katherina (Kahn Forthcoming (a)). Similarly, Doeg is a particularly malevolent biblical character with uncanny resemblances to Iago, known as a liar, traitor, and killer (see Scolnicov 2001: 186–7 for further discussion of this name and for the symbolism of other biblicizing names in Salkinson's *Othello* translation). When considered in the context of the plays' Italian settings, the selection of these biblical names has an important additional bearing on the target text: in contrast to the English originals, in which the personal names (many, of course, laden with their own symbolic or emblematic resonances) serve to add an element of authenticity to the drama by highlighting its foreign setting, the translators' changes transform the characters into inhabitants of an imagined Jewish Italy steeped in biblical associations, subtly evoking the centuries of Italian Jewish literary and scholarly productivity discussed previously.

Othello, Romeo and Juliet, and *The Taming of the Shrew* are all replete with Christian, often explicitly Roman Catholic, references. Unsurprisingly, Salkinson and Elkind systematically remove these references or replace them with Jewish equivalents, a move designed to underscore the Jewishness of the characters populating the Italy of the target texts, in contrast to the ostensibly non-Jewish Italians featuring in the English originals. This tendency is highly visible in *Romeo and Juliet,* which is laden with unambiguously Catholic elements in keeping with its Italian

172   *Lily Kahn*

setting (Weis 2012: 205). One striking example is the explicit reference to Mary appearing in the source text:

Jesu Maria, what a deal of brine

(2.3.65)

Salkinson removes this overtly Christian allusion, which would have been regarded as unsuitable for inclusion in a Hebrew work intended for a Jewish audience:

כַּמָּה מֵי דִמְעָה שָׁפַכְתָּ כַּמָּטָר עַל גַּנָּה

(*kamma me dima šafakta kammaṭar al ganna*
[How much water of tears you have spilled like rain on a garden)
(Salkinson 1878: 60)

A similar case involves the Nurse's mild oath in Act 1, Scene 3:

Susan and she, God rest **all Christian souls,**
Were of an age

(1.3.19–20)

Unsurprisingly, Salkinson deletes this interjection from his translation, unbefitting a Jewish character's idiolect:

וְשׁוֹשַׁנָּה בַּת גִּילָהּ נוֹלְדָה עִמָּהּ בְּשָׁנָה אֶחָת

(*vešošanna bat gilah noleda immah beshana eḥat*
[And Shoshana was her age; she was born with her in the same year])
(Salkinson 1878: 22)

A couple of scenes later, Salkinson replaces Christian festivals with their Jewish counterparts, as when Pentecost (1.5.36) is domesticated as "בְּחַג הַשָּׁבֻעוֹת הַבָּא" (*beḥag hašavu'ot habba* [On the next **festival of Shavuot**]) (Salkinson 1878: 35). On one level, this is a necessary and straightforward translation decision considering that the Jewish festival of Shavuot, which commemorates the giving of the Torah at Mount Sinai, is the historical antecedent of the Christian Pentecost and falls at a similar time of the year, in late spring or early summer. Salkinson would have struggled to find another way of translating the term given the lack of a recognized Hebrew word for "Pentecost", although, on another level, the substitution has the obvious effect of erasing the Christian connotations of the original and replacing them with explicitly Jewish ones tailored to Salkinson's Hebrew-reading audience. Salkinson likewise neutralizes Othello's exclamation, "For **Christian** shame, put by this barbarous brawl" (2.3.168), writing out the Christian content

Representations of Italy   173

with a more generalizing statement: "בּוֹשׁוּ הִכָּלְמוּ מִמְּשׁוּבוֹתֵיכֶם" (*bušu hik-kalemu mimmešuvoteḵem* [Be ashamed, be humiliated by your wicked behaviour]) (Salkinson 1874: 67). Elkind adopts a comparable strategy in his rendition of Petruccio's litany of appellations in *The Taming of the Shrew*. Here,

> the prettiest Kate **in Christendom**
>
> (2.1.186)

is rendered, via an intertextual nod to the Song of Songs (2:14), as

> חָגָא חֲמוּדָה, חָגָא מֵחַגְוֵי סָלַע
> (*haga ḥamuda, ḥaga meḥaggeve sela* [Charming Haga, Haga **from
> the clefts of the rock**])
> (Elkind 1892: 64)

Such adaptations point to a strenuously ideological enterprise of producing a domesticated target text steeped in Jewish culture, reclaiming Shakespeare's version of Italy by modifying his terms, while preserving something of the authenticity and canonicity of his works by keeping the surrounding material more or less unchanged.

In a yet more interventionist stance, Salkinson and Elkind insert Jewish content into lines lacking any particular cultural loading, Italian or otherwise, in the original. This tactic is evident in the description of Katherina and Petruccio's wedding in 3.2 of *The Taming of the Shrew*. In the original, Baptista asks the following question:

> What mockery will it be
> To want the bridegroom when the priest attends
> **To speak the ceremonial rites of marriage?**
>
> (3.2.4–6)

In Elkind's version, these lines read somewhat differently:

> אֵיךְ נִהְיֶה לִשְׂחוֹק!
> כִּי נִפְקַד הֶחָתָן, וְהוּכַן הַכֹּהֵן
> לְסַדֵּר הַחֻפָּה וּבִרְכוֹת הַנִּשּׂוּאִין
>
> (*eḵ nihye liseḥoq!*
> *ki nifqad heḥatan, vehuḵan hakkohen*
> *lesadder haḥuppa uvirḵot hannissu'in*
> [How we will be made a mockery!
> For the bridegroom is missing, when the priest is ready
> To arrange **the wedding canopy and the marriage blessings**])
> (Elkind 1892: 85)

174 *Lily Kahn*

This insertion entirely transforms the wedding into an explicitly Jewish one, complete with a *chuppah*, the traditional canopy under which the couple and close family stand during the ceremony. Moreover, consistent with this Judaizing strategy, the alteration introduces בְּרְכוֹת הַנִּשׂוּאִין (*birkot hannissu'in* [marriage blessings]), the set name for the blessings said during a Jewish wedding. Finally, the Hebrew translation כֹּהֵן (*kohen* [priest]) has very different connotations from its English equivalent, evoking both the priests of the biblical Temple in Jerusalem and their descendants, who retain a special status within the framework of rabbinic Judaism to the present day.

A similar alteration can be seen in the previous act, in 2.1. In the source text, Katherina responds to Petruccio's comment that "women are made to bear" with the statement, "No such **jade** as you, if me you mean" (2.1.202). By contrast, in Elkind's version Hoglah says, "לֹא גֹלֶם כָּמוֹךָ, אִם אוֹתִי תְדַמֶּה" (*lo golem kamoka, im oti tedamme* [Not a **golem** like you, if you have me in mind]) (Elkind 1892: 65). A "golem", a popular concept in Jewish folklore, perhaps dating back to the Talmud (Kieval 2010), is mentioned in medieval mystical works that describe ways of animating inorganic matter in imitation of the Divine. The most famous example of this phenomenon is the Golem of Prague, which was said to have been animated by the Maharal, Rabbi Judah Loew of Prague, in an attempt to protect the Jewish community from anti-Semitic attacks. This type of insertion reinforces the Jewish connotations of the characters and setting, and further distances the target text from any associations with the non-Jewish Italy of the original.

Another intriguing example of such domestication can be seen at the beginning of Salkinson's translation of *Romeo and Juliet*. In the original, the play opens (after the Prologue) with the following lines:

> SAMSON Gregory, on my word, we'll not **carry coals.**
> GREGORY No, for then we should be **colliers.**
>
> (1.1.1–2)

By contrast, the Hebrew version exchanges the coals and colliers with wood and woodcutters:

> שמשי אַחַת דִּבַּרְתִּי גֵרָא, לֹא **נַחְטֹב** עוֹד **עֵצִים.**
> גרא כֵּן דִּבַּרְתָּ, כִּי לָמָּה נִהְיֶה **חֹטְבֵי עֵצִים.**
> (*šimšay*   *ahat dibbarti gera, lo nahtov od eṣim.*
> *gera*   *ken dibbarta, ki lamma nihye hoteve eṣim.*
> [SHIMSHAY On my word, Gera, we shall no longer **cut wood.**
> GERA   You are right, for why should we be **woodcutters?**])
>
> (Salkinson 1878: 1)

Salkinson's substitution of "woodcutters" for "colliers" is in fact an explicitly Judaizing dynamic equivalent. Although not associated specifically

Representations of Italy 175

with Italian Jewry, woodcutting was a common occupation among their Eastern European brethren well into the twentieth century (see Salsitz 2002: 84–7); moreover, it would have been widely recognized among Hebrew readers as a classic form of manual labour due to its appearance in a well-known phrase from Joshua 9: 21, "woodcutters and water carriers". Thus, Salkinson chooses to populate his play with Hebrew-speaking characters whose conception of physical work is rooted in an unambiguously Jewish perspective.

One final aspect of the Judaized Italy worth noting concerns Elkind's treatment of Italian expressions and sentences, which appear on various occasions in *The Taming of the Shrew*. For example, Petruccio and Hortensio conduct the following short exchange in Italian in the second scene of the play proper:

> PETRUCCIO *Con tutto il cuore ben trovato*, may I say.
> [With all my heart, well met]
>
> (1.2.24)

> HORTENSIO *Alla nostra casa ben venuto, molto honorata signor mio Petruccio.*
> [Welcome to our house, my most esteemed Petruccio]
> (1.2.25–26)

Elkind replaces these Italian elements with their equivalent in Aramaic:

> פרץ   ,,בְּרֵעוּת נַפְשָׁאִי מֵיתָךְ לְטַב'' אֲשִׁיבָה.
> גוּנִי ,,בְּרִיךְ אַתְּ בְּמֵיעַלֵךְ לְגוֹ בֵּיתָאִי, מָרָא פֶּרֶץ מָרִי רְחִימָאִי''
>
> (*pere*ṣ   *"bire'ut nafša'i metak leṭav" ašiva.*
> *guni*   *"berik at beme'alek lego vetay, mara fereṣ mari reḥimay"*
> [PERETZ   "With the friendship of my heart, welcome", I respond.
> GUNI   "Blessed are you in your entrance into my house, Mr Peretz, my merciful lord"])
>
> (Elkind 1892: 39)

Elkind's translation of these lines into Aramaic constitutes a fascinating Judaizing strategy. Aramaic and Hebrew are closely related Northwest Semitic languages with similar morphology, syntax, and lexis. Moreover, they share a long history of linguistic contact dating back to the Babylonian Exile of 586–37 BCE, when Hebrew-speaking Judean exiles are believed to have adopted the Aramaic lingua franca of their Babylonian captors (Sáenz-Badillos 1993: 112). Jewish use of Aramaic is thought to have grown more predominant in subsequent centuries until it replaced Hebrew as the main Jewish vernacular in approximately 200 CE (Sáenz-Badillos 1993: 171). Although Aramaic was itself replaced by other spoken languages among the Jews over the course of the first millennium CE, its prominent position in Jewish society was preserved

176 *Lily Kahn*

in the form of a substantial canon of Aramaic-language literature including biblical translations, commentaries, and, most significantly, the Babylonian Talmud, which has occupied a central position in the traditional Jewish educational system up to the present day. Because it was usually studied only by more advanced students, in contrast to Hebrew which was learned from a very early age, Aramaic took on elite and somewhat esoteric connotations among Jews. As such, it was sometimes employed as a substitute for Latin in Judaizing nineteenth-century Hebrew Shakespeare translations (Kahn Forthcoming (b)). However, it was also sometimes utilized in nineteenth-century Hebrew literature as a way of representing the traditional Central and Eastern European Jewish vernacular Yiddish (Even-Zohar 1986: 52).

Elkind adopts the latter approach in his translation, using Aramaic as a Judaized substitute for the Italian appearing in the original English work. In contrast to the source text, in which the Italian expressions serve to inject an element of authenticity into the otherwise exclusively English-language dialogue, these adaptations do not pretend to any sort of realism given that Jewish inhabitants of Italy would not have spoken Hebrew any more than Elkind himself did; rather, they would have employed vernacular languages (typically Italian by the period in which the translations were undertaken). Nevertheless, the use of Aramaic serves as a way of preserving the linguistic difference afforded by these Italian extracts in Shakespeare's play. Yet its function is not to indicate a specific language but rather to signal to Hebrew readers in an abstract way that these elements were uttered in a theoretical vernacular, perhaps the spoken language of Elkind's imagined community of Italian Jews.

The Maskilic Hebrew translators of *Othello*, *Romeo and Juliet*, and *The Taming of the Shrew* were confronted by the unusual challenge of adapting English dramatic works set in Italy and exhibiting explicitly Italian cultural, religious, and linguistic features into ones suitable for a Hebrew-reading Eastern European Jewish audience with a very particular ideology. Instead of viewing locations such as Venice, Verona, and Padua as mechanisms for lending an exotic flavour to the story and perhaps providing audiences with a vicarious travel experience, as in the original Elizabethan and Jacobean context, the Maskilic authors interpreted these settings through the prism of the long-established and prominent Jewish presence in Italy and as such regarded them as suitable candidates for retention within a domesticated target text. Hence, they replaced the non-Jewish Italian characters and cultural context of the originals with Jewish equivalents while maintaining the Italian geographical locations. This technique led to the creation of an identifiably Jewish Italy where characters speak Hebrew and Aramaic, have biblical names, and engage in explicitly Jewish religious practices. The result opens up a unique perspective on the multilateral representation of Italy and the Italian language within the context of an emergent, nineteenth-century global Shakespeare.

Bibliography

Abramson, Glenda, and Tudor Parfitt, eds. 1985. *The Great Transition: The Recovery of the Lost Centers of Modern Hebrew Literature*. Totowa, NJ.

Almagor, Dan. 1975. "Shakespeare in Hebrew Literature, 1794–1930: Bibliographical Survey and Bibliography". *Festschrift for Shimon Halkin*, ed. by Boaz Shahevitch and Menachem Perry. Jerusalem. 721–84.

Armistead, Samuel G., and Joseph H. Silverman. 1965. "Christian Elements and De-Christianization in the Sephardic Romancero". *Collected Studies in Honour of Americo Castro's Eightieth Year*, ed. by M. P. Hornik. Oxford. 21–38.

Baumgarten, Jean. 2005. *Introduction to Old Yiddish Literature*, ed. and trans. by Jerold C. Frakes. Oxford.

Dan, Joseph, and Joelle Hansel. 2007. "Luzzatto, Moses Ḥayyim". *Encyclopaedia Judaica*, 2nd edition, ed. by Michael Berenbaum and Fred Skolnik, 22 vols. Detroit. 13: 281–6.

Elkind, Judah Loeb. 1892. *Musar sorera [The Taming of the Shrew]*. Berditchev.

Even-Zohar, Itamar. 1986. "Aspects of the Hebrew-Yiddish Polysystem". *HaSifrut*, 10.3–4: 46–54.

Hacker, Joseph R., and Adam Shear. 2011. *The Hebrew Book in Early Modern Italy*. Philadelphia.

Harshav, Benjamin. 1993. *Language in Time of Revolution*. Stanford.

Kahn, Lily. 2017. *The First Hebrew Shakespeare Translations: A Bilingual Edition and Commentary*. London: UCL Press.

———— Forthcoming (a). "Biblical Motifs in the First Hebrew Translation of *The Taming of the Shrew*". *Multicultural Shakespeare*, 14.

———— Forthcoming (b). "Domesticating Techniques in the First Hebrew Translation of *Hamlet*". *Hamlet Translations*, ed. by Márta Minier.

Kieval, Hillel J. 2010. "Golem Legend". *YIVO Encyclopedia of Jews in Eastern Europe*. www.yivoencyclopedia.org/article.aspx/Golem_Legend. Accessed 03/07/2014.

Klausner, Joseph. 1952–58. *History of Modern Hebrew Literature*, 6 vols. Jerusalem.

Leviant, Curt, ed. and trans. 2003. *King Artus: A Hebrew Arthurian Romance of 1279*. Syracuse.

Malkiel, David. 2000. "New Light on the Career of Isaac Samuel Reggio". *The Jews of Italy: Memory and Identity*, ed. by Bernard D. Cooperman and Barbara Garvin. Bethesda, MD. 276–303.

Milano, Attilio, Daniel Carpi, Sergio Itzhak Minerbi, Sergio DellaPergola, Lisa Palmieri-Billig, and Yohanan Meroz. 2007. "Italy". *Encyclopaedia Judaica*, 2nd edition, ed. by Michael Berenbaum and Fred Skolnik, 22 vols. Detroit. 10: 795–816.

Nielsen, Bruce. 2011. "Daniel van Bombergen: A Bookman of Two Worlds". *The Hebrew Book in Early Modern Italy*, ed. by Joseph R. Hacker and Adam Shear. Philadelphia. 56–75.

Noy, David. 2000. "The Jews in Italy in the First to Sixth Centuries C.E.". *The Jews of Italy: Memory and Identity*, ed. by Bernard D. Cooperman and Barbara Garvin. Bethesda, MD. 47–64.

Patterson, David. 1964. *The Hebrew Novel in Czarist Russia: A Portrait of Jewish Life in the Nineteenth Century*. Lanham, MD.

178   Lily Kahn

———— 1988. *A Phoenix in Fetters: Studies in Nineteenth and Early Twentieth Century Hebrew Fiction*. Savage, MD.

Pelli, Moshe. 2006. *The Age of Haskalah: Studies in Hebrew Literature of the Enlightenment in Germany*, 2nd edition. Lanham, MD.

Rovang, Paul R. 2009. "Hebraizing Arthurian Romance: The Originality of *Melech Artus*". *Arthuriana*, 19.2: 3–9.

Sáenz-Badillos, Angel. 1993. *A History of the Hebrew Language*, trans. by John Elwolde. Cambridge.

Salkinson, Isaac Eduard. 1874. *iti'el* [*Othello*]. Vienna.

———— 1878. *ram veya'el* [*Romeo and Juliet*]. Vienna.

Salsitz, Norman. 2002. *Three Homelands: Memories of a Jewish Life in Poland, Israel, and America*. With Stanley Kaish. Syracuse.

Scolnicov, Hanna. 2001. "The Hebrew Who Turned Christian: The First Translator of Shakespeare into the Holy Tongue". *Shakespeare Survey*, 54: 182–90.

Shmeruk, Chone. 1988. *Yiddish Literature: Aspects of Its History*. Jerusalem.

Singerman, Robert. 1988. "Between Western Culture and Jewish Tradition". *A Sign and a Witness: 2,000 Years of Hebrew Books and Illuminated Manuscripts*, ed. by Leonard Singer Gold. New York. 140–54.

Tobias, Alexander. 2007. "Samuel David Luzzatto". *Encyclopaedia Judaica*, 2nd edition, ed. by Michael Berenbaum and Fred Skolnik, 22 vols. Detroit. 13: 286–7.

Toury, Gideon. 2012. *Descriptive Translation Studies—and beyond*, 2nd edition. Amsterdam.

Valles, Margot Behrend. 2013. *Judaized Romance and Romanticized Judaization: Adaptation in Hebrew and Early Yiddish Chivalric Literature*. PhD Thesis. Indiana University.

Weis, René, ed. 2012. *Romeo and Juliet*. Arden Shakespeare. London.

Zer-Zion, Shelly. 2010. "Hebrew Theater". *The YIVO Encyclopedia of Jews in Eastern Europe*. www.yivoencyclopedia.org/article.aspx/Theater/Hebrew_Theater. Accessed 22 July 2014.

Zilberberg, Gershon, and Jennifer Breger. 2007. "Printing, Hebrew". *Encyclopaedia Judaica*, 2nd edition, ed. by Michael Berenbaum and Fred Skolnik, 22 vols. Detroit. 16: 529–40.

12 Through the Fickle Glass
Rewriting and Rethinking Shakespeare's *Sonnets* in Italy

Matteo Brera

Not much is known about how Shakespeare's *Sonnets* reached Italy. Most nineteenth- and twentieth-century criticism limited itself to analysis of the poems' content and style without tracing the reception of the work in the Italian peninsula, where Shakespeare's plays had already attained considerable notoriety, even by the end of the eighteenth century. It was only in 1890 that a secondary-school teacher from Palermo, Angelo Olivieri, completed the monumental endeavour of translating Shakespeare's sonnets into Italian. In the introduction to his work, Olivieri mentions "pochissimi Sonetti di Shakspeare tradotti nella nostra lingua" [very few Shakespeare sonnets translated into our language] (Olivieri 1890: xxxvii). Although he merely hints at some previous translations of the sonnets into Italian, Olivieri almost certainly is referring here to Gustavo Tirinelli's essay published a few years earlier in the *Nuova Antologia* (Tirinelli 1878), which appears to be the first ever critical analysis of the *Sonnets* written in Italian.

The task of determining in what edition the *Sonnets* reached Italy—and, most importantly, *when* they were first read by the Italian public—is a problematic one. However, it is most likely that Shakespeare's poems, published in separate editions from the plays, arrived in Italy over the course of the eighteenth century when what Arturo Graf has called "Anglomania" was beginning to announce itself on the Italian peninsula. The cultural revival of interest in English customs led to the discovery of forgotten or hidden literary gems, numbered among which were, presumably, Shakespeare's *Sonnets* (Graf 1911). This *Settecento* fascination with English literary culture established the conditions by which works written in English could be read in their original language rather than via French or German intermediaries, as had hitherto been the case (Scherillo 1892: *passim*; Brognoligo 1891; Brera 2010: 63). These early translators and commentators seem to have been aware of some of the textual difficulties surrounding the original 1609 Quarto, even if their primary sources were most probably relatively recent English editions (De Marchi: 8–11). In the preface to his translations, Olivieri confirms that he had read the *Sonnets* edited by Edward Dowden (published in London in 1881), at the time the newest and most accessible edition

180 Matteo Brera

of Shakespeare's poems circulating in Italy in small paperback format, from which he derived inspiration to pursue his own translating enterprise. Olivieri mentions an outstanding critical work on the *Sonnets*, written by the "eminente critico inglese" [eminent English critic] Dowden (Olivieri 1890: ix), by which he is almost certainly referring to Dowden's *The Sonnets of Shakspere*, an edition that contained neither *Venus and Adonis*, nor *The Rape of Lucrece*, nor *A Lover's Complaint*, suggesting that at the end of the nineteenth century the *Sonnets* circulated in Italy as an independent poetic collection, achieving fame in isolation, on their own merits.

In 1891, Luigi De Marchi, brother of the more famous novelist Emilio, followed Olivieri's poetic-prose *sonetti* with an essay on Shakespeare's poems, some of which he translated in verse form (De Marchi 1891). The translator confirms that the *Sonnets* had been "si può dire completamente ignoti" [almost completely unknown] before 1890, when Olivieri's translation attracted the "attenzione di qualche rivista" [attention of a few journals] (De Marchi 1891: 18; see Ottolini 1921: 351). The complete poetic translation of the sonnets would not appear for a further seven years when, in 1898, a full text was issued by Ettore Sanfelice. This work was preceded by Giuseppe Chiarini's *Studi Shakespeariani* (1896), a pivotal book for the dissemination of Shakespeare's poetry in Italy, in which Chiarini also translated a few fragments from the *Sonnets* to enrich his essay and to elucidate some of the more obscure passages of the source text.

As Anglophilia became entrenched on the Italian peninsula, previously neglected works of English literature were increasingly chosen by Italian scholars and poets for translation. The end of the nineteenth century was a stimulating time for translators: Giosuè Carducci memorably declared in his preface to Sanfelice's translation of Percy Bysshe Shelley's *Prometheus Unbound* (*Prometeo liberato*), "L'Italia [...] non legge Shelley [...] ma, oltre tradurlo, gli prepara monumenti" [Italy does not read Shelley ... besides translating him, though, she also erects monuments to him] (Shelley 1894: xii). The fame that Shakespeare's sonnets enjoyed in Italy during the late nineteenth and early twentieth century, when numerous versions were published (see Brera 2010: 63–67, for a list of translations 1890–2010), has its roots in a renewed Italian impetus to close a perceived cultural gap with the rest of Europe by translating literary classics. Shakespeare's status was particularly stellar at the turn of the century, in part a consequence of the sustained popularity of Verdi's Shakespearean operas.

This chapter focuses on the language and style of the *Sonetti* translated by Angelo Olivieri, Luigi De Marchi, and Ettore Sanfelice, with a view to highlighting the translators' linguistic and stylistic choices, before looking briefly at the twentieth-century translation by Eugenio Montale, in order to outline the "struggle" of rendering Shakespeare's language and prosody into Italian. The language of the first translations was deeply rooted in the

Through the Fickle Glass 181

Italian poetic tradition, but the literary challenge that stimulated translators to bring Shakespeare's poems to the peninsula also prompted them to rethink the sonnets in the light of contemporary tastes.

The First Translations: Imitating Shakespeare (with a Twist)

Enabling an Italian audience to access Shakespeare's poetry, specifically the *Sonnets*, was the main aim behind Angelo Olivieri's translational enterprise, in recognition of the fact that these poems had been translated in most European countries by 1890 with the exception of Italy: Germany, Olivieri recounts, had as many as ten translations, and France, Holland, and numerous other countries could read the *Sonnets* "nei loro rispettivi idiomi" [in their respective languages] (Olivieri 1890: ix). A teacher at *Leonardo da Vinci*, a technical school in Rome, Olivieri conceded that the task of translating Shakespeare had been "a job [that] cost [him] more studies and labour than one could possibly imagine [...] through all sorts of difficulties". In the preface to his translation, dedicated to Francesco Lanza Spinelli, Prince of Scalea, he states his intention of making a translation of the *Sonnets* that was "tanto esatta e fedele, quanto lo permettevano e la differenza grande delle due lingue" [as accurate and faithful as possible given the great difference between the languages], to say nothing of the even greater diversity in the "modo di vedere e di esprimere i sentimenti"—the different ways in which the *Sonnets* were received by Italian readers and the differences between the sixteenth and nineteenth centuries in the perception and expression of feeling (Olivieri 1890: xii). De Marchi's translation of 1891 was also prompted by the desire to popularize Shakespeare's *Sonnets* for Italian readers. A geographer with a passion for English studies, De Marchi translated *Gulliver's Travels* into Italian (Swift 1892) and wrote a few essays, among which *I Sonetti di Shakespeare* reconstructed some of the critical debates around the poems, commenting on their controversial authorship and main stylistic features. The author adds several poetic *intermezzi* to his work, including Italian translations of twenty-four sonnets chosen more or less evenly from across Shakespeare's collection, through which he discusses Shakespearean poetics.

All 154 sonnets were rendered into Italian by Ettore Sanfelice, Giosuè Carducci's disciple and author of a number of poetic translations from the English literary tradition, including a rendering of Shelley's *Prometheus Unbound*. Carducci himself confirmed in the preface to this translation how Sanfelice showed the "generoso ardimento d'una lotta metrica" [generous daring of a metrical battle] with Shakespeare where he was most "intorato" [ireful], namely in the *Sonnets* (Shelley 1894: vii–viii). Sanfelice's title-page stated that he had translated Shakespeare's poems as "Italian sonnets" [*sonetti italiani*], thus implying some sort of adherence to the Petrarchan model. However, he

182 *Matteo Brera*

respects the metric structure of the Elizabethan sonnet, including the final couplet [decasyllabic lines rhyming *ababcdcdefefgg*], instead of choosing the pattern of fourteen rhyming hendecasyllables canonized by Petrarch. Sanfelice Italianized Shakespeare's poems by using a language deeply rooted in Italian literary history, and the following analysis will show how in his renderings—and those by his fellow translators—multiple poetic traditions are at work.

A comparison of Olivieri's and Sanfelice's translations of Sonnet 127, traditionally regarded as the first addressed to the so-called "Dark Lady", is instructive. The original text of Sonnet 127 runs as follows:

> In the old age black was not counted fair,
> Or if it were, it bore not beauty's name;
> But now is black beauty's successive heir,
> And beauty slandered with a bastard shame:
> For since each hand hath put on nature's power,
> Fairing the foul with art's false borrowed face,
> Sweet beauty hath no name, no holy bower,
> But is profaned, if not lives in disgrace.
> Therefore my mistress' eyes are raven black,
> Her eyes so suited, and they mourners seem
> At such who, not born fair, no beauty lack,
> Sland'ring creation with a false esteem;
>   Yet so they mourn, becoming of their woe,
>   That every tongue says beauty should look so.
>
> (Duncan-Jones 2002: 369)

Olivieri's translation seeks in its *mise-en-page* (reproduced below as in the original publication) to preserve the poetic structure of Shakespeare's sonnet, respecting its implicit division into quatrains and a couplet, albeit now in a hybrid kind of strophic prose:

> Negli antichi tempi la bruna non era considerata bella, o se la era, non portava il nome della bellezza; ma ora è la bruna la erede successiva della bellezza, e questa è calunniata con false apparenze:
>
> Dacchè la mano dell'uomo ha usurpato il potere della natura, abbellendo il brutto colla maschera presa in prestito dall'arte, la dolce bellezza non ha più nome, non ha più un sacro recesso, ma è profanata quando non viva nella vergogna.
>
> Perciò gli occhi della mia bella sono neri corvini, quegli occhi che le si addicono tanto; e sembrano portare il lutto per quelle, che non essendo nate bionde, ma non mancando di bellezza, calunniano la natura con false attrattive.

Through the Fickle Glass 183

Pure gli occhi di lei portano il lutto, e questo si addice tanto al
loro duolo, che ogni lingua dice:—la bellezza dovrebbe esser bruna.

(Olivieri 1890: 255)

Angela Locatelli contends that "the pedagogic intent and the romantic
enthusiasm for the wild genius of the Bard are evident" from Olivieri's
translations (Locatelli 1989: 284). The translator's "enthusiasm" announces itself in the accuracy and the detail of Olivieri's poetic glosses
and annotations that reveal a profound knowledge of Shakespeare's
works and scholarship, even if the rendering of each sonnet is rather
pedantic and literal. Olivieri's format, a parallel-text edition reproducing the English original on the facing page, further implies that
the primary aim of his translations was to "explain" Shakespeare's
poetics to the reader. The pedagogic and exegetic intentions of the
translator are clear, as Olivieri unfurls the syntax of the original in
an attempt to make it easily understandable. His prose is somehow
poetic as the lines and words emulate the structure of the Shakespearean sonnet, which is formally preserved in loose strophic units, although lacking any real versification in the Italian. Olivieri's linguistic
texture shows a predilection for words belonging to the prose register ("brutto" [ugly], "occhi" [eyes], "lutto" [grief]) that inevitably
undermine the poetic power of Shakespeare's imagery. Most of his
rendering is a calque of the original, as we see in the hypothetical
"Or if it were", translated unoriginally as "o se la era", and in the
syntagms "with a bastard shame" ("con false apparenze"), "with art's
false borrowed face" ("colla maschera presa in prestito dall'arte"),
"holy bower" ("sacro recesso"), and "eyes [...] raven black" ("occhi
[...] neri corvini").

By contrast, Sanfelice shows a desire to adhere more closely to a contemporary Italian poetic tradition than to Shakespeare's text:

La bruna un tempo non tenean per bella,
  né, bella, di bellezza aveasi il nome;
  ora per succession l'erede è quella
  della bellezza, e questa ha false chiome.

Dacchè la man fè forza alla natura,
  e l'immondo abbellì con la menzogna,
  nome e tempio non ha bellezza pura,
  è profanata, ovver vive in vergogna.

Corvine luci ha la mia dama, e quelle
  bene le stan, chè sembrano in gramaglia
  per le non nate bionde, che, pur belle,
  falsan natura con orpel che abbaglia.

184   *Matteo Brera*

Sì gramaglia al lor duol ben si accomuna
che dice ognun: "Beltà deve esser bruna".

(Sanfelice 1898: CXXVII)

Sanfelice, not unlike Olivieri, contextualized his translation within the poetic tradition of the *contrasti* [verse dialogues], one of which, written by fellow Carducci-follower Severino Ferrari ("Il contrasto della bionda e della bruna"), appears to be the most likely source for the choice here of the synecdochic "la bruna" to translate "black" (Ferrari 1892). To register the re-creation of Shakespeare's poetry within an Italian canon being actively shaped by Sanfelice, and to assess the distance between his translation and Olivieri's, the translation of "with a bastard shame" might usefully be chosen for close analysis. Given that the obvious equivalent for "shame" is "vergogna" in Italian, Olivieri's translation of the phrase as "con false apparenze" is a rather loose one. And Sanfelice opted for a more semantically distinct "ha false chiome". The syntagm seems to descend from Sanfelice's poetic mentor Carducci. It cannot be traced back to any standard nineteenth-century bilingual vocabulary and could not possibly derive from any dictionary to which the translator had access, such as those compiled by Baretti, Comelati and Davenport, Millhouse, Roberts and Melzi, the most commonly used and most reliable English-Italian dictionaries listed by Olivieri in the preface to his study of English verbs (Olivieri 1905: n.p.). According to the *Biblioteca Italiana Zanichelli* (Stoppelli 2010), the syntagm "false chiome" (literally, a wig) is a poetic *hapax* in the Italian tradition and only present in Carducci's "A certi censori":

Ecco Pomponio, a le cui false chiome
E al giallo adipe arguto,
Dolce Pimplea, tu splendi in vista come
Un grosso angel paffuto [...]

(Carducci 1998: 283, ll. 37–40)

The translator makes explicit, through the use of "false chiome", what Shakespeare himself implies: the fashionable habit of sixteenth-century ladies to wear wigs made of hair taken from dead bodies. While Shakespeare insists here—and elsewhere in most of the *Sonnets*—on the ideas of false and true reproduction, legitimacy and illegitimacy, Sanfelice reworked the pairing "bastard shame" to create a more personal image, in a marked departure from the original. Sanfelice opted for linguistic emulation of the most influential Italian poet of the time, thus trying to anchor his translation within Carducci's classicist canon. "False chiome" also derives from the older satirical and iambic tradition associated with Angiolo D'Elci, from whose "Satira Ottava: Le donne", and specifically the phrase

Through the Fickle Glass   185

"false chiome in testa", Carducci most probably took inspiration himself (D'Elci 1817: 154).

A contemporary poetic tradition also surfaces in the versions of the third of our translators, Luigi De Marchi, who did not translate Sonnet 127 among those he deemed relevant for discussing Shakespeare's poetics. Particularly significant for the translator's linguistic and stylistic choices is, however, De Marchi's version of Sonnet 146, particularly when read alongside Shakespeare's original:

> Poor soul, the centre of my sinful earth,
> Feeding these rebel powers that thee array,
> Why dost thou pine within and suffer dearth,
> Painting thy outward walls so costly gay?
> Why so large cost, having so short a lease,
> Dost thou upon thy fading mansion spend?
> Shall worms, inheritors of this excess,
> Eat up thy charge? Is this thy body's end?
> Then soul, live thou upon thy servant's loss,
> And let that pine to aggravate thy store;
> Buy terms divine in selling hours of dross,
> Within be fed, without be rich no more:
>   So shalt thou feed on death, that feeds on men,
>   And death once dead, there's no more dying then.
>
> (Duncan-Jones 2002: 409)

> Povero cor, centro al peccaminoso
> mio fango, e schiavo a sue forze ribelli,
> perché entro te ti consumi affannoso
> e a spese tue il tuo carcere abbelli?
>
> Perché, se breve è la scadenza, spendi
> te stesso per sì effimera dimora?
> E al verme, erede del tuo corpo, rendi
> ogni opra tua? per ciò dato ti fora
>
> un corpo? oh, vivi del tuo servo a danno,
> E la sua pena tu ricchezza aumenti!
> Compra l'eterno col fuggevol anno,
> Dentro ti nutri, e fa che il corpo stenti.
>
> Così morte, che uccide, ucciderai,
> E uccisa morte, tu immortal sarai.
>
> (De Marchi 1891: 43)

The syntax of the poem is perturbed by strong enjambments, above all across ll. 8–9 ("dato ti fora | un corpo"), thus disrupting the syntactic

186   *Matteo Brera*

break expected at the volta, and ll. 1–2 ("peccaminoso | mio fango", also complicated by a hyperbaton), and also ll. 5–6 ("spendi | te stesso") and ll. 7–8 ("rendi | ogni opra tua"). De Marchi's reshaping of the rhythm of the original—most of Shakespeare's sonnets tending to favour end-stopped lines—marks a notable departure from the syntactic habits of the original text. The nervous rhythm of De Marchi's Shakespeare also incorporates some characteristics of the poetry of the Italian *Scapigliatura*, a term deriving from the novel *La Scapigliatura e il 6 febbraio* (1861) by Cletto Arrighi (the pseudonym for Carlo Righetti, 1830–1906), one of the foremost exponents of the movement itself, an avant-gardism that gave rise to later literary vogues like Decadentism and Symbolism. Its members, the *Scapigliati*—most famously perhaps Emilio Praga (1839–1875) and Arrigo Boito (1842–1918), the latter central to the reception of Shakespeare's plays in Italy as librettist for Verdi's *Otello* (1887) and *Falstaff* (1893)—attempted to rejuvenate Italian culture through foreign influences and, above all, the poetry of Charles Baudelaire, favouring a language that was intentionally obscure and privileging gloomy tones.

In this tradition of the *Scapigliati*, and as part of a linguistic texture that privileges the use of common "poeticisms" (Serianni 2001) such as the apocopate "cor" [heart] (l. 1), "fuggevol" [fleeting] (l. 11), and "immortal" (l. 14), the two key words in De Marchi's poem above are, in fact, "verme" [worm] and "fango" [mud]. Shakespeare reflects on the folly of bestowing excessive care on the body ("sinful earth"), the soul's outer covering and ministering servant. In conclusion, he expresses the resolution to attain immortality by nourishing the soul at the body's expense. De Marchi's sonnet gains a decadent twist as the "verme", which will devour the body, triggers the translation of "sinful earth" as "peccaminoso | mio fango" [my sinful mud]. De Marchi must have thought of the Baudelairian worms that inspired Emilio Praga's "Vendetta postuma" (in his 1864 collection *Penombre*), where the poet imagines a "wave of worms" ["sentirai l'onda dei vermi"] devouring his buried lover's heart (Praga 1969: 180, ll. 21–24). The semantic shift towards a "decadentification" of Shakespeare's "only religious sonnet" (West 2007) is completed by De Marchi with the "fango", the mud, that lies at the core of Praga's poetics. The word has a programmatic value in the proemial poem of *Tavolozza* (1862), "Per cominciare":

> chi, col fango battendosi,
> cerca di metter l'ali.
>
> (Praga 1969: 8, ll. 47–48)

In the poetry of the *Scapigliati*, the "fango" is everything that is opposed to spiritual elevation and it is central to one of Praga's most popular poems, "Preludio", where the poet famously promises to sing of "the ideal, drowning in the mud":

Canto [...]
[...] l'ideale che annega nel fango

(Praga 1969: 84, ll. 25–26)

De Marchi's translation, echoing Giacomo Leopardi's "A se stesso", is an original re-interpretation of Shakespeare's sonnet. Leopardi's poem is certainly more of a tonal presence, although it is clearly invoked by the incipit of De Marchi's sonnet ("Povero cor"), recalling the "stanco mio cor" of Leopardian memory (Leopardi 1998: 510, l. 2). De Marchi, furthermore, situates his translation within the Italian poetic canon thanks to the use of the poeticisms "opra" [work] and "fora" [would be]. Luca Serianni notes that "opra" runs throughout the Italian poetic tradition in the nineteenth and twentieth centuries and recurs in authors such as Carducci, Giovanni Pascoli, and Gabriele D'Annunzio, its last certified appearance coming in Montale (Serianni 2001: 100). De Marchi's translation exemplifies the anxiety of experimentation of a translator who operates between tradition and modernity, seeking to surpass in originality both Olivieri's servile translation and Sanfelice's Carduccian imitation of Shakespeare.

From Tradition to Contemporaneity: Wrestling with Shakespeare

Nineteenth-century Italian translations of the *Sonnets* show an interesting leap toward modernity, as far as the language and style of the poems are concerned. While Olivieri aimed chiefly to encourage the dissemination of Shakespeare's sonnets in Italy, rendering them in prose through plain language that only very rarely has poetic traits and paying attention, above all, to grammatical and syntactical cohesion, both Sanfelice and De Marchi included some highly specific elements of contemporary poetics in their translations of Shakespeare. Sanfelice tethered his work to two metric and stylistic pillars: Shakespearean sonnets and Carduccian language. Moreover, he succeeded, with the exception of two sonnets (Sonnets 135 and 136), in creating perfect hendecasyllables, often through metrical virtuosity (synaloepha and enjambment above all), thus respecting both the canonical Petrarchan line and the pattern of the Shakespearean sonnet.

On the one hand, the syntax of Sanfelice's translations coincides, where possible, with the original—and this is what made Carducci speak of "wrestling" or bodily combat ["fare alle braccia"] with Shakespeare (Shelley 1894: vii). On the other, the imagery evoked by the new sonnets is torn between the original and the literary background so familiar to the translator. The Italian sonnets often omit important details from the original, mainly because of the imitative nature of Sanfelice's translation, although he somehow remedies this shortcoming through the insertion of linguistic traits that help to "Italianize" the imagery. In particular,

188   *Matteo Brera*

Giovanni Pascoli is a significant presence in his translation, as in Sonnet 143 in which the "farmyard drama with three characters" (West 2007: 435) is emphasized through the use of rhyme words that link Sanfelice's translation to the Italian poetic tradition of his time. Sanfelice's translation is revealing, even in an analysis of the first two quatrains alone:

> Lo, as a careful housewife runs to catch
> One of her feathered creatures broke away,
> Sets down her babe, and makes all swift dispatch
> In pursuit of the thing she would have stay;
> Whilst her neglected child holds her in chase,
> Cries to catch her whose busy care is bent
> To follow that which flies before her face,
> Not prizing her poor infant's discontent [...]
>
> (Duncan-Jones 2002: 401)

> Ecco, come sollecita massaia
>   corre dietro al pulcin che l'è sfuggito,
>   pon giù il bambino, e affrettasi per l'aia,
>   per raggiungere il piccolo smarrito;
>
> e il bimbo intanto che si vede solo,
>   qua e là cèrcala e grida, ma al pulcino
>   ella sol bada che va inanzi a volo,
>   né ascolto dà al suo povero bambino [...]
>
> (Sanfelice 1898: CXLIII)

Before 1898, when Sanfelice's translation was published, the rhyming words "massaia" and "aia" occurred only twice in the sum of Italian poetry. Other occurrences are found in Praga's "L'anima del vino" (Praga 1969: 133, ll. 17–20), and Giovanni Pascoli's madrigal "Galline" (Stoppelli 2010):

> Al cader delle foglie, alla massaia
> non piange il vecchio cor, come a noi grami:
> ché d'arguti galletti ha piena l'aia;
>
> e spessi nella pace del mattino
> delle utili galline ode i richiami:
> zeppo, il granaio; il vin canta nel tino.
>
> Cantano a sera intorno a lei stornelli
> le fiorenti ragazze occhi pensosi,
> mentre il granturco sfogliano, e i monelli
> ruzzano nei cartocci strepitosi.
>
> (Pascoli 2015: 239)

Through the Fickle Glass 189

There is a link between Pascoli's linguistic *koiné* and the general atmosphere of Sanfelice's sonnets, where the cruelness of the Dark Lady/housewife, who follows the "feathered creature"/youth while abandoning the "babe"/poet, is lost in favour of the representation of a rural scene that would immediately call the *Myricae* to readers' minds. Furthermore, the image of the unruly scamps ("i monelli | ruzzano nei cartocci strepitosi", ll. 9–10) in Pascoli's "Galline" can be linked with Sanfelice's "va inanzi a volo" [flies before her face] (l. 7).

Sanfelice's translation of Shakespeare's "feathered creatures" seems to be indebted to another poem by Pascoli, "Primo Canto", where the same context—and the same rhyme words—are in evidence:

> Galletti arguti, gloria dell'aia
> che da due mesi v'ospita e pasce,
> ora la vostra vecchia massaia,
> quando vi sente, pensa alle grasce [...]
>
> (Pascoli 2002: 782, ll. 19–22)

Another potential echo of Pascoli's phrasing can be found in the final couplet of Sonnet 146, where, in order to translate Shakespeare's polyptoton "And death once dead, there's no more dying then" (Duncan-Jones 2002: 409), Sanfelice refers again to *Myricae* and, more precisely, to the poem "Il pesco":

> si crede
> morta la Morte,
>
> anch'essa [...]
>
> (Pascoli 2015: 573, ll. 7–9)

The polyptoton "morta la Morte" is a *hapax* in Italian literature before Sanfelice, who translates the final line of the sonnet in comparable terms: "Morta la morte, più mortal non sei" (Sanfelice 1898: CXLVI). "Morta la morte" appears as "uccisa la morte" in De Marchi's translation, where the general tone of the sonnet is remarkably *scapigliato*. The overall homicidal, suicidal aura characterizing the final couplet of the sonnet reflects the translator's decision to render a decadent Shakespeare whereby, for instance, even the "outward walls" (l. 4) of the original become a "peccaminoso [...] carcere" [sinful [...] jail] that is the ideal setting for a guilty and lustful *fin-de-siècle* love that has nothing to do with the more spiritual possibilities of Shakespeare's sonnet. The first translators of the *Sonnets* went beyond the limits imposed by the arduous task of condensing Shakespeare's verse into the Italian metrical system, imbuing the new poems with linguistic nuances that would make them easily

190   *Matteo Brera*

readable by an Italian audience, who would see them as lyrics written by a contemporary Shakespeare, sometimes *carducciano*, sometimes *pascoliano*, and sometimes *scapigliato*.

In the twentieth century, "wrestling" with the *Sonnets* became an even more challenging task for Italian translators who attempted to reproduce Shakespeare's poetics. Eugenio Montale, who translated only three sonnets (22, 33, and 48), unhitched his translations from established literary traditions. His rendering of Sonnet 33 merits comparison with its Shakespearean source:

> Full many a glorious morning have I seen
> Flatter the mountain tops with sovereign eye,
> Kissing with golden face the meadows green,
> Gilding pale streams with heavenly alchemy;
> Anon permit the basest clouds to ride
> With ugly rack on his celestial face,
> And from the forlorn world his visage hide,
> Stealing unseen to west with this disgrace:
> Even so my sun one early morn did shine
> With all triumphant splendor on my brow;
> But out alack, he was but one hour mine,
> The region cloud hath masked him from me now.
>   Yet him for this, my love no whit disdaineth:
>   Suns of the world may stain, when heaven's sun staineth.
>
>   (Duncan-Jones 2002: 177)

> Spesso, a lusingar vette, vidi splendere
> sovranamente l'occhio del mattino,
> e baciar d'oro verdi prati, accendere
> pallidi rivi d'alchimìe divine.
> Poi vili fumi alzarsi, intorbidata
> d'un tratto quella celestiale fronte,
> e fuggendo a occidente il desolato
> mondo, l'astro celare il viso e l'onta.
> Anch'io sul far del giorno ebbi il mio sole
> e il suo trionfo mi brillò sul ciglio:
> ma, ahimè, poté restarvi un'ora sola,
> rapito dalle nubi in cui s'impiglia.
>   Pur non ne ho sdegno: bene può un terrestre
>   sole abbuiarsi, se è così il celeste.
>
>   (Montale 1984: 732)

From a prosodic perspective, Montale's version adheres most closely to the pattern of the Shakespearean sonnet, preserving much of the metrical shell of the original. A run of interpolated enjambments—"accendere

Through the Fickle Glass 191

| pallidi rivi" (ll. 3–4), "desolato | mondo" (ll. 7–8), and "terrestre | sole" (ll. 13–14)—contributes to an ascending climax that leads to the progressive loss of the youth, who leaves the scene in the final dactylic *a maiore* line (l. 14). The passion for the lover, obscured by betrayal, is substituted in Montale by an unbridgeable distance between the poetic voice and the loved one, which reminds us, from a stylistic and linguistic point of view, of Montale's own poetics. One key word in the Ligurian poet's translation is the participle "desolato" ("desolate, wasted", for Shakespeare's "forlorn world"), of Eliotesque descent: through this kind of lexis, according to Roberto Orlando, Montale sublimates the imagery of his Shakespearean source to venture, instead, a frozen, rarefied, existential portrait, inherently reminiscent of Montale's poetic signature in *Le occasioni* (1928–1939) (Orlando 2001: 11–12).

Continuing the tradition by which Italian translators of the *Sonnets* mediate their renditions through a filter of contemporary Italian poetic vogues, Montale reworks Sonnet 33 in the context of his *own* evolving poetics, implementing a series of linguistic revisions to his versions between 1933 and 1942, a period during which he was working on *Le occasioni* and *Finisterre* (Orlando 2001: 8–11). The linguistic weave of Montale's sonnet also connects the translation with several other Montalean loci, especially the fourth section of *Le occasioni*, which is, not coincidentally, introduced by a couplet from Shakespeare's Sonnet 5: "Sap check'd with frost, and lusty leaves quite gone, | Beauty o'er-snow'd and bareness every where". The "astro inabissato" [sunken star] of "Stanze" (Montale 1984: 169, l. 7) is reminiscent of the darkening "terrestrial sun" ("terrestre | sole abbuiarsi") depicted in the final couplet of his translation of Sonnet 33 above, while the play of light and darkness is a motif that recurs throughout Montale's Shakespearean translations and his later poetry alike. In "Stanze", there is a "vaneggiante amara | oscurità che scende su chi resta" [delirious bitter | darkness that descends on those who remain] (Montale 1984: 170, ll. 38–40); in "Sotto la pioggia", the poet refers to a "poca vita tra sbatter d'ombra e luce" [little life between the gentle sound of light and shadow], possibly invoking Prospero's tenebrous image of a "little life" (Montale 1984: 171, l. 12); in "Costa San Giorgio", he speaks of "un'altra luce e l'ombra attorno" [another light and the surrounding shadow] that "sfarfalla, poi ricade" [flickers, and then falls] (Montale 1984: 173, ll. 4–5); and in "Il ritorno", he proposes an image pictorially close to the abducted sun/son of his Shakespearean translation—"il sole | che chiude la sua corsa, che si offusca | ai margini del canto" [the sun | which ends its course, which blurs | on the edge of the song] (Montale 1984: 186, ll. 23–25). Montale's version inflects Shakespeare's Sonnet 33 in an unusual, interlaced way, in that it is not only rooted in Petrarchan and Elizabethan poetic traditions but is also infused with the bleak tones of the translator's own wider corpus—a pessimism that would come to saturate his *Bufera* some

192 Matteo Brera

two decades later. As such, Shakespeare becomes subsumed within a broader, personalized poetics.

Bibliography

Brera, Matteo. 2010. "I *Sonetti* di W. Shakespeare in Italia. Osservazioni su lingua e stile delle traduzioni ottocentesche di Angelo Olivieri, Luigi De Marchi, Ettore Sanfelice". *Il Confronto Letterario*, 53: 63–86.

Brognoligo, Gioachino. 1891. "Le imitazioni shakespeariane di Antonio Conti". *Rassegna Padovana*, 1: 5–11.

Carducci, Giosuè. 1998. *Tutte le poesie*, ed. by Pietro Gibellini. Rome.

D'Elci, Angiolo. 1817. *Satire*. Florence.

De Marchi, Luigi. 1891. *I sonetti di Shakespeare*. Milan.

Duncan-Jones, Katherine, ed. 2002. *Shakespeare's Sonnets*. London.

Ferrari, Severino. 1892. *Versi raccolti e ordinati*. Modena.

Graf, Arturo. 1911. *L'anglomania e l'influsso inglese in Italia nel secolo XVIII*. Turin.

Leopardi, Giacomo. 1998. *Canti*, ed. by Franco Gavazzeni and Maria Maddalena Lombardi. Milan.

Locatelli, Angela. 1989. "La prima traduzione italiana dei 'Sonetti' Shakespeariani". *La traduzione del testo poetico*, ed. by Franco Buffoni. Milan. 283–90.

Montale, Eugenio. 1984. *Tutte le poesie*, ed. by Giorgio Zampa. Milan.

Olivieri, Angelo. 1890. *I Sonetti di William Shakespeare tradotti per la prima volta in Italiano. Col testo inglese a fronte riscontrato sui migliori esemplari*. Palermo.

———— 1905. *Studio sui verbi inglesi di uso più frequente e più specialmente quelli che cambiano di significato col cambiare di preposizione. Con numerosi ed opportuni esempi e frequenti citazioni classiche*. Milan.

Orlando, Roberto. 2001. "Montale e i *Sonnets* shakespeariani". *Applicazioni montaliane*. Lucca. 7–40.

Ottolini, A. 1921. "Traduttori di Shakespeare in Italia". *I libri del giorno*, 4: 349–51.

Pascoli, Giovanni. 2002. *Myricae. Canti di Castelvecchio*, ed. by Ivanos Ciani and Francesca Latini. Turin.

———— 2015. *Myricae*, ed. by Gianfranca Lavezzi. Milan.

Praga, Emilio. 1969. *Poesie*, ed. by Mario Petrucciani. Rome-Bari.

Sanfelice, Ettore. 1898. *I 154 sonetti di Guglielmo Shakespeare tradotti in sonetti italiani*. Velletri.

Scherillo, Michele. 1892. "Ammiratori e imitatori dello Shakespeare prima del Manzoni". *Nuova Antologia*. 3rd series, 42, 126.208–238.

Serianni, Luca. 2001. *Introduzione alla lingua poetica italiana*. Rome.

Shelley, Percy Bysshe. 1894. *Prometeo liberato. Dramma lirico in 4 atti*, trans. by Ettore Sanfelice. Turin.

Stoppelli, Pasquale, ed. 2010. *Biblioteca Italiana Zanichelli* (BIZ). Milan.

Swift, Jonathan. 1892. *I viaggi di Gulliver in alcune remote regioni del mondo*, trans. by Luigi De Marchi. Milan.

Tirinelli, Gustavo. 1878. "I Sonetti di Shakespeare". *Nuova Antologia*. 2nd series, 8. 5.228–259.

West, David, ed. 2007. *Shakespeare's Sonnets*. London.

Part III

Twentieth Century to the Present

Originality and Ownership

13 Giovanni Grasso
The *Other* Othello in London

Enza De Francisci

The Sicilian Dialect Player

Giovanni Grasso (1875–1930) was one of the most renowned actors to emerge from Sicily's first official theatre company, the *Compagnia drammatica dialettale siciliana*, founded by director Nino Martoglio in 1902. The set cast included actors such as Grasso, Angelo Musco, Marinella Bragaglia, and Mimì Aguglia, and the repertoire mainly consisted of a variety of plays situated in Sicily and composed by Giovanni Verga (the 1884 *Cavalleria rusticana* [*Rustic Chivalry*], *La Lupa* [*The She-Wolf*] of 1896, and *La caccia al lupo* [*A Wolf's Hunt*] from 1901, each performed in dialect) and by Luigi Pirandello, particularly his dialect plays produced in 1916 (*Pensaci, Giacuminu!* [*Think About It, Giacuminu!*], *Liolà*, *'A birritta cu 'i ciancianeddi* [*Cap and Bells*], and *'A Giarra* [*The Jar*]). Shortly after his debut in 1902, Grasso broke away from this company and performed with a number of actresses, including the aforementioned Bragaglia and Aguglia, both in Italy and in theatres around the world: Spain and South America in 1907; Britain, Germany, Hungary, and Russia in 1908; and, once again, Britain in 1910 (Zappulla Muscarà 1995). His international repertoire drew from a selection of plays not just by authors from Sicily (Verga and Giuseppe Giusti Sinopoli), but also playwrights from mainland Italy (Gabriele D'Annunzio's *La figlia d'Iorio* [*The Daughter of Iorio*] and Paolo Giacometti's *La morte civile* [*Civil Death*]) and from around the world too (Àngel Guimerà's Spanish play *Feudalismo* [*Feudalism*] and Shakespeare's *Othello*) (Walbrook 1911).

From this repertoire, Othello numbered among the more popular roles for Italy's prominent nineteenth-century actors, after inaugural, landmark performances by the renowned Ernesto Rossi (1829–1896) and Tommaso Salvini (1829–1915). While much has been discussed about the international careers of the Italian star actors (the *grandi attori*) and their interpretation of Shakespeare, above all by Marvin Carlson (1985), one actor who has been largely overlooked in existing scholarship is Grasso, who first performed in *Otello*, translated by Carlo Rusconi, at the Lyric Theatre in London on 21 March 1910. To date,

196   *Enza De Francisci*

only Sarah Zappulla Muscarà and Enzo Zappulla have catalogued the critical response Grasso received for his international tours (Zappulla Muscarà and Zappulla 1995). This chapter offers, however, a close analysis of a selection of English newspapers recently made available through the British Library's online *Newspaper Archive*. This material invites a set of questions about the status and legacy of Grasso's enterprise: why would a Sicilian actor choose to interpret Othello in Shakespeare's homeland? How did London audiences respond to this "new" Othello on stage? How did Grasso's interpretation differ from that of his predecessors? And what do the early accounts reveal about his approach to Shakespearean drama? Grasso's decision to perform the Moorish-Venetian general in an explicitly aggressive way must be placed within the wider historical and cultural framework of a newly-united Italy, and needs to be understood in the context of prevailing racial stereotypes of the Sicilian. While, one might argue, Grasso seemed somewhat naïve in exploiting this emerging stereotype of the violent Sicilian (a type closely associated with Africa), he was at the same time skilfully introducing a new kind of realism to the international stage through his interpretation of Shakespeare's Moor of Venice.

Othello and the "Southern Question"

The appeal of the international tour for late nineteenth-century Italian actors was in no small part rooted in Italy's unusual linguistic tradition. Studies conducted by Tullio De Mauro (De Mauro 1995: 41) estimate that, in the wake of Italy's relatively late political unification in 1861, only 2.5% of the population was able to speak the Italian language, based principally on the Florentine dialect, which bore the cultural prestige of Italy's *tre corone* [three crowns], Dante, Petrarch, and Boccaccio (Lepschy and Lepschy 1991); the majority of the populace communicated in local regional dialects. For a medium, such as theatre, so reliant on speech, the lack of a common spoken language would seem to inhibit the growth of an early national theatre. As a result of these socio-linguistic conditions, only two forms of Italian drama met with any notable success in Italy or abroad when, subsequently, they were taken to a global market: the *commedia dell'arte* and the opera, which both subordinate the importance of the spoken word to, respectively, body language and music (Trifone 2007). Victorian England, and specifically London, was a particularly fashionable place in which to perform (Jenkins 1991; Foulkes 1992), attracting many rising stars from around the world, including the French actresses Rachel Félix in 1841 and Sarah Bernhardt in 1879, Italy's *grande attrice* Eleonora Duse in 1893, and the Japanese performer Sada Yacco at the beginning of the twentieth century (Buonanno 1995: 66). Grasso toured London twice in the course of his career: following the enthusiastic response he gained in 1908 for his performances of mainly Sicilian plays, Grasso returned, only two years later, with a new role included in his repertoire, *Othello*.

Othello has, necessarily, had a complex performance history. The Othellos that appeared on British and American stages during the first half of the nineteenth century tended to promote a gallant, noble, heroically-tragic character. The English actor William Charles Macready, who starred as Othello in Warwick in 1829, describes his adopted persona as very much "like us", in an effort to erase cultural and racial difference (Vaughan 1994: 159). However, by the 1870s, in the wake of the America Civil war, *Othello* was no longer the regular feature that it had been in the American South during the first half of the nineteenth century, and was seldom seen except in parodies, or when its eponymous hero was deliberately "whitened" (Vaughan 1994: 160). Similarly, in Britain, which witnessed a continued expansion of its Empire in the last decades of the century and the emergent theory, following the publication of the sixth edition of Charles Darwin's *On the Origin of Species* (1872), of what might be labelled Social Darwinism, the conditions arose for a cultural assumption that "races" could be divided into different categories, such as, in Edward Saïd's terms, the "advanced and backward, or European-Aryan and Oriental-African" (Saïd 2003: 207). In this context, Othello was described in a lecture in 1904 by the Oxford Professor of Poetry, Andrew Cecil Bradley, as someone who "comes before us, dark and grand, with a light upon him from the sun where he was born", leading to the conclusion that "[h]e does not belong to our world" (Vaughan 1994: 158).

Coinciding with this branding of Othello as an "Other", the decades at the turn of the new century saw the arrival *en masse* of Italian migrant communities in London. Grasso was performing in London shortly after a period in which "Italian emigration became a mass phenomenon" in Britain. In 1888–89, Italian immigrants in Britain were described by the Select Committee appointed to adjudicate on foreign immigration as "immoral, illiterate, vicious, and low"—in sum, they were disparaged as "a degraded class, which must cause undesirable results among the surrounding population" (Sponza 1993: 12). In addition, just as Italians were being portrayed as "Other" in turn-of-the-century Britain, so too Sicily and Sicilians were becoming regarded as alien in post-unification Italy, at a time when racialist studies began to emerge in Italy, notably Cesare Lombroso's *L'uomo delinquente* (1876), subsequently translated into English by his daughter in 1911 as *Criminal Man*. Following years of postmortem examinations on criminals, Lombroso advocated a theory of the born criminal, placing the Southern Italian among what he calls a class of "savages". According to Lombroso, having been conquered over the centuries by a number of invading populations,

198 *Enza De Francisci*

including North Africans and Arabs, Southern Italians were predisposed to violent, criminal behaviour.

These years in Italy were marked by intellectual wrangling over the so-called "Southern Question", whose roots lay in the period of the Risorgimento itself. After Giuseppe Garibaldi's triumphant entrance into mainland Italy in May 1860 with his thousand troops—an expedition that ultimately led to political unification a year later—Luigi Carlo Farini, the chief administrator of Southern Italy, wrote despairingly to Camillo Cavour (soon to become Italy's first prime minister) from Molise on 27 October 1860: "Altro che Italia! Questa è Africa!" [Some Italy! This is Africa!] (Moe 2002). From 1861 onwards, Italy faced the challenges of self-fashioning, of constructing a stable national identity. As the Piedmontese statesman and man of letters Massimo d'Azeglio allegedly claimed, "L'Italia è fatta. Restano da fare gli italiani" [Italy has been made. We now need to make Italians]. Yet Italy remained fundamentally fractured between northern and southern spheres: the Mezzogiorno (the southern half, including Sicily, physically detached from the mainland) became a kind of "other".

Popular journals were quick to pick up on this emerging image of Sicily as the *Africa of Italy*. The *Illustrazione Italiana*, published in Milan, hardly ever featured illustrations and articles relating to the South during the first six months of its print run in 1873. However, as unification gathered momentum, not only did Southern Italy feature more regularly, but these representations tended to focus on a distinct brand of southern people. For the Christmas edition in 1890, journalist Raffaelo Barbiera was sent to Sicily to report on his experience in Palermo and the terminology he employs continued to reinforce Sicily's association with Africa. He makes reference to a boy's physical features (black curly hair and olive skin), concluding that "proud haughtiness and cunning are mixed together in the way he looks at you. For all that Norman blood mixed with Moorish blood, the latter is still dominant" (Dickie 1999: 102–4). Images of Sicily's "otherness" continued to proliferate in the *Illustrazione Italiana* throughout the well-known exhibition, the Mostra Etnografica Siciliana at the Esposizione Nazionale in Palermo from 1891 to 1892, inspired by the tradition of the 1851 Great Exhibition at Crystal Palace in London. This exhibition displayed various Sicilian cultural materials, collected by the doctor-turned-folklorist Giuseppe Pitrè, alongside a living exhibit of colonized Ethiopians residing in a fictional village, Villaggio Abissino, "[c]omplete with sand, palms, and huts" (Greene 2012: 300). Through this pairing of Sicily and Africa, this ethnographic exhibition continued to emphasize the "otherness" of the Mediterranean island. Early interpretations of Shakespeare's Othello were in dialogue with such questions of cultural identity, especially so when this "other" role was performed by an actor from the "other" part of Italy.

Grasso in London

Even prior to Grasso's debut on the London stage on 3 February 1908 at the Shaftesbury Theatre, the actor had already been turned into a kind of celebrity by the media. Indeed, his reputation was already sufficiently established that his debut was attended by royalty—King Edward VII, his wife, and the Prince and Princess of Wales. Before touring in London, Grasso had already achieved some notoriety after performing in Paris with his Sicilian repertoire, for which one of his most famous portrayals came in Verga's *Cavalleria rusticana*, in which he performed the role of the betrayed husband Compare Alfio who challenges his wife's lover to a duel. In contrast to Verga's original script, which ends soon after the lover is killed in the feud, Grasso's version allegedly saw the actor return on stage, bloody from the duel, in order to give himself up to two *carabinieri*, declaring in dialect, "Cca sugnu! ... Non scappu!" [Here I am! ... I'm not going anywhere!]—the last of several interpolations to Verga's text. Horrified by Grasso's modifications, Verga wrote to his translator, Édouard Rod, in a letter of 29 January 1908, to express his disgust at what he called Grasso's "caricatura grottesca" [grotesque caricature] of the Sicilian character (Verga 1954: 245–46), and to order the immediate withdrawal of *all* his plays from the actor's repertoire.

Despite Verga's incensed reaction, Parisian audiences were stunned by what they saw, and news of this realist actor quickly spread to London. According to the *Pall Mall Gazette* on 17 January 1908, Grasso's acting moved his audiences to tears:

> Strange and marvellous is the power of this Sicilian peasant who manages to deeply move, indeed to tears, a public as sceptical and frivolous as that of Paris. [...] Such a natural interpretation, so primitively realistic and authentic, has never before been seen in Paris.
> (Zappulla Muscarà and Zappulla 1995: 97)

Even before landing in Britain, Grasso's reputation as an actor of "primitively realistic" sensibilities had already preceded him, and this characterisation—one that paired clearly eulogistic terms of wonder ("strange", "marvellous") and authenticity ("natural", "realistic", "authentic") with a haughty and pejorative rhetoric ("peasant", "primitively") in an uneasy, contradictory balance—was perpetuated in the intervening years before his performance of Othello in 1910.

The *Manchester Courier and Lancashire General Advertiser* on 8 February 1908 was one of the first newspapers to comment on the initial success that Grasso's theatre company gained in London. The company, starring Mimì Aguglia as the leading lady, performed a selection

200 *Enza De Francisci*

of Sicilian plays including Luigi Capuana's *Malìa*, Verga's *Cavalleria rusticana*, and Sinopoli's *La zolfara*:

> The artistic success of the Sicilians is assured. When they opened on Monday at the Shaftesbury in *Malia* [*sic*] it was at once seen that they were great realists, and to-night they show that their success is not confined to one play. They gave a wonderful performance of *Cavalleria rusticana* which, minus music, is more powerful than the opera. Signor Grasso's Turridu is a very strong piece of action, and a big hit was scored by Mme. Aguglia as Santuzza. The second item on the bill was *Zolfara*, a grim little melodrama about the sulphur mines. It, too, is full of blood and fire, and shows the players to the utmost advantage both as tragic and comic actors of great skill.
>
> (Quoted from *The British Newspaper Archive*)

As with the *Pall Mall Gazette* cited earlier, the anonymous critic here points to the actors' realism and the play's defining atmosphere of "blood and fire"—qualities reminiscent of those celebrated in the company's earlier performances in Paris, which suggests that the explicit use of violence in the performances by Grasso's troupe was becoming a kind of signature or trademark. Tellingly, the critic preferred Grasso's theatrical version of *Cavalleria rusticana* to the more famous one-act operatic version by Pietro Mascagni that premièred in 1890 in Rome. Despite the use of dialect in Grasso's rendition, this reviewer was evidently not lost in translation. Indeed, to overcome the obvious language barrier, the actors relied on physical gesture and body movement to communicate with their foreign audience. This privileging of physical techniques of expression has its roots in practical necessity: the absence of a common spoken language in the newly-unified Italy compelled actors to exploit gesture and mime to render their plays accessible even to an Italian audience. According to the same newspaper a few days later, on 17 February 1908, what was distinctive about this company of actors was that they "let themselves go with such Southern abandon, that these Sicilian plays may almost claim to be designated as unique". This reputation for naturalistic immediacy, unmediated, "Southern" authenticity, and an appearance of spontaneous execution of their scenes attracted large audiences to Grasso's performances, proving so commercially successful that "the management at the Shaftesbury is supplying each member of the audience with a card on which may be written the title of his or her favourite play, so that arrangements for future repertoires can be made to suit the wishes of the majority". Part of the growing popularity of Grasso's troupe among English audiences would seem to derive, then, from the performers' ability to play up to emergent stereotypes about the impulsive Sicilian.

In spite of the Shaftesbury Theatre's efforts to ensure that Grasso's most popular Sicilian plays were performed on future tours, it seems that Grasso had another role up his sleeve: Othello. As rumours started to reach London that the star actor would perform this tragic role, latent stereotypical perceptions about cultural and racial affinities between Sicily and Africa were growing even stronger. The *Manchester Courier and Lancashire General Advertiser*, in its commentary on 3 August 1908, is perhaps the first newspaper to announce Grasso's intention of returning to the capital city for his second tour:

> There is some talk of a return to London of Signor Grasso, the famous Sicilian actor, who made a stir when he appeared last season at the Shaftesbury Theatre in company with Madame Aguglio [*sic*]. Should the contemplated arrangement be carried out, his leading lady on this occasion will be Madame Grammatica. They will appear in *Othello*, a tragedy which Grasso is anxious to "present" to a British audience. Doubtless old playgoers who remember the sensation that was made by Salvini in this role will be furbishing up bygone memories. Certainly Grasso seems designed by nature for the part of the jealous Moor. "Can you imagine", says one writer on things dramatic, "that tempestuous leonine creature filling the stage with his transports of jealousy? It would be a tremendous affair, a really appalling spectacle". He does not envy Madame Grammatica as Desdemona in the final scene with Grasso as Othello, and asks with real or affected alarm "would she live to play a second performance?"

What is striking is the immediate association between Grasso's Sicilian identity and his perceived suitability (as if "designed by nature") to play the jealous Moorish general. Indeed, the critic, partially displacing his type-casting on to an interlocutor (real or fictitious), archly suggests that the actor's animalistic rage put the life of the leading lady in danger. To be sure, performing alongside Grasso in this uninhibited, realist vein was a notoriously challenging job. Dramatist and theatre critic Camillo Antona-Traversi offers an account of what he witnessed during a performance of Grasso's interpretation of Capuana's *Malìa* from the previous tour in Paris, in which the actor starred alongside Mimì Aguglia. Traversi recalls Aguglia, returning back stage, screaming in pain for having been grabbed by her hair and flung to the floor by Grasso, crying out, "Mi ucciderà!" [He will kill me!] (Antona-Traversi 1929: 205).

A no less noteworthy feature of the reviewer's commentary on Grasso's mooted performance of Othello is the instinctive comparison to his predecessor, Tommaso Salvini. Salvini was one of the first Italian actors to gain notable critical attention in performing Shakespeare abroad, debuting the role of Othello in London at Drury Lane on 1 April 1875 in an

202   *Enza De Francisci*

Italian translation by Giulio Carcano. Salvini gained a name for himself by experimenting with realist drama and dissolving the illusion of a division between art and reality; he was duly singled out as one of the early actors admired by Russian naturalistic director Constantin Stanislavsky in his 1924 autobiography *My Life in Art*. Even earlier, American author Edward Tuckerman Mason in 1890 produced an account of Salvini's interpretation of Othello, scene by scene, and points to one element of the performance considered particularly unusual and unprecedented: "At the end of the speech he embraces Desdemona more closely, kisses her, and stands with his lips pressed to hers" (Mason 1890: 22).

Over three decades after Salvini's debut in London, Grasso premièred his version of *Otello* at the Lyric Theatre on 21 March 1910, this time in an Italian translation by Carlo Rusconi, with Marinella Bragaglia as Desdemona and Angelo Campagna as Iago (Zappulla Muscarà and Zappulla 1995: 121). One of the first critical accounts of Grasso's interpretation was produced by theatre critic Henry Mackinnon Walbrook (1911), who reviewed the première itself. From his description, what emerges most clearly is that Grasso was enthusiastically welcomed back to London, the audience allegedly "calling and cheering" for him (Walbrook 1911: 210). Walbrook opens his review by describing Grasso's costume and make-up, "[b]earded, brown rather than black", tending to suggest a North African or Arabic Moor, and calls the character a "noble savage" (Walbrook 1911: 210) in terminology that gained currency during the Enlightenment (Harp and Hrdlicka 2015). He gradually moves on to describe a more intimate scene with Desdemona: perhaps to distinguish himself from Salvini's passionate interpretation, Grasso appeared to have favoured a less physical (but possibly more sensual) approach: "And when he kissed her it was not her lips that he kissed, *more Siciliano*, but her hair or her fingers, with a courtly reverence" (Walbrook 1911: 211). The comparisons between Grasso and his predecessor culminate, towards the end of the review, in a consideration of their respective interpretations of the protagonists' death scenes. Walbrook explains that, like Salvini, Grasso "catches Iago by the throat, flinging him to the floor, raising a foot to trample on him, bending over him as though to choke him to death, and finally recoiling and collapsing into a chair in a convulsion of shame and rage", bursting out in "hoarse cries". However, Walbrook later distinguishes Grasso's realism from Salvini's at the very end of the play. Desdemona's murder is described (a little grudgingly) as "realistic enough", taking place behind the curtains, followed by "a thrilling cry of horror and fury at the discovery of Iago's villainy and Desdemona's innocence" (Walbrook 1911: 212–13), but Grasso makes his mark in his approach to Othello's suicide. The death scenes are said to have been "so realistic in all their prolonged details—including a hideous death-rattle—that they were too much for some of the audience"

(Walbrook 1911: 213), hinting at a game of actorly one-upmanship between Grasso and his predecessor, as if Grasso sought to out-Salvini Salvini in conveying these violent acts.

In a similar vein, the *Sheffield Daily Telegraph*, just before the theatre company embarked on their tour of South America, made a similar observation, on 2 April 1910, about Grasso's interpretation of Othello's end, drawing a comparison with Salvini:

> Grasso's death scene as Othello is so realistic that it seems the actual thing and—whether that is desirable or not on the stage—I can recall no other actor or actress, not excluding Sarah Bernhardt, who has conveyed that impression to me. Grasso's treatment is not violent or prolonged, as Salvini's was. In a flash the Othello of Grasso has drawn his scimitar across his throat and fallen flat on his face on the stage. He crawls on all fours to Desdemona's bed, rises with his back to the audience, and with his hands to his throat tries to speak the last beautiful lines. But the words cannot come, they issue only as a loud inarticulate gurgle, and Othello once more falls prone on the stage. The effect would horrify if it did not enthral by its supreme reality. What does Grasso do? To get that effect by sleight of hand he takes a mouthful of water.

Both reviews seem to suggest that Grasso was keen to shock his audience with a technique never before experimented with on stage, and to offer an even more heightened brand of on-stage realism than either Salvini or Bernhardt. A fortnight earlier, the *Western Daily Press*, in a review dated 23 March 1910, located the distinctiveness of Grasso's portrayal in his Sicilian identity:

> We are used to tragic, melodramatic Othello, passionate at times, it is true; but Signor Grasso makes him almost epileptic in his distress and volcanic in his anger. His acting was altogether superb, and although much of it was brutal we must not blame him for displaying the Moor's animal instincts; he merely gives what is to the Southern mind a perfectly natural and accurate description.

Reconciling Grasso's "Southern" bearing with Othello's perceived nobility, the reviewer goes further by suggesting that Grasso brought to life "a real living Othello, a man with all the instincts of a man, a gentleman, and not a mere savage, as too many people persist in believing". Part of the attraction, to critics such as this, of Grasso's Sicilianism is the opportunity it afforded for recuperating Othello from the sub-Saharan barbarousness of "black" interpretations, instead relocating the protagonist's racial identity to the cultural melting-pot of Moorish North Africa and Southern Europe, the implication being that a "brown" Othello

204 *Enza De Francisci*

as portrayed by Grasso could combine Moorish animalism with a redeemable Southern European nobility.

Grasso's "otherness" as a Sicilian, a result of his origins in that liminal territory between Europe and Africa, is hinted at repeatedly in newspaper accounts from the time, in which the Sicilian actors ("them") are consistently counterpointed with indigenous British audiences ("us"). The *Sheffield Daily Telegraph*, on 2 April 1910, stated that "[t]o judge them"—"these players from a sunny land"—"by the same standard as you use for our own actors would be absolutely futile; it would be like comparing one of Pain's firework displays with the titanic efforts of their native Etna, or its sister, Stromboli". For all the immediacy of the performance, Grasso's troupe remains decidedly "other" in its ethos. In a conflation of the realms of "art" and "nature", the same critic adds:

> It is even hard to believe that the Sicilians are artists at all; they are more like a product of nature. You only realise that they are artists afterwards when you think about what you have seen, and feel that you know something more about nature than you did before. Only one thing can make you feel that, and that one thing is art.

Grasso's technique is celebrated as "primal and direct", leading to the claim that "there never was a company of more flagrant melodramatists in this country", even though this praise is tinged with a kind of condescension about the players' Sicilian origins:

> The Sicilians are children of a land wherein passion still lives— where men still right their wrongs by means of the hereditary and tragic Vendetta. Nature in Sicily is less tame than in our country: she does things on a more flamboyant scale, crumbling up cities in the palm of her hand, and spouting flame and molten earth at the sky from the mouths of her burning mountains. The passions of her people are a reflection of the same spirit. Love, hatred, jealousy, revenge are all burning, devastating things. They are primitive and untamed. The peasant of Sicily is to this day something of a faun—beneath the veil of Christianity there still lurks the spirit of the bright Pagan world.

In keeping with other reviewers, this critic, harnessing a eulogistic, sentimental rhetoric of romanticized Sicilian impulsiveness and a more condescending vocabulary of rustic primitivism, makes much capital out of the myth of Sicilian passion and natural spontaneity, a cultural assumption to which Grasso may consciously have played up for crowd-pleasing effect. The article concludes with a final salvo that posits a fundamental, universalizing similitude between Sicilian and English, while reasserting the insuperable cultural differences between the two:

Grasso and his players are a glimpse of a lost age. Every play they produce reveals the same thing, a fierce, primal thing, something as remote from our own day and civilisation as it is near to our own hearts: hence cultured London's ready response. It matters not what play it is: it is just the same in Shakespeare's *Othello* or in a tragedy comedy of Anatole France, as it is in their own folk-plays, *Feudalismo* and *Malia* [*sic*].

A New Othello

Given the extent and consistency of this critical reception, Grasso's performance seems susceptible to a kind of journalistic caricaturing and reductiveness. One notable exception to this trend can be found in a review published in *The World* on 29 March 1910:

> Were I asked to give in one word the salient figure of Signor Grasso's magnificent, nay, wonderful impersonation, I should say, "Restraint". In comparison with certain English actors who have roared and bellowed and hurled themselves and the furniture and Iago about the stage in their paroxysms of fury, this, the most tremendous Othello for three decades past, was the embodiment of self-restraint.
>
> (Quoted in Zappulla Muscarà and Zappulla 1995: 122)

Registering the crucial moments before Grasso's Othello launched into his impassioned outbursts on stage, this reviewer draws attention to the control and craft that undergirds his performance, further suggesting that the actor deliberately gave the impression of "letting himself go" (to return to the *Pall Mall Gazette*'s terms) in these heated scenes, exploiting a skilful dramatic technique based, unexpectedly, on discipline, moderation, and self-possession. It is precisely this unexpected element to Grasso's performances that suggests that, by pushing the boundaries between fiction and non-fiction and by exploiting (even partially) the racial stereotypes of the time, the actor cleverly began to forge a new kind of realism on the London stage—a realism that, arguably, went on to influence foremost practitioners like Stanislavsky, Meyerhold, and Strasberg (see Tcherkasski in Sica 2014). While early accounts and theatre reviews are inclined to place emphasis on Grasso's explicitly violent approach, what is noteworthy here is the description of the moment before his aggressive outbursts on stage, drawing attention to a rather different side to his dramaturgy, based on self-discipline and control.

This Sicilian actor's audacious decision to interpret the role of Othello in Shakespeare's homeland begins to make sense when considered in the context of transnational cultural practices and expectations at the turn of the twentieth century. Presumably what attracted Grasso to this role

206 *Enza De Francisci*

was, to some degree, the opportunities it afforded him to take advantage of the associative pairing of Sicily and Africa that defined many ethnographic prejudices of the time. Privileging a language of physical performance, Grasso narrowed the gap between an actorly Sicilian "them" and a staid British "us". Indeed, none of the critics cited above had any difficulties understanding the foreign language of the script. Grasso's exploitation of contemporary racial stereotypes goes hand-in-hand with his pioneering of a new kind of realism: combining a veneer of animalistic abandon with an underlying discipline of tight control, he garnered a reputation for what one of Italy's foremost twentieth-century writers, Luigi Pirandello, called the "terribile, meravigliosa bestialità di Giovanni Grasso" [terrible, wonderful bestiality of Giovanni Grasso] (Pirandello [1909] 1960: 1168), and in so doing ultimately placed Sicily on the modern Shakespearean map.

Bibliography

Antona-Traversi, Camillo. 1929. *Ricordi parigini*. Ancona.

The British Newspaper Archive, https://www.britishnewspaperarchive.co.uk.

Buonanno, Giovanna. 1995. *A Stage under Petticoat Government: Italian International Actresses in the Age of Queen Victoria*. PhD Thesis. University of Warwick.

Carlson, Marvin. 1985. *The Italian Shakespearians: Performances by Ristori, Salvini, and Rossi in England and America*. Washington.

De Mauro, Tullio. 1995. *Storia linguistica dell'Italia unita*. Rome.

Dickie, John. 1999. *Darkest Italy. The Nation and Stereotypes of the Mezzogiorno*. London.

Foulkes, Richard, ed. 1992. *British Theatre in the 1890s. Essays on Drama and the Stage*. Cambridge.

Greene, Vivien. 2012. "The 'Other' Africa: Giuseppe Pitrè's Mostra Etnografica Siciliana (1891–2)". *Journal of Modern Italian Studies*, 17.3: 288–309.

Harp, Richard, and Steven Hrdlicka. 2015. "The Critical Backstory". *Othello: A Critical Reader*, ed. by Robert C. Evans. London. 15–49.

Jenkins, Antony. 1991. *The Making of Victorian Drama*. Cambridge.

Lepschy, Anna Laura, and Giulio Lepschy. 1991. *The Italian Language Today*, 2nd edition. London.

Lombroso, Cesare. 2006 [1876]. *Criminal Man*, trans. by Mary Gibson and Nicole Hahn Rafter. Durham, NC.

Mason, Edward Tuckerman. 1890. *The Othello of Tommaso Salvini*. With Portraits by Robert Frederick Blum. New York.

Moe, Nelson. 2002. *The View from Vesuvius: Italian Culture and the Southern Question*. Berkeley, LA.

Pirandello, Luigi. 1960 [1909]. "Teatro Siciliano?". *Saggi, poesie, scritti vari*, ed. by Manlio Lo Vecchio-Musti. Milan. 1168–69.

Saïd, Edward. 2003 [1977]. *Orientalism*. London.

Sponza, Lucio. 1993. "The 1880s: A Turning Point". *The Supplement to The Italianist. A Century of Italian Emigration to Britain 1880–1980s: Five Essays*, ed. by Lucio Sponza and Arturo Tosi, no. 13. 10–24.

Stanislavsky, Constantin. 1962 [1924]. "Tommaso Salvini the Elder". *My Life in Art*. London. 265–77.

Tcherkasski, Sergei. 2014. "Twofaced Giovanni Grasso and his Great Spectators or What Stanislavsky, Meyerhold and Strasberg Actually Stole from the Sicilian Actor". *The Italian Method of La Drammatica*, ed. by Anna Sica. Milan. 109–32.

Trifone, Pietro. 2007. *Malalingua. L'italiano scorretto da Dante a oggi*. Bologna.

Vaughan, Virginia Mason. 1994. "Salvini, Irving, and the Dissociation of Intellect". *Othello: A Contextual History*. Cambridge. 158–80.

Verga, Giovanni. 1954. *Lettere al suo traduttore*, ed. by Fredi Chiapelli. Florence.

Walbrook, Henry Mackinnon. 1911. "Grasso as Othello". *Nights at the Play*. London. 210–13.

Zappulla Muscarà, Sarah, and Enzo Zappulla. 1995. *Giovanni Grasso. Il più grande attore tragico del mondo*. Acireale.

14 Shakespeare, Vittorini, and the Anti-Fascist Struggle

Enrica Maria Ferrara

In a 1946 interview with the English journalist Kay Gittings aimed at a British audience, Elio Vittorini (1908–66), one of the most influential Sicilian writers and intellectuals of the Fascist and post-war eras, discussed his English literary models, not least Shakespeare, whose *Titus Andronicus* Vittorini had translated into Italian in 1938 for the new edition of Shakespeare's collected works edited by Mario Praz (Shakespeare 1943: 474–553). Vittorini, who had just published his Resistance novel *Uomini e no* [*Men and Not Men*] (1945) after receiving widespread acclaim for his anti-Fascist novel *Conversazione in Sicilia* [*Conversations in Sicily*] (1938–39), also recalls having read the complete works of Shakespeare, in English, between 1935 and 1936. Throughout the Fascist period, Vittorini had worked for the publisher Bompiani as a translator of English and Spanish texts, also serving as editor for several anthologies of foreign literature (including one of modern American writers, *Americana*), and acquired a reputation for frustrating and circumventing the scrutiny of Fascist censors. Vittorini's *Tito Andronico* is just one explicit manifestation of a broader, more sustained engagement with the English playwright, who enabled Vittorini, in *Conversazione in Sicilia*, to articulate a partially occluded anti-Fascist message.

Considered "il più grande scrittore non solo inglese che si sia avuto dopo i tragici greci" (Vittorini 2008: 334) [not just the greatest English writer, but the greatest writer anywhere, since the Greek tragedians], Shakespeare exerted a special hold over Vittorini due to his ability to reach out to a diverse audience through a type of rhetoric that was comprehensible, at different levels, to both aristocrats and the general public, to intellectuals and laymen alike (Blake 1983: 18). In his 1937 article, "Elogio della cultura popolare", Vittorini argued that Shakespeare's plays could be seen as embodying a "popular culture" otherwise non-existent in Italy. Even factory workers had taken to reading Shakespeare at the beginning of the twentieth century, stimulated by a desire for "culture":

> L'operaio che, con bisogno estraneo alla sua attività di operaio, leggeva Shakespeare e Vico, impersonava la vera tendenza alla cultura.

Shakespeare, Vittorini, and the Anti-Fascist Struggle 209

Egli suscitava un tipo ideale cui tutti cercavano o dovevano cercare di conformarsi. [...] Così il desiderio della cultura era in tutti.

(Vittorini 1997: 1029)

[The factory worker who read Shakespeare and Vico, driven by a need that was alien to his job as a factory worker, was the champion of a true disposition to culture. He evoked an ideal type to which everyone sought or had to conform. [...] Thus, the desire for culture was in everybody.]

It is in this sense that Shakespeare's art was considered politically potent by Vittorini, stimulating social and cultural participation among the working classes.

In post-war Italy, Vittorini often seemed to perform a balancing act between the rival stances forming, as if around a virtual barricade, between, on the one hand, left-wing intellectuals, often former anti-Fascist partisans, advocating a kind of Soviet Communist cultural politics, and, on the other, the democratic forces associated with the Allies and supported by the Catholic Church, severing cultural production from politics. The importance, in Vittorini's poetics, of an artistic idiom accessible to an audience of diverse social, political, and aesthetic leanings is clarified further in an essay on the socially-committed artist, "L'artiste doit-il s'engager?", composed in 1948, in which Vittorini argues that militant artists reveal their social or political commitment through a type of art recognized as "engageant", activating various levels of meaning for different types of public (Vittorini 2008: 519–33). The paragon that Vittorini proposes is Shakespeare:

L'arte moderna non è engageant per tutti come lo era, per alcuni in un modo, e per altri in un altro, per alcuni in una misura e per altri in un'altra, quando Shakespeare, ad esempio, sapeva engager nei gradi e nei sensi più diversi gentiluomini, borghesi, popolo minuto, e cattolici e riformati, oppressori ed oppressi; o non è engageant con effetto immediato.

(Vittorini 2008: 527)

[Modern art is not *engageant* for everyone, *engageant* in one way and to a certain extent for some, and in another way and to a different extent for others, as it used to be, when Shakespeare, for example, was able to *engage* (to varying degrees and at different levels of meaning) gentlemen, the middle class, common people, both Catholics and the Reformed, oppressors and oppressed. Or else, it is not *engageant* with immediate effect.]

210   Enrica Maria Ferrara

The absolute and all-encompassing nature of Shakespeare's "engagement" is attested in its theatrical, performed aspect, which boasts an "effetto immediato" [immediate effect]. As Vittorini explains further on, in giving shape to the myths of popular imagination, Shakespeare's plays produced an "immediate effect" on Elizabethan audiences due, first, to the osmosis between the *engagé* artist and society described by Vittorini as an intimacy between playwright-actor and audience and, secondly, to the theatrical medium itself, which enabled the playwright to return the product of his social engagement to a heterogeneous audience, and to receive an equally immediate acknowledgement of this engagement through unmediated audience response. Given its immediacy and social reach, Shakespeare's theatre, for Vittorini, had the potential to serve the anti-Fascist cause without conveying explicitly anti-Fascist sentiments. The need to circumvent the censor became more pronounced after Mussolini extended his control over Italian stages, passing new legislature on 6 January 1931 (*Nuove norme sulla censura teatrale*), which centralized theatrical censorship, previously left to the initiative of individual prefects (Bonsaver 2007: 58–75). Essentially, "all plays, operas, reviews and all other forms of live theatrical presentation intended for public performance were subject to examination", even if they had previously been staged or published (Griffiths 2005: 77–78). Shakespearean political tragedies (notably *Julius Caesar* and *Macbeth*) received particular attention and were only finally allowed after several textual changes and deletions.

Beyond its political agency, Shakespeare's theatre was also, for Vittorini, the quintessential embodiment of a plurilingual realism. It enabled the expression of multiple registers and varieties of spoken language, and also incorporated that indispensable non-verbal component of communication, body language. In the critical essay *Parlato e Metafora* (1959) (Vittorini 2008: 870–73), Vittorini posits the primacy of theatrical writing for the purpose of realistic representation and pinpoints his reasons in theatre's ingredients of gesture, mime, vocal projection, timbre, and tone; in sum, in the physicality of theatrical language, as opposed to narrative as a literary medium. Given that, in Vittorini's opinion, half of all *viva voce* communication was accounted for by gestural language, an author of a narrative, non-dramatic medium would need to "tradurre in parole [...] una sua scelta di tutto quanto nella realtà di comunicazione è costituito di mimica, di gesti, di sguardi, di pause, di toni, ecc., anzichè di parole" (Vittorini 2008: 872) [translate into words [...] his choice of everything that, in the actual practice of communication, is composed of mime, gestures, glances, pauses, tones, etc., instead of words]. In the case of Shakespeare's theatre specifically, his *engageant* vitality also derived in part from his role as an actor-author, a figure mythologized in Vittorini's novel *Conversazione in Sicilia* as an embodiment of *impegno* [social commitment] (Fischer 2013).

Shakespeare, Vittorini, and the Anti-Fascist Struggle 211

This chapter, which builds upon previous research on the role that Vittorini attributed to Shakespeare's theatre in transmitting a fiercely anti-Fascist message through *Conversazione*'s subtexts (Ferrara 2012: 115–119), aims to further the hypothesis that the Shakespearean artist— an artist who is truly and profoundly *engageant*—constitutes the novel's hidden, "suggellato" [sealed] message. To this end, I will explore the symbolic meanings that references to Shakespeare and his theatre convey in Vittorini's novel, paying particular attention to the allusions to *Macbeth*, *Hamlet*, and *The Tempest* scattered throughout.

Macbeth, Hamlet, and Silvestro's Father: "My Shakespearean Father"

A so-called left-wing or "revolutionary" Fascist, Vittorini had initially been drawn to the Fascist cause by Mussolini's apparent openness towards a socialist agenda and a "corporative" state, although these aspirations floundered with the eruption of the Spanish Civil War in 1936, prompting Mussolini to create a right-wing strategic axis in Europe with General Franco's Spain and Hitler's Germany. Steeped in disillusionment at the failed "revolutionary" project, *Conversazione in Sicilia* was, by Vittorini's own admission, an emotional and intellectual response to this trauma. The novel narrates the story of Silvestro's journey back to his Sicilian homeland from the North of Italy, where he has lived in a state of indifference and apathy even though he is tormented by the images of "massacri sui manifesti dei giornali" (Vittorini 2005: 571) ["slaughters on the newspaper placards" (Vittorini 1949: 13)]. It soon becomes apparent that Silvestro is an alter-ego of the author and that the novel is a journey of both regeneration (like Dante's *Commedia*, Bunyan's *The Pilgrim's Progress*, or Joyce's *Ulysses*) and *nostos*, a voyage back, in this case to his childhood (Bertoni 2009: 83–90). By the end of the journey, following a number of encounters, the protagonist, Silvestro, has undergone a transformation from the indifference and "non-hope" of his Fascist indoctrination to an emotional understanding of "i dolori del mondo offeso" ["the woes of the outraged world"], which will lead him to the discovery of other ideologies that could be embraced as an alternative to Fascism.

Profoundly aware of the need to bypass Fascist censors, Vittorini composed his novel in a style that combined the main components of a social realist novel with the poetic simplicity of fairy-tales and parables, and ample use of symbolism to construct its political allegory (Bonsaver 2000: 84–90). From its opening, *Conversazione* makes reference to Shakespeare's theatre through the character of Silvestro's father, Costantino (Martin 1992; Ferrara 2012, 2014), who becomes a key allegorical figure precisely because of his acting in Shakespearean roles. An actor, poet, and railway worker, Silvestro's father—who triggers his son's

212   *Enrica Maria Ferrara*

journey by sending him a letter in which he announces that he has left his wife for another woman—immediately appears in his son's memory dressed as Macbeth on the grand stage of a city called Venice, to which he has moved in search of a new life.

> [R]ilessi la lettera, e riconobbi mio padre, il suo volto, la sua voce, i suoi occhi azzurri e il suo modo di fare, mi ritrovai un momento ragazzo ad applaudirlo mentre lui recitava il *Macbeth* in una sala d'aspetto d'una piccola stazione [...] Ma la memoria non si aprì in me che per questo solo [...] Non si aprì dunque che appena per questo, e ritornò otturata.
>
> (Vittorini 2005: 573)

> [Re-reading the letter I recognized my father, his face, his voice, his blue eyes, his gestures, and I visualized myself as a boy applauding him while he recited *Macbeth* for railwaymen, in a waiting room at a little station [...] But this was all my memory revealed. [...] No sooner did my memory disclose this than all was dark again.]
>
> (Vittorini 1949: 16–17)

This memory of his father in Shakespearean costume becomes a leitmotif in the novel and is key to decoding the "sealed" message of *Conversazione*. Every time Silvestro's father is mentioned, his name is associated with the plays in which he had acted, through the formulas "Mio padre in *Macbeth*" [My father in *Macbeth*] and "Mio padre in *Amleto*" [My father in *Hamlet*].

An ambivalent figure whose moral position is questionable and opaque—due to his unfaithfulness towards Silvestro's mother and his troubling association with Macbeth—Costantino is not portrayed as the herald of potential answers to Silvestro's questions. In fact, he is immediately replaced by a father-like figure whom the protagonist meets randomly during his train journey from the North—the charismatic Gran Lombardo, who makes a great impression on Silvestro because he seems to be in search of "altri doveri" [other duties]. After this encounter, once the protagonist has landed in Sicily, Silvestro seems to be obsessed by the similarity between his father and the Gran Lombardo, despite the absence of a real physical likeness between the two: "io pensai che mio padre ora somigliava forse a lui sebbene mio padre lo ricordassi giovane, snello, magro, recitando il Macbeth, vestito di rosso e nero" (Vittorini 2005: 586) ["I thought that he possibly resembled my father as he now would have been, although I could remember my father only as a young man, slim and lithe, reciting *Macbeth*, garbed in scarlet and black" (Vittorini 1949: 39)]. Silvestro's father is partially rehabilitated in his son's eyes because of his acting in the role of Macbeth, a suggestion in itself that he had been in search of "other duties" (Ferrara 2012: 108–109).

Shakespeare, Vittorini, and the Anti-Fascist Struggle   213

Vittorini's insistence on the figure of Macbeth, inherently (and dangerously) associated with political assassination, would seem, perhaps surprisingly, to have escaped the attention of the Fascist censors. One explanation is that Vittorini privileges Costantino's affinities with Hamlet over those with Macbeth, in an attempt to promote an archetypal balance between the contemplative and active life (Martin 1992: 304–5). Yet more important than the specific role performed by Costantino is the underlying fact of his being on stage—a Shakespearean surrogate, an actor-author, and (like Shakespeare) a poet too. Costantino's search for "other duties" can therefore be linked, in Vittorini's idealizing, mythic image, to Shakespeare's status as an actor-author of modest extraction and an *engageant* artist.

The idea of Shakespeare's theatre as a "socialist" medium is intimated in *Conversazione* when Silvestro recalls the evenings spent in the company of his father, attending plays performed in the same place, with the same tools, and among the same men, as from his time as a railway worker, possibly in a faint echo of the rehearsing mechanicals from *A Midsummer Night's Dream*: "la recita aveva luogo all'aperto, tra i mietitori venuti dal grano e tra fuochi, tra grida, con mio padre ossesso montato su un palcoscenico di traverse" (Vittorini 2005: 689) ["There, in the open, the recitation took place, amidst the reapers from the wheatfields, amidst flares, amidst cries from the spectators, with my father obsessed and strutting about his stage that was set on sleepers" (Vittorini 1949: 220–21)]. In his list of culturally-significant works deemed sufficiently worthy to be performed, Vittorini reserved a special place for Shakespeare's plays, as confirmed in his 1937 article celebrating the aforementioned "desire" for a cultural participation that animated the working classes. Silvestro's father, Shakespearean actor and railway worker, embodies the only positive ideology to survive the ruin of all other anti-Fascist ideologies encountered and "tested" by Silvestro in the second part of the novel. Shakespeare's theatre is thus invested with a fundamentally revolutionary, anti-bourgeois ethos, the antithesis to a bourgeois theatre fostering a culture of idle, mindless entertainment—a theatre viewed by Vittorini, not least during his time as a militant left-wing Fascist, writing for the party journal *Il Bargello* and actively participating in Mussolini's anti-bourgeois campaigns of 1934 and 1935, as the expression of a spineless intellectual and professional class who engaged with theatre as if it were a "'gioco di società' o insomma passatempo" (Vittorini 1997: 1037) [a "parlour game" or pastime].

Rather than using Shakespeare "on the level of 'histoire' ('story') and 'discourse' ('plot')" to render his work "accessible to the working-classes" (Martin 1992: 302), Vittorini drew upon his oeuvre more subtly to promote a theatrical narrative designed to educate and shape a new anti-bourgeois, anti-Fascist conscience. The anti-Fascist artist, like the "engageant" Shakespeare, produced art that was socially and politically

214   Enrica Maria Ferrara

committed, on its own artistic grounds, with "effetto immediato". This portrait of Shakespeare is invoked in the famous section of the novel in which Vittorini illustrates the role of the "actor-author" in unmasking human illusions as well as in creating and disseminating "simboli per l'umana liberazione" (Vittorini 2005: 688) ["symbols of human liberation" (Vittorini 1949: 219–20)], in turn revealing other lyrical and philosophical links between Shakespeare's theatre and *Conversazione*'s narrative-theatrical project.

Silvestro's Father and Prospero "the Actor-Author"

In the second part of the novel, Silvestro meets three characters, or rather allegorical figures, through whom Vittorini symbolizes ideologies that he sees as potential alternatives to Fascism: the knife-grinder Calogero, symbol of a revolutionary Marxist culture; the saddler Ezechiele, symbol of an idealistic culture; and the cloth-maker Porfirio, symbol of Catholic culture (Bonsaver 2000: 98–100), a series of labourers that perhaps harks back to the opening scenes of *Julius Caesar*, in which representatives of artisanal professions are shown in a position of some resistance to imperial hegemony. None of these ideologies is completely satisfactory to Silvestro, who realizes their inadequacy after spending the evening in a tavern, in the company of the three leaders, surrounded by drunkards whose sorrows, generation after generation, are drowned in wine: "e una generazione beveva dall'altra, dalla nudità di squallido vino delle altre passate, e da tutto il dolore versato" (Vittorini 2005: 685) ["one generation drank from another, from the squalid, winesteeped nakedness of past generations, drank from their torrent of griefs" (Vittorini 1949: 213)].

During this sad bacchanal, however, Silvestro is informed that his father, too, used to spend time in the tavern in which he had even performed a Shakespearean play once, possibly *Hamlet*, featuring Ezechiele and the dwarf publican Colombo in supporting roles. Silvestro's rejection of the sorrowful tavern scene, and his silent escape from it, symbolize his resistance to the strategies proffered by Calogero, Porfirio, and Ezechiele, and his subsequent formulation of a new, alternative ideology centred on the figure of the actor-author embodied by his "Shakespearean father":

> L'uomo rimasto ignudo e inerme andava nella notte e incontrava gli Spiriti, le Belle Signore Cattive che lo molestavano e schernivano, e anche calpestavano. Tutte Fantasime di azioni umane, le offese al mondo e all'umano genere uscite dal passato. [...] E l'uomo che il vino o altro aveva reso inerme era, in genere, preda loro. Diceva: i re, gli eroi. E si lasciava invadere la spoglia coscienza, le antiche offese accettava per glorie. Ma qualcuno, Shakespeare o mio padre

Shakespeare, Vittorini, and the Anti-Fascist Struggle   215

shakespeariano, si impadroniva invece di loro ed entrava in loro, svegliava in loro fango e sogni [...] Qualcuno nel vino e qualcuno no. Un grande Shakespeare, nella purezza delle sue notti di meditazione senza paura, e il piccolo mio padre nella oscurità folle delle sue notti cresciute sotto il vino.

(Vittorini 2005: 688)

[There of a night a defenceless man encountered spirits, the Beautiful and Wicked Ladies who mocked and molested him, and trampled upon him—they who were the phantoms of human actions, of all the insults to the world and humanity, who came back from the past. [...] And they were wont to prey upon a man rendered helpless by drink or by some other means. Imagining himself to be king or hero, such a man would let his conscience be subdued and accept the old insults as if they were honours. Yet another, were it Shakespeare or my Shakespearean father, would subjugate them and enter their bodies, lift them from the mire and inspire them with dreams [...] It might be someone sober or someone drunk: a mighty Shakespeare in his limpid nights of fearless meditation or my humble father in the mad blindness of his wine-sodden nights.]

(Vittorini 1949: 219–20)

Crucial to this passage is the locution "vino o altro" ["wine or other means"], "altro" signifying some "other illusion"—the illusion of Fascist ideology symbolized by the wine poured for the various patrons by the dwarf Colombo, "intellettuale del regime" [Fascist intellectual] (Falaschi 2006: 36). This implicit attack on Fascist rhetoric anticipates the anti-militarist, anti-nationalist argument that permeates the fifth section of *Conversazione*. Vittorini suggests that a common man, confounded and overwhelmed by the wine-illusion of Fascism, could end up seeing glory and heroism where only sorrow and insults are to be found. On the other hand, any artist—even an amateur artist like Silvestro's father—is able to control ghosts and spirits, acknowledge them for what they are, give them a shape and a voice, a local habitation and a name, force them to confess their sins, hopes and sorrows, and finally turn them into "symbols of human liberation".

The artist described by Vittorini is therefore reminiscent of that actor-author, magician and tamer of ghosts and spirits, victim of betrayal and rebel against tyranny and colonization despite being a "tyrant" himself—Prospero (Gurr 2014). While the common man in *The Tempest*, native of the island and son of the "blue-eyed hag" Sycorax, the monstrous Caliban, falls prey to the illusions of wine and becomes a victim not only of the uneducated servants Stephano and Trinculo but also of the spirits incited against them, Prospero, by contrast, is the sober master, wizard and artist, storyteller and fabricator of

216 Enrica Maria Ferrara

dreams who exposes his brother's guilty plot and bears witness to the truth. Prospero and Caliban are ultimately presented as mutually implicated in one another (Bigliazzi and Calvi 2014: 1–30), just as Silvestro's father reconciles the figures of artist (through his proximity to Shakespeare) and common man, a Caliban prone to the allure of "wine" and illusions. Costantino fulfils the role of guide to his son Silvestro who, in the fifth section of the novel, becomes actor-author, speaks to the ghost of his dead brother, enchants all the characters encountered along the way with his music and, finally, reveals his tricks and exposes the metatextuality of the novel he inhabits.

This metamorphosis of the protagonist into his "Shakespearean father" begins soon after he exits Colombo's tavern and gives voice to his idea of the artist as a shaman and actor-author, when he meets the ghost of his soon-to-be-dead brother at the cemetery, an encounter that is the first act of a new "play" that takes shape within the novel. The genesis of this play-within-the-novel lies, roughly speaking, in the dream-like encounter between Silvestro and his brother Liborio, who confesses to being the actor of an inauthentic performance, forced to play a part assigned to him by the mystifying rhetoric of Fascist propaganda; he will, however, show Silvestro a way out of this distorted reality, allowing language to recover its authenticity and real performative potency. Liborio's final wish, akin to a spiritual testament, is that a "Shakespearean artist" will rewrite the play, which he performs alongside all the "vincitori e vinti" [winners and losers] every night at the cemetery:

> "Non siete venuto per la rappresentazione?" disse il soldato.
> E io: "Io non so nulla di rappresentazioni".
> [...]
> Io: "Immagino che soffrono molto. Cesari non scritti. Macbeth non scritti".
> Il soldato: "E i seguaci, i partigiani, i soldati... Soffriamo, signore".
> (Vittorini 2005: 693–94)

> ["Haven't you come to see the play?" asked the soldier.
> "I know nothing about a play".
> [...]
> I: "I expect they suffer much. The unsung Caesars, the unsung Macbeths".
> The soldier: "And their followers, their partisans, their soldiers as well. We suffer, sir".]
> (Vittorini 1949: 228–29)

The scene at the cemetery can therefore be read as a proleptic *mise en abyme* of the role that Silvestro will play towards the novel's end, impersonating that model of actor-author (and even director) to which he has

Shakespeare, Vittorini, and the Anti-Fascist Struggle 217

alluded repeatedly in references to Shakespeare and "my Shakespearean father". Ideally, Silvestro will rewrite Liborio's inauthentic play, free his representation from the yoke of Fascist rhetoric, and bear witness to the piteous destiny of a child-soldier whose only reason for going to war was to "see the world". Here, "unsung Caesars" and "unsung Macbeths" gesture to the place of dead Fascist soldiers in the collective imagination of those who remain. Silvestro not only performs the role of the "actor-author", unlocking all this unwritten potential through his story-telling, but also alludes to the fictional nature of his performance, self-consciously acknowledging Vittorini's proposed strategies for would-be artists seeking to become this Prospero figure, this "Shakespearean father".

After the encounter with Liborio, Silvestro stumbles back home and falls into a deep sleep. When he awakes in his mother's house the following day, readers are catapulted into the ominous meteorology of a Shakespearean landscape invoking, as Hanne notes, the "words spoken by Macbeth just after he dispatches the murderers to kill Banquo" (Hanne 1975: 81). Even more remarkably, the weather appears to have been artificially concocted—as if by magic—when the protagonist notes that the island is being enveloped in eternal night: "Ceneri fredde avvolgevano, nel ghiaccio dei monti, la Sicilia, e il sole non si era levato, non si sarebbe più levato" (Vittorini 2005: 696) ["Sicily and its snow-covered mountains lay under a shroud of cold ash. The sun had not risen, nor would it ever rise again" (Vittorini 1949: 233)]. One cannot help recall Prospero's monologue at the beginning of Act 5, when he addresses the spirits who have assisted him with his magic art on the island "by whose aid [...] I have bedimmed | The noontide sun, called forth the mutinous winds, | And 'twixt the green sea and the azured vault | Set roaring war" (Shakespeare 2002: 5.1.41–44). As in *The Tempest*, in which the island becomes the set of a performance directed by an actor-author who confesses not only to having obscured the sun but also to having awoken the dead ("graves at my command | Have waked their sleepers [...] | By my so potent art", 5.1.48–50), so in *Conversazione* the island turns into a stage on which the protagonist is able to speak to his dead brother and on which the borders between life and death, fiction and reality, are insistently blurred. The premise recalls another late romance, namely *The Winter's Tale*, a play set, of course, mostly in Sicilia, strenuously interrogating the capabilities of art in transcending the boundaries between life and death.

The announcement of Liborio's death to Silvestro's mother by a Fascist officer follows the dimming of light on the island-stage, a moment forcing readers to question the text's realism. Was Silvestro's meeting with his brother just a prophetic dream? How could Silvestro possibly know of Liborio's death before its official announcement? This kind of alienation effect disrupts the reading experience, at least until the moment

218 *Enrica Maria Ferrara*

when Silvestro stages his "rewriting" of Liborio's death through his conversation with his mother Concezione, which, not coincidentally, takes the form of a theatrical dialogue (Vittorini 2005: 700–703). The turning point at which Silvestro begins explicitly to impersonate the role of the actor-author, overlapping with and replacing that of his father, comes in the final scenes that depict the protagonist crying, in a counterpart to the opening of the novel in which Silvestro heard the music of a piper playing, soon after he finished reading his father's letter. Silvestro seemed, there, to be involuntarily haunted by repressed memories of his past:

> e cominciai a sentire in me un lamento come un piffero che suonasse lamentoso. Andavo al lavoro tutte le mattine, per il mio mestiere di tipografo-linotipsta [...] e un piffero suonava in me e smuoveva in me topi e topi che non erano precisamente ricordi.
>
> (Vittorini 2005: 574)

> [I began to hear within me a lament like a pipe's mournful note. I went to work every day as linotype operator [...] all the while within me sounded the pipe and stirred the countless mice, which could not be precisely described as memories.]
>
> (Vittorini 1949: 18)

The music follows Silvestro around until he finally surrenders to its mysterious force and buys a train ticket to Sicily. This sort of enchantment to which the protagonist is subjected—music's inexplicable, virtually supernatural reach—is reminiscent of Prospero's use of music to perform his charms and control his subjects, both humans and spirits (Shakespeare 2002: 5.1.51–54). Costantino's enchantment of his son through the piper's music, which unlocks his repressed memories, is mirrored in Silvestro's final crying, likened to a kind of remembering: "Non piangevo per qualche ragione. In fondo non piangevo nemmeno; ricordavo; e il ricordo aveva quest'apparenza di pianto agli occhi altrui" (Vittorini 2005: 704–705) ["I did not cry for any reason. At bottom, I did not even cry; I remembered, and remembrance seemed tears in the eyes of the others" (Vittorini 1949: 247)].

As Silvestro keeps stirring memories through his tears in the novel's last section, a long queue of people starts forming behind him as if hypnotized by the sound of the invisible piper. These individuals, initially resembling passers-by, suddenly turn out to be all those characters whom Silvestro has encountered along his journey. When he admits that he is not crying "in questo mondo" (Vittorini 2005: 705) ["in this world" (Vittorini 1949: 248)], Silvestro implies that his crying belongs to the world of narrative fiction, the world of ghosts tamed by his father and all other Shakespearean artists—those figments of his imagination, spirits and simulacra encountered at the cemetery, whose destiny is waiting to

Shakespeare, Vittorini, and the Anti-Fascist Struggle 219

be written. In addition, Silvestro's crying may well recall the crying of Gonzalo and the other victims of the shipwreck conjured up by Prospero, brimful of "sorrow and dismay", a spectacle of mourning that would make Prospero's "affections [...] tender" (Shakespeare 2002: 5.1.13–18).

In sum, what Silvestro aims to communicate is that he has followed the path indicated to him from the very beginning of the novel by his acting father and that the play performed by him—*Conversazione*'s novel-play itself—has come to an end. Instead of acting in the role of Macbeth or Hamlet, Silvestro has become, like Prospero, the actor-author or the director-actor-author reciting his part alongside all other characters (the Great Lombard, the young peasant with malaria, the young man from Catania, the knife-grinder, and so on), attempting to find a remedy to "il male del mondo offeso" ["woes of the outraged world"]. In *Conversazione*, the "parola suggellata" ["sealed word"] is, finally, the monosyllable that Silvestro has heard pronounced for the first time by his brother Liborio at the cemetery, the interjection "*Ehm!*"—a phoneme signifying a "precious secret [...] the symbol of the general feeling for which the artist must find a shape" (Bonsaver 2000: 102). This cipher is uttered by all the characters gathered, in a visual echo of the alienating, metatheatrical dénouement of *The Winter's Tale*, around a woman's statue during the final scene. Characters are transformed back into actors—actors compelled to lend their voices and gestures to past "ghosts" or memories. The guttural, monosyllabic utterance "Ehm!" adds another layer to the novel's soundscape, enriching an isle already full of other noises from crying to pipe-music. Through these non-verbal articulations in *Conversazione*, Vittorini champions a new style of writing that might be termed theatrical realism (Ferrara 2014), a verbal equivalent in prose for a stage actor's partially non-verbal idiom. The rhetoric of wonder and the musical poetics of late Shakespeare confirm Vittorini's recourse to *The Tempest*, whose author (like his dramaturgical surrogate Prospero) becomes a figure idealized as the archetype of a socially-committed artist reaching out to a broad constituency in a new style and distinctive idiolect.

Bibliography

Bertoni, Roberto. 2009. "Nóstos e assenza del padre: *Conversazione in Sicilia* e *Notti sull'altura*". *Un secolo per Vittorini. Atti della giornata di studio. Trinity College, Dublino, 18–4–2008*, ed. by Roberto Bertoni. Turin. 83–90.

Bigliazzi, Silvia, and Lisanna Calvi, eds. 2014. *Revisiting* The Tempest. *The Capacity to Signify*. New York.

Blake, Norman Francis. 1983. *Shakespeare's Language: An Introduction*. London.

Bonsaver, Guido. 2000. *Elio Vittorini: The Writer and The Written*. Leeds.

——— 2007. *Censorship and Literature in Fascist Italy*. Toronto.

220   *Enrica Maria Ferrara*

Falaschi, Giovanni. 2006. "Introduzione". In Elio Vittorini, *Conversazione in Sicilia*, ed. by Giovanni Falaschi. Milan. 5–54.

Ferrara, Enrica Maria. 2012. "Vittorini in conversazione con Shakespeare. Teatro e cultura popolare". *Italian Studies*, 67.1: 105–119.

——— 2014. *Il realismo teatrale nella narrativa del Novecento: Vittorini, Pasolini, Calvino*. Florence.

Fischer, Donatella, ed. 2013. *The Tradition of the Actor-Author in Italian Theatre*. Oxford.

Griffiths, Clive. 2005. "Theatrical Censorship in Italy during the Fascist Period". *Culture, Censorship and the State in Twentieth-Century Italy*, ed. by Guido Bonsaver and Robert S. C. Gordon. London. 76–85.

Gurr, Andrew. 2014. "*The Tempest* as Theatrical Magic". *Revisiting* The Tempest. *The Capacity to Signify*, ed. by Silvia Bigliazzi and Lisanna Calvi. New York: 33–42.

Hanne, Michael. 1975. "Significant Allusions in Vittorini's *Conversazione in Sicilia*". *Modern Language Review*, 70: 75–83.

Martin, Stephen. 1992. "Vittorini meets Shakespeare: *Conversazione in Sicilia* and *Hamlet*". *Romance Languages Annual*, 4: 301–306.

Shakespeare, William. 1943. *Tito Andronico*, trans. by Elio Vittorini. *Teatro*, ed. Mario Praz. 3 vols. Florence. 1: 474–553.

——— 2002. *The Tempest*, ed. by David Lindley. Cambridge.

Vittorini, Elio. 1949. *In Sicily*. New York.

——— 1997. *Letteratura arte società. Articoli e interventi 1926–1937*, ed. by Raffaella Rodondi. Turin.

——— 2005 [1974]. *Conversazione in Sicilia*. In *Le opere narrative*, ed. by Maria Corti, 2 vols. Milan. 1: 569–710.

——— 2008. *Letteratura arte società. Articoli e interventi 1938–1965*, ed. by Raffaella Rodondi. Turin.

15 Hamlet's Ghost
The Rewriting of Shakespeare in C. E. Gadda

Giuseppe Stellardi

Carlo Emilio Gadda (1893–1973) was fascinated by the work of Shakespeare throughout the course of his life. There is uninterrupted evidence of this interest, from the earliest known private writings, such as the war diaries of the *Giornale di guerra e di prigionia* (1915–19) in which we find the first of a long series of references (Gadda 1992: 579), to the very last statements, as late as 1972, one year before his death, when Gadda "confesses" to be reading the *Sonnets* (Gadda 2007: 172). In a 1958 interview Gadda names Shakespeare as the *one* writer whose work he would "perhaps" take with him, if he had to leave the planet, never to return (Gadda 2007: 67). The catalogues of what remains of his library (now held in Rome and Milan) reveal the significant presence of the English author, including the complete oeuvre in the original and a collection of all the plays in Italian translation, in addition to several different editions of individual works (among these, three of *Hamlet*, two of *Macbeth*, three of the *Sonnets*), as well as a handful of critical volumes on Shakespeare and Elizabethan theatre. This chapter will try to provide a brief answer to a double question: why was Gadda so interested in the English dramatist, and what was the influence of the latter's work on his own?

Gadda's interest in Shakespeare has not escaped the attention of critics, but for a long time general, ambient awareness failed to give rise to detailed, sustained analyses. After initial hints, cursorily provided by some of the best representatives of early Gaddian criticism (in particular Contini, Roscioni, and later Gorni), it was only after the turn of the new millennium that the relationship between Gadda and Shakespeare became the object of proper investigation. It is easy to understand the reasons why the Shakespearean connection did not—despite its obvious relevance—receive adequate prominence in the early critical approaches. The links between Gadda's unique and unclassifiable style and his literary lineage reveal a complex diagram of diverse preferences and influences. Even just in its "local" components, this inheritance includes the classical Roman writers (Horace in particular); the "macaronic" poetry of the sixteenth century (Teofilo Folengo); and the "Lombard" line, represented by several, contrasting strains (the Enlightenment thinkers;

222 *Giuseppe Stellardi*

Giuseppe Parini; Alessandro Manzoni; the dialectal poetry of Carlo Porta; and the Milanese *Scapigliatura* of the late nineteenth century). Foreign influences were readily detected, notably from French, Spanish, and Russian literature—Rabelais, Flaubert, Balzac, Céline, the Spanish Baroque, Dostoyevsky—but not explored in any greater depth. More subtle or distant, but equally intriguing, consonances and echoes—Joyce, Beckett, Leiris, Faulkner, and Dürrenmatt—have only more recently become objects for analysis.

In all such source hunting, the true significance of Gadda's explicit and constant reference to Shakespeare remained, as it were, drowned in the general noise, taken for granted but under-researched, and, for the most attentive readers, somewhat enigmatic. As an example of this, Guglielmo Gorni suggested (as early as 1972) that it is abroad that one should look for the most original and significant literary stimuli shaping the protagonist of Gadda's *La cognizione del dolore*, among which he specifically names Shakespeare. Yet, curiously, at the same time, he reduces the impact of his pertinent observation by declaring it obvious, reducing it, in the wake of Roscioni, to a matter of mere style, with reference in particular to aspects of the comic and the grotesque (Bertone 2004: 108, 128). It is only more recently that Shakespeare's centrality within the vast array of Gadda's models has started to attract adequate attention, a centrality re-articulated in a theatrical as well as a critical domain, for instance in Fabrizio Gifuni's 2010 *L'ingegner Gadda va alla guerra o della tragica istoria di Amleto Pirobutirro*, a dramatic performance fusing Gadda's *Giornale di guerra e di prigionia* and *Hamlet* in an original *contaminatio* (see Gifuni 2013 for the English translation and additional critical texts).

To be correctly understood, Gadda's relationship to Shakespeare needs to be seen within a broader context. The question of how to classify Gadda's aesthetics remains to this day an open and controversial one: critical opinion is divided over whether to associate him with one or other of the available formulae (Modernist, Postmodernist, Expressionist, and so on), or none at all (see Stellardi Forthcoming). The difficulty arises because of Gadda's reiterated (but contradictory and ultimately unsuccessful) attempts to define his own poetics, and the obvious clash between some of his statements and his actual style. It is this engrained conceptual tension that makes it impossible to reach firm conclusions, but at the same time preserves an aura of originality and uniqueness around Gadda's oeuvre.

These stylistic uncertainties notwithstanding, it is clear that Shakespeare plays a significant part in Gadda's literary imagination (Bonci 2012). The English playwright is a crucial component in the diagram of opposing forces that, combined, constitute Gadda's literary cipher. If this system cannot be reduced to a single poetics, it is because it remains fundamentally fractured between antagonistic principles, which are not, however, hermetically separated. Most obviously among these competing forces, Manzoni sits on one side, representing linguistic and ethical clarity, and life guided by belief, and Shakespeare sits on the other, representing "baroque" complexity, and life subjected to chaos. The two influences are not diametrically opposed: on the contrary, it is most likely *through* Manzoni that Gadda first read Shakespeare, since Manzoni was a noted admirer of the English author (Bonci 2012: Chs. 1.3.2, 2.3). Moreover, there are clear consonances between the ways that the two Italians interpret the English dramatist. For instance, the ethical dimension (and especially the notion of moral responsibility) is something they both hold very dear, even though Manzoni's Christian faith and consequent adherence to a providential vision of human history clearly separates him from Gadda's vision.

From its earliest manifestations, Gadda's interest in Shakespeare reaches well beyond the level of simple aesthetic similitude or stylistic affinity. Shakespeare's impact goes much deeper, and in at least two ways. On the one hand, Gadda is not only attracted to the playwright's mastery of words and inventive ability, but also (and particularly) interested in his *thought*, or *Weltanschauung*. In an adjective dear to Gadda, Shakespeare's work carries "heuristic" meaning, as well as artistic value (and indeed, for him, the two must necessarily combine to create a true work of art). On the other hand, there is in Gadda (as is often the case with his literary allegiances) a strong component of subjective projection and autobiographical identification, in this case not with the dramatist himself but with some of his characters—and one in particular. These two aspects point towards a sort of polarity and opposition—or at least a tension—between universality (the world, and the need to grasp it conceptually) and particularity (the self, and the need to express it emotionally). This contrast is systemically present in Gadda's work.

Gadda's Early Shakespearean Forays: *Racconto italiano* and *Meditazione milanese*

A literary career was not, for the young Gadda, the only or the automatic choice. Whilst his family (and specifically his mother) exerted constant pressure to coerce him into some form of "serious", professional training, he was for a long time drawn to both literature and philosophy. This dual vocation became particularly visible after his return from Argentina (1924), when—at the same time as enrolling in a formal course of philosophical studies—he decided to write a novel, which was provisionally entitled *Racconto italiano di ignoto del novecento* [*Italian Tale by an Unknown from the Twentieth Century*] and remained unfinished. He never completed a degree in philosophy either, but in 1928 he composed a philosophical dialogue (published posthumously), entitled *Meditazione milanese*. Both *Racconto italiano* and *Meditazione milanese*

224   Giuseppe Stellardi

include echoic references to Shakespeare, as well as more fully-fledged ideas that can be directly connected with Shakespeare's *thought*, as expounded in Gadda's later essays—clear proof that the English dramatist was, from very early on, central to Gadda's reflections and very close to both the literary and philosophical chambers of his heart.

One thing that is evident from even a superficial examination of Gadda's writings is the central space occupied, out of the vast Shakespearean canon, by *Hamlet*. The first explicit reference (in a text published during Gadda's life) can be found in *Le meraviglie d'Italia* (1939; see Gadda 1991: 105) and proves that, during his stay in Argentina (1922–24), Gadda had "in his suitcase" a copy of the play and saw a performance of it. In *Racconto italiano* the names of both Shakespeare and Hamlet make striking appearances. The Prince of Denmark takes on the role of a sort of "model character", that is (to quote Gadda's own words from the preparatory notes) someone who is an active agent in the dramatic plot ["gestore del dramma"], who knows what is truly going on ["conoscitore del dramma gestito"], and who provides the link between the particular and the universal, on both a theoretical and practical level ["riallacciatore con l'universale"]. While most characters represent one or two of those fundamental perspectives, very few combine them all. Hamlet is one of those few, and becomes for Gadda not only a great theatrical creation but the very quintessence of dramatic figuration (Gadda 1993: 415), so much so that he finds it impossible to replicate its complexity within a single character in his own projected story, and decides instead to diffract it in two separate figures: first, Grifonetto Lampugnani, the type A character (in Gadda's own classification), who makes the plot move forward, but in the course of the narrative also turns into a type B and begins to discover (still in Gadda's terminology) the "abnormal" under the "normal"; and secondly Gerolamo Lehrer, representing the type C character, the one who overlays a philosophical judgement on events (Bonci 2012: 63).

If *Racconto italiano* constitutes a first, clumsy, and unaccomplished attempt to project burning autobiographical matter onto the screen of literary creation (identifying Shakespeare's *Hamlet* as a possible model), *Meditazione milanese* moves in a different orbit, that of pure philosophical theory. But here, too, *Hamlet* plays a crucial part, and is explicitly cited; in the dialogue, the correspondence of the abstract distinction being/non-being with the ethical dichotomy good/evil is posited as central to Gadda's reflections. The link with his future discussion of Shakespeare (in his 1952 essay, addressed below) is evident and was pointed out by, among others, Elio Gioanola (Gioanola 2004: 55). This correspondence constitutes the lynchpin of his masterpiece, *La cognizione del dolore*. Thus, *Meditazione milanese* acts as the conceptual link between the beginnings of Gadda's narrative ambitions (*Racconto italiano*) and the development of the masterpiece of his maturity. Shakespeare and

Hamlet are central to the entire trajectory, as they constitute a powerful, external validation and artistic manifestation of Gadda's own vision of life (Bonci 2012: 59).

Hamlet, the "Hamletic", and La cognizione del dolore

In Gadda's writings over the course of almost fifty years, Hamlet is not only the first and most frequently quoted of all the plays in the Shakespearean canon; it is also the only one to attract direct, detailed, and extensive critical analysis by Gadda, in one of his most provocative essays. "Amleto al Teatro Valle", published (under a slightly different title) in 1952, and subsequently included in Gadda's most important collection of non-fictional writings (I viaggi la morte, in Gadda 1991), is ostensibly the review of a performance of the play in Rome. In his evaluation, Gadda shows admiration for Vittorio Gassman's Hamlet but criticizes Anna Zareschi, accusing her—interestingly—of portraying the Queen in a far more humane, "maternal", and noble manner than she deserves (Gadda 1991: 543–44). Yet Gadda's essay exceeds the limits of an occasional theatrical review, moving from an evaluation of the performance to a discussion of the philosophical content of the play itself.

It is on the meaning of the term "Hamletic" that Gadda fixates in a highly polemical manner, and with considerable vehemence, betraying a profound and deeply personal involvement. He attacks, in particular, interpretations of the adjective that see in the protagonist simply the embodiment of gnoseological doubt, if not moral vacillation and indecision too. By contrast, for Gadda, "in lui non si contorce il dubbio, chi mai ha inventato questa scemenza? Si palesa invece un dibattito" [it is not doubt that writhes in him—who ever came up with that silly notion? What it turns out to be is, instead, a debate] (Gadda 1991: 539). The core of the essay, arguably, consists of Gadda's contemptuous rejection of what he regards as a superficial and misguided interpretation of the protagonist's predicament and character, as summarized in the idea of so-called "Hamletic doubt", which he regards as a misnomer; Hamlet, for Gadda, is not engaged in a tentative search for truth because, at the moment of his most famous soliloquy, he knows it with absolute subjective certainty (although he still needs the objective final proof that comes through the staged "mousetrap" of the actors' performance). Nor, on the other hand, is he subject to hesitations of an ethical nature. He is not affected by any degree of moral uncertainty concerning his future behaviour: he knows exactly what needs to be done and is simply (but only momentarily) pausing to reflect on the necessity and momentous consequences of his unavoidable actions. The soliloquy is an instance of reflection and self-collection, not hesitation: Hamlet knows that he will not be able to eschew his duty. Nevertheless, the reflective pause is neither futile nor unjustified, given the inevitable

226   *Giuseppe Stellardi*

consequences of his actions. Far from symbolizing doubt and wavering, Hamlet represents and embraces the absolute clarity of ultimate self-sacrifice. The same argument returns in Gadda repeatedly, before and after the 1952 essay, for instance in the reviews "Il Faust tradotto da Manacorda" of 1932 (Gadda 1991: 759) and "Giuseppe Berto, *Il male oscuro*" of 1965 (Gadda 1991: 1200). Most importantly, it can be found in the preparatory notes for his first (complete) published novel, *La cognizione del dolore*, which appeared in instalments between 1938 and 1941, then as a single volume in 1963.

La cognizione contains numerous similarities or convergences with Shakespeare's drama. Manuela Bertone (2004) provides a list of the most striking of these, and shows that, reduced to their bare outlines, *Hamlet* and *La cognizione* are essentially the same story, in which the protagonist knows that the superficial appearance of order and good will disguises a profound sickness poisoning the whole of society. The tragedy inheres not only in the fact that the two protagonists, unlike the rest of their conformist entourage, see with the utmost clarity this state of affairs and feel duty-bound to remedy it, but also and even more poignantly in their awareness that the only possible remedy will necessarily entail terrible consequences. Among these consequences are the destruction of their respective enemies and, at the same time, an assault on what is most sacred in life, represented in both cases by the figure of the mother. The necessary actions of the two heroes will inevitably cause the untying of sacred bonds.

Gonzalo Pirobutirro (the autobiographical protagonist of *La cognizione*) has clear Hamletic traits; a brooding, isolated, melancholic, and eccentric figure, he lives in a state of paroxystic antagonism with his social environment, and with what everybody else regards as "normality" (but which he sees instead as a web of lies). Like Hamlet, Gonzalo too is in possession of by-now-incontestable certainties demanding urgent action ("sapeva, sapeva" [he knew, he knew]; Gadda 1990: 730), and finds himself at a decisive junction of his life. This is particularly evident at the beginning of Ch. 7, where the narrator presents us with a third-person re-enactment of Hamlet's soliloquy. To attack the "parvenze non valide" [invalid appearances] is what the truth/justice imperative dominating Gonzalo's mind requires of him, and what his soul wants, in order to affirm itself as valid substance, rather than an inconsistent shadow: "Negare, negare: chi sia Signore e *Principe* nel giardino della propria anima" ["to deny, deny: to be Lord and *Prince* in the garden of one's own soul"] (Gadda 1990: 703; Weaver 1969: 156; my emphasis). As in *Hamlet*, here too the tragic double bind arises from the fact that the ethical subject's heroic self-affirmation takes the form of an extreme negation: in destroying false appearances, one also destroys every possibility of solidarity, love, and compassion, and nothing remains.

For Gonzalo, as for Hamlet, ethical action unleashes destructive consequences whose implications, both objective and subjective, are unspeakably atrocious, as well as irredeemably immoral: these are symbolized in the (realized or only imagined) killing of the mother. In both cases, she is at the centre of a web of lies, turning life itself into a monstrous comedy. In her kitchen, at the heart of her villa, in the centre of her little kingdom and of the universe, Gonzalo's mother, like a gigantic spider, weaves her net of apparent goodness, bringing the stench of untruth up to her son's very last refuge (his bedroom), depriving him of any remaining space and energy necessary to live in the only way that is possible to him—that is, in a state of disdainful separation from reality. This conflict with the social environment around him might not, after all, prevent life altogether for him, if Gonzalo could at least count on the only ally that he needs in order to set up, in his own secluded space, an alternative world to the bourgeois farce that everybody else calls life: his mother. But his mother, far from being a companion for him on his difficult voyage, reveals herself more and more clearly to be what she has always been: the enemy, the original and deep source of all evil (Wehling-Giorgi 2014: Ch. 3). This present resentment nourishes itself with the memory of remote injustices suffered or imagined, of incomprehensible cruelties on the part of his chief educator, and is also sustained by his secret jealousy toward her other son, preferred by the mother and killed during the war. At the same time, however, she is by definition the source of life itself, the sole dispenser of love, the umbilical cord to reality; to negate the mother, therefore, means to destroy the last bridge to normality, and the last hope of salvation.

So it is for Hamlet, as well; Queen Gertrude, morally complicit (at least in Gadda's judgement) in a horrible crime, is also the principal obstacle to the re-establishment of justice, precisely because her son's natural respect prevents him from hurting her. The necessary and desperate gesture affirming the ethical will of both heroes—a negation of everything that is false, and therefore of *everything* (including for Hamlet Ophelia's innocent love, or for Gonzalo the innocuous and well-meaning propositions of his doctor)—entails the destruction of the very root of life, symbolically represented by the mothers, and also procreative marriage. In his aforementioned essay "*Amleto* al Teatro Valle", Gadda contends that:

> Amleto sente il carattere annichilatore della propria azione, sa di dover cadere lui stesso, nell'atto di operare il cauterio estremo del male, della vergogna e della colpa. Ed è questa, forse, la ragione oscura e profonda per cui egli respinge da sé quella [*viz.* Ophelia] che lo ama riamata (che è nel buio del non sentire e del non essere, etico e fisico)
>
> (Gadda 1991: 541)

228 *Giuseppe Stellardi*

> [Hamlet realizes the annihilating nature of his own actions: he knows that he, too, will have to fall, in the act of applying the extreme remedy to illness, shame, and guilt. This is, perhaps, the obscure, fundamental reason why he rejects the one [*viz.* Ophelia] who, requited, loves him (and who lies in the darkness of unawareness, of non-being—ethically and physically)]

It is noteworthy that, in both cases, what is at stake is marriage—that is, biological continuity obtained with society's blessing: in *La cognizione*, Doctor Higueróa, summoned by Gonzalo to diagnose his obscure illness, is (not very subtly) intent on curing the patient by marrying him off to one of his several nubile daughters.

Admittedly, in Shakespeare's drama, the death of the Queen is accidental, and in Gadda's novel the possibility (contemplated at the stage of planning) of the son's direct responsibility for the attack against his mother is only vaguely intimated. Nevertheless, both mothers are subjected to the outrage and the violence that both sons secretly presaged and desired, as the necessary precondition for the triumph of truth and their own liberation, although of course Hamlet resists the urge as something contrary to nature: "Let me be cruel, not unnatural: | I will speak daggers to her, but use none", he pledges (3.2), following the ghost's injunction not to "contrive | Against thy mother aught" (1.5) (Shakespeare 1975: 148, 74). The most terrible consequences will follow from such unnatural excess against the person of the mother, but also against life itself as represented by her—an entanglement of contradictions and lies, and nevertheless an organic system of relations, duties, and affections. And so it is that Hamlet immediately dies, whereas of Gonzalo's fate nothing is said, although we already know from the dream episode in the third chapter (for Gonzalo too, like Hamlet, is afflicted by "bad dreams") that the disappearance of the mother, rather than heralding psychological freedom and financial emancipation, will only bring Gonzalo increased solitude, despair, and remorse: "tutto era mio! mio! ... finalmente ... come il rimorso" ["everything was mine! Mine! Finally ... like remorse"] (Gadda 1990: 632; Weaver 1969: 82).

Another central similarity uniting Hamlet and Gonzalo concerns the relationship between both protagonists and *thought* itself, which is perceived as entailing something conflicted and unhealthy. In 3.1, the Danish prince states that "the native hue of resolution | Is sicklied o'er with the pale cast of thought" (Shakespeare 1975: 122); in the case of the Marquis Pirobutirro, after uttering a phrase in English that could well be an indirect reference to *Hamlet* ("but I'm ill of thinking", recalling Hamlet's anxieties about "thinking too precisely" in 4.4), Gonzalo launches a tirade against personal pronouns, which he describes as "i pidocchi del pensiero" ["the lice of thought"] (Gadda 1990: 636; Weaver 1969: 85). Thinking, it seems, is part of the illness affecting the two

Hamlet's Ghost 229

heroes, inasmuch as an excess of it becomes paralyzing and prevents necessary and potentially salvific action (see Bonci 2012: Ch. 4; Gioanola 2004). As we have seen, an uncompromising, wholesale rejection of all false appearances, demanded by fidelity to the truth and to oneself, can bring only death. The act of ultimate cognition—and, for Gadda, the gesture of writing *La cognizione*, which itself incorporates and manifests that act—corresponds to that rejection and in part expresses it; to write *La cognizione* means to make explicit the homicidal intentions of Gonzalo-Hamlet. It is an act of total veridiction (at least in intention), barely veiled under a thin layer of fiction.

This, however, is where the two stories diverge. In Shakespeare's tragedy, Hamlet's sacrificial act of redressing is successful (albeit at a terrible price), as it rectifies a perversion in the ethical and political order. If natural succession to the throne is prevented by the Prince's death, healthy blood will nevertheless be restored to power in the person of Fortinbras, thus removing the incestuous and monstrous sickness affecting the realm. By contrast, in Gadda's tragicomedy, Gonzalo's dreams of purification are thwarted; the mother is attacked but not by him or another agent of justice; the evil powers are not in the least affected; and in the end life continues on its foul course, without catharsis or redemption. Ultimately, Gonzalo's negation of false appearances is a "sterile passo" ["sterile footstep"] (Gadda 1990: 703; Weaver 1969: 156).

The destructive but liberating sequence of events that concludes *Hamlet* is necessary for the accomplishment of the intended ethical purpose, and for the completeness of the dramatic plot. This trajectory is missing in Gadda's work, which accordingly (at least from the subjective perspective of the author) fails to achieve its aim. In this respect, Gadda's end-product, *La cognizione del dolore* itself, can only be regarded as incomplete and imperfect. Neither Gonzalo nor his author can fully correspond to their Shakespearean model; the choice in favour of the ethical absolute (or for true life: "to be") has not been brought to its logical conclusion. Gonzalo's life is spared, and so perhaps is that of the mother, but at what price? Interestingly, something similar also happens in Gadda's other novel, *Quer pasticciaccio brutto de Via Merulana* (published in instalments in 1946, then in a single volume in 1957), set in Rome at the time of Mussolini's dictatorship. Having arrived at his own "Hamletic" moment, when justice should be re-established but also when life—this time represented by Assuntina's exuberant vitality—should be imprisoned and mutilated in the name of abstract and uncomprehending principles and on behalf of a false authority, detective Ingravallo hesitates and, almost, repents. The second novel, too, for all its Shakespearean resonances—not least the parallel between detective Ingravallo and Hamlet (Veronese 2013)—concludes without resolution.

To write *La cognizione*, right after his mother's death, is for Gadda something resembling Hamlet's terrible choice in favour of truth and

230 *Giuseppe Stellardi*

justice. But as a gesture of a generalized denial of conventions, affections, and habits, and of the fragile fabric of life (powerfully subsumed in the iconoclastic symbol of the liberating violence against the mother), *La cognizione* is a double-edged sword whose uncompromising intention cannot be fulfilled. The novel in the end embodies imperfection and contamination: a compromise between the exorbitant demands of (subjective) truthfulness on the one hand, and the needs of life on the other. If the former requires total lucidity and the refusal of any concessions, the latter yearns for the restoring balms proffered by art: invention and beauty; sublimation and transfiguration; dream, illusion, and merriment; oblivion.

It is therefore clear that Shakespeare in general and *Hamlet* in particular represent for Gadda not only a precedent in terms of expressive and reflective power, subtlety, and complexity, but also the materialisation of some of the most crucial tensions affecting him personally, both as a man and as a writer. And it is in this essentially autobiographical sense (and not in terms of formal criteria or genre modelling) that *La cognizione del dolore* can legitimately be seen as a rewriting of *Hamlet* first and foremost, notwithstanding the novel's other allusions to *Macbeth*, *King Lear*, and *The Tempest*. In this respect, the crucial essay of 1952 represents the outcome of a process of autobiographical projection—superimposed on an existing and long-standing admiration for Shakespeare—that must have peaked at the time of writing *La cognizione* (in the late 1930s, and, significantly, after the death of Gadda's mother in 1936). The essay can in fact be regarded as a disguised peroration *pro domo mea*, and an implicit defence of Hamlet as Gadda's own double and predecessor.

In summary, what Gadda sees in *Hamlet* and strives to reproduce in his own work, and in his own way, takes the following shape. *Hamlet* offers Gadda the dramatic allegory of a world that is not what it seems, since a veneer of innocuous and well-meaning normality hides a monstrous reality that fundamentally contradicts all illusions. Within this broader context, Gadda dwells particularly on a more specific representation of perverted family relations and, moreover, the most crucial and horrible lie, that of maternal love. Accordingly, Gadda draws out from his Shakespearean model a contrast between life and spirit—life (represented by Ophelia, or by Gonzalo's mother) demands compromise and illusion, but the spirit is uncompromising in its quest for justice, and demands blood. This paradigm involves both an ethical duty, which fundamentally opposes the individual to the social body, and a sacrifice: to redress injustice and to heal a secretly rotten society, the heroic individual must sacrifice everything, including himself. In both *Hamlet* and *La cognizione*, the "illness of thought" recurs as a fundamental clash between idle contemplation and action.

Yet for all the indebtedness to *Hamlet*, what works in Shakespeare does not necessarily work in Gadda, who must forfeit, simultaneously, the stylistic homogeneity of tragedy; the identification of the protagonist as a true hero; and a cathartic solution to the dramatic tensions. Gonzalo is no Hamlet, and his world is beyond salvation. Inevitably *La cognizione*, which Gadda conceives as a modern tragedy (and concludes on a lyrical note), remains imprisoned in a swamp of contradiction and irresolution, both formally and emotionally.

I would propose that *Hamlet* represents for Gadda the lucid awareness of life's intractable complexity, combined with the obstinate pursuit of a (now) impossible ideal of truth and justice. The underlying issue is therefore ethical and socio-ideological, having to do with the very significance and function of literature in society. Writing, for Gadda, only has meaning inasmuch as it delivers a payload of truth. This is where the antithetical drives dominating his inspiration should combine: be it through lyrical intensity, macaronic *contaminatio*, comic enumeration, or baroque proliferation, literature should be the fulfilment of a moral imperative to truthfulness—or, alternatively, it must resign itself to a purely ornamental contribution, which is tantamount to utter futility. The problem is that, for Gadda, this noble task does not ever seem to be successfully accomplished, and what was supposed to be a positive participation in an act of collective improvement turns instead (from his own perspective at least) into an instance of personal, arbitrary, ultimately futile, and ineffective revenge:

> Nella mia vita di "umiliato e offeso" la narrazione mi è apparsa, talvolta, lo strumento che mi avrebbe consentito di ristabilire la "mia" verità, il "mio" modo di vedere, cioè: lo strumento della rivendicazione contro gli oltraggi del destino e de' suoi umani proietti: lo strumento, in assoluto, del riscatto e della vendetta.
>
> (*Intervista al microfono*, in Gadda 1991: 503)

> [In my life as a "humiliated and insulted" human being, narrative, at times, offered itself to me as the instrument to make it possible to re-establish "my" truth, "my" way of seeing—that is, the instrument of vindication against the offences of fate and of its human projectiles; the instrument, in absolute terms, of redemption and revenge.]

Shakespeare, for Gadda, is an inspiration and certainly a master of both style and thought, but he cannot be a model on which to pattern his own writing. The same, however, can be said of all other significant precedents that the writer, in turn, identifies as valid examples of literary achievement: neither Horace, Manzoni, Folengo, Dossi, nor Porta can provide the formula. This is also, perhaps, why the tragic ghost keeps

232 Giuseppe Stellardi

returning, forever unsatisfied; the modern Hamlet cannot die, cannot live, condemned to a destiny even harsher than that of the original Hamlet—a ridiculous, meaningless existence of permanent dissatisfaction. Intriguingly, Gadda's last known mention of Shakespeare does not concern *Hamlet*, but is a reference to the *Sonnets*, in which, a few months before his death, he seems to be looking for an answer. There is no indication that he found one.

La cognizione del dolore shines in the polarized tension between the (negative) impulse for truth and the eternally positive drive of art. Art wins gloriously (albeit narrowly, if one keeps count of all the losses) in a work that ranks among the greatest and the most stunningly beautiful of the twentieth century, but not to the extent that it can unshackle, or forever appease, the restless and homicidal ghost of Hamlet.

Bibliography

Bertone, Manuela. 2004. "'Nel magazzino, nel retrobottega del cervello / Within the book and volume of my brain': per l'*Amleto* di Carlo Emilio Gadda". *Gadda. Meditazione e racconto*, ed. by Cristina Savettieri, Carla Benedetti, and Lucio Lugnani. Pisa. 105–136.

Bonci, Roberto. 2012. *"La distanza intercorrente tra la noia e la poesia". Carlo Emilio Gadda interprete di Shakespeare.* Unpublished Thesis. University of Bologna.

Gadda, Carlo Emilio. 1990. *Romanzi e racconti—I*, ed. by Raffaella Rodondi, Guido Lucchini, and Emilio Manzotti. Milan.

——— 1991. *Saggi Giornali Favole e altri scritti—I*, ed. by Liliana Orlando, Clelia Martignoni, and Dante Isella. Milan.

——— 1992. *Saggi Giornali Favole e altri scritti—II*, ed. by Claudio Vela, Gianmarco Gaspari, Giorgio Pinotti, Franco Gavazzeni, Dante Isella, and Maria Antonietta Terzoli. Milan.

——— 1993. *Scritti vari e postumi*, ed. by Andrea Silvestri, Claudio Vela, Dante Isella, Paola Italia, and Giorgio Pinotti. Milan.

——— 2007. *"Per favore, mi lasci nell'ombra". Interviste 1950–1972*, ed. by Claudio Vela. Milan.

Gifuni, Fabrizio. 2013. *Gadda goes to war*, ed. Federica G. Pedriali. Edinburgh.

Gioanola, Elio. 2004. *Carlo Emilio Gadda. Topazi e altre gioie familiari.* Milan.

Shakespeare, William. 1975. *Amleto (edizione bilingue)*, ed. by Gabriele Baldini. Milan.

Stellardi, Giuseppe. Forthcoming. "'In nome di quale poetica?': l'antipoetica di Gadda". Special issue of *Cuadernos de Filología Italiana*, on Gadda.

Veronese, Cosetta. 2013. "Tragedia e commedia shakespeariana nel *Pasticciaccio*". *Un meraviglioso ordegno. Paradigmi e modelli nel Pasticciaccio di Gadda*, ed. by Maria Antonietta Terzoli, Cosetta Veronese, and Vincenzo Vitale. Rome. 57–87.

Weaver, William. 1969. Carlo Emilio Gadda, *Acquainted with Grief.* London.

Wehling-Giorgi, Katrin. 2014. *Gadda and Beckett. Storytelling, Subjectivity and Fracture.* London.

16 "The rest which is *not* silence"

Shakespeare and Eugenio Montale

Camilla Caporicci

The fact that Eugenio Montale knew and loved Shakespeare's work needs no demonstration. He composed several translations of Shakespeare's plays and poems: besides an unpublished version of *Julius Caesar*, he translated some fragments from *A Midsummer Night's Dream* (published in 1948 in *Quaderno di traduzioni*); from the *Sonnets*, Sonnets 22 and 33 (first published in 1944 in *Città*) and Sonnet 48 (first published in 1947 in *L'immagine*); *Hamlet* (published by Mondadori in 1949); and *The Comedy of Errors, Timon of Athens*, and *The Winter's Tale* (all three in the Sansoni series edited by Mario Praz in 1964). Moreover, he commented on Shakespeare's oeuvre in many of his prose works, most notably in a series of articles now collected in the volume *Il secondo mestiere: Prose 1920–1979* (1996), invariably expressing the utmost admiration for his work. It is surprising, therefore, that the deep and unquestionable influence that Shakespeare's output exercised over Montale's poetry remains almost entirely unexplored by critics. In fact, the critical literature on the relationship between Montale and Shakespeare has so far focused exclusively on Montale as Shakespeare's translator, and particularly as translator of selected *Sonnets* (Isella 1988; Meoli Toulmin 1971; Erspamer 1990; Scaglione 2007; Lonardi 1980; Orlando 2001). These forays, though valuable, typically do not take into account the range of other Shakespearean echoes found in Montale's output. The aim of this chapter is to bridge this gap in the critical literature on the subject, casting light on the influence of Shakespeare's work on one of the greatest Italian poets of the last century.

Letters to Clizia

Montale's relationship with Shakespeare is intrinsically bound up with his meeting with the American scholar Irma Brandeis, who was to become not only his lover but also his most influential muse, "Clizia" (the pseudonym, or *senhal*, adopted by Montale for her, as if she were the beloved courtly-love object of a troubadour poet). That is not to suggest that the poet did not know Shakespeare's work before his contact with Brandeis. In fact, Montale's interest in English literary culture, though

234 Camilla Caporicci

certainly increasing from the 1930s onwards (Barile 1990), appears to trace back some years before this encounter. However, not only does his first known engagement with Shakespeare—the translation of the fragments from *A Midsummer Night's Dream*—date to 1933 (Montale 1948), the same year as his meeting with Brandeis, but the letters he sent her between 1933 and 1939 attest the importance of Shakespeare's voice within the fluid and polymorphous Anglo-Italian idiolect used in the exchanges between the two lovers.

On more than one occasion do we find Montale addressing Irma with a Shakespearean "Hail to Thee" (Montale 2006), commenting on Beethoven's Fifth Symphony with an ironical "too much ado for nothing" (Montale 2006: 37), or expressing his discontent with Fascist Italy by parodically echoing Miranda's exclamation in *The Tempest*: "As for me, my bottom aches—in the Brave—New—World" (Montale 2006: 113). Hamlet's famous question resounds many times throughout the letters, especially when the problematic nature of the relationship with Brandeis surfaces: "I don't think another man could love you as I do; but am I worth while? *That's the question*" (Montale 2006: 58). Moreover, in expressing a principle crucial to his poetry, the "miracle" that breaks the wall of necessity and allows the "chosen few" to escape (Montale 2012: 193), Montale reuses *Henry V*'s "happy few" motif (Shakespeare 2005: 4.3.60): "necessity is the Rule; but the miracle, the *contingenza* [contingency] exists also [...] for the 'happy few'. I don't think I belong; but the happy few *do* exist. I hope you, Irma, will belong" (Montale 2006: 48).

Here, Montale's references to Shakespeare are mainly used to embellish the epistolary language directed to his English-speaking muse, connoting a shared cultural horizon deeply rooted in Shakespeare's work, as Brandeis' diaries likewise clearly reveal (Brandeis 2008). They appear as formulaic quotations, the outcome of a sort of casual intertextuality that, while not indicating any specific knowledge of Shakespeare's work on the part of Montale, implies a cultural prestige that Shakespeare had attained and enjoyed among learned Italian readers in the middle decades of the twentieth century. Yet, crucially, these references also show the poet's tendency to associate Shakespeare's poetry with Brandeis, in a way that leaves a trace in Montale's own poetry.

Le occasioni and *La bufera e altro*

In the two collections dominated by the figure of Clizia, *Le occasioni* and *La bufera e altro*, Montale counters the pain of reality with highly lyrical language whose primary virtue is its own aesthetic value. Clizia's angelic splendour redeems the world by offering the poet a glimpse of a higher universe, just as the lyrical climax, with its aesthetic surplus, redeems an ontologically and linguistically indifferent quotidian reality. In this poetry, beauty—of the female "tu" and of language itself—is still

"The rest which is not *silence*" 235

able to save the world. It is precisely in order to increase these reserves of beauty that Montale turns to the Shakespeare of *Romeo and Juliet*, the *Sonnets*, *A Midsummer Night's Dream*, and *The Tempest*. Shakespearean echoes integrate themselves in a synergistic fashion into the poet's language, enhancing poetic expression at those moments of aesthetic or existential sublimity that represents the "miracle" in these collections.

In some cases, such as *Punta del Mesco*, the reference to Shakespeare is no more than a vague or impressionistic hint, yet it comes endowed with powerful effect. Here, the light-bringing epiphany of the female figure—whether she be the same figure of *Il balcone* identified by Montale first as Clizia (Motolese 2007) and then Arletta (Rebay 1976), or Maria Rosa Solari (Greco 1980: 46)—combines the memory of Leopardi's Nerina in the *Ricordanze* with that of Shakespeare's Juliet, rising like the sun at the window. Thus, Montale's own window becomes the frame of his beloved's luminous visage, which brings daylight into an otherwise dark world:

> Brancolo nel fumo,
> ma rivedo: ritornano i tuoi rari
> gesti e il viso che aggiorna al davanzale
>
> (Montale 2012: 178)

> [I grope in smoke,
> but once again I see: rare gestures of yours
> return, and the face dawning at the window
>
> (Montale 2012: 179)]

The Shakespearean echo strengthens the salvific beauty that corresponds to the beloved's redeeming epiphany, which is aesthetically enriched by the semantic surplus brought to the reader's mind by the recollection of Juliet's iconic appearance.

A comparable Shakespearean reference is to be found in the ninth motet, featuring a much more explicit quotation from *The Tempest*: "Luce di lampo | invano può mutarvi in alcunché | di ricco e strano. Altro era il tuo stampo" ["In vain can the lighting | change you into something rich | and strange. You were stamped from another mold"] (Montale 2012: 152, 153). In order to express the mystery and preciousness of Clizia's protean nature, Montale borrows from Ariel's homage to metamorphosis: "Nothing of him that doth fade | But doth suffer a sea-change | Into something rich and strange" (1.2.402–404). The allusion is highly self-conscious, as it appears in a letter to Irma in which Montale confirms that in the motet "è incluso un verso di Shakespeare: something of rich and strange, o qualcosa di simile che ho ricordato a memoria" (Montale 2006: 259) [a Shakespearean verse is included: something of rich and strange, or something similar, which I know by heart]. One may suppose that the memory of this

236   Camilla Caporicci

specific verse could have lingered in the poet's mind thanks to its presence not only in Percy Shelley's Roman epitaph, but also in the work of Gabriele D'Annunzio who, as Isella points out, quotes it in many of his writings (Isella 2006: 63). The currency of this Shakespearean phrase in the Italian cultural system allowed Montale to count on the fact that at least some of his readers would recognize its source. In this way, the Shakespearean echo integrates itself into the motet's metamorphic image system, and adds a mythical aura to Clizia's miraculous essence.

The link between Clizia and Shakespearean memory also finds expression in the parallels that Montale establishes with Shakespeare's *Sonnets*. That the *Sonnets* might have influenced the *Occasioni* and the *Bufera* is not surprising, given Montale's deep knowledge of these poems, three of which he translated, and that he considered "uno dei monumenti di Shakespeare" (Montale 1996: 164) [one of Shakespeare's monuments]. Moreover, Montale himself signals the intertextual role of the *Sonnets* in the poems dedicated to Clizia. Not only did he include a partially cryptic dedication at the start of the collection, "to I. B.", but also referred to that same I. B. as the "only begetter", both explicit references to the mysterious dedication prefacing the 1609 Quarto of the *Sonnets*: "To. The. Onlie. Begetter. Of. These. Insuing. Sonnets. Mr. W. H.". Montale defines his addressee in this way in an interview with Gianfranco Contini (Contini 1974: 70), and again many years later in the poem *Domande senza risposta*. Yet the first attestation of this reference is found much earlier, in the handwritten epigraph on the copy of the *Occasioni* that he sent to Irma in November 1939: "to the Only Begetter | the Only Idiot | E. M. | 6 XI 1939" (Bettarini 2006: xxxv). Even more importantly, he makes his indebtedness to the *Sonnets* explicit in the epigraphic quotation that introduces the fourth section of the *Occasioni*—"Sap check'd with frost, and lusty leaves quite gone, | Beauty o'ersnow'd and bareness every where. Shakespeare, *Sonnets*, V" (Montale 2012: 171). Montale frequently uses this paratextual technique in order, as Orlando points out, to indicate the text under the influence of which the relevant poems have been written (Orlando 2001b: 55).

Evidence of Montale's enduring "loyalty" to the *Sonnets* (Orlando 2001a: 40) can first be found in the motets composed between 1937 and 1939—the same years in which Montale wrote the ninth motet with its quotation from *The Tempest*. However, the references to the *Sonnets* differ from Montale's use of *The Tempest*. The latter case shows what could be called an "allusive" reference, one that is intentionally used in order to have a specific effect on readers and can only work if it is recognized by them as a poetic formula drawn from a specific literary text (Blasucci 2002a). On the other hand, the references to the *Sonnets*, and in one case to *A Midsummer Night's Dream*, appear as "not allusive", but rather as perfectly autonomous references (Blasucci 2002a: 215). These "not allusive" references do not rely on the reader's identification of the

"The rest which is not *silence*" 237

source, but are instead the more or less conscious outcome of the influence exercised by the poet's cultural background on his creative process. Here, Montale does not refer to the *Sonnets* in order to generate, through the reader's recognition of the source, a specific intertextual effect; these echoes, probably prompted by the link established in Montale's mind between Brandeis-Clizia and Shakespeare, are not clear quotations of well-known and recognizable Shakespearean expressions, but appear instead as impressionistic allusions emerging from a sort of assimilative process, through which they become part of the poet's own language.

While referring to Orlando's illuminating work on the formal and thematic affinities between the *Sonnets* and Montale's *Occasioni* and *Bufera* (Orlando 2001a), this chapter ventures original analysis of some instances of Montale's use of Shakespeare, beginning with the motet "Non recidere, forbice, quel volto":

> Non recidere, forbice, quel volto,
> solo nella memoria che si sfolla,
> non far del grande suo viso in ascolto
> la mia nebbia di sempre.
>
> Un freddo cala… Duro il colpo svetta.
> E l'acacia ferita da sé scrolla
> il guscio di cicala
> nella prima belletta di Novembre.
>
> (Montale 2012: 160)

> [Scissors, don't cut that face,
> all that's left in my thinning memory.
> Don't change her great listening look,
> into my everlasting blur.
>
> A chill strikes… The harsh blow slices.
> And the acacia, wounded, peels off
> the cicada's husk
> in the first November mud.
>
> (Montale 2012: 161)]

Here we find echoes of two Shakespearean works. First, we have both a lexical and thematic affinity with *A Midsummer Night's Dream* (a text that Montale had already translated when he composed the motet). The image of the scissors cutting off the beloved's existence is crucial to both poetic texts. In Montale's translation of the *Dream*, we find Piramo (Pyramus) exclaiming: "Venite, furie insane, e recidete I questo stame" [Come, terrible Furies, and cut this thread], and then Tisbe (Thisbe) invoking death from the furies "se reciso avete I nel sangue,

238 *Camilla Caporicci*

con le forbici, il suo fiore" (Montale 1990: 738) [as you have bloodily cut, | with scissors, his flower], corresponding to Bottom's and Flute's lines "Approach, ye furies fell. | O fates, come, come, | Cut the thread and thrum" (5.1.279–81), and "Since lion vile hath here deflowered my dear" (5.1.287). Moreover, Piramo, his thread severed by the scissors' stroke, affirms "e scenda sulla lingua | il gelo" (Montale 1990: 739) [and a chill strikes | the tongue], corresponding to Bottom's line "Tongue, lose thy light" (5.1.299), which might remind us of the motet verse "A chill strikes ... The harsh blow slices". Finally, the botanical imagery is retained: just as Piramo's life is represented by a flower clipped by the scissors, so the wounded acacia symbolically signifies Montale's amputated memory. In the image of the blade cutting the beloved's visage from memory and "confounding" it in a blur, there lies an echo of Sonnet 63, in which Shakespeare affirms that he is fortifying "Against confounding age's cruel knife, | That he shall never cut from memory | My sweet love's beauty" (ll. 10–12).

The influence of the *Sonnets* is even stronger in the poems composed between 1938 and 1939. For instance, the Shakespearean motif of the beloved's "breaking" through the clouds—found in Sonnets 33 and 34—is echoed in Clizia's epiphanies, merging in Montale's mind with Juliet's light "breaking" through the window (2.1.44), attesting his preference for the verb "to break" [*rompere*] for references to the beloved's epiphanies. This is visible in *Il tuo volo*—"Se rompi il fuoco" ["if you break the fire"] (Montale 2012: 224, 225)—and in *Notizie dall'Amiata* (1938-1939), where Clizia's luminous icon "breaks" through the cloudy window: "il quadro | dove tra poco romperai" ["the frame through which | you soon will break"] (Montale 2012: 202, 203).

The *Sonnets* continue to resonate in *La bufera e altro*. In this phase of his poetic *cursus*, Montale's poetic expression veers towards a Petrarchan kind of poetry (Montale 1976: 567–68), but one that appears to "passa[re] anche attraverso l'esperienza dei sonetti shakespeariani" [be filtered through the experience of the Shakespearean sonnets] (Mengaldo 1978: xxxv). Montale's chromatic discourse appears newly significant in the light of Shakespeare's shift in addressee across the *Sonnets*, from the "fair" young man traditionally identified in the main body of the collection to the "dark" mistress of the final portion. A similar shift is found in Montale's poetry, with the entrance of a muse very different from the solar, angelic Clizia—namely, *Volpe* [The Fox]. This is most evident in *Lasciando un "Dove"*, a poem that reminds us of Shakespeare's transitional Sonnet 127: "In the old age black was not counted fair | Or if it were, it bore not beauty's name; | But now is black beauty's successive heir" (ll. 1–3).

> Una colomba bianca m'ha disceso
> fra stele, sotto cuspidi dove il cielo s'annida.

"*The rest which is* not *silence*"   239

Albe e luci, sospese; ho amato il sole,
il colore del miele, or chiedo il bruno,
chiedo il fuoco che cova, questa tomba
che non vola, il tuo sguardo che la sfida.

(Montale 2012: 242)

[A white dove descending dropped me here
among memorial stones, under spires where the sky nests.
Dawns and lights, adjourned. I've loved the sun,
color of honey; now I want the dark,
I want the brooding fire, this unsoaring
grave, your gaze of defiance.

(Montale 2012: 243)]

The first part of the poem is dominated by Clizia's chromatic symbolism: the white dove (in a play on the noun "colomba" [dove] and the adverb "dove" [where]), the sky, the lights, the colour of honey, and the sun. Then the switch—*leaving* a dove, as the title-word "Lasciando" suggests—is introduced, exactly as in Shakespeare's sonnet, by the word "now" (l. 4, "or" in the Italian). A new desire for the dark emerges, corresponding to the sensual and earthly nature of this new dark muse. By this, I do not mean to imply a clearly-delineated dichotomy between the two addressees as we have in Shakespeare—though Montale himself seems to confirm it (Cima 1977: 194)—but only to suggest that there is a certain affinity between Shakespeare's and Montale's shifts in addressee. This affinity is revealed in the specific echoes of *Lasciando un "Dove"*, the colour shifts in which appear to influence the chromatic characterization of other poems: the golden sun becomes "blind" (Montale 2012: 271) and "black" (257); the beloved's signs penumbral, likened to "black cloud" (287), "black trout" (243), "black duck" (289); and the muse herself appears equally darkened at times (247), with wings of ebony (285).

With the exception of the quotation from *The Tempest* and, partially, from *Romeo and Juliet*, Shakespeare's presence in the *Occasioni* and the *Bufera* appears, essentially, to consist of a subtle net of impressionistic echoes. Hardly perceptible to the average reader, these "not allusive" references do not indicate any specific intertextual intention. However, they clearly imply a certain degree of internalization of Shakespearean language on the part of Montale, whose poetry bears the signs of this influence on both thematic and formal levels.

Satura and Onwards

Montale's use of Shakespearean references changes greatly in the second part of his output, namely in the collections from *Satura* onwards—a collection whose very title points to its dual trappings as both something

240 *Camilla Caporicci*

satirical and, in the word's Latin etymology, a "mixed dish" or compilation of assorted fragments. The allusions grow in number and become much more explicit, in line with Montale's general tendency when quoting in this period: "From *Satura* onward the examples of allusivity" become both "more frequent and explicit, part of the parodic and satiric mechanisms" of late Montale (Blasucci 2002a: 213). At the same time, these clearly "allusive" references, for the most part, cease to be signs of an effective and internalized source of inspiration. Instead, they become intentionally recognizable elements that establish a dialogic relationship between the two texts in a strictly metapoetic sense. This change is part of the more general passage from the rigorous lyricism of the early works to the dry and prosaic style of *Satura* and the following collections, in which Montale adopts a "discursive register" replete with "satiric and parodic tonalities", a development consistent with his rejection of an increasingly degenerate "historical-sociological reality" comprising mass culture, consumerism, and "optimistic scientism" (Blasucci 2002b: 105).

Montale's growing pessimism manifests itself in the choice of plays to which he refers. Abandoning the Shakespeare of love and magic, Montale turns increasingly to Shakespeare's tragedies of loss, decrepitude, and death: *King Lear* and *Hamlet*. In the letters, references to *Hamlet*—limited to the canonical "to be or not to be" motif—were used by Montale as a belletristic commonplace to adorn his epistolary language. The older, more bitter Montale appears to have an enhanced understanding of the play's ontological-theological reflections and nihilistic undertones—perhaps developed when translating the play, published for Mondadori (1949). Montale's poem "Si può essere a destra" ends with the poet as a sort of modern Hamlet: "Alas, poor Yorick, che teste di cavolo | noi siamo (e questa resta | la nostra sola certezza)" (Montale 1990: 684) [Alas, poor Yorick, what cabbageheads | we are (and this remains | our only certainty)]. The quotation, in English, may indicate an affinity between Montale's and Hamlet's personal philosophies, yet it also signals an ironic reduction of the source. Montale addresses Yorick's skull with entirely colloquial language, almost banal in the infantile image of cabbageheads, which suggests a grotesque comparison between the rounded vegetable and the dead man's skull. The quotation implies modern poetry's surrender and failure to compete with an artistic past, which it can confront only through a degraded form of ironic citation. On the other hand, it is precisely this degradation of the original poetic myth that, by divesting it of its aura of untouchable authority, brings it closer to the modern poet. A similar process of de-idealization and humanization of poetic authority is at work in many of the poems that exemplify this pronounced metapoetic vein in Montale's late collections. In *Le storie letterarie*, for instance, Montale resumes a discourse begun in prose in the article "Sotto il nome di Shakespeare sarebbe nascosto Lord Derby" (Montale 1996: 1162), returning to the theory that "Shakespeare" represented a collaborative circle of Elizabethan authors, thereby undercutting the myth of the colossal, solitary poet-genius and, consequently, bringing him closer to the misery of the modern poet.

The acute pessimism of late Montale also defines his use of Shakespeare when he turns to the theme of love. With the exception of the reference to Cordelia in *Morgana*—"Ahimé figlia adorata, vera mia | Regina della Notte, mia Cordelia, | mia Brunilde" ["Alas, my adored daughter, my true | Queen of the Night, my Cordelia, | my Brunhilde"] (Montale 2012: 658, 659)—where the figure of Lear's daughter is evoked in a positively lyrical sense, Shakespearean references lack such *tendresse* and suggest something prosaic, devoid of lyrical sublimity. In the "suite" *Dopo una fuga*, which tells the story, according to Montale (Montale 1980: 65), of a last love between a young woman (Laura Papi) and an old man, the seventh poem reads:

> Girovagai lentamente
> l'intera lunga giornata e riflettevo
> che tra re Lear e Cordelia non corsero tali pensieri
> e che crollava così ogni lontano raffronto.
> Tornai col gruppo visitando tombe
> di Lucumoni, covi di aristocratici
> travestiti da ladri, qualche piranesiana
> e carceraria strada della vecchia Livorno.
> M'infiltrai nei cunicoli del ciarpame. Stupendo
> il cielo ma quasi orrifico in quel ritorno.
> Anche il rapporto con la tragedia se ne andava ora in fumo
> perché, per soprammercato, non sono nemmeno tuo padre.
> (Montale 2012: 408)

> [All day long I wandered slowly about, musing
> that Lear and Cordelia had no such thoughts as these,
> and that even the most remote comparisons crumbled.
> I returned with the group, after visiting
> the tombs of Lucumos, dens of aristocrats
> disguised as thieves, and prison streets
> à la Piranesi, in old Livorno. I burrowed
> my way through rabbit holes of trash. The sky
> was stupendous but almost terrifying
> on the way back. Even the link with tragedy
> dissolved in smoke since, in any case,
> I'm not even your father.
> (Montale 2012: 409)]

242   Camilla Caporicci

Montale ventures a comparison between the speaker's personal relationship with Laura and that found in *King Lear*, only to highlight the inadequacy of such similitudes that inevitably "crumble" on closer analysis: intergenerational, familial love between father and daughter in *King Lear* sits uneasily beside the erotic tension that characterizes the relationship between the "old dotard" and Laura (Montale 1980: 1035), more befitting of the perverted lusts found in *The Winter's Tale*'s source, Greene's *Pandosto*. In a previous draft, the earlier wording of the line "Lear and Cordelia had no such thoughts as these" made explicit the unwholesome nature of the attraction: "tra re Lear e Cordelia, certo non corsero impuri | pensieri" (Montale 1980: 1033) [King Lear and Cordelia surely had no impure | thoughts]. The comparison draws attention to the present as an inferior, debased simulacrum of a tragic, anterior model. The drama of modern life, according to Montale, falls short of the greatness of the past: it is no more than a puppet show, a "cabaret" hastily staged, a "two-bit film" (Montale 2012: 643), the small-screen standing in for the grandeur of the bygone stage whose tragic myths are "way above us, unreachable" (Montale 2012: 491).

The eighth poem of this "suite" presents another striking Shakespearean echo:

> Non posso respirare se sei lontana.
> Così scriveva Keats a Fanny Brawne
> da lui tolta dall'ombra. È strano che il mio caso
> si parva licet sia diverso. Posso
> respirare assai meglio se ti allontani.
> [...]
> So che se mi leggi
> pensi che mi hai fornito il propellente
> necessario e che il resto (purchè *non sia* silenzio)
> poco importa.
>
> (Montale 2012: 408)

> [I can't breathe when you're not here.
> So Keats wrote to Fanny Brawne, plucked
> by him from oblivion. It's strange,
> but my case is different, *si parva licet*.
> I breathe rather better when you're not here.
> [...]
> If you're reading me, I know you're thinking
> you've provided me with the stimulus I needed,
> and that everything else (providing *it's not* silence)
> doesn't much matter.
>
> (Montale 2012: 409)]

"The rest which is not *silence"* 243

In this poem, Montale reflects upon the loss of both Papi and his never-forgotten Brandeis, and expresses this absence through a *pastiche* in which we find two English authors whom, in the letters to Brandeis, Montale had quoted to declare his passion for her. While in Letter 20 he proclaimed to love her with the same sensuality with which Keats loved Fanny Brawne (Montale 2006: 34), in Letter 39 he declared, "if I dream you I don't dream your Soul, I dream your lips, your eyes, your breast, and the rest which is *not* silence. I daresay that the rest is the *best* and Shakespeare knew it" (Montale 2006: 77). The references in the poem thus work on an overt, intertextual level for the reader's sake, and on a more intimate, perhaps less conscious, level, reflecting the persistence of these authors in the poet's memory, in which they are intrinsically related to Brandeis. Moreover, both references establish a "distinctive" relationship with the source, in a technique that Montale uses regularly in his late collections (Orlando 2001a: 43): the negation of a poetic passage, which is evoked only to be challenged by a diametrically opposite assertion—"I breathe rather better when you're not here", "*not* silence". Montale again recalls one of Shakespeare's most recognisable formulae (Hamlet's final words), made almost banal from overuse, and intentionally overturns it, distancing himself from the source. As he had done in the preceding poem with *King Lear*, Montale deprives his sources of their original aura and makes them part of the prosaic and disillusioned tenor of his poetry.

Finally, as Clizia's figure overlaps with those of his other addressees, the poet brings back into the foreground, in *Domande senza risposta*, the motif of the "onlie begetter" (notably retaining the original spelling of his borrowed phrase): "Mi chiedono se ho scritto | un canzoniere d'amore | e se il mio onlie begetter | è uno solo o è molteplice" ["They ask me if I've written | a *canzoniere* of love poems | and whether my 'onlie begetter' | is one or many"] (Montale 2012: 592, 593). Even here, the motif seems exhausted, denuded of its specific intertextual value. Lacking the specificity that linked it to the figure of Clizia-Brandeis in the early collections, the "onlie begetter" becomes, not without a touch of irony, a literary commonplace, a generic synonym for a poetic inspirer, in whom, now, many figures merge almost indistinguishably.

Given the two main types of reference that Montale uses to engage with Shakespeare's texts—"allusive" and "not allusive"—Shakespeare's voice could be said to perform a double role in the poet's work. In Montale's early poetic collections, especially in *Le occasioni* and *La bufera e altro*, Shakespearean echoes, deeply connected to the figure of Clizia, appear mainly as the outcome of a cultural influence exercised by Shakespeare over Montale's creative processes. Shakespeare's influence—explicitly acknowledged by the epigraphic reference to Sonnet 5—works not on an overt plane but "from the inside", integrating itself in Montale's language and contributing to the construction of his poetry both on thematic and formal levels. In this sense, we can talk of a positively synergic form of intertextuality, in which a Shakespearean voice works in the same direction as the primary text, enhancing its poetic potential and purposes.

From *Satura* onwards, the intertextual dynamic operating in Montale's poetry changes greatly. Perhaps reflecting Shakespeare's heightened, more extensive presence in the Italian cultural panorama, Shakespeare's voice is now perceived as a major authority within a common cultural heritage, and used as such. The explicit references to Shakespeare's most recognisable expressions are clearly aimed at establishing a metatextual relationship with the source, which is usually deprived of its original context and connotations, and "reduced" in order to fit the prosaic tenor of late Montale. Through this process, Montale distances himself from a source that, because of its cultural status, he rejects as alien to and unattainable by modern poetry, which can now confront Shakespeare only through a poetics of negative citation. While Shakespeare's presence among the great poetic voices that Montale challenges is in itself a sign of the status he had acquired in both the official poetic canon and in Montale's personal pantheon, the reduction of his figure through demolishing, metapoetic quotations questions and resists Shakespeare's poetic authority, divesting it of its aura of untouchability, and humanizing it for the modern poet and reader alike.

Bibliography

Barile, Laura. 1990. *Adorate mie larve: Montale e la poesia anglosassone*. Bologna.

Bettarini, Rosanna. 2006. "Introduzione". In Montale 2006. vii–xli.

Blasucci, Luigi. 2002a. "Appunti per un commento montaliano". *Gli oggetti di Montale*. Bologna. 203–27.

———— 2002b. "Percorso di un tema montaliano: il tempo". *Gli oggetti di Montale*. Bologna. 87–111.

Brandeis, Irma. 2008. *Irma Brandeis (1905–1990). Profilo di una musa di Montale*, ed. by Marco Sonzogni, trans. by Domenico Iannaco, Barbara Pezzotti, Marco Sonzogni, and Giulia Zuodar. Balerna.

Cima, Annalisa. 1977. "Le reazioni di Montale". *Eugenio Montale*, ed. by Annalisa Cima and Cesare Segre. Milan. 192–201.

Contini, Gianfranco. 1974. "Pour présenter Eugenio Montale". *Una lunga fedeltà. Scritti su Eugenio Montale*. Turin. 59–75.

de Rogatis, Tiziana, ed. 2011. Eugenio Montale, *Le occasioni*. Milan.

Erspamer, Francesco. 1990. "I sonetti dell'esperienza. Montale traduttore di Shakespeare". *Quaderni d'italianistica*, 11: 269–85.

Greco, Lorenzo. 1980. *Montale commenta Montale*. Parma.

Isella, Dante. 1988. "Montale e il giovane poeta Guglielmo Crollalanza". *Annali della Scuola Normale Superiore di Pisa*, 18: 1371–86.

———— ed. 2006. Eugenio Montale, *Mottetti*. Milan.

Lonardi, Gilberto. 1980. "Fuori e dentro il tradurre montaliano". *Il vecchio e il giovane e altri studi su Montale*. Bologna. 144–63.

Mengaldo, Pier Vincenzo. 1978. "Introduzione". *Poeti italiani del Novecento*. Milan. xiii–lxxvii.

Meoli Toulmin, Rachel. 1971. "Shakespeare ed Eliot nelle versioni di Eugenio Montale". *Belfagor*, 26: 453–71.

Meriano, Francesco. 1982. *Arte e Vita. Con tre carteggi di Umberto Saba, Eugenio Montale, Gabriele D'Annunzio*, ed. by Gloria Manghetti, Carlo Ernesto Meriano, and Vanni Scheiwiller. Milan.

Montale, Eugenio. 1944. *Motivi. Città* (7 December 1944). Rome.

—— 1947. *L'immagine*. Rome. 1: 114–115.

—— 1948. *Quaderno di traduzioni*. Milan.

—— 1949. *Amleto, principe di Danimarca*, trans. by Eugenio Montale. Milan.

—— 1964. *La commedia degli errori, Timone d'Atene, Racconto d'inverno*, trans. by Eugenio Montale. William Shakespeare, *Tutte le opere*, ed. by Mario Praz. Florence.

—— 1976. *Sulla poesia*, ed. by Giorgio Zampa. Milan.

—— 1980. *L'opera in versi*, ed. by Rosanna Bettarini and Gianfranco Contini. Turin.

—— 1990. *Tutte le poesie*, ed. by Giorgio Zampa. Milan.

—— 1996. *Il secondo mestiere: Prose 1920–1979*, ed. by Giorgio Zampa. Milan.

—— 2006. *Lettere a Clizia*, ed. by Rosanna Bettarini, Gloria Manghetti, and Franco Zabagli. Milan.

—— 2012. *The Collected Poems of Eugenio Montale 1925–1977*, trans. by William Arrowsmith, ed. by Rosanna Warren. New York.

Motolese, Matteo. 2007. "Per le 'Occasioni': una lettera inedita di Eugenio Montale ad Alfredo Gargiulo". *Bollettino di Italianistica*, n. s., 4: 183–92.

Orlando, Roberto. 2001a. "Montale e i 'Sonnets' shakespeariani". *Applicazioni montaliane*. Lucca. 7–40.

—— 2001b. "Reminiscenze maledette! Per una tipologia della 'citazione distintiva' nell'ultimo Montale". *Applicazioni montaliane*. Lucca. 41–66.

Rebay, Luciano. 1976. "Sull'autobiografismo di Montale". *Innovazioni tematiche e linguistiche della letteratura italiana del Novecento*, ed. by Vittore Branca, Robert J. Clements, Cesare De Michelis, Stephan Di Scala, Olga Ragusa, and Michael Ricciardelli. Florence. 73–83.

Scaglione, Giuseppe. 2007. "Le traduzioni shakespeariane in Eugenio Montale e Giovanni Giudici". *Gli scrittori d'Italia. Il patrimonio e la memoria della tradizione letteraria come risorsa primaria*. Proceedings of the XI ADI National Congress, Napoli, 26–29 September 2007 (www.italianisti.it).

Shakespeare, William. 2005. *The Oxford Shakespeare. The Complete Works*, ed. by Stanley Wells, Gary Taylor, John Jowett, and William Montgomery, 2nd edition. Oxford.

17 Giorgio Strehler's *Il gioco dei potenti*

A Shakespearean Master Finds His Voice

Mace Perlman

Fu proprio grazie a Shakespeare che il Piccolo ed io stesso definimmo una dimensione che ci ha seguito nel tempo. Al suo contatto, problemi di estetica e di storia divennero estremamente consistenti, la lezione di Bertolt Brecht divenne concreta assai più [con *Coriolano*] che con la rappresentazione dell' *Opera da tre soldi*. Per la prima volta riuscimmo a mettere in scena quel teatro della storia, quel teatro dialettico, quello scontro delle classi in movimento, senza per questo dimenticare mai la dimensione dell'umano, del privato del carattere nella storia.

—Strehler 1992: 31

[It was precisely thanks to Shakespeare that the Piccolo Teatro and I myself defined a breadth of vision which has never left us. Through contact with him, problems of aesthetics and history became remarkably palpable, and the lesson taught by Bertolt Brecht became much more concrete [in the case of *Coriolanus*] than it had with the performance and staging of *The Threepenny Opera*. For the first time we succeeded in staging that theatre of history, that theatre of dialectics, that clashing of classes in movement, while nonetheless never forgetting the human dimension, and the private world of the character in the midst of history.]

Much has been written on the great Shakespearean masterpieces of Giorgio Strehler's maturity—his *King Lear* (1972) and *Tempest* (1978)—and about Strehler's indebtedness to Shakespeare more broadly (Lombardo 1992, 1998; Tempera 2004). But very little exists, in English or in Italian, to document his *Il gioco dei potenti* or *The Game of the Powerful* (1965, 1973, 1975), which was an adaptation of the *Henry VI* trilogy, presented in two nights, *Un trono e un popolo* [*A Throne and a People*] and *La guerra delle due rose* [*The War of the Two Roses*]. This massive undertaking prefigured by two decades his only project of comparable size and ambition, the mounting of both parts of Goethe's *Faust* (1988–91). *Il gioco* represented a total commitment to the staging of Shakespearean history: it required every skill and resource Strehler could muster; and it promised to present the public with "feasts, fairs, battles, rebellions, throne-rooms, executions, love, hate, vengeance, deception, apparitions, skulls, grave-diggers, cannon shots" (Hirst 1993: 72). As the director recounts:

> *Il gioco dei potenti* rappresentò un salto coraggioso nel buio, una specie di ricapitualazione scorretta ma potente e vasta del mondo di Shakespeare, anche se certo coraggio della "scrittura" su Shakespeare—che non ripeterei mai più—ebbe una sua ragione interiore nel mio lavoro di teatro.
> (Strehler 1992: 32–33)

> [*Il gioco* represented a courageous leap into the unknown, a sort of potent and vast recapitulation of Shakespeare's world, wrong-minded, even if a certain courage to "write" on Shakespeare's behalf—something I would never repeat—had its own reason for being and internal logic in the context of my work in the theatre.]

It was clearly an overreaching on Strehler's part, yet it was also an essential moment in his growth as a director of Shakespeare (see Fig. 17.1). It serves as a fundamental bridge between the earlier productions of *Julius Caesar* and *Coriolanus*, tragedies reimagined as history plays, and the two great Shakespeare productions of his later years (*King Lear* and *The Tempest*).

Figure 17.1 Giorgio Strehler directing Valentina Cortese as Queen Margaret and Renato De Carmine as Henry VI, 1964–65 (Luigi Ciminaghi/ Piccolo Teatro di Milano—Teatro d'Europa).

248 *Mace Perlman*

Faithful and even overly self-effacing, Strehler always defined his role as that of a mere interpreter, never as deserving the name of creator. *The Game of the Powerful* represents the great stretching of Strehler's theatrical wings—even where he failed, he was laying the groundwork for the magisterial productions which were to follow.

Strehler (1921–1997) has been called "the single most important figure in post-war Italian theatre" (McManus 2008: 441). As McManus points out, he was more than just a director—he was an actor, scholar, *dramaturg*, and scenographer. His moral commitment to the act of theatre-making as a dialogue with society, and not mere entertainment, made for shows that expected and received total engagement from their audiences while never failing to entertain. It is no small wonder in this regard that he and Brecht were such easy and immediate admirers of one another's work. Although Strehler is well known for his stagings of works by Goldoni, Brecht, Pirandello, and Chekhov, Shakespeare was from the very beginning a fundamental fixture and a touchstone in his life as a director.

Over the first eight seasons in the life of the Piccolo Teatro di Milano— the repertory theatre that Strehler cofounded in 1947 with Paolo Grassi and Nina Vinchi—he directed ten of Shakespeare's plays: *Richard II, The Tempest, Romeo and Juliet* (1948); *The Taming of the Shrew* (1949); *Richard III* (1950); *1 Henry IV, Twelfth Night* (1951); *Macbeth* (1952); *Julius Caesar* (1953); and *Coriolanus* (1956). Strehler, by his own admission, was in the thrall of a youthful exuberance that began to wane in the early-to-mid 1950s. These were the years of his encounters with Brecht, and he was beginning to come to terms with the complexity of Shakespeare's language and themes in a deeper way.

In his early productions, including his *1 Henry IV* (1951) for the Roman amphitheatre on the banks of the Adige in Verona, he was, as he conceded, overly concerned with recreating the form of a Globe-inspired "Elizabethan" playhouse. This design had developed from the two-level, polygonal facade created by the designer Gianni Ratto for *Richard II*; and Laurence Olivier's recreation of the Globe in his recent film of *Henry V* (1944) exerted its influence as well (Astington 2004: 63–64). As he researched a new aesthetic and a new stage-space for playing, Strehler was also exploring a new approach to storytelling deeply influenced by Brecht. His production of *Julius Caesar* (1953), which predated the influence of Brecht, nonetheless laid the foundations for a new approach to staging Shakespeare's history plays. Strehler recognized the need to explore both the power struggle between Caesar and the Republican conspirators on the one hand, and the human drama of a shattered friendship between Cassius and Brutus on the other. This dialectic tension between the public and the private, the political and the personal, the collective and the individual lay at the heart of Brecht's productions, and it would carry Strehler through his subsequent *Coriolanus* and onwards to his *Il gioco dei potenti*.

Giorgio Strehler's Il gioco dei potenti 249

Julius Caesar posed challenges which were practical as well as drama-turgical. Aesthetically, the show took Strehler and his scenographer, Piero Zuffi, in a new direction, abandoning the Elizabethan stage of earlier productions for a "transfigured" ["trasfigurata"] and sobre Roman-style design and an "emblematic synthesis of realistic elements" ["sintesi em-blematica di dati realistici"] (Bentoglio 2002: 68). As Strehler recounts:

> In un grande vuoto in una specie di teatro romano, estatico e calci-nato, si svolse questa rappresentazione tragica con una grande con-centrazione e parsimonia di mezzi.
>
> (Strehler 1992: 25)

> [In a great void in a sort of Roman theatre, ecstatic and covered in lime, this tragedy unfolded with great concentration and a parsi-mony of means.]

Finally, Strehler gave musical resolution to the public-private dialectic of the play, directing the actors "in slow and austere rhythms and whis-pered tones of intimate realism" during the conspiracy; and contrasting this conspiratorial music with the martial tones of those who would oppose them, exploding into brief moments of robust eloquence—as during the funeral oration of Mark Antony (Bentoglio 2002: 69).

With *Coriolanus* (1956), Strehler built upon many of his discoveries from the earlier production. As in the case of *Julius Caesar*, Strehler recast this play not so much as the personal tragedy of a wronged pro-tagonist, but as a political drama with very human elements, where his-torical forces met the personalities of individuals. Openly influenced by his meetings with Brecht, who was also studying this play at the time, Strehler recounts:

> Ricordo che una sera a Berlino trovai su un tavolo del Maestro il *Coriolano* aperto. [...] "Mio caro ragazzo, sarà meglio che tu lo riguardi il *Coriolano* di Shakespeare. È molto diverso da quello che si dice". Mi indicò alcuni punti fondamentali [...] La rilettura av-venne solitaria e fu la scoperta ancora nuova, ma pure ovvia, che il "lavoro culturale" intorno alle opere di Shakespeare non solo presenta dei vuoti paurosi ma ha delle connotazioni estremamente partigiane, condizionate da lontano e che essa si riflette altrettanto ovviamente sulle traduzioni di Shakespeare. Si ritornava al versante della traduzione, ma non solo come fatto letterario, qui come fatto letteralmente "ideologico".
>
> (Strehler 1992: 26)

> [I remember one evening in Berlin I found on one of the Maestro's tables an open copy of *Coriolanus*. [...] "My dear boy", he said,

250 Mace Perlman

"you would do well to have another look at Shakespeare's *Coriolanus*. It's quite different from what people say about it". He led me in the direction of a few fundamental points [...] My re-reading was a solitary one and led me to a discovery which, although new, should have been obvious, that the "cultural work" around Shakespeare's plays not only presents us with terrible gaps but also has extremely partisan connotations, conditioned by long habit. The same applies, of course, to [our] translations of Shakespeare. We returned to investigate things from the perspective of translation, but not only as a literary question, now literally as a matter of "ideology".]

Interestingly, when Strehler later saw the Berliner Ensemble's own production of *Coriolanus*, posthumously directed according to Brecht's instructions, he was impressed by its size but ultimately disappointed. Luciano Damiani's design for the Piccolo had been marked by a clarity and a simplicity which were to become the hallmarks of the Piccolo's future work; and the "people of Rome" and scenes of war were represented by no more than twenty actors, all students. The Berliner's battle scenes were marvellously choreographed by a Japanese Noh actor, Kita Kenze, and involved hundreds onstage; yet, to Strehler's eye, they seemed to show more and evoke less. Most importantly, the key scene between Volumnia and Coriolanus, so essential to the play and a nexus in Strehler's production, which tellingly interwove the personal with the political, was cut altogether (Strehler 1992: 30).

Strehler had directed a production of Shakespeare practically every year from 1948 onwards, and the gap of three years between *Julius Caesar* and *Coriolanus* represented a significant pause for reflection on the director's part. He was to take almost a decade between *Coriolanus* and his next Shakespearean production, a reduction and adaptation of the *Henry VI* trilogy, *The Game of the Powerful*. Strehler has written that he felt something come to a close with *Coriolanus*. In a way, he felt it to be the most fully realized of all his Shakespeare (Strehler 1992: 29). And yet he felt the need somehow both to recapitulate all he knew and to take a leap into the void, to let go of the text somewhat, deconstructing and reconstructing the words in order to explore ever more deeply the inherent theatricality of Shakespeare's drama.

Much has been written about the Brechtian influence on several major adaptations of the *Henry VI* plays that emerged during the 1960s, including Peter Hall's and John Barton's *The Wars of the Roses* at the RSC (1963); Strehler's own production (1965); and Peter Palitzsch's *Der Krieg der Rosen*, performed at Stuttgart (1967). As James N. Loehlin explains:

Brecht's epic dramaturgy provided a justification for the construction of the plays, which retain the episodic narrative of the chronicles in place of an Aristotelian unity. Brecht's theatrical practice, with its

Giorgio Strehler's Il gioco dei potenti   251

attack on comforting illusions, encouraged a stark design style well suited to the plays' emblematic groupings and gritty details. Finally, Brecht's method of political analysis served as an alternative to the prevailing academic interpretation of the plays as conservative homilies on divine providence and the dangers of rebellion.

(Loehlin 2004: 134)

All these imperatives could be said to have applied to Strehler's *Coriolanus*, and indeed that production was far more Brechtian than *Il gioco*. What had changed since 1956 were the immense social upheavals of the new decade, the war in Vietnam, and the profound mistrust of institutional authority, all of which lent an urgent relevancy to this story of civil war and the lust for power. Most significant of all perhaps was the impact of Jan Kott's *Shakespeare Our Contemporary*, which officially appeared in England in 1964 but was already circulating in underground proofs during the RSC rehearsals (Loehlin 2004: 135, referencing Pearson 1990: 26).

Strehler was in personal contact with Kott, and certainly Kott's book was a major impetus behind Strehler's need to revisit the question of Shakespearean history. Kott's vision of history seemed to allow for no escape. Strehler, while acknowledging the violence, the perfidy, and the lust for power which were so evident to Kott, also sees something more in Shakespeare:

> Perhaps all the plays of Shakespeare are to be seen as a grand allegory of history in which [...] all these forces are seeking a power which corrupts and hates and at the same time may close the bloody circle of history [...] My view is that Shakespeare had a pessimistic view of history, but not a pessimistic vision of man [...] All the great personages of Shakespeare are in dialectic with history, with fetishes of power.
>
> (Berry 1989: 126)

For the first time with *Il gioco*, Strehler listed himself as the primary adapter of the text and as the primary designer of both set and costumes, together with his collaborators Carlo Tommasi for set and Enrico Job for costumes. It was a bold leap without precedent as befitted the most ambitious of all his productions to date, and *Il gioco* was to bear his personal signature in every aspect. Choosing to present the production in the space of the Teatro Lirico, a stage significantly wider and deeper than the Piccolo's, Strehler envisioned a kind of rough circus, staged even more minimally than his *Coriolanus*.

The primary scenic element was a wooden, slightly raked stage floor, hexagonal or octagonal in shape (recollections vary), and vaguely recalling the polygonal space of the Elizabethan stage-house. Gone were the

Figure 17.2 Franco Graziosi as the choral figure of L'Attore (The Actor), 1964–65 (Luigi Ciminaghi/Piccolo Teatro di Milano—Teatro d'Europa).

façades of his early productions, the arches or door-openings for exits and entrances. Instead, a tiny Globe was placed on the open stage for certain scenes featuring "the Actor", a kind of choral figure, a metatheatrical reference to the Elizabethan player, a commentator on the action, speaking words drawn from other Shakespeare plays, mostly the histories (see Fig. 17.2). The production not only announced itself as a play, Brechtian-style, but as a play by Shakespeare, and further announced that play as a metatheatrical commentary on the nature of history itself.

The stage was thus transformed into one enormous playground, *Il gioco* of the title, within which there were "three separate stages resembling circus rings on which various scenes took place simultaneously". A tent-like covering to the stage created the impression of "a roundabout when the fair has closed" (Hirst 1993: 73). The play opened with the simultaneous scenes of Henry V's funeral and the young Henry VI's coronation. Recalling Claudius' "With mirth in funeral and with dirge in marriage" (*Hamlet*, 1.2.12), the demands of politics leave little space or time for private grief: no sooner has the ceremonial send-off for the old Henry begun than the new, not-yet-ready child Henry is brought on stage. To heighten the strangeness of the event, the cardinal presiding over the funeral must also lead the royal baptism and coronation, rushing from one side of the stage to the other. (One is reminded not only of Arlecchino's divided consciousness from Strehler's famous productions of Goldoni's *Servant of Two Masters*, but also of how Hamlet

Giorgio Strehler's Il gioco dei potenti   253

recalls his father's recent funeral: "the funeral baked meats | Did coldly furnish forth the marriage tables" (*Hamlet*, 1.2.179–80)). While the funeral proceeded with lines from the play, the baptism-cum-incoronation moved forward in ecclesiastical Latin.

Ogni tanto il bambino piange e la cerimonia si arresta mentre la nutrice deve cullarlo e cantargli, piano, una ninna nanna popolare. Il bambino allora si acquieta e ride. La cerimonia può riprendere.

Entrano in un certo punto nella cerimonia funebre, i messi ad annunciare sventure di guerra. I nobili si strappano di dosso gli abiti da lutto e appaiono già vestiti sotto in abito da guerra, senza le spade e gli elmi. [...] Resta solo, per poco accanto al catafalco, di spalle, a pregare, il cardinale. Poi anch'egli si svolta e annuncia al pubblico che egli è restato soltanto perchè in questo modo, durante l'assenza dei signori, sarà più facile per lui impadronirsi del potere [...] La seconda cerimonia [...] il cardinale impone al bambino la corona [...] pesante, cruda anche se costruita alla misura dell'infante [...] subito quando gli viene imposta in capo piange, e non riesce a sostenerne il peso.

(Strehler 1964a: *Appunti*, parte prima,
primo schema, primo quadro)

[Ever so often, the child cries and the ceremony stops while the nursemaid has to cradle and sing to him, softly, a popular lullaby. The child, in response, calms down and laughs. The ceremony can start up again.

Enter messengers, at a certain point in the funeral ceremony, to announce military defeats. The nobles rip their mourning clothes from their backs to reveal war-like clothing beneath, ready to go, lacking only swords and helmets. [...] A lone figure remains, for a short while by the catafalque, his back to the audience, in prayer: the cardinal. Then he too turns and announces to the audience that he's remained only because, that way, in the absence of the *signori* (the nobles), it will be easier for him to seize power [...] The second ceremony [...] the cardinal forces the crown upon the child [...] heavy, crude even though made to the infant's measurements [...] as it's forced on his head, he cries, and is unable to bear the weight of it.]

From this very first scene, Strehler lays before the audience both the imperatives of the state and, in contrast, the all-too-human reality of the vulnerable child-king. This stark juxtaposition of the public and political with the private and personal continues throughout Strehler's production, most tellingly in those scenes invented, or rather expanded, in Strehler's retelling of Shakespeare's tale.

The scene of the choosing of sides (*1 Henry VI*, 2.4) for the future War of the Roses shows Strehler's imagination at work (see Fig. 17.3). Placing rose

254 *Mace Perlman*

bushes, red and white, centre-stage, Strehler makes the living plants the mute witnesses to the nobles' will to power. Having first inserted York's soliloquy of ambition to the throne from 2 *Henry VI* (1.1), Strehler has two gardeners remove the throne, replacing them with flowering bushes; and York, rather than closing his monologue with a rhetorical finish, is interrupted mid-thought by the appearance of this new reality. The "powerful" enter, joining York from various sides, and engage in a mute dance, likened in Strehler's notes to "una specie di dolce passeggiata tra i fiori" [a pleasant sort of stroll amongst the flowers] (Strehler 1964a: *Appunti*, parte prima, IIIo quadro, 4). In Strehler's performance script, York "sniffs and admires the flowers while from various corners of the stage, with an indolent and purposeless gait, enter the various *potenti*. They look at one another with suspicious eyes and smiles on their lips. Small nods of their heads. But no one speaks" ["annusa e ammira i fiori mentre da vari lati entrano con passo indolente come senza meta, vari potenti. Tutti si guardano con occhi sospettosi e bocche sorridenti. Piccoli cenni dal capo. Ma nessuno parla" (Strehler 1964b: *Copione*, prima giornata)]. Tellingly, between his earlier notes and this final script, Strehler has added this detail, so reminiscent of Hamlet's uncle, of broad smiles to hide the pretendants' suspicious eyes.

Always pointing to a dialectic, to a contrast which illuminates, Strehler's conclusion to the scene is also his greatest invention: "The naked rosebush remains on stage, its branches twisted and cut, branches which the gardeners gather together and carry off, as if the scene presented us with a funeral bier. The faint music of an oboe accompanies the scene. The stage remains empty for a moment. Then silence and darkness" ["Resta sulla scena il roseto nudo, di rami contorti e tagliati, che i giardinieri raccolgono e portano via, come se fosse una spoglia mortuaria. La tenue musica di un oboe accompagna la scena. Persiste un attimo la scena vuota. Poi silenzio e buio" (Strehler 1964a: *Appunti*, parte prima, IIIo quadro, 5)]. The bushes, which in Shakespeare's text appear to be no more than a symbolic convention, are transformed by Strehler's *mise-en-scène* into a living victim. Perhaps thinking back to his early production of *Richard II*, in which the living garden is compared to the state of England, likening its health or decay to the well-being of the commonwealth, Strehler makes us feel for the living limbs that are lopped off by the unfeeling Vernon, the music of the gardeners' shears recalling the clanging of swords and the ringing descent of the guillotine, and the simple picking of flowers a kind of decapitation, leaving behind the bare, ruined "corpse" of the rosebush with its tangled limbs.

Exposing the unfeeling dance of the "powerful", Strehler follows the lead of Shakespeare's writing, reading their soliloquies mostly only for their outer form and public rhetoric and avoiding any humanizing exploration of their psychology. Instead, when it comes to inner life, he concerns himself more with his "personaggi popolari", his lower-class characters. Yet in his treatment of the murder of Humphrey, Duke of

Figure 17.3 The *potenti* and the rosebush, 1964–65 (Luigi Ciminaghi/Piccolo Teatro di Milano—Teatro d'Europa).

Gloucester, he manages both to focus on his lower-class murderers for thought and inner life, and also to awaken our sympathy for this particular member of the class of the *potenti*. Strehler's choices for this scene break with all our expectations, engaging us with a playful, yet trenchant, dialectic to achieve a masterful and surprising alienation effect. Gloucester, the young king's protector, is arguably the most sympathetic of all the *potenti*, and he must be eliminated by those who would seize the throne (*cf.* Strehler 1964a: *Appunti*, parte prima, IXo quadro, 13; Strehler 1964b: *Copione*, Xo quadro—"INTERMEZZO").

Surprisingly, given its importance, Shakespeare's text avoids depicting the actual murder altogether; one might, in fact, consider it the great unwritten scene of *2 Henry VI*. Instead, Shakespeare gives us the following exchange:

First murderer
    Run to my lord of Suffolk; let him know
    We have dispatched the Duke as he commanded.

Second murderer
    O that it were to do! What have we done?
    Didst ever hear a man so penitent?

Enter Duke of Suffolk

First murderer
    Here comes my lord.

256   *Mace Perlman*

SUFFOLK
Now sirs, have you dispatched this thing?

FIRST MURDERER
Ay, my good lord, he's dead.

SUFFOLK
Why, that's well said. Go, get you to my house.
I will reward you for this venturous deed.
The King and all the peers are here at hand.
Have you laid fair the bed? Is all things well,
According as I gave directions?

FIRST MURDERER
'Tis, my good lord.

SUFFOLK
Away, be gone!   *Exeunt the Murderers*
(Shakespeare 2001: *2 Henry VI*, 3.2.1–14)

This brief encounter importantly includes payment for services rendered, and a detail, both realistic and poetic, which Strehler expands into an entire scene. Suffolk's only question, other than the terse and politic "have you dispatched this thing?", is an odd query which appears to be the object of Strehler's evident interest: "Have you laid fair the bed?".

Strehler's assassins, like two commedia "zanni", had received an advance on their later payment from Suffolk, with the assurance that the rest will be paid "upon delivery" ["il resto dopo!" (Strehler 1964a: *Appunti*, parte prima, IXo quadro, 12)]. Treated by their employer "like two starving dogs" ["*come due … cani affamati*" (*Ibid.*)], they run down and violently seize the tossed coins of their down-payment, then advance upstage on tiptoe, clutching two large, white pillows. The silent Duke, peacefully asleep in bed, is wheeled in from the back and arrives downstage centre. We recognize these two as a pair of zanni, or commedia servants, both by their aspect and by their comic execution of the coin-chasing "lazzo" (gag or interlude). Strehler presents us with a tall and menacing first zanni, giving him a long red feather reminiscent of blood, and he gives us a carefree second zanni, with the great paws and haunches of an animal. Yet these are no mere professionals but, in Strehler's imagination, theatrical artists, and their artwork will culminate with a brilliantly detailed routine, both chilling and grotesque, the "laying fair of the Duke's bed".

All through the scene, Strehler uses contrast and dialectic to heighten the audience's awareness of the action's essential strangeness. Pervaded by and played out in a deathly silence, even if punctuated by the "theatrical

Giorgio Strehler's Il gioco dei potenti   257

cry of a night-bird" and an "offstage theatrical rain, with distant thunder" (Strehler 1964b: *Copione*, Xo quadro, 1L), the scene is both comic and terrifying. These are "artists of violent death", a name by which the two are "well-known, and not for nothing, among their circle" (*Ibid.*: 2L). Masters not only in the execution of their killing, they are just as importantly masters in the framing and presentation of their artwork. The audience is not simply witnessing the tragic murder of a good man, nor are we simply watching a grotesque comedy. Strehler understood that the scene must, above all, fulfil its purpose as political commentary and metatheatrical spectacle. We are made behind-the-scenes witnesses to the making of spin: "artists" are being paid to "lay fair the bed".

Following the black comedy of the actual murder, the two must now compose the tableau, aesthetically and theatrically. After the tall one plucks a feather from his hat, holding it to the Duke's face to be sure he is dead, the two consider their work, with heads inclined over the bed. They prepare "una macabre messa in scena" [a macabre *mise-en-scène*]. Strehler continues:

> Il tema è: "morte nella notte di un malato di cuore". Sfanno un poco le lenzuola, rovesciano sul fianco il corpo del duca, gli tirano fuori un braccio, aprendogli le dita della mano come se avesse voluto tirare il campanello del letto, che scende al baldacchino, e non ci fosse riuscito; buttano a terra un cuscino, fanno un minimo disordine. Poi si allontanano verso l'avanscena e guardano un attimo inclinando la testa come due artisti [...] non sono però soddisfatti; si riavvicinano al letto, compiano alcune correzioni di posizione, la testa viene inclinata più naturalmente, una gamba piegata meglio. [...] Il corpo del duca assassinato resta là, nell'ombra che invade la scena fino ad inghiottirla del tutto. Pioggia, tuono e lampo in quinta, sordi e lontani.
> (Strehler 1964b: *Copione*, prima giornata, Xo quadro, 1L–2L)

> [The theme is: "death in the night of a man with a weak heart". They muss up the sheets a little, turning the duke's body over on its side. They pull out an arm, opening the fingers of the hand as if he had wanted to pull on the bell hanging from the canopy at his bedside, but was unable to; they throw a cushion to the floor, creating a little disorder. Then they move down to the lip of the stage and assess for a moment with a tilt of the head like two artists [...] but they're not satisfied; and they go back to the bed, making a few corrections in his position—the head needs to be tilted more naturally, a leg given a more convincing bend. [...] The body of the assassinated duke remains where it is, in a shadow which invades the stage until swallowing it up whole. Rain, thunder, and lightning in the wings, muffled and faraway.]

In spite of the grotesque and comic nature of the scene, Strehler paints these two men with sympathy: they are human, perhaps more so than the *potenti* who have hired them.

This same sympathy allowed Strehler to give depth and humanity to another major figure in the *gioco*, a character not often associated with these qualities. Jack Cade, the leader of a "people's" rebellion, appears in Shakespeare's text as a grotesque and comic vulgarian, overblown in his political pretensions. Often interpreted as little more than a brutal buffoon, Palitzsch's Cade, for example, "was purely a tool of the York faction, 'just as power-hungry, brutal and butcherlike as the feudal nobility'" (Zander 1983: 270, quoted in Loehlin 2004: 146). Hall and Barton depicted Cade as a "charismatic, shifty demagogue", and indeed, in the later scenes, Cade was "frightening [...] using a Hitlerian style of oratory and engaging in brutal violence even against his own followers" (Loehlin 2004: 142). In spite of this essentially dark interpretation, Hall and Barton's rebel leader was "sometimes comic but never ridiculous and his promise to the people that the realm would be held in common was meant, and taken, seriously" (*Ibid.*: 139). Strehler, too, took the rebellion and its aspirations seriously; and for all Cade's faults, he found his story moving and tragic. In a rehearsal note dated May 25 (for the 1973 restaging of the *Gioco* in Salzburg), Strehler writes: "Jack Cade o la tragedia della 'classe'. Nessuno come W. Sh. ha scritto per rappresentarla la vera tragedia di una rivoluzione del popolo" (Strehler 1992: 58) [Jack Cade or the tragedy of "class". No one has written or represented onstage like W. Sh. the true tragedy of a people's revolution].

Figure 17.4 Glauco Onorato as Jack Cade, leader of the people's rebellion, 1964–65 (Luigi Ciminaghi/Piccolo Teatro di Milano—Teatro d'Europa).

Giorgio Strehler's Il gioco dei potenti 259

Figure 17.5 Cade and his followers, 1964–65 (Luigi Ciminaghi/Piccolo Teatro di Milano—Teatro d'Europa).

This compassion for Cade's plight would never have been possible for the young Strehler who at first reading considered *Coriolanus* a "fascist, reactionary" play, and its tribunes devoid of any redeeming qualities (Strehler 1992: 26). Instead, the maturing artist discovered in Cade "uno dei grandissimi personaggi shakespeariani sconosciuti o misconosciuti" [one of the greatest unknown or misunderstood Shakespearean characters]. The revolt of Jack Cade "assumeva i caratteri di un processo storico di una contemporaneità sconvolgente. [...] Rivoluzione realistica, tradita da se stessa quasi, con un eroe positivo-negativo che ha i tratti della ribellione e già della prevaricazione dittatoriale" (Strehler 1992: 32) [assumed the qualities of an astonishingly contemporary look at the historical process. [...] A realistic revolution, betrayed by itself almost, with a positive-negative hero who bears the features of rebellion and already the prevarication of a dictator] (see Figs. 17.4–17.7).

Perhaps the most striking example of Strehler's compassionate dialectic at work is his rendering of the scene in which Cade finally meets his death in the garden of Alexander Iden, esquire of Kent (*2 Henry VI*, 4.10). In Shakespeare's text, Cade enters the garden alone, a solitary figure, exhausted and desperate, railing against ambition and seeking only some sustenance. Strehler devised a brilliant way to show us Cade's suffering and his humanity. Cade, who with the brutality of a rebellious peasant had sent men to death for the crime of literacy, is now simply a man, half-naked and starving to death. In place of the garden named

Figure 17.6 Cade trying out the trappings of royalty, 1964–65 (Luigi Ciminaghi/Piccolo Teatro di Milano—Teatro d'Europa).

Figure 17.7 Cade commandeers the throne, 1964–65 (Luigi Ciminaghi/Piccolo Teatro di Milano—Teatro d'Europa).

in the text, all we see in Strehler's staging is a poor shack, lit by "a cold sun which rises with difficulty" to illuminate the straw of its thatched roof (Strehler 1964b: *Copione*, prima giornata, XVIIIo quadro, 1T). A terribly poor boy appears, shod in wooden clogs, and tenderly cradling a small black lamb in his arms, who bleats while the boy pets him with

Giorgio Strehler's Il gioco dei potenti 261

long, caressing strokes. "The two love one another", reads Strehler's stage direction (*"I due si vogliono bene"*). While boy and lamb play together, Cade appears in the wings. We hear a distant bagpipe, and Cade's first words, "My Kent!" (*Ibid.*), establish the bitter recognition that he is home, and yet not home, as Strehler notes: he feels the impulse to laugh, the script tells us, yet hardly has the strength to do so.

Cade, on all fours, makes for the lamb; but he is stopped by the terror-stricken boy, who clasps the animal to his chest and runs. By the time the exhausted Cade gathers himself up and approaches the pair, it is clear that his compassion, despite his brutality, will not allow him to sacrifice the animal.

> I due si fissano a lungo [...]
>
> CADE—Hai qualche cosa da darmi da mangiare, eh? Non mangio da cinque giorni ... (Il bambino fa un cenno che non capisce e non sente. L'altro ripete) Erba ... insalata ...
>
> (Il bambino fa capire con qualche piccolo suono che non può parlare nè sentire. È nato così ...)
>
> (*Ibid.*: 2T)
>
> [The two stare at one another for a long time. [...]
>
> CADE—Have you got something to give me to eat? I haven't eaten for five days ... (The boy makes a sign that indicates that he cannot understand or hear. The man repeats.) Grass ... salad ...
>
> (The boy makes it clear with some little sound that he can neither speak nor hear. He was born that way ...)]

At Cade's gestures, the boy finally understands, and he exits to find Cade some food, leaving the rebel to watch over the lamb.

After this long, invented scene, it is clear where the audience's sympathies will lie when Iden enters; and Strehler cuts Shakespeare's initial dialogue between the two to a bare minimum. Instead, his description of their battle speaks volumes about the meeting of two classes and the relative human cost of their conflict to each: "Facing each other down are brute force and fencer, degraded beast and holiday hunter [...] Cade charges like a crazed buffalo. Iden is almost amusing himself with feints and counter-feints" ["Sono di fronte la forza bruta e lo schermidore, l'abbruttito e il cacciatore di passatempo [...] Cade carica come un bufalo impazzito. Iden quasi si diverte con finte e controfinte" (*Ibid.*: 3T)]. Strehler follows Shakespeare's text, but chooses to extend Cade's dying speech with a coda: "It's been five days now that I've gone without eating" ["Sono cinque giorni che non mangio"]. This dying consideration will

262   Mace Perlman

haunt us, long after we have left the theatre, to think and rethink the rebel's death. The scene ends with the deaf-mute child crying, propped up against the exit, while his "lamb strains against its rope". "They drag off Cade's body like a slaughtered bull, leaving behind a long red stripe which crosses the wooden stage [...] The bagpipe plays softly. Then silence. Blackout" ["trascinano via, come un bue amazzato, il cadavere di Cade che lascia una lunga riga rossa sul palcoscenico. [...] L'agnellino tira la corda. La cornamusa suona piano. Poi tace. Buio" (*Ibid.*: 4T)].

No example could better serve to illustrate Strehler's artistry than the scene of Cade's death with which the director chose to end his first night of the *Gioco*, a first night entitled *A Throne and a People*. It was the culmination of all his work on Shakespeare up to that point in his career. In the compelling use of light, so attuned to nature's original; in the script's indications of characters' gestures and their relative positioning in space; and in the musical approach to language and the psychological approach to sound, we perceive the first stirrings of Strehler's mature artistry. His sensitive and attentive eye, ear, mind, and heart all function as one to create a whole greater than the sum of its parts, preparing ground for the two Shakespearean masterpieces to follow as a kind of culmination to his life's work: *Re Lear* (1972, *King Lear*) and *La tempesta* (1978, *The Tempest*).

Beginning his career with a more-or-less literal referencing of the space and material reality of Shakespeare's Globe as he knew it, Strehler increasingly experimented with the stage as a play-space, culminating in the plank-traversed earthen "pigsty" of *Re Lear* and the island-as-stage and stage-as-island of *La tempesta*, passing by way of the rough circus space of his *Gioco* productions. Playful in his approach, he nonetheless always used play to serve a greater purpose, to draw the audience's attention to the larger questions of a society rife with contradictions. In exploring the ongoing dialogue between individual and collective, in laying bare the mask-roles which society forces the individual to play, Strehler was forever striving to delve deeper even while creating highly pleasurable entertainment, fulfilling what the director referred to, following Brecht's lead, as theatre's "gastronomic" function.

Always attempting to serve the world of the play, Strehler consistently devoted his energies to the work of the ensemble, eschewing the Italian model of a star-driven production even as early as 1950, with his ground-breaking approach to *Richard III*. If Strehler ever found his Richard Burbage, it was in the actor Tino Carraro, who amazingly played Brutus, Coriolanus, Lear, and Prospero, along with many other leading roles, including Mackie Messer in Strehler's first *Opera da tre soldi* [*The Threepenny Opera*] (1956); yet Carraro was notably absent from *Il gioco*. Renato de Carmine as King Henry VI; Valentina Cortese and later Andrea Jonasson as Queen Margaret (exceptionally, both were Strehler's life-partners as well as his Margarets);

Giorgio Strehler's Il gioco dei potenti   263

Corrado Pani as Richard, Duke of York; and Franco Graziosi as both Humphrey, Duke of Gloucester, and "the Actor", a kind of choral storyteller incorporating texts from other of Shakespeare's histories: all were consummate protagonists in their given roles, yet all served a larger, epic structure that prevailed over the question of any individual performances. With his productions of *Il gioco dei potenti*, Strehler stretched in ways he had never before attempted, and perhaps never would quite attempt again.

> Credo veramente che Shakespeare, appena lo si avvicini con una media disponibilità di cuore, richieda a noi un *assoluto impegno*, una ricerca di verità molto fonda, di rapporti molto densi, domandi una meditazione totale sul mondo e sulle cose [...] E che in questo senso Shakespeare diventi anche una specie di spartiacque tra chi sul teatro gioca e chi al teatro crede invece come una forma insostituibile di Verità e Poesia.
>
> (Strehler 1992: 15)

> [I truly believe that once one approaches him, even from a great distance, even with only a half-opened heart, Shakespeare requires of us an *absolute dedication*, a deep seeking-after of truth and the great density of human relationships; he demands from us a total meditation on the world and on things [...] And I believe that in this sense Shakespeare becomes a kind of great divide, a parting of the ways between those who play at making theatre and those who instead believe in the theatre as an irreplaceable form of Truth and Poetry.]

Walking a theatrical tightrope, Strehler adopted an approach to directing Shakespeare driven by two equally powerful imperatives. On the one hand stood Strehler the interpreter: a rigorous fidelity to text and an abiding concern for—and belief in—the author's intentions. On the other—and despite all his objections to the contrary—stood Strehler the creator, Strehler the adapter. One senses that Strehler, in retrospect, felt that with *Il gioco* the latter had overwhelmed the former, and that too many liberties had been taken. Yet even that hesitation, even that doubt, reveals the full depth of Strehler's own dialogue with himself. This was the true measure of his greatness, and the source of his work's vitality: that he was forever reaching further, forever seeking out an elusive balance, forever engaged in a living, and compassionate, dialectic. Like the "negative capability" that Keats identified in Shakespeare, Strehler's art could juggle opposing forces without falling to one side or the other, with a generosity of spirit and imagination that never required a definitive answer or final certainty to his ever-pressing questions. This combination of rigor with compassionate imagination may be Strehler's greatest contribution of all.

264 *Mace Perlman*

Bibliography

Astington, John H. 2004. "Elizabethanism in Verona: Giorgio Strehler's *Henry IV, Part I*". *Shakespeare and the Mediterranean*, ed. by Tom Clayton, Susan Brock, and Vicente Forés. Newark. 63–74.

Bentoglio, Alberto. 2002. *Invito al teatro di Giorgio Strehler*. Milan.

Berry, Ralph. 1989. "Giorgio Strehler" [interview, 1974]. *On Directing Shakespeare: Interviews with Contemporary Directors*. London. 120–29.

Hirst, David L. 1993. *Giorgio Strehler*. Cambridge.

Kott, Jan. 1964. "The Kings". *Shakespeare Our Contemporary*, trans. by Boleslaw Taborski. London. 3–55.

Loehlin, James N. 2004. "Brecht and the rediscovery of *Henry VI*". *Shakespeare's History Plays: Performance, Translation and Adaptation in Britain and Abroad*, ed. by Ton Hoenselaars. Cambridge. 133–50.

Lombardo, Agostino. 1992. *Strehler e Shakespeare*. Rome.

—— 1998. "Strehler e Shakespeare". *Giorgio Strehler o la passione teatrale: l'opera di un maestro raccontatoa da lui stesso al III Premio Europa per il Teatro a Taormina Arte*, ed. by Andrea Nanni. Milan. 52–57.

McManus, Donald. 2008. "Giorgio Strehler". *The Routledge Companion to Directors' Shakespeare*, ed. by John Russell Brown. New York. 441–56.

Pearson, Richard. 1990. *A Band of Arrogant and United Heroes: The Story of the Royal Shakespeare Company Production of The Wars of the Roses*. London.

Shakespeare, William. 2001. *King Henry VI, Part 3*, ed. by John D. Cox and Eric Rasmussen. Arden Shakespeare. London.

—— 2002. *Henry VI, Part Two*, ed. by Roger Warren. Oxford.

—— 2003. *Henry VI, Part One*, ed. by Michael Taylor. Oxford.

—— 2012. *The RSC Shakespeare: Henry VI, Parts I, II, and III*, ed. by Jonathan Bate and Eric Rasmussen. New York.

Strehler, Giorgio. 1964a. *Appunti per la regia del* gioco dei potenti. Unpublished notes, Archivio storico del Piccolo Teatro di Milano. Milan.

—— 1964b. *Copione per Il gioco dei potenti*. Unpublished working script, Archivio storico del Piccolo Teatro di Milano. Milan.

—— 1974. *Per un teatro umano: Pensieri, scritti, parlati e attuati a cura di Sinah Kessler*. Milan.

—— 1992. *Inscenare Shakespeare*. Rome.

—— 2007. *Giorgio Strehler: Introduction, entretiens, choix de textes, et traduction par Myriam Tanant*. Arles.

Tempera, Mariangela. 2004. "Rent-a-past: Italian responses to Shakespeare's histories (1800–1950)". *Shakespeare's History Plays: Performance, Translation and Adaptation in Britain and Abroad*, ed. by Ton Hoenselaars. Cambridge. 115–32.

Zander, Horst. 1983. *Shakespeare "bearbeitet": Eine Untersuchung gam Beispiel der Historien: Inszenierungen 1945–75 in der Bundesrepublik Deutschland*. Tübingen.

18 Shakespeare behind Italian Bars

The Rebibbia Project, *The Tempest*, and *Caesar Must Die*

Mariangela Tempera

In a climate of overcrowding, dwindling state and EU funding, and institutionalised boredom, the Italian prison system has routinely embraced theatre programmes, drawing on a basic modicum of resources needed to stage plays. Of the inmates involved in such thespian ventures, quite a few develop a genuine interest for the plays, and some even start professional acting careers upon release. As the directors of the programmes are understandably eager to point out, the level of recidivism among ex-convicts who were involved in theatrical activities is far below average. With the exception of the masterly portraits of Neapolitan life by Eduardo De Filippo (known commonly just as "Eduardo"), the works of major Italian playwrights are usually considered either too cerebral (like those by Luigi Pirandello) or too far removed from the culture and language of the inmates (like Carlo Goldoni's eighteenth-century Venetian plays) to be performed in prison. Shakespeare's greatest hits, on the contrary, are deemed more suitable for the programme than those of most other European playwrights. Translated into modern Italian or, more frequently, into a variety of dialects, the plays become linguistically accessible to the composite prison population and offer roles that can be successfully adapted to suit the personalities of the inmate players. Moreover, a Shakespearean corpus of plays from which to draw ensures that productions profit from the added cultural value enshrined, in Italy, in the name of their originating author: in the bid for a limited amount of press attention available for prison theatre programmes, Shakespeare's name trumps any other playwright's.

The longest-running project had its origins in 1988 at La Fortezza, a prison located in Volterra (Tuscany), under the auspices of Armando Punzo, whose most successful adaptation remains *Mercuzio non vuole morire* (2012) [*Mercutio Doesn't Want to Die*], in which the character deeply resents Shakespeare's decision to kill him off early in the play in order to concentrate on the sentimental love story between Romeo and Juliet. This reimagining of Shakespeare's play attests two transformative possibilities that might, to borrow Douglas Lanier's terms, be classified as both *"revisionary narrative*, in which the new narrative begins with the characters and situation of the source but changes the plot" and

266   *Mariangela Tempera*

"reoriented narrative, in which the narrative is told from a different point of view" (Lanier 2002: 83). Performed by the director himself, this Mercuzio is recuperated from an ancillary position in the margins to occupy a space centre-stage. Punzo's Mercuzio, "a poet and a theatre artist" and thus a surrogate for both Shakespeare and Punzo, represents the values of poetry and culture that can only survive if the entire community supports them: he "embodies" and is "defined as" what could be called a "principle of great literature in Italo Calvino's *American Lessons* (1988)", such that sparing him from the death envisioned for him by Shakespeare means "saving both poetry and theatre" (Mancewicz 2012: 549). Combining the techniques of street theatre and circus, Punzo—a director noted for his "intertextual approach to the script" and fondness for a "disruptive though liberating energy" (Mancewicz 2012: 554)— involves the spectators in the play, first in the courtyard of the Fortezza, where they mingle with the inmates, and then through the town of Volterra itself. Created at a moment when the future of the theatre programme was under threat, the production is both a Shakespearean adaptation and a politicised reminder to local administrators and the town's populace alike of the cultural and professional utility that the theatre programme offers La Fortezza's convicts. The *Compagnia della Fortezza*, the prison theatre's ensemble, selects plays to adapt with care, privileging a collaborative *esprit de corps* that responds to the concerns of inmates and local inhabitants in equal measure. The Shakespearean material adapted for performance is "chosen to question reality" and is "dismantled-fragmented" [*sic*] in keeping with the group's "collective contributions" (Puppa 2013: 75).

Building on the success of Punzo's work at La Fortezza, Paolo and Vittorio Taviani's film *Cesare deve morire* (2012) [*Caesar Must Die*] met with unexpected acclaim and shifted the critical lens from La Fortezza and Volterra to Rebibbia, making it a household name among progressive intellectual audiences. Located on the periphery of Rome, Rebibbia is a huge prison complex that includes an all-male high-security wing that has become the venue for a series of theatre-related activities, and the prisoners' productions are typically showcased in a purpose-built theatre inside Rebibbia. In 2003, Fabio Cavalli, a theatre director from Genoa, agreed to supervise the work of the *Compagnia dei Liberi Artisti Associati di Rebibbia Nuovo Complesso* [Company of the Free Associated Artists of the Rebibbia New Wing], an ensemble that included drug dealers, murderers, and inmates with connections to organized crime. After his first successful staging of one of Eduardo De Filippo's plays, Cavalli proposed Shakespeare's *The Tempest*, in De Filippo's translation, as the next project. Initially unfamiliar with the play and indifferent to the iconic status of its author, the actors required a great deal of convincing, but eventually agreed. Following the success of this version of *La Tempesta*, which premièred in 2005,

De Filippo would exert further influence on the Rebibbia troupe in an adaptation of *Julius Caesar*.

When Giulio Einaudi, a leading Italian publisher, asked him to contribute his version of a Shakespeare play to the series *Scrittori tradotti da scrittori* [*Writers Translated by Writers*], De Filippo chose *The Tempest* and made the task of translation even harder by abandoning the colloquial, contemporary dialect characteristic of his own works in favour of classical, seventeenth-century Neapolitan. From his rendering of the very first lines, he makes it clear that he will take liberties with the letter of the original and inject robust doses of local colour. Thus, the Boatswain's "Heigh, my hearts!" speech (Greenblatt 1997: 1.1.5–7) becomes "Guagliú, curríte. Faciteve curaggio: 'a Maronna 'a Catena nce aiuta. [...] Guagliú, facímmece annòre: símmo Napulitane!" (De Filippo 1984: 5) [Come on, lads, hurry up. Take heart: the Virgin of the Chain will help us [...]. Let's prove ourselves, lads: we're Neapolitan!]. Through cuts and additions to the original, he portrays Prospero essentially as a loving father and a forgiving victim (rather than the somewhat sinister magus obsessed with revenge who has intrigued Shakespearean critics for centuries), and turns Ariel into a street urchin ["scugnizzo"] and prankster ["burlone"] (De Filippo 1984: 187).

More disturbingly, in 2.2, De Filippo expands on Stephano's orders ("Kiss the book" and "Come on, then; down and swear") and on Caliban's response ("I'll kiss thy foot. I'll swear myself thy subject", 2.2.134–145) to introduce echoes of an initiation ceremony for an underground crime syndicate like the *camorra*: "Te voglio addenucchiato pe' fa' lu giuramento" [I want you on your knees to swear], "Avanti, faje lu dovere tujo: vàsa!" [Come on, perform your duty: kiss!], "Li pede te li scarfo e te li vàso" [I'll warm your feet with my breath and kiss them] (De Filippo 1984: 100). He is familiar with the sinister connotations that a word like "respect" can acquire: Stephano's "The poor monster's my subject, and he shall not suffer indignity" (3.2.34–35) becomes "Stu povero mostro è suddito mio e se rispetta lu cane pe' lu patrone!" (De Filippo 1984: 117) [This poor monster is my subject and you should respect the dog because of the master]. Replete with a wealth of footnotes for readers unfamiliar with the Neapolitan dialect, the book was published in 1984, shortly before De Filippo's death, after he had managed to leave a recording of his translation, albeit without ever seeing it staged.

Even for those Rebibbia inmates who were native speakers of Neapolitan, learning lines from De Filippo's version was a challenge, and in some cases a simplified version of the text needed to be adopted. Of the lines in the text (running to over an hour and a half in performance) that required cutting, the most sophisticated grafts of classical Neapolitan onto the living language were the first to go. Cavalli cast Cosimo Rega as Prospero and, perhaps predictably, Benneth Uche Emenike, the only African convict who had signed up for the theatre programme, as

268 *Mariangela Tempera*

Caliban. Emenike, a Nigerian who held a degree in chemistry and was fluent in both English and Italian, embraced De Filippo's lines without difficulty, and gave his Caliban comic and exotic twists while leaving the audience in no doubt that he could just as easily have made an excellent Prospero. Salvatore Striano offered an interpretation of Ariel as the wily Neapolitan street urchin envisaged by De Filippo and, playing the role of Miranda, professional actress Valentina Esposito was called upon by Cavalli to speak her lines in standard Italian, even conducting a brief exchange in English with Caliban.

By 2005, large numbers of asylum-seekers braving the Mediterranean on rickety, overcrowded boats had turned shipwrecks from literary themes into evening-news material. Dominated by a bare-chested, heavily-tattooed Boatswain, a well-choreographed opening scene leaves the castaways stranded on an island where, like the inhabitants, they will become prisoners, the iconography of bunk beds with hanging ropes, soon to be occupied by Alonso and his entourage, reinforcing this suggestion. Tweaks to the text of Shakespeare's original are readily in evidence in this 2005 production: Ariel compensates for the lack of special effects with lively Neapolitan songs and dance routines, but does not even attempt "Full fathom five" (1.2.400–408), potentially out of keeping with the character as rebranded by De Filippo; the love between Ferdinand and Miranda is kept completely chaste; Stephano and Trinculo bring a Roman flavour to their scenes through their distinctive accents, but still play up every possible *camorra* reference in the translation; and De Filippo's recorded voice speaks the epilogue, lending his authority to the production and reasserting the intermediary, filtering presence of the translator at this crucial, valedictory moment in Shakespeare's oeuvre in which questions of the speaker's legacy, the surrendering of claims to ownership and title-holding, the collaborative involvement of the audience in the fiction-making, and the possibility of release from crimes coalesce ("Dateme la libertade [...] liberare mene", De Filippo 1984: 182).

Just as De Filippo had felt free to add Neapolitan references to the Shakespearean base text, the convicts liberally interpolated repeated reminders of their own status in De Filippo's script. Thus, Ariel's request for his liberty at 1.2.246 ("La libertà!", De Filippo 1984: 36) is qualified with an aside in Cavalli's version [Liberty, *so to speak*] that elicits the expected sympathetic response from the audience. In his utopian world, Cavalli's Gonzalo not only admits "no name of magistrate" (Greenblatt 1997: 2.1.149) but also, in another addition, no prisons nor prisoners (De Filippo 1984: 74–75). Instead of "I shall no more to sea, to sea" (2.2.39), Cavalli's Stefano breaks into "La ballata del Miché", a famous 1961 song by Fabrizio De André, which opens:

> Quando hanno aperto la cella
> era già tardi perché

Shakespeare behind Italian Bars   269

con una corda sul collo
freddo pendeva Michè

[When they opened the cell door
it was too late because
with a rope round his neck
Miché was hanging dead]

Ordinarily quick to respond with laughter to every irreverent *contaminatio* of the Shakespearean source text with borrowings from modern popular culture, most of the Rebibbia spectators received this song in grim silence, alert to the oblique reference to the suicide rate in Italian prisons, buried in De André's characteristically dark, jaunty homage to the socially marginalized and politically disenfranchised. Such interpolations in Cavalli's version gesture to a combination of "reverent recognition and playful revisionism" with respect to the Shakespearean source text, and give rise to what (to borrow another set of terms from Lanier) could be considered "a Shakespeare recast in the forms and practices of popular culture" (Lanier 2002: 55).

The equipoise that characterizes this interplay with the Shakespearean source is broadly in keeping with De Filippo's rationale as translator. In his note on translation that appears at the close of his edition ("Nota del traduttore"), De Filippo recognises the exigencies involved in translating a text that is removed—linguistically and chronologically—from his audience, and the additional imperative to remain close to the source text:

Ho cercato d'essere il piú possibile fedele al testo, come, a mio parere, si dovrebbe essere nel tradurre, ma non sempre ci sono riuscito [...] altre volte ho sentito il bisogno di aggiungere alcuni versi per spiegare meglio a me stesso e al pubblico qualche concetto.
(De Filippo 1984: 186)

[I have tried to remain as faithful to the text as possible, as, I believe, you should when translating, but without always succeeding [...] at other points I have felt the need to add some lines in order to explain an idea more clearly, both to me and to the audience.]

Attentive to this duality, De Filippo also acknowledges the bivalence of the Neapolitan dialect chosen for his translation. With one foot in the seventeenth century and another in the present, De Filippo's chosen medium bridged the temporal and cultural gap between his contemporary readership and his early modern source:

Quanto al linguaggio, come ispirazione ho usato il napoletano seicentesco, ma come può scriverlo un uomo che vive oggi; sarebbe

270 Mariangela Tempera

stato innaturale cercare una aderenza complete ad una lingua non usata ormai da secoli. Però ... quanto è bello questo napoletano antico [...] con la sua muscialità, la sua dolcezza [...] e con una possibilità di far vivere fatti e creature magici, misteriosi, che nessuna lingua moderna possiede piú!

(De Filippo 1984: 187)

[As for the language, I took as my inspiration seventeenth-century Neapolitan, but used it as someone would who is living today; it would have been unnatural to look for complete fidelity to a language not spoken for centuries. And yet ... how beautiful this old Neapolitan is [...] with its own musicality, and sweetness [...] able to bring to life magical and mysterious events and creatures in a way no modern language is anymore!]

By a clever bivalent device, De Filippo captures the source's alien antiquity at the same time as rendering the text legible and accessible to a modern audience. Rather than seeking to convey merely the substance or content or plot of the source, De Filippo's Neapolitan rendition translates something of the musicality and wonderment of Shakespeare's play, the connotations of awe and the marvellous built into Shakespeare's aural landscape, recreating the original's rhetoric of wonder and forgiveness through the seemingly distracting, obfuscating filter of a local, early modern dialect.

Under Cavalli's direction, the Rebibbia Company continued to produce theatrical work rooted in the Shakespearean canon (including a version of *Hamlet* in 2007) that was appreciated by spectators but went largely unnoticed by critics. The Rebibbia's critical fortunes were revived when the Taviani brothers, two internationally-established film directors in their eighties, started attending their performances and consequently commissioned a production of *Giulio Cesare* that would come to form the core of their new film. Cavalli had countenanced an adaptation centred entirely on the rehearsals, *Giulio Cesare alla prova* [*Julius Caesar in Rehearsal*], but the Taviani brothers took full control of the operation and imposed their own vision. The final product, *Cesare deve morire*, which met with acclaim at the 2012 Berlin International Film Festival, was a short film (76 minutes), but not a "docufiction", as the Taviani brothers repeatedly emphasized: "Everything was performance. Everything was scripted. It's a movie. A peculiar movie, yes, but still a movie" (Gilbey 2013). In other words, this film should not be considered an Italian equivalent of *Shakespeare Behind Bars*, a documentary film directed by Hank Rogerson in 2005 detailing the nine-month gestation of a production of *The Tempest* (featuring prisoners from Luther Luckett Correctional Center in LaGrange, Kentucky, and overseen by Curt Tofteland) that has become a kind of touchstone for

Shakespeare behind Italian Bars   271

all media presentations of Shakespearean performances in prison. The non-Shakespearean lines in *Cesare deve morire* were based on material that the Taviani brothers had gathered from conversations with the inmates and were incorporated into a script by the directors, to be memorized and performed for camera within 35 days, a demanding task for performers required to adapt to the working practices of an unfamiliar medium. By contrast, the Shakespearean scenes had been first translated into the performers' dialects (mainly Neapolitan, but also Roman, Sicilian, and Apulian) and thoroughly analysed and mastered over a period of six months of rehearsals under Cavalli's guidance such that, by a curious paradox, the inmates were more convincing when inhabiting the roles of Shakespeare's ancient Romans than when playing themselves.

The film opens in colour with the close-up of an actor (Salvatore Striano) performing on stage an abridged version of Bruto's suicide scene (from *Julius Caesar* 5.5) in Neapolitan. A massive, imposing Stratone (Shakespeare's Strato) reluctantly holds the dagger and bemoans the death of his leader, before we cut to the tribute over Bruto's body paid by Antonio and Octavio (who appropriates some of Antonio's lines), followed by general applause on the part of an enthusiastic audience. Without any prior knowledge of its subject matter, a viewer would assume that this introductory sequence shows the end of a professional performance of *Giulio Cesare*. Only after witnessing the audience leaving under surveillance and the actors meekly allowing themselves to be marched off-stage by guards, who take them through a series of locked gates, do we realize that the first scene has taken place inside a prison and the actors are inmates. At this point, five minutes into the film, the location is revealed as the high-security wing of Rebibbia.

Given that many of its ancient monuments have been reduced to ruins and are often off-limits to film crews, Rome is far from ideal as a film location for Shakespeare's Roman plays. Filmmakers have either reconstructed its ancient splendour in studios (for example, Joseph Mankiewicz's 1953 *Julius Caesar*), sought out striking corners that have nothing to do with the Empire (the Palazzo della Civiltà del Lavoro in Julie Taymor's 1999 *Titus Andronicus*), or selected another city altogether (Belgrade in Ralph Fiennes's 2011 *Coriolanus*). The Taviani brothers shot their film in a place that both is and is not Rome. About halfway through the film, two aerial views of Rebibbia (one at night and one by daylight) remind the spectators of how claustrophobically self-contained this ghastly, brutally functional 1960s group of buildings is. The Shakespearean scenes are rehearsed in several corners of the huge complex. The barren spaces lend themselves to an evocation of Elizabethan staging practices, a connection deliberately underlined by a close-up of a board on which an inmate has printed "The Philippi plain" as if in imitation of early modern scene-changing props. As for the costumes, they are no more Roman than those portrayed in the famous

272   Mariangela Tempera

1590s Peacham drawing (preserved in the "Longleat Manuscript") of a scene from *Titus Andronicus*. In rehearsal, only Cesare is wrapped in a sort of white sheet that recalls a Roman tunic; all the other performers are in everyday clothes, supplemented by an assortment of cloaks over the course of the performance, though at each turn the directors take every opportunity to remind viewers that the setting is inescapably that of Rebibbia. In the rehearsal of the assassination scene, when Bruto inflicts "the unkindest cut of all", the camera lingers on the bent blade of the tin dagger that he pretends to pull out of Cesare's body, a gesture to the prison authorities' strictures on the use of anything resembling a real weapon.

Following the brief, introductory excerpt from the end of a performance, the bulk of the film recounts, in a flashback that starts six months earlier, the auditions and rehearsals of *Giulio Cesare*, and is beautifully shot in black and white. Cavalli is shown auditioning inmates, announcing that they will all take part in the play, before naming his choices for the main roles: Giulio Cesare (Giovanni Arcuri), Cassio (Cosimo Rega), Bruto (Salvatore Striano, who, we later gather, had already been released in 2011 and begun a successful acting career), Marcantonio (Antonio Frasca), Decio (Juan Dario Bonetti), and Lucio (Vincenzo Gallo). Each inmate is framed in close-up while his crimes and his sentence are superimposed on the screen. Surprisingly, it is the two most unassuming prisoners, Rega (Cassio) and the harmonica player Gallo (Lucio), who have committed murders so brutal as to earn on their files the dreaded stamp, "*fine pena: mai*" [end of prison sentence: never], although their participation in *Cesare deve morire* probably helped precipitate a more lenient sentence. As Cavalli notes, "the theatre from this point of view is very important because it allows you to stop being anonymous" (De Benedetto 2012–13: 413). Given the relatively early moment in the film at which their criminal records are revealed (far sooner and more matter-of-factly than in *Shakespeare Behind Bars*), audience sympathy becomes far more challenging. Viewers start expecting connections between the performers' lives in crime and the Shakespearean roles they are asked to play, and through a clever mix of original scenes and lines from *Julius Caesar*, the directors fuel these expectations.

Two interpolated episodes apparently bring us tantalizingly close to the pre-Rebibbia lives of the convicts, only to leave us disappointed. In the first, Striano, whom we have seen obsessively practising Bruto's lines, suddenly breaks down at "O, that we then could come by Caesar's spirit, and not dismember Caesar!" (2.1.169–70). After much prompting, he admits that, with words that were "different but the same", a friend of his had expressed a similar reservation, resenting, and possibly disobeying, his boss's order to kill a snitch, for which he was consequently derided both by Striano and the rest of the gang. Since, in the *camorra*, refusing to obey an order to kill necessitates being killed in turn, the

Shakespeare behind Italian Bars 273

question to Striano—"What happened next?"—was shorthand for asking whether Striano himself had been assigned the task to eliminate his friend. With a cutting gesture of his arm, Striano signals his unwillingness to offer further details and abruptly brings the curtain down on the play-within-the-film he has barely outlined. By contrast with Cavalli's *Tempest*, a late play in which violence is threatened but averted, assassinations plotted but foiled, and danger deflected into forgiveness, *Giulio Cesare* resists these consolations of romance and pastoral, and *Cesare deve morire* insists on the inescapable proximity of fictional representation and lived experience in the actions of its inmate players. The second "autobiographical" scene equally reminds viewers of how precarious the atmosphere of good-natured camaraderie actually is in a prison setting. While Arcuri and Bonetti rehearse Decio's attempt to convince Cesare to go to the Capitol (2.2.58–105), Arcuri suddenly steps out of character and accuses Bonetti of having betrayed him in the past. After a weak attempt at returning to the rehearsal, Bonetti in turn becomes aggressive. Gallo (Lucio) points out to Cavalli that an outburst of violence would mean the end of the theatre project and urges him to intervene, but the director is completely out of his depth, his theatrical authority suddenly rendered useless. Rega (Cassio), the ruthless lifer, takes over and follows the fighters out of the room, returning a few moments later to signal to a distraught Cavalli that all is under control. We are left in no doubt about the means used to quell the outburst of violence so quickly; the cathartic remedy of Shakespearean language was clearly ineffective on this occasion.

While watching these two scenes that apparently open a window into the prisoners' past, we should, of course, recall the directors' warning, "Everything was scripted", and avoid confusing Striano and the other convicts with "Striano & Co.", fictional characters (albeit based on real people) who, like Shakespeare's ancient Romans, only live their lives of words in performance, their "lofty scene acted over | In states unborn and accents yet unknown" (to borrow Cassius' words from 3.1). What prevents us from fully understanding the past events that are alluded to in these two episodes is a directorial decision, not the reticence of the inmates. By leaving so much unsaid and unseen, the Taviani brothers tell us that we will only see the public face of the convicts, the one they choose to show us, not their true present and past lives. They also ensure that the theme of betrayal, raised by the Shakespearean scenes and further elaborated upon in the subtext of Striano's tale and in Arcuri's outburst, receives full attention. Prior to doubling as the Roman rabble, the convicts who do not belong to the company fill the Rebibbia night air with whispered complaints against the prison authorities. Before we move on to the daylight assassination scene, "for a few seconds, a close-up of a self-satisfied Caesar is superimposed upon the image of the prison building, which cogently furthers the identification of 'Caesar'

274   Mariangela Tempera

with a 'monstruous' prison system" (Calbi 2014: 246). They are only too glad to cheer Bruto and shout "Freedom" from their cells overlooking the inner courtyard where an uninterrupted run-through of 3.2 is filmed, although, of course, they are just as readily won over by Antonio. Since in other parts of the film they show a complete lack of interest in the theatre workshop, this sequence (where every inmate finds his place in Shakespeare's text and all work together collaboratively) should probably be considered the result of the directors' decision to indulge in a brief, audience-pleasing flight into a fantasy world that momentarily transcends the drab reality of interpersonal relationships in a prison setting.

As the rehearsals unfold, we realize that, although there are no direct references to *The Tempest* in this film, Cavalli's 2005 production (which also featured Rega, Striano, Arcuri, and Carusone) forms an important subtext for *Cesare deve morire*. The aerial shots of Rebibbia establish it as an island-prison within Rome, akin to Prospero's prison-island. The parallel is underlined by the only colour shot within the black-and-white sequence when, returning to his cell, Gallo stares at a postcard that suddenly acquires colours—a Mediterranean island on a sunny day, the foil for the island-prison we are about to see in a night-time aerial view. Within the Rebibbia complex, the camera repeatedly returns (in a possible filmic echo of Peter Greenaway's 1991 *Prospero's Books*) to the very small room that houses the prison library and pans over the meagre collection of books on its few shelves. The throbbing heart of the New Wing is here, where the inmates gather not only to study their Shakespeare but also to undertake other mental journeys inspired by their engagement with *Julius Caesar*. When Arcuri picks up Caesar's *De Bello Gallico* and wonders why on earth he had hated it so much in school, we are encouraged to attribute to these volumes, like Prospero's, a transformative, magical property capable of remoulding the readers who come into contact with them. As in their *Tempesta*, the inmates here are attentive to possible parallels with Naples, a city more familiar to some inmates than Rome. As Bruto and Cassio rehearse their version of 2.1, Cassio supplements Bruto's "Rome, shameless city" with the ad-libbed line, "You too, my Naples, have become a shameless city", before appending an apologetic aside to the director: "Looks like this Shakespeare had actually lived in my hometown". Since most of the text is translated into Neapolitan, this sense of topographic dislocation is not unexpected, but the script elaborates on it further. Later in the film, Bruto tells his cellmates how the angry Roman crowd has set fire to the houses of the conspirators and banished them: "Just like my homeland, Nigeria", is the reaction of an African inmate. The cultural authority embedded in the Shakespearean source text becomes endlessly appropriable, apt for relocation and recontextualistion.

The emphasis on books and Naples is not the only connection between this script and De Filippo's translation of *The Tempest*. Just as De Filippo had preferred seventeenth-century to contemporary Neapolitan, Cavalli insists that his actors should translate Shakespeare's lines into their own dialects, but "not a vulgar dialect, a dialect spoken by aristocrats". De Filippo had managed to insert subtle references to the language and the ceremonies of the *camorra* in the unlikely context of *The Tempest*, a task considerably less problematic in *Julius Caesar*. Antony's sardonic taxonomy of "honourable men" effortlessly becomes "uomini d'onore" [men of honour], but with an additional nod to the Sicilian mafia: "Baciamo le mani" [We kiss your hands]. The Neapolitan playwright obliquely intrudes into the Shakespearean text. As Bruto struggles to master the lines of his monologue (2.1.10–34), the phrase "It must be by his death" (2.1.10) becomes "Adda murì" [He must die] and is repeated as "Adda murì, mò, mò" [He must die right now] at the end of the speech. The syntactical construction perhaps recalls De Filippo's most famous line: "Adda passà 'a nuttata" [The night will pass, eventually]. Pronounced at the end of De Filippo's 1945 comedy *Napoli milionaria*, it has acquired currency in standard Italian as a proverb signifying that even the worst situation will ultimately end. The connection with De Filippo is further foregrounded shortly afterwards. The conflicting views of Decio, Casca, and Cinna about the point on the horizon where the sun will rise (2.1.100–110) are fully rehearsed and then commented upon by the baffled convicts: what sort of idiots would argue over the rising sun when they are about to kill their boss? In the scene, Bruto's "And every man hence to his idle bed" (2.1.116) becomes "Ch'a sprecammo a fa' 'sta nuttata? Andiamo a dormì" [Why are we wasting this night? Let's go to bed]. The clear implication, from this thicket of De Filippo intertexts and half-echoes, is that the night that envelops Rome under Caesar will eventually pass, but for the sun to rise, the tyrant must die.

And yet, after Cassio has committed suicide, unaided and with the effortless air of a "uomo d'onore", Bruto speaks some of the very few lines lifted *verbatim* from the original—"O Julius Caesar, thou are mighty yet" (5.3.93–95)—thus bringing Cesare very pointedly back into the play. In much greater detail than in the abridged version of the scene shown at the start of the film, Bruto is shown doing the rounds of his friends, begging them to help him to die until Stratone complies. As the camera frames Bruto's dead body, we expect the final speeches to start, but instead Cesare comes in from the wings and, with an intriguing smile on his face, takes Striano's hand, lifting him up for the curtain call. He had done the same at the beginning, but, by now, we are far better equipped to register the complexity of the persona that the Tavianis had created for Arcuri in his portrayal of Cesare. At this moment, poised on the threshold between the world of the characters and that of the actors, Arcuri signals Cesare's final victory.

276 *Mariangela Tempera*

Cesare deve morire does not quite end with the upbeat note of the thunderous applause that greets the conclusion of the performance from the audience gathered in the prison to watch the play. The camera then follows Rega (who had performed the role of Cassio) back to his empty cell, which he enters while musing, "Ever since I knew art, this cell has become a prison". The final frames show him making himself a cup of Neapolitan coffee. The convicts who shouted "I do not want to die!" in Punzo's *Mercuzio non vuole morire* expressed a healthy will to resist a system that takes punishment well beyond the limits established by the law. In *Cesare deve morire*, the directors foreground the plight of those who succumb to despair. In 2011, out of about 68,000 inmates in Italian prisons, at least 66 committed suicide. The Rebibbia Company is made to perform Bruto's suicide twice—not necessarily the first scene that comes to mind when one thinks of Shakespeare's *Julius Caesar*. The words that in the original Brutus whispers to his friends are spelt out by Striano four times: "Help me to die!". Given that, in an overcrowded cell, even killing oneself requires the complicity of other inmates, this interpolation gestures to the directors' desire to address the issue of suicide in custody without openly antagonizing the prison authorities. Just as during the Risorgimento, when anti-Austrian sentiments were voiced by Giulio Carcano through his translations and by Giuseppe Verdi through his adaptation of *Macbeth*, so these two twenty-first-century Italian artists have turned to Shakespeare to bypass censorship, and to draw on the cultural authority of his presentation of ancient Rome to speak to and comment on the present, in a revisionary, circuitous *translatio* that brings the narrative full circle.

Bibliography

Calbi, Maurizio. 2014. "'In states unborn and accents yet unknown': Spectral Shakespeare in Paolo and Vittorio Taviani's *Cesare deve morire* (*Caesar Must Die*)". *Shakespeare Bulletin*, 32.2: 235–53.

De Benedetto, Susanna. 2012–13. "*Giulio Cesare* a Rebibbia: il teatro come esperienza di libertà. Conversazione con Fabio Cavalli". *Stratagemmi*, 24/25: 407–14.

De Filippo, Eduardo. 1984. *La Tempesta*. Turin.

Gilbey, Ryan. 2013. "Paolo and Vittorio Taviani: 'For us it was cinema or death'". *The Guardian*, 1 March 2013: www.theguardian.com/film/2013/mar/01/taviani-cinema-or-death.

Greenblatt, Stephen, ed. 1997. *The Norton Shakespeare*. New York.

Lanier, Douglas. 2002. *Shakespeare and Modern Popular Culture*. Oxford.

Mancewicz, Aneta. 2012. "*Mercuzio non vuole morire* (review)". *Shakespeare Bulletin*, 30.4: 548–54.

Puppa, Paolo. 2013. "Theatre as Prison, Prison as Theatre". *Differences on Stage*, ed. by Alessandra De Martino, Paolo Puppa, and Paola Toninato. Newcastle-upon-Tyne. 68–76.

19 Shakespeare, Tradition, and the Avant-garde in Chiara Guidi's *Macbeth su Macbeth su Macbeth*

Sonia Massai and Chiara Guidi

Introduction

Chiara Guidi is arguably one of the most exciting directors currently working with Shakespeare in Italy. Along with Romeo Castellucci and Claudia Castellucci, Guidi cofounded Socìetas Raffaello Sanzio (SRS) in 1981 (Kelleher et al. 2007; Sacchi 2014). The company soon rose to international prominence for its radical attack on theatrical traditions and conventions that reduce performance to derivative spectacle by being bluntly text-centred. By choosing to engage with Shakespeare, the company singled out one of the most established and venerated bodies of play-texts associated with mainstream European theatrical traditions. Their *Amleto: La veemente esteriorità della morte di un mollusco* [*Hamlet: The Vehement Exteriority of the Death of a Mollusc*] (1992), *Giulio Cesare: Da Shakespeare e gli storici latini* [*Julius Caesar: From Shakespeare and The Latin Historians*] (1997), and *Ophelia* (1997) each jettisoned familiar plot-lines, characters, and most of Shakespeare's dialogue in favour of striking stage images which, while inspired by the Shakespearean source texts, were specifically meant to counteract the formidable influence exerted by the long history of Shakespeare's reception in Western theatre. As Bridget Escolme explains, "SRS replace naturalistic acting with a performance that liberates the early modern dramatic text from the limitations of psychological coherence ... and re-sensitise the spectator to Shakespeare's over-produced texts, [by] present[ing] us with the raw material that goes to make up drama—text, body, mise-en-scène, the work of performance" (Escolme 2005: 138).

Guidi, who curated voice and sound in most SRS productions up to 2004, has since taken on directorial roles, both as director of individual productions and as artistic director of theatre festival events in Italy and in Europe. *Macbeth su Macbeth su Macbeth: Uno studio per la mano sinistra* (henceforth *MsMsM*) [*Macbeth on Macbeth on Macbeth: A Study for the Left Hand*] premièred at the Orizzonti Festival in Chiusi in Siena in summer 2014. The stage action in *MsMsM* is arranged into sixteen sequences and each sequence foregrounds the real or imaginary object or place that marks the trajectory of Macbeth's fall. Most prominent among them are "la pietra d'inciampo" [the stumbling block] (see Fig. 19.1) associated with the weird sisters, because they "stop" Macbeth and Banquo's "way" in 1.3, and also with Malcolm's investiture in 1.4, which Macbeth describes as the "step | On which [he] must fall down, or else o'er-leap, | For in [his] way it lies" (Clark and Mason 2015: 1.4.48–50); also, "il cerchio d'oro" [the golden round] (see Fig. 19.2) invoked by Lady Macbeth in 1.5, which is simultaneously the crown Macbeth aspires to wear and the symbol of that god-like state of being, the "single state of man" (1.3.142), which Macbeth paradoxically forfeits as he gives way to his desire to be king; "la porta" [the gate] in the porter's scene in 2.3; and, of course, "il pugnale" [the dagger], the most enduring symbol of a play that, according to William Hazlitt, was Shakespeare's greatest "for the wildness of the imagination" (Hazlitt 1992: 422). The stage, a vast expanse of darkness, is an ideal backdrop against which Guidi's minimalist props emerge when brightly lit, sometimes insistently, as with the golden round, sometimes intermittently, as with the dagger, which, as a result, acquires a genuinely ghostly quality, hovering between being and not being. These conditions are reminiscent of Trevor Nunn's highly acclaimed RSC production at the Other Place in 1976, which included black walls and floor in the playing area, around which a single chalk circle separated both audience from actors and stage from off-stage (Mullin 1987: 350–59).

Three female actors—the 2014–2015 cast included Chiara Guidi, Anna Lidia Molina, and Agnese Scotti—share a selection of speeches and lines originally spoken mostly by Macbeth, Lady Macbeth, Banquo, the Porter, and the weird sisters. The repetition of key lines and phrases, accompanied by Francesco Guerri's cello, draws the audience's attention

Figure 19.1 "The stumbling block"; *Macbeth su Macbeth su Macbeth* (2014), dir. by Chiara Guidi; production photograph by Luca Del Pia.

Figure 19.2 "The golden round"; *Macbeth su Macbeth su Macbeth* (2014), dir. by Chiara Guidi; production photograph by Luca Del Pia.

to the musical and acoustic qualities of specific words, including, most noticeably, "re" [king], which is conveniently similar to a range of personal pronouns in Italian—*me* [me], *te* [you], *le* [her], or *se* as in *sé stesso* [oneself]. The repetition of key words in turn produces a suggestive soundscape that prevents language from becoming a mere vehicle for the literal and literary meaning of Shakespeare's original dialogue. Also arresting is the interweaving of the bodies of the three women in the third sequence ("la pietra d'inciampo", the stumbling block), where they lie face down on top of each other, with their arms and legs becoming more and more entangled as they struggle to get back on their feet (see Fig. 19.3). This startling stage image, along with the sharing of lines originally spoken by different characters, reinforces Guidi's fundamental

Figure 19.3 Chiara Guidi, Anna Lidia Molina, and Agnese Scotti: interweaving bodies; *Macbeth su Macbeth su Macbeth* (2014), dir. by Chiara Guidi; production photograph by Luca Del Pia.

intuition that Macbeth, Lady Macbeth, and the weird sisters are inextricably linked, both as psychic reflections of each other and in their use of distinctively idiomatic language and phrases, including, most prominently, Macbeth's and the weird sisters' references to the interchangeable qualities of "foul" and "fair" in the opening scenes of the play, or Lady Macbeth's and Macbeth's apostrophes in 1.4 ("Come, thick night") and 3.2 ("Come, seeling night"). Rather than reducing *Macbeth* to a moral fable, Guidi's adaptation proves strikingly original in its suggestion that Macbeth's "vaulting ambition" is not only about becoming king but also about becoming fully and absolutely himself. Macbeth's profoundly human inability to "be the same in [...] act and valour, | As [he is] in desire" (1.7.40–41) becomes a metaphor for the theatre, which is always and inevitably suspended between being and not being, between reality and fiction. Hence the subtitle of Guidi's adaptation (*Uno studio per la mano sinistra*, "A Study for the Left Hand"), whose relevance is powerfully conveyed by the third and fourth sequences, when the three women take turns to bind their right arms behind their backs. Every action thus becomes strenuous and self-conscious, a stunning visual counterpart for Macbeth's disabling realisation that "nothing is, but what is not" (1.3.144).

Guidi gave talks about *MsMsM* and her forthcoming project inspired by *The Tempest* at King's College London in October 2014 and February 2015. The interview that follows is the product of an ongoing conversation between Guidi (CG) and Massai (SM) begun in early 2014.

Shakespeare, Tradition, and the Avant-garde 281

"Nothing is, but what is not"

[SM] You have often told me that you are drawn to Shakespeare because of the rich, expansive, and evocative quality of his language. And yet *MsMsM* departs from theatrical traditions that monumentalize Shakespeare by scrupulously reproducing the texts of his plays on stage as closely as possible to how they were originally printed in the late-sixteenth and early-seventeenth centuries and to how they have been edited for readers ever since. Can you explain whether your approach enhances or undercuts the cultural value generally ascribed to Shakespeare's words and what role the book as prop plays in *MsMsM*?

Figure 19.4 "The book of the play" falls apart; *Macbeth su Macbeth su Macbeth* (2014), dir. by Chiara Guidi; production photograph by Luca Del Pia.

282 Sonia Massai and Chiara Guidi

[CG] Macbeth's line "nothing is, but what is not" (1.3.144) suggests the impossibility of staging the play in its entirety and as it was originally printed in the Folio edition of 1623. *Macbeth* invites us to look simultaneously at *and* through the material world, including the materiality of the play as a book, so that we can detect at once what is visible and what is invisible, or what is immaterial and nevertheless real. The book as prop is introduced at the very beginning of *MsMsM*. After a short sequence called "Falso Inizio" [False Start], when the lights are still on in the auditorium and we look lost and call out Macbeth's name, as if we were literally "looking for Macbeth", the lights go out as we exit upstage left and right. When I re-enter, I carry a book that falls apart when I open it (see Fig. 19.4). Several pages fall on to the stage, suggesting my obsessive exploration of Shakespeare's words but also my need to cannibalize the text and those textual, editorial, and critical traditions which, while ensuring its survival and its incremental cultural value over the last four centuries, can prevent a fresh and more experimental approach to the play. The book is then displayed on a low pedestal downstage, where it remains in full view of the audience until it gets tied to the back of the throne, after Duncan is murdered. My line "Ora hai tutto" [Now you have everything] hints at an overlap between Macbeth's temporary illusion of fulfilment and the modern adapter's illusory sense of ownership over Shakespeare's play (see Murphy 2000: 10–25 for how the book has been used in recent cinematic adaptations of Shakespeare).

That line, "Nothing is, but what is not", is also a reminder that a play that includes a ghost among its characters cannot but privilege the immaterial over the material dimensions of reality. Banquo's tremendous power in 3.4 stems from his being present and absent at once. Macbeth's line is therefore an injunction to stage what cannot be staged; it is a challenge that directors of the play must face and it was certainly my starting point, as I decided what lines or words from the play I could use as building blocks for my stage production. Hence the title of my production: *Macbeth on Macbeth on Macbeth*.

My decision to use Macbeth's line as a starting point for my production was also due to the fact that it stems from Macbeth's first encounter with the weird sisters. Their main function is to help us understand that what we read about in the text of the play—Macbeth, his desire, and whatever else lies within Macbeth—predates us as well as the written (and the printed) word. The weird sisters reveal what lies within Macbeth with the suddenness and the clarity of a torch lit in a dark cave. The rhetorical power of their prophecies is such that we, like Macbeth, cannot ignore them. And the rhetorical power of their words is not conceptual but material: their words literally "stop our way". They are a scandal, a breach in nature that defies the senses, a rip in the texture of reality that makes us question the relationship between the body and the world, between the body and what else is in it, thus opening

Shakespeare, Tradition, and the Avant-garde   283

up new ways of reading and interpreting the world that go beyond a conventional mapping of reality, beyond established epistemologies. So Macbeth's journey and the play start with a stumbling block: the words spoken by the weird sisters.

Their words are also a stumbling block for Western theatre because *Macbeth* is all about staging what cannot be seen. How should one stage a ghost? If the ghost is personated by an actor or represented through special effects that are registered by the senses, the ghost is not a ghost. *Macbeth* forces theatre to rethink itself and what defines it as a specific art form, as a distinctive language and medium. By using thoroughly metatheatrical terms and images in *Macbeth*, such as Macbeth's famous analogy in 5.5—"Out, out, brief candle, | Life's but a walking shadow, a poor player, | That struts and frets his hour upon the stage | And then is heard no more"—Shakespeare invites us to reread and reinterpret what we take for granted. I believe that *Macbeth* exceeds the familiar reading of the tragic hero's fall as a moral fable. The main source of the cathartic power of this tragedy lies in its potential to free up the gaze. Hence my decision to open my production by staging the physical stumbling of the three female actors on an invisible step, which is then marked by adhesive tape. That is the spot where we stumble. That is the spot where we begin. The actor needs to learn how to stumble. The stumbling must be so well-rehearsed, so perfectly performed, as to look real.

[SM] Your reference to the ambiguity between reality and fiction, between what is and what is not, in *MsMsM* seems also central to the performance philosophy that has made SRS so distinctive, even within the context of European avant-garde and experimental theatre. Your actors, as much as your spectators, learn to share a very different actorial and spectatorial strategy from conventional playacting and playgoing, which implies a suspension of belief in what is taken to be real, rather than a suspension of disbelief in the fictive quality of theatrical performance. How has this performance philosophy impacted on specific aspects of your production of *Macbeth*?

[CG] Every time I embark on a new project, I consider how the project engages my sense of what is real and what is fictional. I feel what is real to me and then I pretend to feel it. I forge the stage language that I am going to share with my actors and my audiences by shuttling between reality and fiction. I think of this stage language as syntax, as a very precise set of images, words, and sounds, connected to each other by a grammar devised for each project through practice. *Macbeth* highlights the tension between being and pretending to be, which is central both to the actor's mode of being on stage and to our way of being in the world. The actor puts on a costume, metaphorical armour, and then takes it off, thus shuttling between being and not being. Except in *Macbeth* the actor is confronted by a character who cannot be, or pretend to be, king, thus disturbing our ability to tell apart reality and fiction. The real turns out to be unreal, when one, Macbeth-like, cannot quite play a role that others perceive as real.

I became obsessed with *Macbeth* when I realised that, besides questioning the purpose of playing, as much as the purpose of being, it also offers powerful images that cut across perceived gender differences. The blood that stains the hands of those who have taken a life—"Out, damned spot! Out, I say. [...] Here's the smell of blood: all the perfumes of Arabia will not sweeten this little hand" (5.1)—is a symptom of genuine fragility but also of a moral sensibility that is as much at the core of Lady Macbeth's character, who speaks these lines, as of Macbeth's character, who is similarly haunted by the sight of his bloody hands ("What hands are here? Ha! They pluck out mine eyes. | Will all great Neptune's ocean wash this blood | Clean from my hand? No, this my hand will rather | The multitudinous seas incarnadine, | Making the green one red", 2.2; see Fig. 19.5). A play that is generally taken to polarize masculinity and femininity is in fact an exploration of their interconnectedness, which incidentally reminds me of Prospero's revealing comment about Caliban, as a "thing of darkness", which he acknowledges as his own, thus merging, instead of juxtaposing, the civilizing master and his monstrous servant—two seeming opposites are, once again, revealed as essentially interlocking subject-positions, as one and the same. Hence my decision to devise a production of *Macbeth* for three female actors. The three women, who are always on stage, can initially be taken to represent the weird sisters. But that is a red herring. They are indeed the weird sisters, insofar as they are the

Figure 19.5 "What hands are here?"; *Macbeth su Macbeth su Macbeth* (2014), dir. by Chiara Guidi; production photograph by Luca Del Pia.

Shakespeare, Tradition, and the Avant-garde   285

stumbling block that forces Macbeth and Lady Macbeth to test their desire to be (king and queen), but they are also three female actors testing the boundaries of their desire to play Shakespeare in the context of (or rather in opposition to) mainstream theatrical traditions that marginalize women as actors or theatre makers.

Stopping the Way

[SM] In this important respect, your production moves beyond feminist readings of the play, which have focused more specifically on how the play itself represents femininity as either powerful but transgressive or normative but ultimately ineffective by polarizing the weird sisters and Lady Macbeth, on the one hand, and Lady Macduff, on the other (Chedgzoy 2001). Your production seems instead to focus on the play's intrinsic metatheatricality in order to make a bold statement about the overwhelming weight of a theatrical tradition that threatens to crush not only a type of theatre that seeks to express itself through new forms and a new language, but also female actors who dare to move centre-stage, especially when what is being re-represented on that stage is Shakespeare, a cornerstone of Western European theatre. I was particularly moved by your staging of the "Birnam Wood prophecy" in the tenth sequence, "La Trave" [The Beam], when a large beam is lowered on top of the three women, until they come dangerously close to being crushed by it. Could you tell us more about this moment and whether there were other moments in your production which similarly draw the audience's attention to the physical structure of the stage and, by association, to the power structures that shape contemporary Italian theatre as an institution?

[CG] Once our right hands are tied behind our backs we cannot move, let alone act, naturally. This simple stratagem foregrounds the challenge we face when we play Shakespeare. It is genuinely quite hard to pick up the golden round off the stage floor and then to secure it to the rope required to lift it by using only our left hands. This stratagem becomes the "step" that "stops our way" and our point of entry into the play. Halfway through my production, a large beam descends from above. The beam comes to rest on our shoulders and slowly crushes us to the floor. The architectural structure of the theatre suddenly becomes visible and it does so to paralyze us, just as Birnam Wood moves to paralyze Macbeth. While the women are trapped under the beam, two men, our technicians Giovanni Marocco and Stefano Cortesi, the former visibly older than the latter, enter, accompanied by a black dog, and take it in turns to sit on the golden chair. Giovanni sits first, placing the golden round on his head. He then stands up and hands the golden round to Stefano, who sits down. Giovanni and Stefano's dumb-show is a reminder of "the show of eight kings" that occurs in 4.1 in Shakespeare's play. A new king succeeds the

286 *Sonia Massai and Chiara Guidi*

former king. The king is dead; long live the king. This unthinking succession, this unthinking fashioning of identity, is the world our Macbeth cannot inhabit. *Macbeth* strikes me as a static play, paradoxically structured around a circular movement, which is perpetual, never-ending. Each motion leaves Macbeth and Lady Macbeth dead, but the desire to be king is passed on. This circular movement sounds a melancholy note in the play and informs my sense of the unattainable in my own work.

I am also aware that the play was written at a time when James I was deeply invested in the demonization of the traditional medical lore associated with wise women in medieval and early modern European cultures. James condemned this type of traditional knowledge in his work on *Daemonologie* (1597), where he describes the grotesque and monstrous character of the witch, who concocts potions that are believed to harm rather than cure. Lady Macbeth's brutality as a mother figure reminds me of the character of the witch, as demonized by James. The queen is a witch. The witches in *Macbeth* are therefore simultaneously on the heath (and beyond Macbeth) and at court (and within Macbeth). Shakespeare tricks James. The king is naked and he is not aware of it. The play is the stumbling block that stops the king's way. The play is also the stumbling block that stops unthinking figures of authority, within and beyond the fictive world of Shakespeare's tragic hero.

I should also explain that my obsession with *Macbeth*, which has drawn me to the play repeatedly, over the years, like a child who needs to listen to the same story over and over again, stems from my need to seek Lady Macbeth and her candle-lit, nightly visitations. I await her confession. It is through Lady Macbeth's confession that the play becomes intimately feminine. The woman at the core of the play bares her soul. She is tasked with this crucial role, which is the crucial role of the sort of theatre SRS has championed since its inception, and the sort of theatre I wish to make as a female director of Shakespeare.

[SM] I am intrigued by the fact that, having curated sound and voice in most SRS productions prior to 2004–2005, you have entrusted Francesco Guerri and his cello to conjure a soundscape that accompanies and complements the voice of the three women in your production. I wonder whether the music, sound, and voices that one hears in *MsMsM* play a slightly different role from earlier SRS Shakespearean productions and whether Guerri's presence on stage modulates and qualifies the role of the three women in any way.

[CG] Music and sounds are often more expressive than words, although their power to communicate obviously depends on our willingness and our ability to listen. My dramaturgy has always been informed by my interest in the epiphanic power of music—hence my recurrent collaborations with musicians and phoneticians. I do not use music to comment

Shakespeare, Tradition, and the Avant-garde   287

or to heighten sentiment, which is the main role of a soundtrack. I am, rather, committed to forging music as a language in its own right, whose main objective on stage is to conjure an image into life. Music has the unique power of drawing the gaze to an image, which may otherwise go unnoticed. As in other SRS productions, the audience in *MsMsM* sees by listening, because stage images are enfolded in sound. This is why I believe prosody to be so central to verse drama and to my approach to it. Verse binds the body (the signifier) and the meaning (the signified) of words together, while the metrical rhythm of verse modulates the concepts expressed by words.

Unlike other plays by Shakespeare, *Macbeth* requires music and sound to ensure that its dialogue is effectively lifted off the page and given new life on stage. It is the ghostly quality of Macbeth's world that seems to me to be best re-presented through the language of music (and the fact that Prospero's magic in *The Tempest* requires Ariel and Ariel's songs is no mere coincidence). But what music, what sound, can help an actor attune her voice to the soundscape in *Macbeth*? Only a close analysis of the atomic structure of the matter individual words are made of can help an actor's voice become one with the words she utters, as in an alchemical reaction between voice and text. I am once again reminded of *The Tempest* and of Prospero's insistent request that his orders be carried out by Ariel "to point" (1.2), that is, point by point.

I collaborated with Francesco Guerri long before I started working with the other two actors. Guerri's cello is first and foremost a potent symbol on stage: the bow and its movement remind me of the dagger and the obsessive replaying of the stabbing of Duncan in Macbeth's memory. And, at the end of *MsMsM*, the bow is set on fire, following Francesca Grilli's suggestion, to emphasize the alchemical combination of text and voice, of printed words and sound, which informs the entire production. The fire keeps burning and its brightness marks a new beginning, a new dawn, as the show draws to an end. Guerri's cello was supported by Giuseppe Ielasi's electro-acoustic sound, which helped us stage that palpable quality of silence, the suspension of sound, which is a prerequisite of any attempt to signify through music. As in earlier SRS productions, music shapes the space within which a play-text is conjured back to life through performance.

Birth and Rebirth

[SM] Your archaeological approach to Shakespeare's text, your painstaking exploration of the layers of meanings produced by the material quality of words as sounds, has produced haunting readings of specific moments in *Macbeth* that have all but disappeared from modern theatrical interpretations of the play. One case in point is your staging of the porter scene, which is now mostly staged as a comic set piece and used

288 *Sonia Massai and Chiara Guidi*

to bring some light relief straight after the dark heart of the tragedy (the murder of Duncan in 2.2). In your production, the porter scene draws on local references in Shakespeare's text that are directly linked to the Harrowing of Hell motif as represented, for example, in medieval mystery plays. Can you explain how you researched and staged the porter scene, the significance of the main stage images in it, and how this moment in your production fits in with your overall approach to the play?

[CG] In Shakespeare, words are intimately connected to their material form and therefore evoke images. I believe that this feature of Shakespeare's language is due to the fact that he was an actor, as well as a playwright. Only by acting Shakespeare does one become aware of the material texture of his words and their ability to conjure stage images. When I read Shakespeare, I first *see* his words and then *think* about them.

In *Macbeth*, the porter scene juxtaposes the bloody hand of the murderer with the knocking hand. I have always been drawn to images of doors where the handles are replaced by living hands covered with gold paint. When I started working on *MsMsM*, I remembered these images and decided to have a hole carved through the wooden door that is lowered onto the stage at the beginning of the ninth sequence, so that I can thrust my hand and forearm, covered with gold paint, through it and knock on it, loudly and repeatedly, throughout this sequence. The gold paint suggests that the knocking hand is linked to the hand that touched the king and that is now soaked in royal blood, because everything about the king in my production is golden—the golden round, the golden chair, and now the knocking hand (see Fig. 19.6). This way the accuser and the accused, the party who judges and the party who is judged, are inextricably linked.

The door with a hand as handle harks back to the combination of tragic and comic registers in the porter scene in Shakespeare. It also combines (moral) opposites, thus speaking to the central concern in a play where being and not being, fair and foul, coexist. The door is hellgate but it also ushers in a new role for Macbeth, a role that Macbeth will be unable to perform. There is another door in my production, albeit a symbolic one, which has a similar function. In the twelfth sequence, "Il Pavimento Appeso" [The Hanging Floor], we use a pulley to lift the heavy black cloth that covers the stage. At this point in the production, the heavy, hanging material functions like an opening, a passageway, and by passing through it we enact a sort of (re)birth. I believe that the much debated references to Macbeth's and Lady Macbeth's children in the play may in fact refer to the process of birth and rebirth generated by both hands, the bloody hand of the murderer who strikes the body of the king and the knocking hand that attempts to awaken the (new) king.

Figure 19.6 "The knocking hand"; *Macbeth su Macbeth su Macbeth* (2014), dir. by Chiara Guidi; production photograph by Luca Del Pia.

[SM] The link between the bloody hand and the knocking hand in the porter's scene is in keeping with your sense that Macbeth, Judas-like, through an act of preordained betrayal, is instrumental in ushering in a (re)birth and, arguably, the rise of a new line of kings culminating with the accession of James I to the throne of England in 1603. More generally, by eschewing a traditional reading of *Macbeth* as a moral parable, *MsMsM* exemplifies a productive and challenging type of "ethic" theatre, because, as Nicholas Ridout has recently put it, "[it] confront[s] its spectators with something that [can]not be assimilated by their existing understanding of the ethical" (Ridout 2009: 67). Thinking about your current work on *The Tempest*, I am equally struck by the originality of your approach, because it moves the play away from familiar

290 Sonia Massai and Chiara Guidi

post-colonial or neo-colonial contexts, within which the play continues to be revived on the world stage, and focuses instead on its characters' ability (or inability) to feel and to know the world around them empathetically. I wonder whether you could explain in more detail how your approach to *The Tempest* eschews the manifestly political (as much as *MsMsM* eschews the manifestly moral) and strives instead, quoting Ridout again, to "issue a demand [that audiences do] not know how to answer" just as yet (Ridout 2009: 67).

[CG] I agree with Ridout entirely, because I also believe that art is primarily meant to raise questions which, in turn, prompt further questions. Questions like births and rebirths, which force us to change. Is this not Macbeth's fate? And is it not Prospero's as well? These characters share our yearning for (forbidden) knowledge and our desire to choose and to act beyond the limits of what we are generally conditioned to regard as ethical. The tragic tension associated with self-knowledge and self-realization shapes these plays' characters and has forced audiences over the last four centuries to confront the same questions and desires. Hence my sense that identifying the significance and the impact of *Macbeth* and *The Tempest*, or of Shakespeare more generally, on a specific political or interpretative context is too limiting, albeit culturally and historically enlightening.

The epilogue spoken by Prospero at the end of *The Tempest* reinforces my sense that this play, like *Macbeth*, challenges its audience to consider questions that they do not know how to answer yet. Prospero has fulfilled his master plan. Ariel's song, like alchemy, has wrought what representation alone cannot express. And yet, by the end of the play, Ariel's song, like Prospero's words, suffers a contraction. Prospero and, more generally, the play do not offer the release granted by a happy ending. This contraction, very much like labour pains, signals a new beginning. I think of all great literary masterpieces as portals or openings, from which new questions emerge, endlessly, forcing us to embrace uncertainty and change as the only possible way of being.

Conclusion

Guidi's highly creative and inspiring reworking of this most familiar of Shakespearean plays sheds light both on important aspects of the critical and theatrical reception of *Macbeth* in the English-speaking world and on the dynamics of cultural exchange in contemporary performance within and beyond it. Guidi's understanding of the early Jacobean context within which the play was first written and performed seems, for example, to depart from earlier theories going as far back as the eighteenth century, according to which Shakespeare wrote *Macbeth* to flatter James

Shakespeare, Tradition, and the Avant-garde 291

I, and is more in keeping with a recent tendency to read the play as ideo-logically ambiguous, as Sandra Clark and Pamela Mason have explained in their Arden 3 edition of the play: "While Shakespeare's choice of an episode from Scottish history featuring the character of Banquo whom James believed to be his ancestor can hardly be accidental, it can also be argued that the play is at the least ambivalent in its handling of topics close to the King's heart" (Clark and Mason 2015: 21). In this respect, Guidi seems interestingly attuned to current interpretative approaches within the wider field of Shakespeare studies.

Similarly, Guidi's visceral approach to Shakespeare's text is a far cry from the type of avant-garde theatre that simply rejects the authority of canonical texts, in keeping with Hans-Thies Lehmann's definition of "postdramatic theatre" (Lehmann 2006). Guidi's need to cannibal-ize Shakespeare's text and her precision in analysing and dissecting individual lines or phrases were interestingly anticipated by Orson Welles when he defended his highly original approach to the play in his 1936 "Vodoo *Macbeth*" as follows: "Any director who directs a Shakespeare play or film can only realize a small part of it [...] All we can do is grasp at or bite off a little bit, but what we grasp must be true and undistorted. I am entirely against distortion in a Shakespear-ean production" (quoted in Kliman 2004: 121). Genuinely creative appropriations—even across different media and languages—seem to capitalize on, rather than resist or undermine, the cultural capital accrued by "master texts" like Shakespeare's plays: in other words, the most productive reworkings of Shakespeare, on the contemporary Italian stage and beyond, suggest that cultural exchange is at its most productive when it prompts a dialogue between enduring traditions and the shock of the new.

Bibliography

Chedgzoy, Kate, ed. 2001. *Shakespeare, Feminism and Gender.* Basingstoke.
Clark, Sandra, and Pamela Mason, eds. 2015. *Macbeth,* Arden Shakespeare. London.
Escolme, Bridget. 2005. "Performing Human: The Socìetas Raffaello Sanzio". *Talking to the Audience: Shakespeare, Performance, Self.* London. 129–150.
Hazlitt, William. 1992. *The Characters of Shakespeare's Plays* [1817]. *The Romantics on Shakespeare,* ed. by Jonathan Bate. London. 307–10.
Kelleher, Joe, Nicholas Ridout, Claudia Castellucci, Romeo Castellucci, and Chiara Guidi. 2007. *The Theatre of Socìetas Raffaello Sanzio.* London.
Kliman, Bernice W. 2004. *Shakespeare in Performance: Macbeth,* 2nd edition. Manchester.
Knights, L. C. 1933. *How Many Children Had Lady Macbeth? An Essay in the Theory and Practice of Shakespeare Criticism.* Cambridge.
Lehmann, Hans-Thies. 2006. *Postdramatic Theatre.* London.

292 Sonia Massai and Chiara Guidi

Mullin, Michael. 1987. "Stage and Screen: The Trevor Nunn *Macbeth*". *Shakespeare Quarterly*, 38: 350–9.

Murphy, Andrew. 2000. "The Book on the Screen". *Shakespeare, Film, Fin de Siècle*, ed. by Mark Thornton Burnett and Ramona Wray. Basingstoke. 10–25.

Ridout, Nicholas. 2009. *Theatre & Ethics*. Basingstoke.

Sacchi, Annalisa. 2014. *Shakespeare per la Socìetas Raffaello Sanzio*. Pisa.

Afterword

Shakespeare, an Infinite Stage

Paolo Puppa

From a position of relative obscurity for much of the eighteenth century, Shakespeare, untutored poet-playwright from a literary backwater in Northern Europe, enjoyed a revival of critical fortunes around the turn of the nineteenth century, his reputation gradually re-evaluated by, *inter alia*, Sturm und Drang writers privileging ecstasy of the passions, a cult of the natural genius, and individualism of feeling, thought, and expression. Increasingly, Shakespeare was deracinated from the materiality of stage space, a world in which the playwright was organically linked to fellow actors and an intimately-placed audience, to be reconceived of as a poet, *the* poet, sacralized in a book. Thus canonized, Shakespeare's versatile poetics were tailored to the critical biases of successive commentators: his writing was likened by Keats to the moods of the sea; for Bakhtin his high and low scenes, comic and tragic, cohabited in a carnival of hybridity pre-empting Dostoyevsky's dialogism; and later twentieth-century critics conscripted him as a spokesperson for a postmodern poetics encompassing, variously, Lionel Abel's *Metadrama* (1963), Julia Kristeva's notions of intertextuality (1969), and Gérard Genette's *Palimpsestes* (1982), favouring a polyphonic scanning between hypertext and hypotext. Building on this critical tradition, this volume's methodologies run the gamut from comparative literature to performance history, reception theory, translation studies, and even socio-ethnological approaches, tracing Shakespeare through a seemingly "infinite variety" of literary and dramatic negotiations.

Shakespeare was embraced in mid-nineteenth-century Italian repertoires, his works newly accessible through the prose translations of Carlo Rusconi and verse renditions by Giulio Carcano, the multilingualism of Shakespeare's originals sacrificed to the reductive demands of a linguistic culture favouring high, homogeneous registers. Italian neoclassical critics maligned the use of subplots, prologues, choruses, rhythmic shifts between verse and prose, and generic hybridity (denouncing the intrusion of comic roles like *Hamlet*'s gravediggers, *Macbeth*'s porter, or Lear's Fool, in works classified as tragic), preferring instead a uniform idiom and unidirectional structure. As Robert Henke's chapter in this volume demonstrates, Shakespeare's high tragedies and even late

294 *Paolo Puppa*

Shakespeare (perhaps even *last* Shakespeare, in *The Tempest*) show an untroubled recourse to types and modular structures derived from the *commedia dell'arte*, just as, in Mukherji's account, *Cymbeline* is suffused with tragicomic polyphony and stylistic ambiguity in a distinctly Italian tradition, befitting a play that counterpoints British and Italian identities. The result is one in which dialectic reigns—a proto-cubist method that collocates, without necessarily reconciling, different angles and multiple points of view. And all of this long before Pirandello.

Due in large measure to Verdi's passion for him, Shakespeare, sung rather than spoken, fostered the conditions for the triumph of the "great actors", following the bold but flawed attempts at adaptation by Gustavo Modena. Hence the performative tradition of a dominant actor-protagonist: Ernesto Rossi's Hamlet, Tommaso Salvini's bloody and noble Othello, and Adelaide Ristori's narcissistic Lady Macbeth. Pioneering a physical, bodily form of communication, these *grandi attori* were in a sense authors in themselves, transcending language barriers and mediating a foreign text through a kind of translation. In Duse's personal library, Anna Sica has uncovered books annotated with declamatory symbols, offering yet another interpretative model for these great actors: as librettists treated the raw texts of Shakespeare's plays, so these actors adopted a utilitarian approach, selecting scenes of personal interest or melodramatic potential, paying little heed to the growing climate of philological fidelity and scandalizing critics with independent, bespoke interpolations. This kind of creative infidelity continues with Ettore Petrolini's parodies and pastiches in the early twentieth century, or metatheatrical rewritings ranging from the expressionist, multilinguistic Giovanni Testori to the nihilistic, sardonic Carmelo Bene. It was not until 1943, in a project coordinated by Mario Praz, that complete, faithful translations of Shakespeare's plays would become available, in versions no longer centred (or dependent) on the ego of a great actor.

Several directorial visions grapple with the idea of the totality of a play; in the case of Strehler, the totality of a trilogy, as discussed in Mace Perlman's account. Obsessed with Shakespeare, Strehler turned his hand to an adaptation of the *Henry VI* trilogy, recast as *Il gioco dei potenti* (1964–65), in which history is staged in the form of a play, drawing on pan-European sources and influences, from Boccaccio and the *commedia dell'arte* to Strehler's beloved Brecht. The final contribution to this volume, adopting a more irreverent approach, sees Chiara Guidi, in conversation with Sonia Massai, unpack her production of *Macbeth*. Guidi seems to cannibalize even Shakespeare's weighty paper textuality, an approach to his canonicity that may recall Charles Marowitz's *Hamlet* (filmed in 1969)—a compressed collage of the play, sparse, fractured, stylized, experimental.

These chapters all address the mechanics of artistic adaptation and exchange: the multiplicity of layers, the vertiginous movement of

Afterword 295

passages from one system to another, the discovery of a Shakespeare hitherto hidden, a continuous network of reductions, amplifications, and interpolations. The history of successive Italian versions of the *Sonnets* (discussed by Matteo Brera) reveals the difficulties of finding another linguistic system and other prosodic rules for housing Shakespeare's poetry. The phenomenon might be extended to Edoardo Sanguineti's *Sonetti* (1997), a musical-poetic pastiche reworked into a neo-futuristic rap form. The ongoing motif is one of accommodated resistance—of tension between adaptation and original that both preserves and circumvents difference. Giovanni Grasso triumphed with his legendary *Otello* of 1910 in London through a synergy of body language and words; the first translations into Hebrew, in the late nineteenth century, overcame the formidable limitations of a written (rather than a spoken) language; and Eduardo translated *The Tempest* into seventeenth-century Neapolitan (a dialect, no less!). Given these linguistic experiments and artistic liberties, one might conclude with Luigi Meneghello's deftly humorous and aptly-named *Trapianti* [*Transplants*] (2002), a poetic defence of the local Malo dialect as a medium better suited than formal Tuscan for translating Elizabethan poetry; the musicality of this local idiom uncovers something obscure, latent, and hidden, in the cornucopian density of the Shakespearean text.

List of Contributors

Susan Bassnett is Professor of Comparative Literature at the University of Warwick and the University of Glasgow, and has published extensively on translation, world literature, theatre history, and postcolonialism, pioneering what has been called "the cultural turn" with André Lefevere. Recent books include an expanded fourth edition of *Translation Studies* (Routledge, 2014 [1980]), *Reflections on Translation* (2011), and *Translation* (for the New Critical Idiom series, Routledge, 2014). She is the new President of the British Comparative Literature Association and a Fellow of the Royal Society of Literature, the Institute of Linguists, and the Academia Europaea.

Matteo Brera is Lecturer at Utrecht University. He has published extensively on the translation of English classics (Sidney, Shakespeare, Milton) into Italian. His current research focuses primarily on ecclesiastical and political censorship in European literature. On this topic, he has recently published the monograph *Novecento all'Indice: Gabriele D'Annunzio, i libri proibiti e i rapporti Stato-Chiesa all'ombra del Concordato* (Storia e Letteratura, 2016). Other research interests include the history of the Italian language, the history of ideas, European opera, popular music, contemporary Italian poetry, and Italian migrant experiences in the American South.

Giovanna Buonanno is Assistant Professor of English Literature at the University of Modena and Reggio Emilia, where she teaches modern and contemporary literature in English. She is the author of *International Actresses on the Victorian Stage* (Modena, 2002) and has published widely on modern and contemporary English and Italian theatre, intercultural drama, and black and Asian British women's writing. Her current research focuses on transnational women's writing in English.

Camilla Caporicci is Humboldt Fellow at the Ludwig-Maximilians-Universität München, carrying out a project on Renaissance love poetry. She is author of *The Dark Lady. La rivoluzione Shakespeariana nei Sonetti alla Dama Bruna* (2013) and several articles and book chapters. Recent publications include "'Breaking the rules': The

298   *List of Contributors*

subversive nature of Shakespeare's sonnets to the Dark Lady", *InVerbis* (2016); "'My Female Evil': A reading of Sonnet 129 and 144", *Annali di Ca' Foscari: Serie Occidentale* (2015); "'Your Painted Counterfeit': The *paragone* between portraits and sonnets in Shakespeare's work", *Actes des congrès de la Société française Shakespeare* (2015); "The Tyranny of Immaterialism: Refusing the Body in *The Winter's Tale*", *Sederi Yearbook* (2015): "'Dark Is Light'. From Italy to England", *Shakespeare and the Italian Renaissance* (2014); "Shakespeare e Giulio Romano: fonti e problemi", *Rinascimento* (2013).

Celia R. Caputi (formerly Daileader) is Professor of English at Florida State University and author of *Eroticism on the Renaissance Stage: Transcendence, Desire, and the Limits of the Visible* (Cambridge, 1998); *Racism, Misogyny, and the Othello Myth: Inter-racial Couples from Shakespeare to Spike Lee* (Cambridge, 2005); and some two dozen articles and book-chapters on Renaissance literature, feminist theory and criticism, critical race studies, and the Italian influence on early modern English drama. Prof. Caputi was a semi-finalist in Italy's Concorso Lingua Madre for her autobiographical essay, *Come l'ago della Bussola*, which has been published in *Lingua Madre Duemilatredici: Racconti di donne straniere in Italia* (Edizioni SEB27, 2013).

Rocco Coronato is Associate Professor of English Literature at the University of Padua. He has published *Shakespeare's Neighbors: Theory Matters in the Bard and His Contemporaries* (2001); *Jonson Versus Bakhtin: Carnival and the Grotesque* (Rodopi, 2003); *La mano invisibile: Shakespeare e la conoscenza nascosta* (2011); *La linea del serpente: caos e creazione in Milton, Sterne e Coleridge* (2012); *Intorno a Shakespeare: re e confessori, marinai e vedove, delinquenti e attori* (2013). His work in progress deals with the relationships between Shakespeare and Caravaggio, the application of complexity theory to literary interpretation, and the digital humanities.

Enza De Francisci is Lecturer in Translation Studies at the University of Glasgow. She has published widely on theatre translation, performance history, and dialect literature in several peer-reviewed journals including *Italian Studies*, *The Italianist*, *Modern Language Review*, and *Pirandello Studies*, for which she edits theatre reviews. She has completed a monograph, *A "New" Woman in Verga and Pirandello: From Page to Stage* (forthcoming), and is assisting with the Leverhulme-funded research network "Re-imagining Italianità: opera and musical culture in transnational perspective".

John Drakakis is Emeritus Professor of English at the University of Stirling and Visiting Professor of English at the University of Lincoln. He is editor of *Alternative Shakespeares* (1985), the editor of *The Merchant of Venice* for the Arden 3 series, and has edited volumes

List of Contributors   299

on *Shakespeare's Tragedies, Antony and Cleopatra*, and (jointly) on *Tragedy, Gothic Shakespeares*, and *Macbeth*. He is general editor of the *New Critical Idiom* series, general and contributing editor of the major revision of Geoffrey Bullough's *Narrative and Dramatic Sources of Shakespeare*, and has contributed numerous book chapters, articles for learned journals, and reviews. He is an elected Fellow of the English Association, an Honorary Fellow of Glyndwr University, Wrexham, and holds an honorary doctorate from Blaise Pascal University in Clermont Ferrand.

Enrica Maria Ferrara is Adjunct Assistant Professor of Italian at Trinity College Dublin and has published widely on Italian and Comparative Literature. Recent publications include a monograph on Italo Calvino and the theatre, *Calvino e il teatro: Storia di una passione rimossa* (Oxford, 2011), and a volume on realism and the interaction of theatrical and narrative discourses in twentieth-century Italian literature, *Il realismo teatrale nella narrativa del Novecento: Vittorini, Pasolini, Calvino* (Florence, 2014).

Chiara Guidi is an actress, director, playwright, and cofounder, with Claudia and Romeo Castellucci, of the *Societas Raffaello Sanzio*, an avant-garde theatre company producing performances at major international festivals and theatres across the world since its inception in 1981. She is pursuing personal research on the centrality and role of the voice as a dramatic vehicle.

Giulia Harding is a retired BBC Radio journalist who has made a hobby of studying links between John Florio and Shakespeare for the past thirty years. She contributes to an Anglo-Italian website on the subject: http://www.Shakespeareandflorio.net.

Robert Henke is Professor of Drama and Comparative Literature at Washington University. He is author of *Pastoral Transformations: Italian Tragicomedy and Shakespeare's Late Plays* (Delaware, 1997), *Performance and Literature in the Commedia dell'Arte* (Cambridge, 2002), and *Poverty and Charity in Early Modern Theater and Performance* (Iowa, 2016). With Eric Nicholson, he has co-edited *Transnational Exchange in Early Modern Theater* (Ashgate, 2008) and *Transnational Mobilities in Early Modern Theater* (Ashgate, 2014). He is editor of the early modern volume of *A Cultural History of Theatre* (Bloomsbury, forthcoming 2017) and presently writing a book on Shakespeare and early modern Italian theatre.

Lily Kahn is Reader in Hebrew and Jewish Languages at University College London. Her main research areas are Hebrew in Eastern Europe, Yiddish, and other Jewish languages. She is also interested in global Shakespeare, comparative Semitics, and endangered languages.

300 *List of Contributors*

Her publications include *The Verbal System in Late Enlightenment Hebrew* (Brill, 2009), *Colloquial Yiddish* (Routledge, 2012), *The Routledge Introductory Course in Biblical Hebrew* (Routledge, 2014), *A Grammar of the Eastern European Hasidic Hebrew Tale* (Brill, 2015), and *The First Hebrew Shakespeare Translations: A Bilingual Edition and Commentary* (UCL Press, 2017).

Sonia Massai is Professor of Shakespeare Studies in the English Department at King's College London. She has published widely on the history of Shakespeare's transmission on stage and page. Her publications include her book, *Shakespeare and the Rise of the Editor* (Cambridge, 2007), collections of essays on *Shakespeare and Textual Studies* (Cambridge, 2015) and *World-Wide Shakespeares: Local Appropriations in Film and Performance* (Routledge, 2005), and critical editions of *The Paratexts in English Printed Drama to 1642* (Cambridge, 2014) and John Ford's *Tis Pity She's a Whore* for Arden Early Modern Drama (2011).

Subha Mukherji was educated in Calcutta, Oxford, and Cambridge, and teaches English at the University of Cambridge. She has published widely on Renaissance literature and Shakespeare, and more specifically on law and literature in early modern England, tragicomedy, epistemology and literature in the Renaissance, and the poetics of space across periods and cultures. Her book-in-progress is *Questioning Knowledge in Renaissance Literature*. She is also editing *Blind Spots of Knowledge in Shakespeare and His World*, and co-editing *Knowing Faith: Literature, Belief and Knowledge in Early Modern England*. She is Principle Investigator on the five-year, ERC-funded, interdisciplinary research project, "Crossroads of Knowledge in Early Modern England: The Place of Literature".

Mace Perlman, who trained as a mime under Marcel Marceau and as an actor under Giorgio Strehler, contributed the chapters "Reading and Interpreting the Capitano's Multiple Mask-Shapes" and "Giorgio Strehler's *Arte*: A Commedia Master Directs Shakespeare" to *The Routledge Companion to Commedia dell'Arte*, edited by Judith Chaffee and Olly Crick (Routledge, 2015); and "Reading Shakespeare, Reading the Masks of the Italian Commedia: Fixed Forms and the Breath of Life" as an epilogue to *Transnational Exchange in Early Modern Theater*, edited by Robert Henke and Eric Nicholson (Ashgate, 2008). He is working to create an Academy of Renaissance Theatre, a cultural institution comprised of a professional company of transnational players together with a school of theatre, language, and Renaissance culture.

Sandra Pietrini is Professor of Theatre History at the University of Trento. She oversees the online iconographic meta-archive *Shakespeariana*, a work in progress run by the Laboratorio Teatrale. She has published

List of Contributors 301

internationally, and her monographies include *Spettacoli e immaginario teatrale nel Medioevo* (2001), *Fuori scena: Il teatro dietro le quinte nell'Ottocento* (2004), *Il mondo del teatro nel cinema* (2007), *L'arte dell'attore dal Romanticismo a Brecht* (2009), and *I giullari nell'immaginario medievale* (2011), in addition to a critical edition, *L'Amleto di Cesare Rossi* (2015).

Paolo Puppa, formerly Professor in Theatre History at Venice's Cà Foscari University, is a specialist in modern and comparative theatre, and has written critical works on Pirandello, Fo, Rolland, Ibsen, Rosso di San Secondo, D'Annunzio, Morselli, Goldoni, Brook, and Duse. He co-edited *A History of Italian Theatre* (Cambridge), *Encyclopedia of Italian Literary Studies* (Routledge), and *Differences on Stage*, which was awarded the George Freedley Memorial Award for 2014. Puppa is author of *Il teatro dei testi: la drammaturgia italiana nel Novecento* (2003) and *Teatro e spettacolo nel secondo Novecento* (2004). His latest publications include *La voce solitaria* (2010), *Racconti dal palcoscenico: Dal Rinascimento a Gadda* (2011), and *La Serenissima in scena: Da Goldoni a Paolini* (2014).

Anna Sica is Associate Professor in Theatre History at the University of Palermo, specializing in nineteenth- and twentieth-century drama, as well as acting and directing. She is a specialist in the Commedia dell'Arte, contemporary Italian drama, and in North American and Russian theatre. She has edited *Uptown-Downtown: New York Theatre from Tradition to Avant-garde* (2005) and *The Italian Method of La Drammatica* (2014), and is author of *The Murray Edwards Duse Collection* (2012) and *La drammatica-metodo italiano* (2013). Her essays have been published in *Biblioteca Teatrale*, *New Theatre Quarterly*, and *Nineteenth Century Theatre and Film*. She is a member of the International Federation for Theatre Research and current board member of the Massimo Opera House, Palermo.

Chris Stamatakis, Lecturer in Renaissance Literature in the Department of English at University College London, is author of *Sir Thomas Wyatt and the Rhetoric of Rewriting: Turning the Word* (Oxford, 2012) and has written on the Earl of Surrey, Gabriel Harvey's Italian reading, and early Tudor literary criticism (*Oxford Handbooks Online*). Works in progress include a monograph on the influence of Italian literature on sixteenth-century English poetry and poetics; essays on prefatory sonnets and the transmission of Petrarch in England; and an edition for Oxford University Press of Thomas Nashe's *Christs Teares ouer Ierusalem*.

Giuseppe Stellardi studied in Pavia and Paris and worked in Cape Town and Lancaster before joining Oxford University. His main research interests are in modern Italian literature. He has written on Dossi,

302   *List of Contributors*

Tarchetti, Michelstaedter, Svevo, Gadda, Moravia, Eco, Morante; on Deconstruction (Derrida); *Pensiero debole* (Vattimo); and metaphor. He has published a book on metaphor in Derrida and Heidegger, another on the work of Carlo Emilio Gadda, and a translation in English of Carlo Michelstaedter's *La persuasione e la rettorica*. With Emanuela Tandello-Cooper, he has recently edited the proceedings of a conference on Italo Svevo and is currently working on temporality in twentieth-century Italian literature.

Mariangela Tempera was Professor of English at the University of Ferrara and has written extensively on Renaissance drama, Shakespeare and film, and Shakespeare in performance. She is author of *Feasting with Centaurs: "Titus Andronicus" from Stage to Text* (1999); was chief editor of the series "Shakespeare dal testo alla scena" (Clueb, Bologna); founder and director of the "Shakespeare Centre" in Ferrara; and cofounder of the Italian Association of Shakespearean and Early Modern Studies (IASEMS).

René Weis is Professor of English at University College London. His Shakespeare publications include editions of *King Lear* (Longman), *Henry IV, Part 2* (Oxford), and *Romeo and Juliet* (Bloomsbury Arden Shakespeare). He is the author of *The Yellow Cross* which has been translated into seven languages. His *Shakespeare Revealed: A biography* was published by John Murray. His most recent book, *The Real Traviata: The Song of Marie Duplessis,* appeared from Oxford University Press in 2015.

Index

acting method xv, 16, 18, 20, 54–7, 61, 127, 131, 132, 151–64, 195–206, 210–12, 219, 249, 250, 277–80, 283, 285, 287; *see also* gesture; mime

actors: transnational movements of 8, 10, 12, 18, 54, 56–7, 61, 133, 153, 155–6, 195, 199–206

adaptation: by early modern playwrights 41, 47, 61, 70–71; for the stage 15, 126, 131, 132–5, 263; of culture 9, 166–7, 173, 276; of Shakespeare's language 14, 120–21, 132, 173, 176; of Shakespeare's plays 14, 19–20, 113–14, 118–20, 121–2, 131–5, 140, 154, 176, 246, 250, 265–7, 270, 276, 277–81, 294; reception and 97, 114; resistance to 21, 137, 140, 263, 282, 294–5; *see also contaminatio*; cultural exchange; domestication; imitation; translation

Aguglia, Mimì 195, 199–200, 201

Alfieri, Vittorio 122, 158

Algarotti, Francesco 114, 121

Alleyn, Edward 57

allusion: cultural 35, 169, 172; historical 142; literary 19, 27–9, 43, 44, 50, 65, 69, 99, 119, 122; 211, 216–17; 230, 235–7, 239, 240, 243

Aramaic 17, 175–6

Archer, William xvi, 158, 159, 164

Aretino, Pietro 10, 36, 43, 46–9, 100; *Il Marescalco* 47–8, 49; *I modi* 12, 46–9

Ariosto, Ludovico 14, 41, 44, 53, 60, 100, 117

Aristotle 13, 65, 66, 72, 76, 80, 81, 83, 84, 90; unities of 117, 128, 130, 141, 250–1

Armin, Robert 53, 137

Ascham, Roger 2, 11, 32, 99

authenticity 20, 101, 119, 134, 137–50, 156, 164, 171, 173, 176, 199–200, 216

avant-gardism 20–21, 186, 277–91

Bakhtin, Mikhail 2, 293

Baldini, Gabriele xiii

Bancroft, Richard 81, 82

Bandello, Matteo 31, 97

Baretti, Giuseppe 1, 117–18, 119, 121, 127, 184

Baudelaire, Charles 186

Bazzoni, Giunio 126, 130

Beckett, Samuel 140, 222

Bene, Carmelo 294

Berardinis, Leo de xvi

Bernhardt, Sarah 156, 196, 203

bilingual texts xiii, 1, 2, 31, 34, 184; *see also* parallel-text editions

Boccaccio, Giovanni 8, 97, 102–3, 196, 294

Boito, Arrigo xv, 16, 145–9, 157–9, 160, 162, 186

Bonucci, Antonio xiii

book trade 7, 10, 168, 180

Bragaglia, Marinella 195, 202

Brandeis, Irma 19, 233–5, 236, 237, 243

Brandes, Georg xii

Brecht, Bertolt 20, 123, 246, 248–52, 262, 294

Bruno, Giordano 11, 29, 34–5, 36

Burbage, James 57

Burbage, Richard 57, 137, 262

Cammarano, Salvatore 137, 139

Capuana, Luigi 200, 201, 205

Carcano, Giulio xiv, xv, 15, 16, 125–6, 129–35, 138, 202, 276, 293

304 *Index*

Carducci, Giosuè 17, 152, 180, 181, 184–5, 187, 190
Cary, Henry Francis xi, xii
Castiglione, Baldessar 4, 8, 65–6, 68, 75
Catholicism 42, 54, 70, 101, 171, 209, 214
Cavalli, Fabio 20, 266–75
censorship 15, 50, 121, 129, 131, 140, 142, 208–13, 276
Chapman, George 4, 6–7
Chekhov, Anton 156, 248
Christianity 67, 70, 84–7, 89, 92, 94, 166–7, 169, 171–2, 204, 223
Cicero 67, 73, 108
Cinthio, Giambattista Giraldi: *Gli Hecatommithi* xv, 31, 97, 125, 146, 147, 158
Clubb, Louise George 11, 53, 60, 62
Coleridge, Samuel Taylor 35, 146
collaboration 14, 15, 17, 116, 247, 266, 268, 271, 274; *see also* translation, collaborative
collation 2, 6, 9, 37
commedia dell'arte 10, 12, 20, 29, 54–63, 196, 256, 294
contaminatio 3, 16, 17, 28, 158, 169, 170–1, 173, 175, 182–92, 222, 231, 235, 237–8, 252, 269, 271; *see also* adaptation; hybridity
Conti, Antonio 113–14, 116, 118
Corneille, Pierre 114, 130
Coryate, Thomas 54, 57
cosmopolitanism 6–8, 14, 42, 44, 45, 81, 91, 118; *see also* transnationality
Covell, William 96, 98–100, 103
Croce, Benedetto 157
cultural exchange: dynamics of xi–xii, 3–5, 9, 291; economics of 2–4, 84–6, 91, 109; history of xi, 10; metaphors of 2–3, 5; multilateral 3, 14, 18, 176, 182; resistance to 3, 19, 21, 43, 101, 102, 109, 121, 125, 144, 172, 180–92, 229–32, 242–4; *see also* adaptation; translation

D'Agostino, Nemi xiii
Daniel, Samuel 4, 7, 75, 99–100
D'Annunzio, Gabriele 152, 157–8, 161, 187, 195, 236
Dante 8, 14, 120–1, 158, 196; *Divina Commedia* xi, xii, xiii, 74, 211; translated into English xi–xii
Darwin, Charles 148, 197

De André, Fabrizio 268–9
decadence 157, 186, 189
De Filippo, Edoardo xvi, 20, 265–76
D'Elci, Angiolo 17, 184–5
De Marchi, Luigi 17, 179–81, 185–7, 189
dialect xvi, 5, 8, 17, 20, 36, 175–6, 195–6, 199–200, 222, 265, 267, 269–271, 275, 295
dialectic 5, 10, 19, 42, 83, 246, 248, 249, 251, 254–5, 256, 259, 263, 294
dictionaries 1, 2, 8, 11, 28, 35, 184
disegno 12, 68, 71
domestication 16, 38, 45, 83–94, 117, 166–76, 187, 189–90, 295; *see also* adaptation
Dowden, Edward 179–80
drammatica, la 16, 151–64
Drayton, Michael 125
Ducis, Jean-François xiii, 119–20, 122
Dudley, Robert, Earl of Leicester 6, 11, 32, 33, 34, 57
Duse, Eleonora xv–xvi, 8, 16, 151–64, 196, 294

Edmunds, Bridget 96, 97, 100, 102, 103
Edmunds, John 96, 99, 103
Eduardo *see* De Filippo, Eduardo
Elkind, Jacob 16, 167–71, 173–6
Eliot, T. S. xii, 191
Elizabeth I, Queen 12, 32, 54, 56, 69
enargeia 99, 108–9
energeia 131
engageant poetics 209–13, 248; *see also* Shakespeare, William, political appeal of
Escudier, Léon 138, 144–5
exchange *see* cultural exchange
experimentalism 27, 132, 187, 277–91, 294

Faccio, Franco 145, 158
fantasies 12, 18, 42, 58, 90, 92–3, 104, 274
Fascist Italy 18, 208–19, 234, 259
Field, Richard 35, 37
Fiorentino, Giovanni 37, 85
Fletcher, Giles 99
Fletcher, John 11–12, 37, 40–51, 105
Florence xi, 10, 42, 89, 122, 143, 144, 153, 170
Florio, John 1–2, 3, 4, 8, 11, 27–38, 47
Florio, Michael Angelo 31, 32

Folengo, Teofilo 221, 231
fragments 59, 66, 72–4, 167, 180, 233, 234, 240, 266
French classical theatre xiii, xiv, xv, 15, 113, 115, 122, 127–8, 130; *see also* neoclassicism
French translation 97; role in mediating Shakespeare's works xiii, 15, 56, 114, 119, 128, 130, 148–9, 179; *see also* translation, intermediary

Gadda, Carlo Emilio 19, 221–32
Garibaldi, Giuseppe 7, 198; *see also* Italian unification; Risorgimento
Garrick, David xiii, 14
Gascoigne, George 41, 60
Gatti, Hilary xiv
Gattinelli, Gaetano 153, 158, 159
German Shakespeare xii, 14, 114, 133, 179, 181; *see also* translation, intermediary
gender politics 11–12, 42–51, 54, 58, 89, 92, 93, 96, 104, 278, 283–6
genius 3, 14, 15, 115, 117, 123, 125, 127, 129, 150, 183, 241, 293
Genoa 42, 102, 133, 145, 266
genres, mixture of 3, 28, 59, 62–3, 109, 113, 114, 117, 118, 293; *see also* contaminatio; tragicomedy
gesture: stage language of 8, 16, 54, 56, 154–7, 196, 200, 210, 212, 219, 261, 262, 273, 277, 295; *see also* acting method; mime
ghosts 18–19, 144–5, 215–16, 218, 219, 228–32, 278, 282, 287; *see also* memory
Giacometti, Paolo 129, 195
Globe Theatre 13, 54, 137, 142, 248, 252, 262
Goldoni, Carlo 116–17, 248, 252, 265
grande attore 8, 14, 15, 120, 126, 131–3, 135, 195, 294; tradition of xiv, 113, 122, 127, 135
Grasso, Giovanni 18, 195–206, 295
Greene, Robert 31, 32, 242
Gritti, Francesco xiii, 122
Guarini, Giovanni Batista 10, 37, 105–6, 107

Harvey, Gabriel 55–6, 58, 59
Haydocke, Richard 69
Heaney, Seamus xii

Hebrew culture 16–17, 85, 142, 166–76; *see also* Jewish identity
Henslowe, Philip 33
Heywood, Thomas 12, 55
Hoby, Thomas 4, 8–9
Holinshed, Raphael 101, 128
Horace 117, 221, 231
hybridity xv, 3, 5, 13, 117, 182, 234, 293; *see also* contaminatio

imitatio see imitation
imitation 4–5, 66, 67, 74, 114, 116, 117, 122, 130, 187, 271; rivalrous (*aemulatio*) 150, 181, 184, 187, 247; *see also* adaptation; translation
incompletion *see non finito*
ingegno 12, 68, 123, 125
intermediaries *see* translation, intermediary
intertextuality 2, 9, 10, 11, 17, 19, 32, 47, 101, 102, 173, 191, 234–44, 266, 275, 293
Italian Englishman 5, 56
Italianicity *see* Italianism
Italianism xii, 10, 11, 12, 13, 42–3, 47, 50, 102–3, 105–7, 109, 118, 179
Italian Shakespeare: emergence of xiii–xiv, 10; theatricality of xvi, 12, 20, 252
Italian unification 7–8, 153, 196–8, 200; *see also* Risorgimento
Italy: aesthetic idea of 101–9; *Anglomania* in xii, 118, 179–80; emergence of nation state 7–8, 153; experimentalism in xvi, 132, 187, 202, 203, 262, 282–3, 294, 295; Southern *see* Southern Italy

James, Henry xv
James I, King 101, 142, 286, 289, 290–1
Jewish identity 16–17, 33, 43–4, 71, 83–7, 92, 94, 166–76; *see also* Hebrew culture
Johnson, Samuel 1, 14, 35, 118, 149
Jonson, Ben 12, 49, 54–5, 58, 59, 89, 125; *Epicoene* 12, 43, 47, 49; *Every Man in His Humour* 89; *Volpone* 54–5, 57, 59, 62, 100, 104, 105–6

Keats, John 139, 242, 243, 263, 293
Kemp, Will 10, 53, 57, 61, 137
Kott, Jan 251

306 Index

language-learning 1, 11, 28, 29, 32, 37, 115; manuals 1, 8, 28–9, 32, 37
Leoni, Michele 14, 126, 127, 128, 129, 130
Leopardi, Giacomo 17, 187
Le Tourneur, Pierre 119, 128
Lewkenor, Lewis 82, 91
lexicography 11, 28, 127, 168; see dictionaries
Livy 80–1, 97, 102
Lomazzo, Giovanni Paolo 12, 69, 74
Lombardo, Agostino xiii
Longfellow, Henry Wadsworth xi

Machevil 83, 85, 91
Machiavelli xvi, 41, 80, 83–5, 88
Magalotti, Lorenzo 115, 125
Mantua 42, 54, 56, 61, 81, 168, 169, 170
Manzoni, Alessandro 15, 19, 122–3, 128–9, 130, 222, 223, 231
Marlowe, Christopher 83, 85, 91
Marowitz, Charles 294
Marrapodi, Michele 9, 48–9
Marston, John 37, 55
Mascagni, Pietro 141, 200
mattatore xiv, xvi; see also *grande attore*
Melchiori, Giorgio xiii
memory: intertextual 18, 187, 219, 235–6, 238, 243; personal 18, 161, 212, 218, 219, 227, 236, 238; theatrical 201, 271, 287; see also intertextuality
Menichelli, Francesco 118, 122
metatextuality and metatheatre 19, 49, 216, 219, 244, 252, 257, 268, 283, 285, 294; inset plays and xiii, 55, 169, 216, 273
metre see verse
Mezzogiorno see Southern Italy
Michelangelo 12, 65–76
Middleton, Thomas 12, 55
Milan xiv, xv, 15, 58, 125, 130, 145, 157, 158, 198, 221, 222, 223–4, 248
Milton, John 118, 125
mime 145, 152, 200, 210; see also acting method; gesture
mise-en-page 8, 17, 182–3; see also parallel-text editions
Modena, Gustavo 152, 159, 294
Montaigne, Michel de 4, 28, 33, 35
Montale, Eugenio 19, 180, 187, 190–2, 233–44

Morrocchesi, Antonio xiii, 118, 122
Mountain, Roger 97, 100, 109
Murray, John 116–17
music and musicality xiv, xvi, 20, 21, 122, 137–50, 219, 249, 270, 278–9, 286–7, 295; see also opera
Mussolini, Benito 210, 211, 213, 229

Naples xv, 58, 139, 153, 163, 274, 275; *camorra* underworld of 267, 268, 272, 275
Nashe, Thomas 31–2, 53, 55
national identity 4–7, 11, 42, 45, 158, 169–70, 171, 176, 198
nationhood: emergence of 3, 5–7; see also transnationality
Neapolitan versions of Shakespeare xvi, 18, 20, 36, 265, 267–71, 274–5, 295
neoclassicism 15, 113–20, 123, 128, 130, 152, 157–9, 163, 164, 293
neologism 2, 4, 7, 8, 11, 27, 28, 36, 57–8, 122
Neoplatonism 12, 65–76
networks: interlingual 15, 117; professional 10, 11, 14, 29, 32–3, 35, 37, 113, 115, 116, 117, 138, 145, 157; publishing 33, 35, 37, 118; theatrical 37
Noh 20, 250
non finito 12, 66, 68, 72–6, 229
novella xi, 31, 53, 96, 97, 146

Olivieri, Angelo 9, 17, 179–84, 187
opera: Shakespeare repurposed for xii, xiv, xv, 16, 120, 126, 137–50, 180, 196
origin and originality 2, 4, 5, 7, 17–18, 20, 99–101, 119, 120, 187, 222, 272, 280, 282, 289–91, 295
"Otherness" 7, 18, 42, 44, 94, 197–8, 204; see also racial alterity
Ovid 72, 108
Ovidianism 13, 48, 72–4, 75, 97, 99, 100, 103–5
ownership 17, 18, 20, 21, 121, 129, 268, 274, 282, 291

Padua xii, 6, 11, 40, 41, 42–3, 61, 81, 168, 169, 176
Painter, William 97, 103, 106
parallel-text editions 1, 8–9, 11, 28, 34, 37, 183
paratexts 14, 19, 236; prefatory 31–3, 35, 37, 38, 65–6, 69, 75, 99,

114, 116–18, 126, 128, 129, 130, 179–81, 184, 236
parody 19, 46, 50, 58, 61, 70, 88, 100, 116, 197, 234, 240, 294
Pascoli, Giovanni 187, 188–9, 190
Pasqualigo, Luigi 10, 61
pastoral 10, 12, 37, 53, 59, 62–3, 273; see also tragicomedy
Peacham, Henry 69, 272
personalisation 17, 115, 184, 191–2, 230–2, 233–5, 239, 243, 272–3
Petrarch, Francis 8, 14, 58, 99, 182, 196; see also Petrarchanism
Petrarchanism 11, 17, 58, 99–100, 181–2, 187, 191, 238
Petrolini, Ettore 294
Pettie, George 97, 103
Piave, Francesco Maria 142–4
Piccolo Teatro 246, 248, 250, 251
Pirandello, Luigi 195, 206, 248, 265, 294
Pisa 42, 61, 170,
Place, Pierre-Antoine de la xiii, 114, 119
Plato see Neoplatonism
Platter, Thomas 13–14
Plautus 30, 33, 53, 60, 61
Pliny 67, 70, 72, 73
Plutarch 32, 97
poetics: comparative 12, 17, 19, 101–9, 118, 121, 128, 130, 179, 181–91, 219, 231, 222, 244, 293
polylingualism 1–2, 6–8, 10, 27–8, 31, 32, 34, 35, 36, 37, 44, 45, 116, 117, 175–6, 184, 210, 234, 293, 294
Pope, Alexander 117, 118
Praga, Emilio 17, 186–7, 188
Praz, Mario 208, 233, 294
prompt-books 16, 152, 153, 158–63
prosody see verse
Protestantism xii, 1, 10, 54, 70, 209
proverbs 10, 11, 29, 30, 34, 36, 275
puns 21, 27–8, 36, 38, 43, 76, 85
Punzo, Armando 265–6, 276

Quintilian 75, 108
quotability 19; see also allusion

racial alterity 5, 13, 18, 87, 90, 108, 146, 147, 149, 196–206; see also Hebrew culture; Jewish identity; national identity; "Otherness"
Racine, Jean 66, 130
Rankins, William 5
realism 18, 176, 196, 199–206, 210, 211, 217, 219, 249, 256, 259

reading habits 2, 7; parallel 8; see also collation; parallel-text editions
reception: belatedness of xii, 4, 180–1; philological xiii, 118, 127, 130, 158, 294
reduction 120, 126, 132–3, 183, 187, 240, 242, 244, 250, 267, 293, 295
republicanism 13, 80
republic of letters 7, 116
Riccoboni, Luigi 151–2
Ricordi, Giulio 137, 145
Risorgimento 15, 127, 129–30, 135, 142, 198, 276; see also Italian unification
Ristori, Adelaide xiv, 8, 15, 126, 131, 132–4, 152, 153, 163, 294
Rolli, Paolo 7, 115, 116, 118, 125
Romani, Felice xiv, 120
Roman New Comedy 53, 55, 58, 60; see also Plautus; Terence
Rome 13, 20, 42, 43, 44, 80–1, 100–2, 108, 109, 157, 167, 181, 200, 225, 229, 250, 266, 271, 274, 275, 276
Rossi, Ernesto xiv, 8, 131, 153, 195, 294
Rowe, Nicholas 14, 119
Rusconi, Carlo xiv, 16, 126, 130, 138, 195, 202, 293

Salkinson, Isaac Eduard 16, 167, 168–76
Salvini, Tommaso xiv, xv, 8, 131, 152, 153, 195, 201–3, 294
Sanfelice, Ettore 17, 180, 181–5, 187–9
Scapigliatura 186, 189–90, 222
Schiller, Friedrich von 138, 139
Schlegel, August Wilhelm von xii, 123
Serpieri, Alessandro xiii
Shakespeare, William: aesthetic and cultural iconicity of 14, 18, 113, 116, 118, 120, 122, 173, 208, 234, 243–4, 265, 274, 276, 277, 281–2; as actor-author 18, 137, 210, 213–19, 288; critical reception of 14, 179, 181, 225, 230, 233, 281–2; dominance of tragedies xiv, 118, 125–6, 129, 231, 240; global reputation of xii–xiii, xiv, 176, 196; inimitable style of 114, 115, 116, 119–21, 123, 127, 131, 248; Italianness of xii, xvi, 10; musical poetics of 150, 219, 262, 270, 279, 287, 295; on film 20, 248, 266, 270–6, 291; political appeal

308 *Index*

of 127–9, 132, 158, 162, 208–19, 209–13, 248–51, 257–8, 266; reception on page 10, 14, 15, 16, 113, 115, 118–22, 126, 132, 135, 138, 166, 293; reception on stage xiii, 10, 14, 15, 113, 115, 118–19, 126, 132, 135, 138, 152, 162, 210, 293; rhetoric of wonder in 66, 199, 206, 219, 270; theatricality of xvi, 20, 61, 250–2, 283; translated by non-English-speaking translators xiii, 116, 119, 138; translated by scholars xiii, 180; *see also* genres, mixture of; reception; untranslatability

Shakespeare's characters: Brabantio 62, 68, 90, 91, 92; Caliban 63, 215, 216, 267, 268, 284; Cleopatra 16, 151, 157–62; Coriolanus 262; Desdemona xv, 58, 70, 71, 72, 163; Hamlet 115, 137, 138, 153, 211–14, 219, 224–32, 240; Iachimo 13, 100, 102–9; Iago xv, 12, 16, 34, 58, 62, 66–7, 71–2, 74–6, 88, 90, 91, 94, 146–9, 171, 202; Imogen 13, 100, 102–9; Jaques 58, 60; Juliet 16, 151, 154–7; King Lear xv, 242; Lady Macbeth xiv, 15, 126, 132–5, 137, 145, 163; Lavinia 71, 104, 105; Macbeth 134–5, 137, 139, 145, 211–13, 219; Ophelia 62, 89–94, 120, 163–4, 227–8, 230, 277; Othello xv, 13, 18, 58, 62, 70, 71, 73, 74, 146–7, 153, 195–8, 200–5, 293, 294; Polonius 59, 62, 63; Prospero 18, 215–19; Shylock 13, 33, 83–7, 89, 92, 167

Shakespeare's sources: later return to xv, 18, 20, 146, 147, 158, 286, 288

Shakespeare's works: *All's Well that Ends Well* 37, 97; *Antony and Cleopatra* xiv, xv, 80, 94, 157–62; *As You Like It* 58, 137; *Comedy of Errors, The* 30, 53, 60, 233; *Coriolanus* xiv, 80, 118, 246–51, 259–71; *Cymbeline* 13, 37, 97, 100–9; *Hamlet* xiii, xiv, 1, 18, 19, 62, 113, 115, 116, 118, 119–20, 121–2, 138, 211–14, 221–2, 224–32, 233, 234, 240, 243, 252–3, 293–4; *Henry IV, Parts 1–2* 141; *Henry V* 234; *Henry VI, Parts 1–3* 19–20, 246, 250–63; *Julius Caesar*

xiii, 20, 80, 114, 115, 116, 210, 214, 233, 247–9, 267–76; *King Lear* xiv, 129, 139–41, 230, 241–2, 246–7; *Love's Labour's Lost* 27–8, 29, 34–6, 58, 61, 62, 66; *Lucrece* 5, 33, 68, 91, 97, 102, 103, 180; *Macbeth* xiv, 15, 16, 18, 20–1, 101, 118, 125, 126, 128, 131–5, 138, 139, 141–5, 149, 150, 158, 162–3, 210, 211–13, 217, 219, 221, 230, 248, 277–91; *Measure for Measure* 31, 37; *Merchant of Venice, The* xiv, 13, 34, 36, 37, 81, 83–7, 89–94, 146, 167; *Merry Wives of Windsor, The* 141, 161; *Midsummer Night's Dream, A* 10, 53, 213, 233, 234, 235, 236, 237; *Much Ado about Nothing* xiv, 31, 62, 66, 167, 234; *Othello* xiv, xv, 1, 12, 13, 16, 18, 31, 37, 62, 66, 68, 70–5, 81, 83, 87, 89–94, 118, 125, 126, 131, 137, 140, 145–9, 167, 168–73, 176, 195–8, 200–6; *Richard III* 34, 66; *Romeo and Juliet* xiii, xiv, 14, 16, 41, 50, 81, 97, 146, 154, 167–72, 174–6, 178, 235, 239, 248, 265; *Sonnets* 9, 17, 19, 179–92, 221, 232, 238; *Taming of the Shrew, The* xiv, 3, 11–12, 16–17, 34, 40–51, 58, 59, 60, 61, 62, 167, 168–71, 173, 175, 176, 248; *Tempest, The* xvi, 12, 17–18, 19, 20, 21, 28, 62–3, 67, 68, 149, 211, 215, 217, 219, 230, 234, 235, 236, 239, 246–8, 262, 266–70, 273–6, 287, 289–90, 294, 295; *Timon of Athens* 97, 233; *Titus Andronicus* 71, 80, 103–5, 208, 271–2; *Twelfth Night* xvi, 30–1, 53, 62, 137, 248; *Two Gentlemen of Verona, The* 61; *Venus and Adonis* 33, 99, 100, 103, 105; *Winter's Tale, The* 1, 5, 18, 37, 217, 219, 233, 242

Shelley, Percy Bysshe 180, 181, 236
Sicilian identity 8, 18, 195–206, 208, 211–12, 217–18, 271, 275
Sidney, Sir Philip 6, 11, 12, 29, 34–5, 65, 66, 70, 75, 99
Sinopoli, Giuseppe Giusti 195, 200
Smith, Joseph 116
Smith, Sir Thomas 81–3, 90
Somma, Antonio xv, 139

Index 309

Sormani, Giacomo 126, 130
Southern Italy 8, 18, 167, 197–200, 203–6; *see also* Sicilian identity
Staël, Mme Germaine de 15, 127, 128, 129
Stanislavsky, Constantin 154, 156–7, 202, 205
Stratford Jubilee xiii, 14
Strehler, Giorgio xvi, 19–20, 246–63, 294
Sutcliffe, Matthew 54, 58

Tarlton, Richard 31, 32, 33, 53
Tasso, Torquato 10, 100
taste xiv, xvi, 7, 15, 115, 119–20, 122, 127, 132–3, 145, 157, 172, 181, 200
Tate, Nahum xiv
Taviani, Paolo and Vittorio 20, 266, 270–6
Terence 53, 61,
Testori, Giovanni 294
Thomas, William 28, 81
Tieck, Ludwig xii
Tolstoy, Leo xii
tragicomedy 10, 12, 13, 37, 62, 105–7, 117, 229, 293–4
translation: collaborative xiii, 116, 119, 122, 132, 138, 143, 148; constraints of xiii–xiv, 159, 187; intermediary 2, 3, 8, 30, 56, 114, 119; prose versus verse xiv, 118, 121, 126, 128, 182–3, 187, 219, 293; role of in cultural exchange 2; *see also* adaptation; cultural exchange; untranslatability
translatio studii 2, 276
transnationality 3, 7; emergence of 11, 42; *see also* cosmopolitanism
travel 6, 11, 14, 28, 31, 43, 44, 45, 54, 57, 58, 61, 63, 69, 81, 102, 125, 176
typography 8–9; *see also mise-en-page*

untranslatability 3, 13, 14, 15, 117, 119, 121, 130, 134, 139–41, 148, 181, 183; *see also* translation

Valentini, Domenico xiii, 116, 118
Varchi, Benedetto 68, 73
Vasari, Giorgio 67, 68, 69, 73, 75
Venice xii, 13, 29, 34, 42, 54, 62, 104, 116, 145–6, 168, 169, 176, 196, 212; myth of 81–94
Verdi, Giuseppe: operatic renderings of Shakespeare xii, 16, 137–50, 180, 294; *Falstaff* xv, 141, 145, 150, 158, 186; *Macbeth* xv, 16, 138, 139, 142–5, 149, 150 276; *Otello* xv, 16, 137–8, 145–50, 158, 186
Verga, Giovanni 195, 199–200
vernacular culture, renovation of 6, 15, 16, 37, 119, 127, 129, 166, 175–6, 180, 181, 186
Verona xii, 41, 42, 81, 154, 155, 168, 169, 176, 248
Verri, Alessandro 1, 118–21
verse 14; difficulty of translating into 14, 15, 180, 181–2, 187, 189, 293; formal approaches to 181–2, 187, 190; translation into 15, 129, 130, 131, 143, 152, 153, 159, 180, 182, 186
Vittorini, Elio 18, 208–19
Volkoff, Alexandre 155–7
Voltaire 1, 7, 114–19, 122, 126–8
vulgarity *see* taste

Wagner, Richard 141, 145, 149, 157–8
Wilson, Robert 11, 32–3, 38
Wolfe, John 8–9, 10
Woolf, Virginia 40, 42

Zeuxis 67–8, 70, 73, 74
Zuccaro, Federico 12, 68